TEACHER'S BOOK

THE OXFORD
Picture
Dictionary

JAYME ADELSON-GOLDSTEIN, NORMA SHAPIRO, AND RENÉE WEISS

Oxford University Press

Oxford University Press
198 Madison Avenue, New York, NY 10016 USA
Great Clarendon Street, Oxford OX2 6DP England

Oxford New York
Auckland Bangkok Buenos Aires Cape Town
Chennai Dar es Salaam Delhi Hong Kong
Istanbul Karachi Kolkata Kuala Lumpur
Madrid Melbourne Mexico City Mumbai
Nairobi São Paulo Shanghai
Taipei Tokyo Toronto

OXFORD is a trademark of Oxford University Press.

ISBN 0-19-470060-7
Copyright © 1998 Oxford University Press

No unauthorized photocopying.

Editorial Manager: Susan Lanzano
Art Director: Lynn Luchetti
Editor: Shirley Brod
Senior Designer and Project Manager: Susan P. Brorein
Production: Alan Barnett, Inc.
Production Editor: Klaus Jekeli
Art Buyer: Donna Goldberg
Pronunciation Editor: Sharon Goldstein
Cover design by Silver Editions

Printing (last digit): 10 9 8 7

Printed in Hong Kong

Illustrations by: David Aikins, Doug Archer, Craig Attebery,
Garin Baker, Sally Bensusen, Eliot Bergman, Mark Bischel, Dan
Brown / Artworks NY, Roy Douglas Buchman, George Burgos /
Larry Dodge, Rob Burman, Carl Cassler, Mary Chandler, Robert
Crawford, Jim DeLapine, Judy Francis, Graphic Chart and Map
Co., Dale Gustafson, Biruta Akerbergs Hansen, Marcia
Hartsock, C.M.I., David Hildebrand, The Ivy League of Artists,
Inc. / Judy Degraffenreid, The Ivy League of Artists, Inc. / Tom
Powers, The Ivy League of Artists, Inc. / John Rice, Pam Johnson,
Ed Kurtzman, Narda Lebo, Scott A. MacNeill / MACNEILL &
MACINTOSH, Andy Lendway / Deborah Wolfe Ltd., Jeffrey
Mangiat, Suzanne Mogensen, Mohammad Mansoor, Tom
Newsom, Melodye Benson Rosales, Stacey Schuett, Rob
Schuster, James Seward, Larry Taugher, Bill Thomson, Anna
Veltfort, Nina Wallace, Wendy Wassink-Ackison, Michael
Wepplo, and Don Wieland.
Thanks to Mike Mikos for his preliminary architectural sketches
of several pieces.

References
Boyer, Paul S., Clifford E. Clark, Jr., Joseph F. Kett, Thomas L.
Purvis, Harvard Sitkoff, Nancy Woloch, The Enduring Vision: A
History of the American People, Lexington, Massachusetts:
D.C. Heath and Co., 1990.

Glassman, Bruce S., Editor, The MacMillan Visual Almanac,
New York: Macmillan, 1996.

Grun, Bernard, The Timetables of History: A Horizontal Linkage
of People and Events, (based on Werner Stein's Kulturfahrplan),
New York: A Touchstone Book, Simon and Schuster, 1946,
1963, 1975, 1979.

Krantz, Les, and Jim McCormick, Peoplepedia, New York:
Henry Holt Co., 1996.

Larsen, David E., Editor-in-Chief, Mayo Clinic Family Health
Book, New York: William Morrow and Company, 1990.

Panati, Charles, Extraordinary Origins of Everyday Things, New
York: Harper and Row, 1987.

Statistical Abstract of the United States: 1996, 116th Edition,
Washington, DC: US Bureau of the Census, 1996.

The World Book Encyclopedia, Chicago: World Book Inc., a
Scott Fetzer Co., 1988.

Toff, Nancy, Editor-in-Chief, The People of North America (Series),
New York: Chelsea House Publishers, Main Line Books, 1988.

Trager, James, The People's Chronology, A Year-by-Year Record
of Human Events from Prehistory to the Present, New York:
Henry Holt Reference Book, 1992.

Wright, John W., Editor, Universal Almanac, Kansas City: Andrews
and McMeel, Universal Press Syndicate Company, 1996.

Acknowledgments

We are grateful to the Oxford University Press publishing
team for their support and skillful work throughout the
writing of the Oxford Picture Dictionary Teacher's Book.
Our special thanks to:

Lynne Barsky, whose ability to edit and smile at the
same time started us out on the right foot,

Shirley Brod, whose teaching skills, clear directions,
and wry remarks helped us each step of the way,

Klaus Jekeli, whose intelligent queries and well-placed
comments kept us on our toes, and

Susan Brorein, whose design sense worked miracles
with space, text, and art, no small feat.

We would also like to acknowledge Arthur Custer, Jon
Van Horn, and Phil Lee, of The Sun Group and Full
House Productions, as well as Rick Adamson, Sally
Woodson, Larry Robinson, Madelon Thomas, Jeff
Woodman, Karla Hendrick, Akira Tana, Kate Pak,
DeMarest Gray, George O. Brome, Eileen Galindo, David
Crommett, and David Grunner for their wonderful work
on the accompanying Focused Listening Cassette.

We owe a debt of gratitude to the following gifted
teachers and writers: James Asher, Sharron Bassano,
Marianne Celce-Murcia, Mary Ann Christison, Rod Ellis,
Sandra Fotos, Irene Frankel, Madeline Hunter, Mary
Hurst, Sadae Iwataki, Spencer Kagan, Stephen Krashen,
Vicki Nagel, James Popham, K. Lynn Savage, Tracy Terrell,
and Penny Ur. We are grateful to have known these
people personally or through their writing and it is an
honor to acknowledge their influence in our teaching
and in this work.

We dedicate this book to our colleagues in TESOL.

Contents

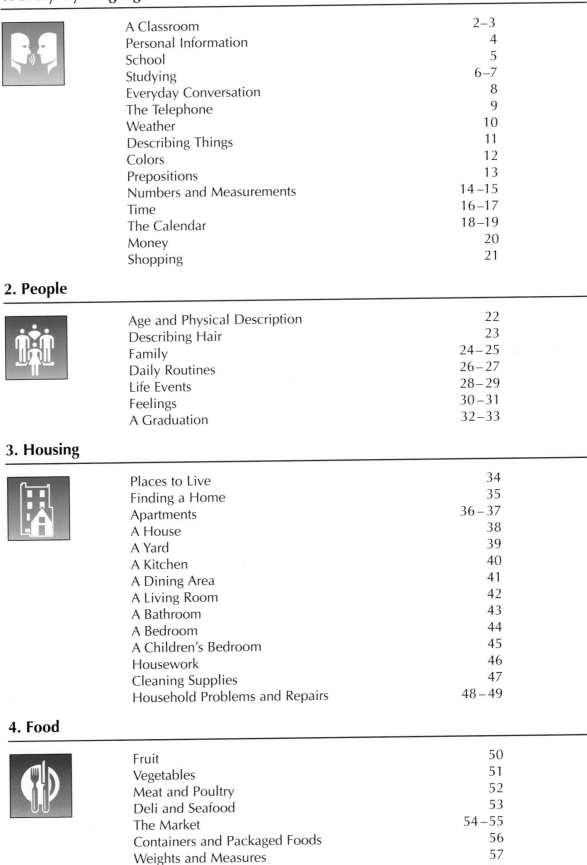

Contents

Contents

Introduction

Welcome to **The Oxford Picture Dictionary Teacher's Book.** This teacher's guide is designed to provide you with the framework for communicative vocabulary lessons based on *The Oxford Picture Dictionary.*

WHAT IS THE OXFORD PICTURE DICTIONARY?

The *Dictionary* is a comprehensive vocabulary resource, containing over 3,700 words, each defined by engaging art and presented in a meaningful context. The *Dictionary* enables your students to learn and use English in all aspects of their daily lives. Each page or pair of pages in the *Dictionary* represents a topic, covering home and family, the workplace, the community, health care, the world, or areas of study. These topics are organized into twelve thematic units based on the curriculum of beginning and low-intermediate level English language coursework.

HOW DOES THE PICTURE DICTIONARY WORK?

The Oxford Picture Dictionary uses a variety of visual formats, each suited to the topic being represented. Where appropriate, word lists are categorized and the page is divided into sections, allowing you to focus your students' attention on one aspect of the topic at a time.

In the word lists:

- nouns, adjectives, prepositions, and adverbs, are numbered;

- verbs are bolded and identified by letters;

- targeted prepositions and adjectives within phrases are bolded.

The Oxford Picture Dictionary Program includes this **Teacher's Book** and accompanying **Teacher's Book Focused Listening Cassette**, the **Beginning Workbook**, the **Intermediate Workbook**, the **Dictionary Cassettes** (giving pronunciation of each word in the *Dictionary*), **Classic Classroom Activities** (a black-line master activity book), **Read All About It 1** and **2** (the *Dictionary* readers), and a set of *Dictionary* **Overhead Transparencies**.

WHAT'S IN THIS BOOK?

The Oxford Picture Dictionary Teacher's Book contains a page-for-page reproduction of the *Dictionary.* Each topic is annotated with topic notes, teaching tips, and a variety of activities within each lesson plan.

In addition to the picture pages, all the other pages of the *Dictionary* appear in the *Teacher's Book* as well, including:

- an alphabetical index listing all words and topics in the *Dictionary;*

- a pronunciation guide and a phonetic listing for each word in the index;

- a map index including pronunciation of all geographical names in the *Dictionary;*

- a verb guide listing all of the verbs presented in the *Dictionary* with their present, past, and past participle forms.

Underlying the lessons in this book is an awareness that our students come to each class with a wealth of knowledge, a variety of learning styles, and a long shopping list of language needs. Naturally, your students' needs and your personal teaching style will ultimately dictate how you use the *Oxford Picture Dictionary* in your classroom. There are, however, a number of time-tested teaching concepts that work well in most situations and provide the framework for the lessons in the *Teacher's Book:*

1. Previewing the subject matter of a lesson with the class helps a teacher assess what the students already know and what they need to learn.

2. Visuals help students learn language.

3. Students need a variety of practice activities to help them learn new language.

4. Students' communication skills benefit from working with their classmates in different group configurations.

With these concepts in mind, the lesson plans for each topic include different ways to introduce and teach the new vocabulary, as well as a variety of meaningful exercises and communicative activities that will help your students practice using the new words in context. Total Physical Response (TPR) activities, Early Production questions, chalkboard activities, conversation practice, substitution drills, problem solving, cooperative group work, and vocabulary games are just some of the activities featured in the lessons.

This *Teacher's Book* is divided into the following sections, which all form part every lesson:

- **TOPIC NOTES:** interesting aspects of the topic and pertinent cross-cultural issues;

- **TEACHING TIPS:** related vocabulary, grammar, spelling, pronunciation, and usage points, as well as suggested teaching strategies for the topic;

- **INTRODUCE THE TOPIC:** surveys, stories, and brainstorms to preview the topic and assess students' prior knowledge;

- **TEACH THE NEW WORDS:** ideas for teaching the vocabulary using the student's *Dictionary* page;

- **PROVIDE PRACTICE:** guided activities that include whole-class categorizing, focused listening, paired conversations, and interview questions;

- **EXPAND THE LESSON:** communicative activities that include problem solving, discussion questions, idioms, cooperative group work, drawing activities, and writing activities;
- **GAMES:** team driven activities including chain drills, spelling bees, and definition bingo.

In addition, at the beginning of each new topic page in this book you will find references to the appropriate *Workbook* and *Classic Classroom Activities* pages for the topic, as well as the related *Dictionary* pages.

HOW DO I USE THIS BOOK?

The sections outlined above comprise two separate areas on the pages of this *Teacher's Book*. The TOPIC NOTES and TEACHING TIPS sections are found in the shaded boxes, and the remaining sections make up the lesson plan portion of the book.

You will want to consider your students' skill levels and their familiarity with the vocabulary when deciding which activities to use. Sections are in the same order from page to page, and activities within each section, which vary, are laid out in ascending order of difficulty. You can pick and choose from these activities, while maintaining a constant lesson framework of introducing, teaching, practicing, and expanding the topic vocabulary. The procedures for using each of the lesson plan sections is described in detail below.

WHAT ARE THE TOPIC NOTES?

TOPIC NOTES are a springboard into every *Dictionary* topic, providing background information, clarifying vocabulary, and previewing interesting aspects of the topic. The TOPIC NOTES are organized into three areas.

- **In the U.S.** provides you with relevant information that focuses on social, economic, or political trends. This information is especially appreciated by students who need familiarity with the culture and cross-cultural issues specific to the U.S.

  In the U.S., students usually **raise their hands** to answer a question, make a statement, or volunteer for a task. Teachers then call on the students whose hands are raised. [Classroom, pp. 2-3]

- **Definitions** are provided for specific words on a *Dictionary* topic that students might need extra help in understanding. These words may have more than one meaning, or they may frequently appear as part of an idiomatic or colloquial phrase.

  A **receipt** is the consumer's proof of purchase and is required for returns in many stores. [Shopping, p. 21]

- **Fact Files,** identified by the icon ▭, include historical or cultural footnotes, intriguing trivia, or demographic trends.

▭The most frequently sung music in the world is "Happy Birthday to You." [Music, p. 120]

WHAT ARE THE TEACHING TIPS?

This section includes a list of related vocabulary, teaching notes on language forms and functions that apply to the new vocabulary, and suggestions for teaching the topic.

- **Related Vocabulary** provides 10 to 14 additional words or expressions that are associated with each *Dictionary* topic. You can use these words as additional support in presenting the topic. Note that some of the words may have an asterisk. For example, windy* appears as a Related Vocabulary word on page 66, *Clothing II*. The asterisk means that the word *windy* can be found on the word list of another page in the *Dictionary* (in this case on page 10, *Weather).*

- **Grammar** highlights a grammar point that corresponds to the topic vocabulary. Teaching grammar contextualized within the vocabulary rather than in an isolated, artificial form, is more purposeful and motivating for your students.

  Grammar: Note that *down* can be a preposition. *He walked down the stairs.* The word *downstairs* is used as an adverb in *Take the elevator downstairs,* and may also be used as an adjective as in *He has a downstairs office.* [Prepositions of Motion, p. 105]

- **Spelling** includes tips about word endings, homonyms, doubling consonants, and forming plurals.

  Spelling: Irregular plurals
  man—men, woman—women, child—children, baby—babies [Age and Physical Description, p. 22]

- **Pronunciation** includes practice with vowels, consonants, stress, intonation, register, and reduced forms. Stressed words or syllables are always bolded for clarity.

  Pronunciation: Stress and intonation
  Demonstrate the stress and rising intonation in clarification questions. *Did you say* **Sam***? The class begins* **when***?* **Who** *is going to school?* [Everyday Conversation, p. 8]

- **Usage** gives the common conventions associated with specific vocabulary.

  Usage: Dates in the U.S. are usually written in month-day-year order, e.g., May 7, 1988—abbreviated 5-7-88. [Personal Information, p. 4]

- **Lightbulb icons** 💡 indicate a strategy you can use to review, practice, or expand upon the *Dictionary* topic. Ideas include pages to review prior to teaching the lesson, additional visual aids, culminating activities, and ways to involve the community.

💡 Review or expose students to the words *pounds, ounces,* and *weigh* so that they can talk about amounts. [Meat and Poultry, p. 52]

💡 As a culminating activity, have students share recipes from their cultures. Duplicate and bind the recipes to create a class cookbook. [Food Preparation, p. 58]

- **The warning icon** ⚠ points out cautionary advice about the topic or specific vocabulary. Warnings are given for topics or words that require cultural, racial, or ethnic sensitivity, are culture-bound to the U.S., or are gender specific. This icon will also warn you when students may be unfamiliar with a concept or vocabulary item due to their backgrounds.

⚠ For immigrant students, talking about their families can be painful if they are separated from them. [Family, pp. 24-25]

HOW DO I INTRODUCE THE TOPIC?

The first stage of each lesson plan in this book is called INTRODUCE THE TOPIC. The activities in this section help you set the scene for your students, enabling them to preview the words and concepts they will be learning. These "opener" activities focus the class on the lesson and help you assess what vocabulary your students already know.

The lessons in this book have two or three ways for you to introduce the topic. For some activities, such as telling a story, drawing a picture, or acting out a situation, students are not required to do more than just listen or answer simple questions. During these kinds of activities students' *Dictionaries* are closed. In this way, distractions are minimized.

Draw a calendar for the week on the board. Talk about your schedule. *On Monday I have an appointment with the doctor. Tuesday is my mother's birthday…* [Calendar, pp. 18-19]

Other kinds of introductory activities, such as whole-class brainstorms or class surveys, require that students take on a more active role. For these activities students' *Dictionaries* are open, but the word lists are covered. Visual prompts provided by the *Dictionary* pictures will lead to full class participation.

Ask students to brainstorm a list of clothing items while you record the items on the board. Working from the list, ask students to stand if they are wearing a particular item. [Clothing I, pp. 64-65]

HOW DO I TEACH THE NEW WORDS?

Once students have some familiarity with the topic, you can TEACH THE NEW WORDS from the *Dictionary* word list. Of course, there is no one way to teach vocabulary. Teachers employ a variety of methods with great success. An important point to remember in order

for beginning-level students to effectively process and integrate the vocabulary is to limit the number of new words presented at one time to between 10 and 15. For those students who are familiar with most of the words in a particular topic, you may want to teach some of the new words from the Related Vocabulary list that appears under the Teaching Tips section.

In the TEACH THE NEW WORDS section the specific activities for a topic depend upon the type of vocabulary presented on the *Dictionary* page. Many of the activities in this section are based on language acquisition theory which suggests vocabulary is learned best in context and that students need a receptive period before they are required to speak. During these activities students look at their *Dictionaries* and either cover up or use the word list. The things you say to the students are indicated in italics, while their answers (from the word lists) are in parentheses.

The following types of teaching activities are included:

- **Total Physical Response (TPR)** allows both you and your students to demonstrate the vocabulary. Students respond to the TPR commands without having to produce the language right away. This technique is especially useful for teaching the verb pages.

Act out and give a series of commands using students' school supplies. *I put the pencil on my book. Put the pencil on your book.* [Prepositions, p. 13]

- **Describing words** so that students can identify them on the *Dictionary* page gives students a chance to hear the words in meaningful sentences.

Ask students to identify the number of a particular picture based on your description. *You stand on it and ride the waves toward the beach. It's a surfboard.* (#3) [Beach, p. 155]

- **Having students "listen and repeat"** gives them an opportunity to hear each word several times and practice its pronunciation.

Say each word and have students repeat the word and point to the correct picture. [City Streets, pp. 88-89]

- **Asking *yes/no* or *or* questions** about the vocabulary allows students to give one-word responses.

Ask students a series of *or* questions about the vocabulary. *Is the U.S. in North America or South America?* (North America) [The World Map, pp. 124-125]

After teaching the new words, it is essential for teachers to check students' comprehension of the words. Checking for comprehension allows you to ascertain at what point students are ready to move on toward the more communicative, student-centered activities. See page xiv for more information on comprehension checks.

HOW DO I PROVIDE PRACTICE?

Because learning vocabulary requires varied and repeated exposure to the new words, the section PROVIDE PRACTICE includes many different activities. You may decide to use all of these activities or limit them to the ones that best suit your class. Students will continue to learn and become more proficient using the vocabulary as they practice it in different contexts, often not even being aware that you have stopped "teaching the new words."

The exercises outlined here begin with simple Chalkboard Activities allowing students to practice with one- or two-word responses. The Conversations allow students to use the words in sentences within a controlled setting, and the Interview Questions give students more freedom in their responses. While all of the activities give students practice in both listening and speaking, the last activity in this section, Listening, gives students specific listening practice.

- **Chalkboard activities** are done with the whole class and involve categorizing, labeling, and sequencing. Students' books can be open or closed.

  Categorizing. Students group vocabulary based on categories which you've written on the board. There is an example in italics underneath each category heading. Students can randomly call out words which you then write on the board, or work by themselves or in pairs to make lists on a separate sheet of paper.

  Have students categorize vocabulary.

Shapes	**Solids**
triangle	*sphere*

  [Mathematics, p. 118]

  Labeling. Students label a simple drawing you have put on the board or on the overhead projector. Students can either come to the chalkboard and tell you where to put the label, or copy the drawing and work with a partner.

  Draw a large outline of a body. Have students come to the board and write the parts of the body on the outline. [The Body, pp. 74-75]

  Sequencing. Students sequence a series of *Dictionary* phrases that you have put on the board. Students can come to the chalkboard and number the phrases in order, tell you how to number them, or copy the phrases on a piece of paper and work with a partner to put them in order.

Have students tell you the order in which these things usually happen:

___start school

___get married

_1_ be born

___have a baby

___graduate

[Life Events, pp 28-29]

- **Conversations.** Students practice the conversations in order to use the vocabulary in a controlled setting. Words within the dialog that may be substituted are written in italic and underlined. Substitutions from the *Dictionary* page for these words appear below each conversation. In some conversations, words to be substituted are in italics and inside brackets. Here students can substitute freely, including using information about themselves.

  Put models on the board and practice. Make appropriate substitutions.

  A: Who likes to *make lunch* in your house?

  B: Usually I do. Sometimes my *[husband]* does.

  G. take the children to school, L. go to the market, N. clean the house, O. pick up the children, P. cook dinner [Daily Routines, pp.26-27]

To conduct a successful conversation activity, follow these steps.

1. Read the conversation aloud. Indicate the two speakers by the way you are facing or by gesturing with your hands (left hand out to indicate one speaker, right hand out to indicate the other) or by changing your tone. Ask students to guess where the conversation might be taking place and who could be talking, e.g., *in a market, a checker and a customer.*

2. Write the conversation on the board and model it with a student volunteer.

3. Have two students model the conversation.

4. Put a list of substitutions on the board next to the conversation and model the pronunciation of the words. Have two volunteers do the conversations again, making one or more substitutions.

5. Have students practice the conversation in pairs. Monitor their progress by walking around the room.

   HELPFUL HINT: Have more advanced students use the conversation as the beginning of a role play that they can then present to the class.

Introduction

- **Interview Questions.** These personalized questions provide a degree of unpredictability even though the answer does not require a long response. They can be used for class discussions, pairwork, or writing. You can use all the questions, or choose the ones which are most appropriate for your class.

  1. Which job skills do you have?

  2. Which ones would you like to learn?

  3. Which ones do not interest you?

  4. Do you prefer to learn on-the-job or in classes? Why?

  [Job Skills, p.140]

To conduct a successful interview activity you can do any of the following things:

1. Ask the questions to the class as a whole, calling on volunteers. You can repeat a student's answer before asking another student the same question. *Marta has three brothers. How many brothers do you have?* (In this example, you can also ask another student to repeat what Marta said.) To show students their similarities and differences, take a poll and write down the various answers given and the numbers of students corresponding to each one.

2. When using the questions for pair work, chose the questions you find appropriate to your class and write them on the board. Have students copy them on a piece of paper. Answer any questions they might have. Pair students and have them ask and answer the questions, not necessarily in order. Students can report back what their partner says.

3. Interview questions are also an excellent source for writing practice. Once again, choose the questions appropriate to your class and write them on the chalkboard. Have students write their answers in complete sentences. Pair students and have them exchange papers. Give students guidelines for feedback appropriate to their level and your lesson. One possibility might be: *Read your partner's paper and put an "X" next to the answer you find most interesting.* Or, another possibility: *Read your partner's paper and check to see if each sentence begins with a capital letter and ends with a period.* Have students discuss their responses with their partners. If you like, collect their papers.

- **Listening.** These focused listening tasks are a part of each lesson in the Teacher's Book. For these tasks, you either work with the material on the page or play a recorded listening passage from the **Teacher's Book Focused Listening Cassette** ▭.

The tapescripts for the cassette passages begin on page 209. In several cases, a single recorded listening passage has the vocabulary from two related topics. For example, *Colors,* page 12, and *Prepositions,* page 13, share the

same tapescript, but have different listening tasks.

In a listening task, your students listen for specific vocabulary and do such tasks as point to either the picture or the word in their *Dictionaries,* write the words or their numbers on a separate sheet of paper, or check off the category of each word they hear. All the listening passages, both those on the tape and those appearing in the lesson plan, include some language that students recognize but may not be able to produce, as well as some entirely unfamiliar language. The task is usually simple (writing numbers, pointing to pictures, drawing, or taking short notes) to allow students to focus on the act of listening rather than on how to do the task.

Listening: ▭ #27, p. 219

"The Patient Doctor" While a patient talks about an exam, students point to the pictures that are described. [Clinics, p. 84]

In addition to the taped listening exercises, these teacher-read listening activities are featured within the lesson plans:

Checklist. Students make a checklist with two or more headings. While you say the items, students make a check under the appropriate heading. When you're finished, students tell you their tallies.

Headings: *Saying "Hi"* and *Saying "Bye."* Sample Sentences: *Hi, Javier; G'nite; Good afternoon; See you tomorrow, Kim;* etc. [Everyday Conversation, p. 8]

Definitions. Students hear the definition of a word while looking at the *Dictionary* page, then write the number of the word or the word itself on a separate sheet of paper.

This cloth covers the dining room table. (tablecloth) *This has sugar in it.* (sugar bowl) Etc. [Dining Room, p. 41]

Interactive Dictation. Students hear a set of sentences related to the topic and are encouraged to interrupt using specific clarification strategies in order to take down the sentences correctly.

Dictate orders from the coffee shop menu. Speak naturally and encourage students to ask for clarification. *(Did you say white or wheat toast?)* Have student volunteers write the orders on the board and have the class check for correct spelling using page 61.

1. *I'll have two scrambled eggs with sausage, wheat toast, and a cup of decaf.* [A Coffee Shop Menu, p. 61]

Listen and Point. Students point to the pictures as you say the vocabulary words.

1. *Point to the whale, the largest mammal.* (#29) 2. *Point to the sea lion sitting on a rock.* (#34) Etc. [Marine Life, Amphibians, and Reptiles, pp. 130-131]

Listen and Write. Students listen to sentences related to the topic and write down only the target information (weather conditions, dates, etc.).

Have students listen and write the adjective in each sentence. E.g.:

1. *That music is too **noisy** for me.* **2.** *That cup is **empty**. Please refill it.* Etc. [Describing Things, p. 11]

To conduct a successful focused listening activity follow these steps:

1. Review the specific vocabulary for which students will be listening. Focused listening teaches listening skills, not new words.

2. Preview the situation or context of the listening passage. This helps students anticipate or predict what they will hear.

3. Demonstrate the task and treat the first item as an example in order to further assist student's prediction skills. Directions are an important part of listening skill development and it is important to go over the directions for both the recorded and nonrecorded listening passages.

4. Speak at a natural speed with normal stress and intonation when you are reciting the listening script. (The cassette listening passages already do this for you.)

5. Interrupt the listening passage to create opportunities for students to tell you what they've heard and how they've responded to the listening task. *What number are you pointing to? What did you write for #2?*

6. When students' answers vary, write the different responses on the board and have students listen to the segment again until the class reaches a consensus on the best answer. Usually three to five repetitions are enough for the students to "hear" the answer.

7. Give students an opportunity to hear the entire passage one last time to show them the growth in their listening skills.

The *Focused Listening Cassette* allows students to hear the same information the same way, each time you play the tape. (We teachers have a tendency to emphasize the words we want our students to hear.) The passages are spoken with the natural speed, intonation, and rhythm your students will hear outside the classroom. With the listening cassette, you can control how much of each passage your students hear at one time. In addition, by using the pause and rewind buttons on your tape recorder, you permit your students to listen again and again to specific sections, phrases, or words in the passage.

The listening cassette contains a variety of voices, accents and sound effects creating a dramatic and entertaining listening experience. This will motivate students to continue listening even when they don't hear or understand every word.

HELPFUL HINT: It is not uncommon for students to feel stressed during a listening activity. They often wait to answer until they hear or see other students' answers. You can lessen their anxiety by treating the entire listening activity as an example. Telling students what they will hear and then having them listen for it is a good way to reassure students that they can understand English spoken at normal speed. Demonstrate how often they will get to hear the passage by repeating one segment of a listening passage five times. As students gain confidence, you can gradually decrease the number of samplings until you are giving students only one sampling for each listening activity.

EXPAND THE LESSON

The type of activities in the EXPAND THE LESSON section allows students to use the target vocabulary in conjunction with previously acquired language, and helps them to "take ownership" of the vocabulary. Tasks such as solving a problem, deciphering an idiom, or expressing opinions and reaching a consensus increase students' communicative competence in the workplace, at social events, and in their daily community interactions.

The grammatical accuracy expected during expansion activities is a matter of teaching philosophy. Many of these activities involve students' taking a risk by sharing their ideas publicly. Overt or frequent error correction may prevent the student from speaking up again. However, accuracy does play a role in how comprehensible students are to each other as well as to people outside the classroom. Your task in these activities is to evaluate a student's response as much for the strength of the message as for the strength of the form.

You can structure these activities for success by giving students an accurate model for expressing their opinions and providing language that will enable them to agree with, disagree with, question and expand upon each other's opinions. As students do more and more of these kinds of activities, they build up a repertoire of formulaic language that they can use.

Each lesson plan in this book includes at least one expansion activity. (For topics covering two pages, there are often three or more such activities.) The main activities in this section are described below. Note: Some one-of-a-kind activities appear occasionally but are not included here. For them, step-by-step procedures are described completely in each instance.

- **Problem Solving**. This activity asks students to consider difficult situations and then brainstorm possible solutions. Students learn to analyze and think critically in the course of solving the problem.

  Max makes money for his family. He's 25 years old and works full-time. He wants to learn new job skills but doesn't have time. What advice can you give him? [Job Skills, p. 140]

Introduction

Karl Simms is afraid of hospitals. His doctor just told him he has to have his gall bladder removed. This is a simple operation, but Karl doesn't want it because he is too scared to go to the hospital. What advice would you give Karl? [A Hospital, pp. 86-87]

There are three stages to a problem-solving activity:

1. Introduce the problem.

2. Have students restate the problem.

3. Have students suggest solutions.

To introduce the problem, you can read the problem to the class, write the problem on the board and have students read it, or act out the situation with two or three students. (This last option is easiest for beginning-level students to understand.) Whatever your method of presenting the problem, students need time to restate the problem in their own words before trying to provide solutions. You may need to ask questions to elicit the restatement. *Who are we talking about? What does he do now? What does he want to do? What does he need to do? What's stopping him?*

Once the class has grasped the gist of the situation, they can brainstorm their solutions in a variety of ways:

- Individual students from the class can take turns calling out possible solutions as you record them on the board.

- In small groups, four to five students can take turns proposing solutions, while a group recorder writes the ideas down.

- Students, in pairs, can take a minute or two to think of a solution, explain their solution to one another, and then team up with another pair to share their ideas. These foursomes can then decide on which solution they want to share with the class at large.

- **Discussion Questions.** These questions are designed for both whole-class or small-group discussions. They have more than one possible answer and require higher level critical thinking and language skills than the Interview Questions from the PROVIDE PRACTICE section. Answers often reflect students' cultural backgrounds.

Psychologists advise U.S. parents they should not criticize their teens' clothing choices unless they are unhealthy or unsafe. Is this good advice? Why or why not? [Clothing I, pp. 64-65]

Do you think it is appropriate to wear exercise wear in public? Why or why not? [Clothing III, p. 67]

In some of these questions the language is more appropriate for the low-intermediate learner. The learner at this level will be able to rely on a larger vocabulary than the beginner, and will be able to handle small-group discussions. Beginners will perform better in whole-class discussions, especially if you have provided a few model structures that students can use such as, *I think it's a good idea for people to wear exercise wear in public because it's comfortable.*

Here are some ways you can set up discussions.

- Write one question on the board and have students jot down their ideas. Survey the class for students' responses. *How many people said it was a good idea? How many people said it wasn't?* You can then run the whole-class discussion by calling on volunteers to share their individual opinions and asking people who disagree to say why.

- Divide the class into small groups of 4 to 5 students. Give students a time limit and have them discuss their answers to the question. A group recorder can take notes, and a group reporter can give the group's answers.

- Write 2 to 4 questions on the board and have students choose the one they'd like to discuss. Then group students according to the questions they chose and have them share responses.

HELPFUL HINT: Discussions, both small-group and whole-class, require the teaching of turn taking, disagreeing, agreeing, and participation skills. Often a few outspoken students will dominate the discussion unless there are some pre-arranged structures that prevent them from doing so. You could ask a dominating student to be the recorder in a discussion; set a time limit for each student's response; or pass around a talking stick (or other object) in group and class discussions, so that only the person holding the stick can talk. In addition you will find it helpful to teach language that encourages participation (*Just a minute Tom. Sam what do you think?*), expresses disagreement (*I don't agree with you. I think…*), and expresses agreement (*That's a good point. I agree except for…*).

- **Language Workout.** Here students look at topic-related idiomatic and colloquial phrases and deduce their meaning from context. To introduce these sentences, you can write the idioms on the board and elicit the possible meanings from the class, or tell a short story that includes the Language Workout sentences and discuss the meaning of the target phrases.

I really miss my friend Hong. I haven't seen him in a month of Sundays. [Calendar, pp.18-19]

Use the idiomatic expressions where appropriate throughout your lesson and applaud your students' efforts to use the expressions as well.

HELPFUL HINT: To further encourage students to use this language in their speech, you can collect all the Language Workout idioms from one *Dictionary* unit and write them on one side of the board. Then write the meanings of the idioms in scrambled order on the opposite side of the board and have students match the meaning to the idiom.

- **Speeches**. Students at all levels create one minute talks on a theme related to the *Dictionary* topic. First, students fill in cloze sentences on the topic, such as those below, and then put phrases together into a short speech that they will give to the class.

    _____ is the best place to visit! The most popular tourist attraction there is _____. The best time to visit is in the _____ (spring, summer, fall, winter) because you can _____. [North America and Central America, pp. 122-123]

These speeches are an excellent opportunity for students to get experience preparing a presentation in English, and students profit as much from listening to the speeches as they do from giving them.

- **Drawing Activities.** Students design or draw something related to the *Dictionary* topic and then share the results with the whole class or their groups. This gives students a chance to personalize and expand the use of the vocabulary.

    Extraterrestrial! Have each student draw a picture of a being from outer space, e.g., a head with three eyes, two mouths, one ear, etc. After each student has drawn an extraterrestrial, the students take turns describing their beings to their partners. [Body, pp. 74-75]

Drawing activities often allow beginning-level students to perform at a level equal to or higher than advanced-level students.

HELPFUL HINT: Once the drawings are finished, students can get further language practice by asking about or commenting on each other's work.

- **Writing Activities.** Students use the vocabulary in communicative writing assignments such as descriptive paragraphs, letters, or classified ads.

    Have students imagine they are the landlord of an expensive apartment building. Have them write a classified ad for one apartment. Have volunteers describe their apartment and how wonderful it is. [Apartments, pp. 36-37]

HELPFUL HINT: In writing activities, students can be placed in pairs, with the higher-level student writing both partners' ideas.

GAMES

GAMES are additional enrichment activities where students can practice the language they have learned. The variety of games within the *Teacher's Book* was selected on the basis of their "play-ability," ease of instruction, and adaptability to numerous topics within the *Dictionary*. There is an assortment of games familiar to teachers and students (charades, scrambled words, scavenger hunts, and memory games) along with some variations on classic ESL activities such as spelling bees, bingos, brainstorms, and chain drills. Some games are for whole-class teams, others for small groups, and still others for pairs.

The GAMES section follows the EXPAND THE LESSON section on most of the two- page *Teacher's Book* topics. Since two-page topics in the *Dictionary* contain from 30 to 60 vocabulary words, students benefit from the additional practice that the games afford. Every game contains step-by-step numbered directions which assist in setting up, conducting, and monitoring the activity.

Games help students review and practice previously learned vocabulary in an engaging way, assist in evaluating how easily students can manipulate or recall the vocabulary, and also serve as a culminating activity for *Dictionary* topics within a particular unit. The inherent characteristics of games such as forming teams, taking turns, working toward a common goal, and—of course—winning, all contribute toward a highly communicative activity.

While certain games appear on certain topic pages, they are not exclusive to that topic. The following games can easily be adapted for use with many different *Dictionary* topics.

- **A-Z Brainstorm.** Students memorize vocabulary and choose a recorder to write words alphabetically, as group members randomly call them out. The group with the most correct words wins.

    Have students in groups of 4-5 study the personal hygiene products on pages 76-77 for 2 minutes and then close their books. Recorders for each group write the letters of the alphabet vertically down the side of their papers. Then they write down the vocabulary words by the appropriate letter as the rest of the group calls them out. Call time after 5 minutes… [Personal Hygiene, pp. 76-77]

- **Backward Dictionary.** Student teams listen to descriptions of target vocabulary and try to guess the word.

    Give definitions or descriptions of the vocabulary words to one team at a time. *They hold the body up. Sometimes they get broken. They show up in X rays. What are they?* (bones) [The Body, pp. 74-75]

- **Charades.** Students act out vocabulary words for their teams.

    Write different household problems on slips of paper and put them into a box or hat. Students take turns picking a problem, and act out fixing it… [Household Problems, pp. 48-49]

- **Class Go-Around.** Students take turns listening to a sentence that features target vocabulary, repeating the sentence and adding new vocabulary, building an oral "chain."

   Begin by saying *Ceila lost the rent check. She looked in the elevator.* A student volunteer repeats the two sentences and adds another phrase. *Ceila lost the rent check. She looked in the elevator and in the hallway.* The next volunteer repeats this, and adds vocabulary again... [Apartments, pp. 36-37]

- **Definition Bingo.** Students write dictated vocabulary on a grid, then listen for definitions, circling the words they hear until they get four in a row.

   Dictate 16 life events. Have students write them into squares in random order. Give a sample definition. *You meet your teacher and classmates on the first day.* Check and be sure all students have circled *start school* on their papers... [Life Events, pp. 28-29]

- **Questions Only!** Students work in groups to study a *Dictionary* topic and write questions about the page.

   Have students look at pages 62-63 and come up with as many questions as they can about the scene. *(Where is the busperson going?)* Recorders write their groups' questions on the board. The group with the most correct questions wins. [Restaurant, pp. 62-63]

- **Spell Check.** Students work in teams to study the spelling of words and write them correctly.

   Tell the first student on each team a word from pages 138-139 and have him or her write it on the board. If the word is spelled correctly, the student earns a point for his or her team and may sit down. Team members who make a mistake go to the end of the line to have another chance... [Jobs and Occupations, H-W, pp. 138-139]

- **Word Links.** Student teams study vocabulary words for two minutes, then take turns writing them in crossword style.

   Write the word *rhinoceros* horizontally on the board. Have a volunteer from Team A come up and write a connecting word vertically, using any letter in the word *rhinoceros*... [Mammals, pp 134-135]

To ensure a successful game-playing experience:

1. Demonstrate the game with student volunteers.

2. Play the game against the class before dividing into student teams.

3. Make sure students have sufficient exposure to the vocabulary.

4. Do a comprehension check on the directions. *Do you write horizontally or vertically? How long do you have to come up with an answer?*

5. Emphasize that cooperation often results in a "win."

6. Set a *firm* time limit.

   HELPFUL HINT: Students need an opportunity to take charge of class activities. Certain games may foster fierce competitiveness, where shy students fade into the background and only dominant voices are heard. To counteract this, emphasize the cooperative aspects of the games and utilize the classroom management strategies described below.

CLASSROOM MANAGEMENT STRATEGIES

Comprehension Checks

   Before beginning any activity that practices the new vocabulary, it is important to be sure students understand the vocabulary on the page. Here are three ways to check for students' understanding.

- Conduct a **silent drill.** Ask *yes/no* questions where the whole class answers silently, raising one finger for *yes*, two for *no*. E.g.: *Is #3 a blouse? Is the woman in the pink dress dancing?*

- Do a short **listen and point** activity. Have students cover the word list. Call out different vocabulary words and have students point to them as you say them. *Point to the park. Look for the bank. Point to the bank. Do you see the courthouse? Point to the courthouse.* Walk around the room checking where they are pointing on the page.

- Ask the whole class **short answer** questions. Have students cover the word list. Ask questions which require one- or two-word answers such as: *What do we call the number and street where we live? What are three things you see in the kitchen?* If the same students keep responding, go around the room, giving each student a chance to answer a question. If students cannot respond, review the vocabulary.

Pairwork

   In pairing students and assigning roles, you may wish to use a variety of techniques. It is a good idea to encourage students to work with as many different people as possible and to vary the methods of making this work. You can assign pairs randomly by handing out playing cards and having students with the same numbers find each other. Or pair students who have different first languages.

   By assigning roles for pairwork, you make the context of the lesson clearer. There is less confusion if all students have roles before they begin.

For example, when doing a conversation, clearly define who is speaking, such as a landlord and a tenant, an employee and an employer, etc. Have students decide who will take each role. If the roles are not explicit, such as with two friends talking, have the student with the longest name, shortest hair, etc., be "A" while the other partner is "B."

With Interview Questions, designate one student as the "teacher" and the other as the "student." (Students enjoy being given the role of "teacher.") You can also name one student an interviewer, such as Barbara Walters, and name the other student a famous person, such as a current actor or political leader. Set a time limit and have students switch roles.

Groupwork

Groupwork goes more smoothly if groups are assigned in some way and if group members have certain responsibilities. The ideal groups have some degree of heterogeneity in terms of ethnicity, language, gender, age, and ability. If a teacher alternates allowing students the freedom to choose their own groups, with putting students into specific groups, students soon realize that there are many learning situations in the class.

To create groups of mixed ability in classes with regularly attending students, you can make name cards ahead of time and place them on the desks. Students find their name cards to know where they sit. Where students do not come regularly, randomly give out playing cards. Have all the ones, twos, etc., find each other. Designate an area of the classroom where each number will sit.

Each time students are grouped, be sure they introduce themselves to one another (if they don't know one another's names). Have them share a little information about themselves before they begin the activity.

Another approach to groupwork is to assign various tasks to group members. Possibilities include recorder, timekeeper, reporter, reader, English monitor, and observer. One way to assign roles easily is to keep a numbered list of these roles on a chart in the room. Tell students which role numbers they will need for a particular activity and have them choose numbers.

Overhead Projectors (OHPs)

Teachers fortunate enough to have an OHP in their classroom will find using transparencies very helpful. By copying the conversations, the interview and discussion questions, problem-solving topics, or idioms and expressions from the Language Workout section onto a transparency, the entire class can focus on the portion of the activity you are modeling or explaining. You can also mask part of the transparency. This focuses students' attention on the part of the lesson you are talking about.

You may also want to use the *Oxford Picture Dictionary Overhead Transparencies*, which reproduce every page of the monolingual English edition of the *Dictionary*. By selectively masking and/or pointing, you can focus students on any part of the page. You can mask parts of an illustration, drawing attention to certain items; or you may wish to mask the words. You can gradually introduce the word list, uncovering each word as you say it.

In addition, some teachers use cutouts of small circles, X's, or animals, and place them directly on the transparency to talk about location. *Where is the X? It's on the bookcase. Where is the cat? It's on the sofa.*

Quiet Signals

Setting up a *Quiet* signal with your class is the fastest way to stop any activity when students are actively engaged. Teachers have been known to use a variety of signals for students to be quiet: a raised hand, a bell, a train whistle, flicking the lights on and off. Anything is better than using your voice, which needs to be saved for instruction!

Monitoring

While students are working together, walk around the room to assess how they are doing. It is best to be as unobtrusive as possible. This is a time for you to make mental or actual notes of where students are having difficulty, to listen for grammar and pronunciation problems, to see how they ask for clarification, etc. Rather than correcting individual students, wait a day or two and do a lesson based on the errors you have heard or observed.

Workbooks, pp. 2–3
Classic Classroom Activities, Unit 1
Related Dictionary Pages
• School, p. 5
• Studying, pp. 6–7
• Prepositions, p. 13

TOPIC NOTES

In the U.S., students usually **raise their hands** to answer a question, make a statement, or volunteer for a task. Teachers then call on the students whose hands are raised.

A **chalkboard** is also called a *board* and sometimes a *blackboard. Whiteboards* use special markers rather than chalk.

TEACHING TIPS
Related Vocabulary

instructor*   school supplies
professor   AV equipment
learner   transparency
dry-erase board   call on someone

Grammar: These verbs are irregular in the past: *stand/stood, write/wrote, take/took,* and *put/put.*
Introduce possessive adjectives: *my/his/her/our/your(plural)/their*
Make new commands for verbs I–L.

☼ Teach the words *door, window, cabinet, closet,* and other special features of your classroom. Combine verbs F–J with these objects to make new commands, e.g. *Open the door.*

⚠ When demonstrating verbs A–L, avoid asking *What am I doing?* until the present continuous has been taught. Ask, *What do I do after I open my book?*

A Classroom

1. chalkboard   3. student   5. teacher   7. chair/seat
2. screen   4. overhead projector   6. desk

A. Raise your hand.   **B. Talk** to the teacher.   **C. Listen** to a cassette.   **D. Stand up.**

E. Sit down./Take a seat.   **F. Point** to the picture.   **G. Write** on the board.   **H. Erase** the board.

  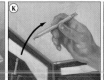

I. Open your book.   **J. Close** your book.   **K. Take out** your pencil.   **L. Put away** your pencil.

2

INTRODUCE THE TOPIC

Describe your classroom as though you were a real estate agent talking about its various features. *This green chalkboard is perfect for writing. And here we have six wonderful pieces of white…* Pretend to forget a target word every now and then, in order to assess what language students already know.

Ask students their opinions about the classroom. *Is this a big room? Do you like the desks? chairs? Do you like to look at the chalkboard or the overhead projector and screen?* (Point to the objects to ensure comprehension.)

Write these three words on 3" x 5" index cards: *chalkboard, chair, desk.* Ask a volunteer to place the cards on or near the correct objects in the classroom.

TEACH THE NEW WORDS

Walk around the room collecting as many of the items featured on pages 2 and 3 as you can. Name each item as you collect it. *I'm looking for a pencil. Oh, here's a pencil.* When you have 8–10 school supplies, call out *Whose pencil is this?* Students raise their hands as you say, *Oh, it's Jorge's pencil. Here's your pencil, Jorge.*

PROVIDE PRACTICE
Chalkboard Activities

△ Have students categorize vocabulary.

Listen to	Read	Write with/ Draw with
cassette	book	pencil

△ Have students sequence the actions.
_____ **Close it.**
_____ **Write in it.**
_____ **Put away your pencil.**
_1_ **Sit down.**
_____ **Take out your pencil.**
_____ **Open your notebook.**

Conversations

△ Put models on the board and practice. Make appropriate substitutions.

A: Is this your *seat?*
B: No, it isn't. I think it's *[Katya's].*
   6. desk 11. cassette player 18. pen
   19. marker 20. pencil 22. textbook

A: Did you hear what the teacher said?
B: She said, *"Stand up."*
   E. Sit down. E. Take a seat. I. Open your book. J. Close your book. K. Take out your pencil.

A: My *textbook* is missing!
B: I see it. It's over by the *teacher.*
A: Oh, thank goodness!
   23. workbook/8. bookcase
   24. binder/28. dictionary
   26. spiral notebook/29. picture dictionary

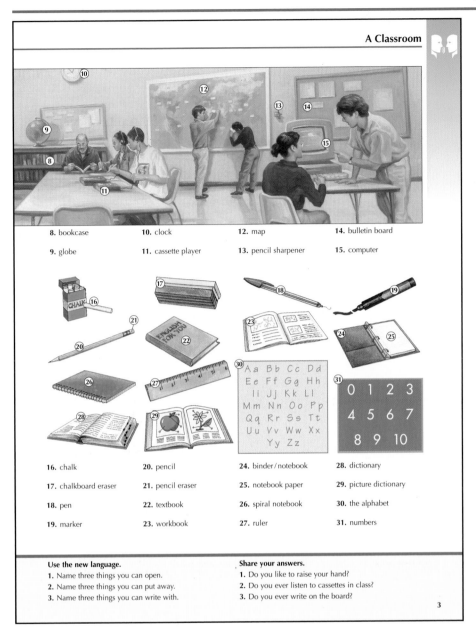

A Classroom

8. bookcase
9. globe
10. clock
11. cassette player
12. map
13. pencil sharpener
14. bulletin board
15. computer

Aa Bb Cc Dd
Ee Ff Gg Hh
Ii Jj Kk Ll
Mm Nn Oo Pp
Qq Rr Ss Tt
Uu Vv Ww Xx
Yy Zz

0 1 2 3
4 5 6 7
8 9 10

16. chalk
17. chalkboard eraser
18. pen
19. marker
20. pencil
21. pencil eraser
22. textbook
23. workbook
24. binder / notebook
25. notebook paper
26. spiral notebook
27. ruler
28. dictionary
29. picture dictionary
30. the alphabet
31. numbers

Use the new language.
1. Name three things you can open.
2. Name three things you can put away.
3. Name three things you can write with.

Share your answers.
1. Do you like to raise your hand?
2. Do you ever listen to cassettes in class?
3. Do you ever write on the board?

3

Interview Questions

1. Which school supplies do you have with you today?
2. Do you prefer to write with a pen or a pencil?
3. Do you prefer to write with markers or chalk?
4. Do you prefer to use a binder or a spiral notebook?
5. What are the three most important tools in a classroom?
6. How many letters or characters are in the alphabet in your language?
7. Which items in the picture of the classroom do you have at home?

Listening: 📼 #1, p. 209
"Whaddya Need?" Have students listen and point to the objects on pages 2 and 3.

EXPAND THE LESSON
Problem Solving
△ Have students brainstorm solutions.
Nathan raises his hand every day to answer the teacher's questions. The teacher always calls on other students. What can Nathan do?

Discussion Questions
1. Do you think computers will take the place of teachers in the future?
2. Which book do you think is most important for learning English?
3. Is it important for a teacher to teach every page in a textbook? Why or why not?

Drawing Activity
△ Have students in small groups draw a picture of the ideal classroom and then share their pictures with the class.

GAMES
Charades
1. Write the verbs A–L on slips of paper and put them into a box or hat.
2. Divide the class into two teams.
3. Students take turns picking a word and acting it out for their teams.
4. Teams get a point for each word they guess.
5. The game ends when all the slips are gone.

Spell Check
1. Divide the class into two teams.
2. Give teams 10 minutes to study the spelling of the words on pages 2–3.
3. Have teams line up on either side of the room.
4. Give the first student on each team a word from the pages and have him/her write it on the board.
5. Team members who spell the word correctly sit down and earn a point for their team.
6. Team members who make a mistake go to the end of the line, so that they can have another chance.
7. The game ends when all the members of one team are seated.

Scavenger Hunt
1. Post a list of ten classroom items that students may have: a blue pen, a red dictionary, a plastic ruler, a broken pencil, etc.
2. Group students in fours, and have a recorder in each group copy the list.
3. Have students look up any words they don't know in their dictionaries.
4. Groups try to find as many items on the list as possible from within their own group by asking and answering the question: *Do you have…?*
5. Compare the results of the scavenger hunt with the whole class.
6. Discuss which items were easy and which items were impossible to find.

Option: You can give students a new list and have them search for items at home.

3

Unit 1　Personal Information　page 4

Workbooks, p. 4
Classic Classroom Activities, Unit 1
Related Dictionary Pages
- Numbers, pp. 14–15
- Family, pp. 24–25
- Life Events, pp. 28–29

TOPIC NOTES

In the U.S., people usually refer to friends, family, and colleagues by their **first names**. Employers, doctors, and teachers are addressed by their title, such as Professor, or by Mr., Ms., Mrs., or Miss. before the last name.

Women in the U.S. commonly use their father's **last name** until they marry, and then they take their husband's last name. Some married women keep their father's name or hyphenate their father's last name and their husband's last name, e.g. Jones-Smith.

TEACHING TIPS
Related Vocabulary

age*	marital status
married*	single
divorced*	widowed
spouse	education
job experience	languages spoken
driver's license number	

Usage: Dates in the U.S. are usually written in month-day-year order, e.g. *May 7, 1988* abbreviated *5-7-88*.

- ☼ Teach the numbers 1–10 to make giving personal information easier.
- ☼ Teach students a spelling alphabet to make their oral spelling more comprehensible: *A as in apple, B as in boy, C as in cat,* etc.
- ⚠ Many students do not know their addresses and telephone numbers. Ask students to bring them to class before you begin.

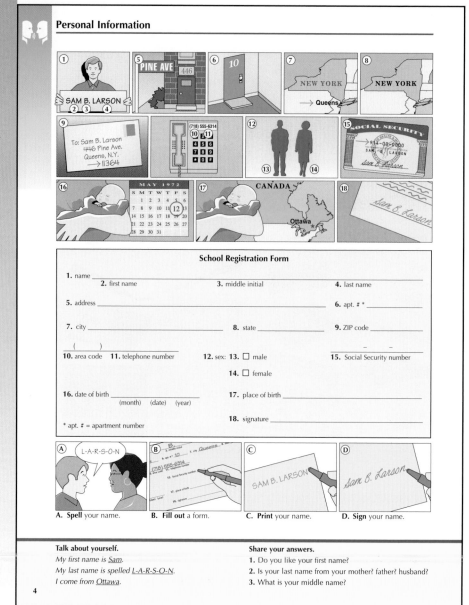

Personal Information

School Registration Form

1. name _____
2. first name
3. middle initial
4. last name
5. address _____
6. apt. # * _____
7. city _____
8. state _____
9. ZIP code _____
(___)
10. area code　11. telephone number
12. sex:　13. ☐ male
14. ☐ female
15. Social Security number _____
16. date of birth _____
 　　(month)　(date)　(year)
17. place of birth _____
18. signature _____
* apt. # = apartment number

A. **Spell** your name.　B. **Fill out** a form.　C. **Print** your name.　D. **Sign** your name.

Talk about yourself.
My first name is Sam.
My last name is spelled L-A-R-S-O-N.
I come from Ottawa.

Share your answers.
1. Do you like your first name?
2. Is your last name from your mother? father? husband?
3. What is your middle name?

4

INTRODUCE THE TOPIC

Talk about your own personal information. Begin with your name. *My name is Nancy Dustin Thomas. My first name is Nancy. My last name is Thomas. That is my husband's last name. My last name before I was married was Dustin.*

Draw pictures of your house or apartment building, a telephone, and a Social Security card with fictitious identifying numbers and talk about them.

Ask students to look at the dictionary page. Talk about Sam Larson. Point out his address, telephone number, etc.

TEACH THE NEW WORDS

Ask students a series of *yes/no* questions about the pictures. *Is the man's name Sam?* (yes) *Is his area code 718?* (yes) *Is his birthday in April?* (no)

PROVIDE PRACTICE
Chalkboard Activities

△ Write categories on the board. Students call out information about themselves.

Place of Birth	**Birthday**
Sonora, Mexico	*March 4, 1975*

△ Write specific information and have students tell you what it is.

(916) 555-2326	*telephone number*
72385	*ZIP code*
July 3, 1945	_____

Conversations

△ Put models on the board and practice. Make appropriate substitutions.

A: What is your name?
B: My name is *[Bich Duc Lee]*.
A: What's your *address*?
B: It's *[51 Flat St.]*.

11. telephone number 15. Social Security number 16. date of birth 17. place of birth

Interview Questions

1. What kinds of papers do you usually sign?
2. Do you like to write in handwriting or print letters in English?

Listening: Listen and Write

△ Have students write down a student's personal information as you dictate it. E.g.:

1. *His name is Dan Nickel. D-A-N N-I-C-K-E-L*
2. *His address is 430 2nd Street.*
3. *The city is Las Vegas.* Etc.

EXPAND THE LESSON
Discussion Question

Most people are careful about giving out their telephone number. Is your telephone number a secret?

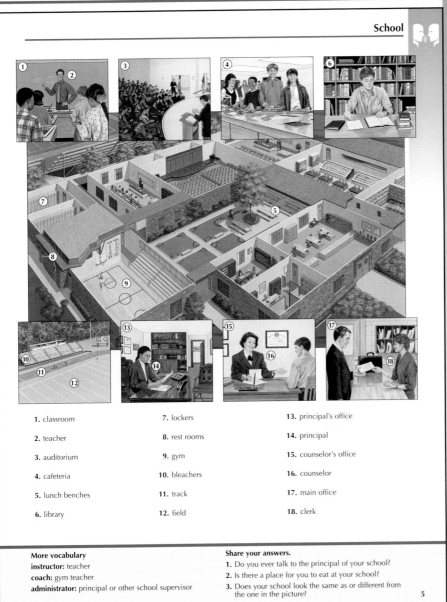

School

1. classroom
2. teacher
3. auditorium
4. cafeteria
5. lunch benches
6. library
7. lockers
8. rest rooms
9. gym
10. bleachers
11. track
12. field
13. principal's office
14. principal
15. counselor's office
16. counselor
17. main office
18. clerk

More vocabulary
instructor: teacher
coach: gym teacher
administrator: principal or other school supervisor

Share your answers.
1. Do you ever talk to the principal of your school?
2. Is there a place for you to eat at your school?
3. Does your school look the same as or different from the one in the picture?

5

Workbooks, p. 5
Classic Classroom Activities, Unit 1
Related Dictionary Pages
• A Classroom, pp. 2–3
• A Graduation, pp. 32–33
• Types of Schools, p. 112

TOPIC NOTES

In the U.S., most students attend public, tax-supported institutions. Local school districts operate elementary and secondary schools, but most school funding and policies are in the hands of the states.

Lockers are found adjacent to **gyms,** where students change their clothes for athletic classes. Many secondary schools install lockers in the corridors so students can store books and other personal items.

📁 The PTA (Parent–Teacher Association) is one of the oldest nationwide school organizations.

💡 Invite your school's counselor or other support staff to discuss relevant information with your students.

TEACHING TIPS
Related Vocabulary

teacher's aide	assembly
dean	portable classroom
volunteer	orientation
homeroom	student pass
periods	faculty lounge

Spelling: Homonyms
Principal has two meanings: 1. (n) the head of a school, 2. (adj) the most important. The homonym *principle* means a basic truth, law, or belief.

💡 Review the school registration form on page 4 to help students complete school paperwork.

INTRODUCE THE TOPIC

Tell a story about your first day at a new school. *I couldn't find my locker! My teacher was angry when I was late.*

Describe the location of several places at your school. Deliberately make mistakes and have students correct you. *The library is next to the gym, right?*

TEACH THE NEW WORDS

Ask students to call out the number of each picture you describe. *Teams play soccer and football here.* (#12)

PROVIDE PRACTICE
Chalkboard Activity

△ Have students categorize vocabulary:

Inside	Outside	Both
auditorium	*field*	*teacher*

Conversations

△ Put models on the board and practice. Make appropriate substitutions.

A: Excuse me. Where is the *field*?
B: Follow me. I'm going there too.
   3. auditorium 4. cafeteria 6. library
   7. lockers 8. rest rooms 9. gym

A: Did you hear about the new *teacher,* [Mr. Percy]?
B: Yeah, I heard [he's] really [strict].
A: Shhh! There [he] is, over by the *rest rooms!*
   14. principal/13. principal's office
   16. counselor/15. counselor's office
   18. clerk/17. main office

Interview Questions

1. Which rooms and places are there at your school?
2. Who do you talk to the most—the principal, counselor, or clerk?
3. Where is the quietest place in your school? the noisiest place?

Listening: Listen and Write

△ Dictate sentences that include the target language. Have students write the school places or people they hear. E.g.:
1. *The **main office** is room 101.*
2. *Get an application from the **clerk.*** Etc.

EXPAND THE LESSON
Discussion Questions

1. How would you like to change your school? What do you like best about your school?
2. Where are the best places for new students to make friends?

Language Workout

△ Copy this sentence on the board and discuss its meaning.
He *ditched school* to go to a mall.

5

Unit 1 Studying page 6

Workbooks, pp. 6–7
Classic Classroom Activities, Unit 1
Related Dictionary Pages
• A Classroom, pp. 2–3
• School, p. 5
• English Composition, p. 113

TOPIC NOTES

In the U.S., students sometimes work with **partners** or in small **groups** to **share** information and learn from each other. This is often referred to as cooperative learning.

⚠ Students may not be used to this strategy, and may need to hear the benefits of working together.

Class work is an assignment that can be completed during class time.
Homework is an assignment that students complete outside the classroom.

TEACHING TIPS
Related Vocabulary

index	respond
word list	evaluate
assignment*	translate
assist	distribute
find a word	make a check
memorize	

Grammar: Separable verbs
These verbs are separable, two-word verbs: *look up, pass out, fill in, cross out.* Demonstrate these by using the full form and then replacing the noun with a pronoun, thus changing the word order: *Fatima, look up "daisy" in the dictionary. Look it up in the index. Jung, pass out these papers. Please pass them out to everyone.* Etc.

Studying

Dictionary work

A. **Look up** a word.   B. **Read** the word.   C. **Say** the word.

D. **Repeat** the word.   E. **Spell** the word.   F. **Copy** the word.

Work with a partner

G. **Ask** a question.   H. **Answer** a question.   I. **Share** a book.   J. **Help** your partner.

Work in a group

K. **Brainstorm** a list.   L. **Discuss** the list.   M. **Draw** a picture.   N. **Dictate** a sentence.

6

INTRODUCE THE TOPIC

Write a word from the dictionary that you feel sure students will not know. Have students tell you how to find out what the word means.

Ask students how they learn new words (e.g., write them in a list, repeat them three times, etc.). Ask them if they like to learn or study alone, with a partner, or in groups.

Demonstrate the verbs *read, say, repeat, spell, ask, answer, help, draw, talk, circle, cross out, underline, match,* and *correct* to assess what students already know. Have students close their books and identify what you're doing.

TEACH THE NEW WORDS

Act out each of the sequences on the two pages. Do only one sequence at a time. Then have student volunteers demonstrate the actions as you give the commands.

PROVIDE PRACTICE
Chalkboard Activities

△ Have students categorize vocabulary:

Actions	Things
share	*book*

△ Have students sequence the actions.

_____	**Check** your work.
_____	**Fill in** the blank.
_____	**Collect** the papers.
_____	**Correct** your mistakes.
_____	**Follow** the directions.
_____	**Discuss** the answers.
_1_	**Pass out** the papers.

Conversations

△ Put models on the board and practice. Make appropriate substitutions.

A: How do you learn new vocabulary?
B: I *say* each new word three times.

   D. repeat E. spell F. copy

A: What did the teacher say to do?
B: She said to *ask a question*.

   H. answer a question I. share a book
   J. help your partner K. brainstorm a list
   L. discuss the list M. draw a picture, etc.

A: You didn't follow the directions!
B: Aren't we supposed to fill in the blanks?
A: No, you have to *circle the answers*.

   T. mark the answer sheet U. cross out the words V. underline the words W. put the words in order X. match the items

Interview Questions

1. How do you learn new words?

2. Which new words have you learned this week?

3. Do you like to ask questions? What are some typical questions you ask every day?

4. Do you like to work with a partner? Name three partners you have worked with.

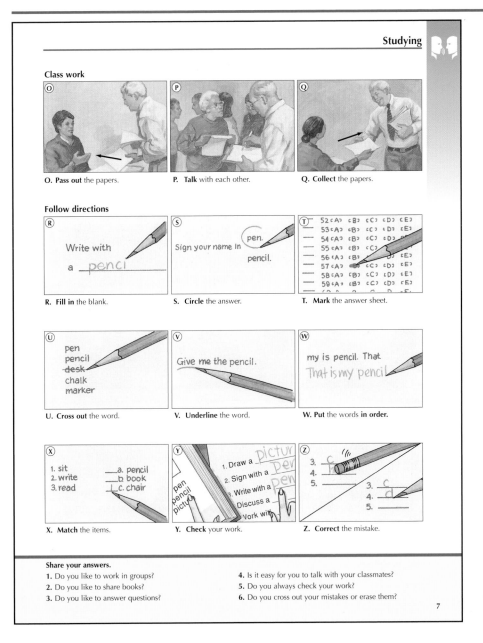

Studying

Class work

O. **Pass out** the papers.

P. **Talk** with each other.

Q. **Collect** the papers.

Follow directions

R. **Fill in** the blank.

S. **Circle** the answer.

T. **Mark** the answer sheet.

U. **Cross out** the word.

V. **Underline** the word.

W. **Put** the words **in order**.

X. **Match** the items.

Y. **Check** your work.

Z. **Correct** the mistake.

Share your answers.

1. Do you like to work in groups?
2. Do you like to share books?
3. Do you like to answer questions?
4. Is it easy for you to talk with your classmates?
5. Do you always check your work?
6. Do you cross out your mistakes or erase them?

7

5. Do you like to work in groups?
6. Do you like to draw? Name something you can draw.
7. Do you like to talk with your classmates?
8. Do you usually check your work?
9. Do you like it when the teacher dictates sentences?
10. Do you prefer to discuss things in a large group, in a small group, or with a partner?

Listening: 🔊 #2, p. 209
"What Do I Do?" Students listen and follow the directions given by the instructors.

EXPAND THE LESSON
Problem Solving
△ Have students brainstorm solutions.

1. *A friend never gets 100% on his spelling tests. How can he do better?*

2. *Ana has a hard time following directions at work. She is embarrassed to tell her supervisor that she doesn't understand his directions. Her supervisor is angry because Ana makes many mistakes. What can you tell Ana to help her?*

3. *A group of four people has to brainstorm a list and one person in the group does not want to work. What advice do you have for the group members?*

Discussion Questions

1. How many words do you think a person can learn in one day?

2. Who is responsible for a student's learning, the teacher or the student?

3. What are some ways you can study English outside the classroom?

Vocabulary Building

1. Divide students into groups of six.

2. Identify a leader in each group.

3. Give the leaders six blank 3" x 5" cards each and have them copy these commands off the board (one command per card):
   A) Copy it.
   B) Look it up.
   C) Read it.
   D) Repeat it.
   E) Spell it.
   F) Say it.

4. Erase the board and write five words on the board that are new to the class but can be found in the picture dictionary.

5. Have leaders, in their groups, deal out the command cards and choose a word from the list on the board.

6. Tell students they will have 10 minutes to study their new word using study skills on their cards.

7. The person with card "A" calls out the command *Copy it* and all group members copy the new word. The person with card "B" says *Look it up* and all the group members look up the word. Continue with all cards.

8. Once a group finishes, they pick a new word and repeat the process.

Take a Test/Make a Test

1. Copy this test on the board and have the class take it together.

   Sample Test: Studying pp. 6–7
   Match.
   1) Ask   _____ a story
   2) Talk to   _____ the answer
   3) Discuss   _____ your partner
   4) Fill in   _____ the papers
   5) Pass out   _____ a question

   Cross out the word that doesn't belong.
   6) discuss   ask   talk to   write
   7) circle   share   mark   underline

   Fill in the blank.
   8) _____ your book with your partner.
   9) Put these words in _____.
   10) The opposite of "ask" is _____.

2. Divide the class into groups of four. Assign each group a dictionary page that they've already studied.

3. Assign a recorder for each group. Tell groups they have 30 minutes to create a test for their page(s) based on the sample test they've just taken.

4. Monitor the group work and make suggestions for revisions.

5. Collect the tests and administer one daily as a review activity.

Unit 1   Everyday Conversation   page 8

- Weather, p. 10
- Feelings, pp. 30–31
- Clothing I, pp. 64–65

TOPIC NOTES

In the U.S., short conversations, or "small talk," about weather, the speakers' locations, or popular entertainment are very common.

A **compliment** is usually accepted with *Thank you.* Sometimes a compliment is followed by a request for more information. *I love your sweater. Where did you get it?*

TEACHING TIPS
Related Vocabulary

make conversation	apology
pay a compliment	gratitude
small talk	introduction
How do you do?	Nice to meet you.
My pleasure.	Same here.
Thank you very much.	You're welcome.

Pronunciation: Stress and intonation
Demonstrate the stress and rising intonation in clarification questions: *Did you say **Sam?** The class begins **when? Who** is going to school?*

- Demonstrate colloquial and reduced speech forms for greetings such as *What's up? G'nite. Howarya?* Ask students to share greetings they've heard outside class.

- ⚠ Present the language on this page over a period of two or three days, and reintroduce it frequently.

Everyday Conversation

A. **greet** someone

B. **begin** a conversation   C. **end** the conversation

D. **introduce** yourself   E. **make sure** you **understand**   F. **introduce** your friend

G. **compliment** your friend   H. **thank** your friend   I. **apologize**

Practice introductions.
Hi, I'm <u>Sam Jones</u> and this is my friend, <u>Pat Green</u>.
Nice to meet you. I'm <u>Tomas Garcia</u>.

Practice giving compliments.
That's a great <u>sweater</u>, <u>Tomas</u>.
Thanks <u>Pat</u>. I like your <u>shoes</u>.
Look at **Clothing I,** pages **64 – 65** for more ideas.

8

INTRODUCE THE TOPIC

Demonstrate different greetings, introductions, and leave-takings as you walk around the room. (Students should have their books closed.) *Hi there, Sun Yee! See you later. I'm going over here to talk to Fruzan. How are you, Fruzan? Fruzan, this is Julio. Julio, Fruzan.*

Ask students to share how they say "Hello" in their native languages. Have the whole class try greeting each other in different languages. (This activity can be done with other expressions, like *good-bye, thank you,* or *I'm sorry* as well.)

TEACH THE NEW WORDS

Act out the conversations on the page for the class. Change voices with each speaker. Have students point to each word as you say it.

PROVIDE PRACTICE
Chalkboard Activities

△ Have students categorize vocabulary:

Greetings	**Leave-takings**
Hello	*Good-bye*

Conversation

△ Put models on the board and practice. Make appropriate substitutions.

A: Hello, my name's *[Jack]*.
B: Nice to meet you. I'm *[Max]*.
A: How do you *greet someone* in your language?
B: We say *["jambo"]*.
  B. begin a conversation C. end the conversation D. introduce yourself, etc.

Interview Questions

1. Do you like to begin conversations?
2. Do you like making introductions?
3. Do you give compliments often?

Listening: Checklist

1. Have students make checklists with the headings *Hi* and *Bye*.
2. Say the sentences below, while students make a check under the appropriate column.
3. Have students tell you their tallies. (The correct tally is 6 *Hi's* and 4 *Bye's*.)

Hi, Javier!	*Have a great weekend.*
How are you?	*Hello there!*
G'nite!	*See you tomorrow, Kim.*
Good evening!	*Let's talk tomorrow.*
Can we talk?	*Good afternoon.*

EXPAND THE LESSON
Problem Solving

△ Have students brainstorm solutions. *Ten minutes after Sara meets a person, she can't remember his or her name. What can she do to remember names?*

The Telephone

1. telephone/phone
2. receiver
3. cord
4. local call
5. long-distance call
6. international call
7. operator
8. directory assistance (411)
9. emergency service (911)
10. phone card
11. pay phone
12. cordless phone
13. cellular phone
14. answering machine
15. telephone book
16. pager

Using a pay phone

A. **Pick up** the receiver.
B. **Listen** for the dial tone.
C. **Deposit** coins.
D. **Dial** the number.
E. **Leave** a message.
F. **Hang up** the receiver.

More vocabulary
When you get a person or place that you didn't want to call, we say you have the **wrong number**.

Share your answers.
1. What kinds of calls do you make?
2. How much does it cost to call your country?
3. Do you like to talk on the telephone?

9

Workbooks, p. 9
Classic Classroom Activities, Unit 1
Related Dictionary Pages
• Everyday Conversation, p. 8
• Numbers and Measurements, pp. 14–15

TOPIC NOTES

In the U.S., the telephone is the most popular way to communicate. Portable and **cellular phones** have made phone use in airplanes, cars, and remote areas routine.

The use of automated telephone systems means that callers more often push buttons to access "menu information" and less often actually reach an **operator**.

Emergency service (911) allows you to place a call where human life or property is in jeopardy and prompt aid is essential.

TEACHING TIPS
Related Vocabulary

area code*	beeper
fax number	voice mail
out-of-order	caller ID
rotary phone	touch tone phone
unlisted number	toll-free
busy signal	call waiting

Grammar: Separable verbs
Pick up, call up, and *hang up* are separable verbs. *Hang up the phone. Hang it up. Call him up.* (*Call up* means to call on the phone.)

☼ Teach the cardinal numbers on page 14 so that students can practice making mock calls.

⚠ Alert students if there is a charge for directory assistance in your area.

INTRODUCE THE TOPIC

Bring in a copy of a phone bill. Talk about the charges. *I made five long-distance calls after 8:00 P.M. It costs less to call at night. I call 411, directory assistance, if I don't know a number.*

Ask students about their telephone habits. Take an informal survey. *How many phone calls do you make each day? Do you have a cordless phone? Did you use a pay phone this week?*

TEACH THE NEW WORDS

Draw a large telephone pad. Call out the actions as you make a call. *I'm making a local call. First, I pick up the receiver. Now I'm dialing the number.* Have students come to the board and practice making calls as you call out the numbers.

PROVIDE PRACTICE
Chalkboard Activities

△ Have students brainstorm a list of people or places for these calls:

Local Call	411	911
friend	library	fire department

Conversations

△ Put models on the board and practice. Make appropriate substitutions.

A: Operator.
B: I'm having trouble making this *local call*.
A: All right. Did you *listen for the dial tone?*
  5. long-distance call/C. deposit coins
  6. international call/D. dial the number

A: Do you hear that sound?
B: Yes, I do. I think it's that *telephone*.
  11. pay phone 12. cordless phone
  13. cellular phone 16. pager

Listening: Scrambled Commands

△ Students cover the vocabulary and write the letter for each command you give. E.g.:
  1. *Leave a message.* (E)
  2. *Pick up the receiver.* (A) Etc.

EXPAND THE LESSON
Discussion Questions

1. What emergency and personal telephone numbers do you know?
2. Is it better to call directory assistance or look in the phone book?
3. What information do you give when you leave a message?

Language Workout

△ Copy these sentences on the board and discuss their meanings.
  1. I can't talk now. I'll *get back to you* later.
  2. Bob's really angry. He *hung up on me*.

9

Unit 1   Weather   page 10

Workbooks, p. 10
Classic Classroom Activities, Unit 1
Related Dictionary Pages
- Numbers and Measurements, pp. 14–15
- Clothing, pp. 64–67
- Natural Disasters and Emergencies, pp. 102–103

TOPIC NOTES

In the U.S., the weather, a universal topic of conversation, provides a common icebreaker—*Isn't it a nice day today?*

Extreme weather like **heat waves** and **snowstorms** are important news events. Meteorologists try to predict these conditions before they arrive. **Smog,** the result of air pollution, is a combination of smoke and **fog.**

📁 Thermometers measure **temperature** in degrees. The centigrade, or Celsius, scale is used in most countries outside the U.S. The Fahrenheit scale is used in the U.S. Here are the conversion formulas:
$$°C=5/9(°F - 32)$$
$$°F=9/5(°C + 32)$$

TEACHING TIPS
Related Vocabulary

fair	barometric pressure
breezy	chance of precipitation
overcast	windchill factor
drizzle	flurries
sleet	partly cloudy
blizzard	first-stage smog alert

Usage: Some temperature words are also used to describe feelings. *I'm freezing.* Or, *Her forehead feels hot.*

💡 Review pages 64–66, *Clothing I–II,* so students can discuss what to wear for different weather conditions.

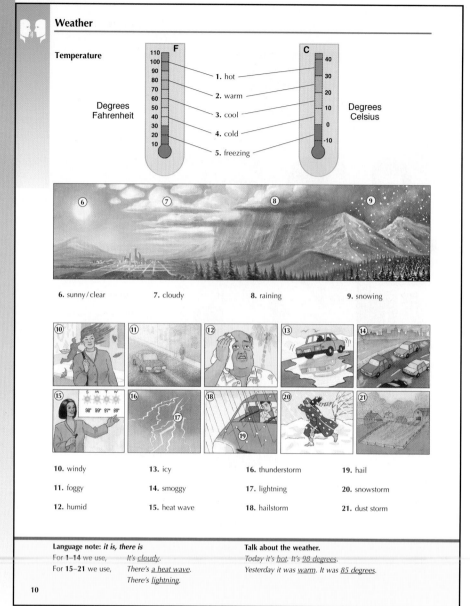

Weather

Temperature

1. hot
2. warm
3. cool
4. cold
5. freezing

Degrees Fahrenheit   Degrees Celsius

6. sunny / clear   7. cloudy   8. raining   9. snowing

10. windy   13. icy   16. thunderstorm   19. hail
11. foggy   14. smoggy   17. lightning   20. snowstorm
12. humid   15. heat wave 18. hailstorm   21. dust storm

Language note: *it is, there is*
For **1–14** we use,   *It's cloudy.*
For **15–21** we use,   *There's a heat wave.*
                        There's lightning.

Talk about the weather.
Today it's hot. It's 98 degrees.
Yesterday it was warm. It was 85 degrees.

10

INTRODUCE THE TOPIC

Bring in accessories (an umbrella, sunglasses, etc.). Talk about weather conditions as you select items. *It's so sunny I need my sunglasses.*

Act out a TV weather forecast, putting temperatures and symbols on the board. *Friday's high will be 98° under sunny skies.*

TEACH THE NEW WORDS

Ask students a series of *or* questions about the pictures. *Is #3 cool or cold?* (cool) *Is #19 rain or hail?* (hail)

PROVIDE PRACTICE
Chalkboard Activities

△ Have students categorize vocabulary:

Good Weather	**Bad Weather**
sunny	*freezing*

Conversations

△ Put models on the board and practice. Make appropriate substitutions.

A: What's the weather like today?
B: It's *sunny*.
  6. clear 7. cloudy 8. raining 9. snowing
  10. windy 11. foggy 12. humid 13. icy
  14. smoggy

A: You're back! How was *[Buenos Aires]?*
B: Terrible! We had *a heat wave* for five days!
  16. thunderstorms 17. lightning 19. hail
  20. a snowstorm 21. a dust storm

Interview Questions

1. What's your favorite weather?
2. What is the weather like in January in your native country?
3. What types of weather are dangerous to drive in?
4. Does smoggy weather affect you?

Listening: Listen and Write

△ Have students write the weather and temperature as you give different forecasts. E.g.:
  1. *It's partly cloudy and 68°.*
  2. *Tomorrow, look for 15" of snow.* Etc.

EXPAND THE LESSON
Problem Solving

△ Have students brainstorm solutions. *There's a heat wave and your air conditioner is broken. How can you stay comfortable?*

Language Workout

△ Copy these sentences on the board and discuss their meanings.
  1. I'm feeling *under the weather* with this flu.
  2. George only calls when he needs something. What a *fair-weather friend!*

Describing Things

1. little hand
2. big hand
3. fast driver
4. slow driver
5. hard chair
6. soft chair
7. thick book / fat book
8. thin book
9. full glass
10. empty glass
11. noisy children / loud children
12. quiet children

13. heavy box
14. light box
15. neat closet
16. messy closet
17. good dog
18. bad dog
19. expensive ring
20. cheap ring
21. beautiful view
22. ugly view
23. easy problem
24. difficult problem / hard problem

Use the new language.
1. Name three things that are thick.
2. Name three things that are soft.
3. Name three things that are heavy.

Share your answers.
1. Are you a slow driver or a fast driver?
2. Do you have a neat closet or a messy closet?
3. Do you like loud or quiet parties?

11

Workbooks, p. 11
Classic Classroom Activities, Unit 1
Related Dictionary Pages
• Age and Physical Description, p. 22
• Describing Clothes, p. 71
• Doing the Laundry, p. 72

TOPIC NOTES
Little and **big, fast** and **slow** are examples of adjectives used to describe an objective, measurable situation.

Beautiful and **ugly** are examples of adjectives used to describe more subjective situations.

TEACHING TIPS
Related Vocabulary

tiny	dull
large*	sharp
tidy	smooth
quick	rough
vacant	straight
inexpensive	crooked

Grammar: Comparatives and superlatives
The comparative and superlative forms of adjectives are made in three different ways.
1. Add -er and -est to one-syllable words: An ambulance is **faster** than a bus. An airplane is the **fastest** way to travel.
2. Add more and most to two-syllable words: The gold ring is **more expensive** than the silver one. That diamond ring is the **most expensive** of all.
3. Use a different word for irregular adjectives, such as **good.** My dog is **better** than yours. Jane has the **best** dog in town.

⚠ Expose students to alternate definitions for these words: cheap (poorly made), light (pale color), and soft (quiet).

INTRODUCE THE TOPIC
Describe your classroom, leaving some sentences open-ended as though you'd forgotten the words. Look at my desk— papers everywhere! It's always…(messy). See if students can supply the missing word(s).

TEACH THE NEW WORDS
Ask students a series of or questions about the pictures. Look at #7. That dictionary has 900 pages. Is it thick or thin?

PROVIDE PRACTICE
Chalkboard Activities
△ Have students categorize vocabulary:

1. **People**   **Things**
   noisy   hard

2. **Positive** **Negative** **Neutral**
   quiet   noisy   thick

Conversations
△ Put models on the board and practice. Make appropriate substitutions.

A: Tell me about your new watch.
B: It's _expensive_.
   1. little 2. big 3. fast 4. slow 20. cheap
   21. beautiful 22. ugly

A: How's your [English] class?
B: It's pretty _good_. What about your class?
A: It's OK. The place is really _noisy_.
   18. bad/22. ugly
   23. easy/15. neat
   24. difficult/16. messy

Interview Questions
1. Name some fast and slow animals.
2. Is English easy or difficult to learn? Why?
3. Name a beautiful place to visit in your native country.

Listening: Listen and Write
△ Have students listen and write the adjective in each sentence. E.g.:
   1. That music is too **noisy** for me.
   2. That cup is **empty.** Please refill it.
   3. She's a **slow** driver. Etc.

EXPAND THE LESSON
Discussion Questions
1. Which language is the most difficult to learn? Why?
2. What expensive gift would you like to receive?
3. How can you be a good person?

Problem Solving
△ Have students brainstorm solutions. You are a very neat person. Your roommate is very messy. How can you live together without an argument?

Workbooks, p. 12
Classic Classroom Activities, Unit 1
Related Dictionary Pages
• Describing Hair, p. 23
• Clothing, pp. 64–67

TOPIC NOTES

In the U.S., colors help define our political, cultural, and social identity. **Red, white,** and **blue** are symbolic of our national unity; **white** and **black** represent life-cycle events such as weddings and funerals; and **pink** and **blue** are often chosen to identify gender from the time of birth.

Red, yellow, and **orange** are warm tones. **Green, blue,** and **purple** are cool tones.

📁 Clothing, caps, or small pieces of material such as ribbons are worn to identify special clubs or organizations. Team colors and gang colors are strong group identifiers.

TEACHING TIPS
Related Vocabulary

gold	navy blue
silver	hot pink
neutral colors	primary colors
neon	secondary colors
bright	metallic colors
faded	color-blind

Usage: We ask questions by saying *What color is it?* (not *What color does it have?*) We answer *It's blue.* (not *It's a blue color.*)

Pronunciation: Silent *-e*
Practice target words with silent letter *e: orange, purple, white,* and *blue.* The vowel combination *ei* in *beige* is pronounced [ā], as in the word *gray.*

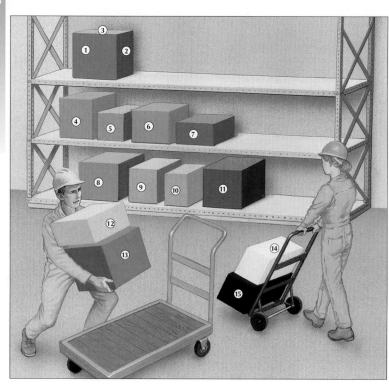

Colors

1. blue
2. dark blue
3. light blue
4. turquoise
5. gray
6. orange
7. purple
8. green
9. beige
10. pink
11. brown
12. yellow
13. red
14. white
15. black

Use the new language.
Look at **Clothing I,** pages 64–65.
Name the colors of the clothing you see.
That's a dark blue suit.

Share your answers.
1. What colors are you wearing today?
2. What colors do you like?
3. Is there a color you don't like? What is it?

12

INTRODUCE THE TOPIC

Tell a colorful story about a Fourth of July celebration. Describe the *gold* and *blue* band uniforms, the *red, white,* and *blue* flags, and the fireworks.

Bring in several clothing ads. Have students help you decide what to buy. *Do you like this brown jacket? What color goes with these blue pants?*

TEACH THE NEW WORDS

Ask students a series of *or* questions about the pictures. *Is box #10 red or pink?* (pink) *Is box #11 beige or brown?* (brown)

PROVIDE PRACTICE
Chalkboard Activity

△ Have students categorize vocabulary:

Things in a Park	On a Highway
green grass	*white signs*

Conversations

△ Put models on the board and practice. Make appropriate substitutions.

A: Do you have this *[sweater]* in purple?
B: Sorry. It only comes in *blue* or *white*.
   4. turquoise/5. gray
   8. green/9. beige
   10. pink/11. brown

A: I'd like to buy a dozen red roses, please.
B: Sorry, we're out of those. How about *yellow* ones?
   10. pink 14. white

Interview Questions

1. What colors are you wearing today?
2. What's your favorite color?
3. What is your least favorite color?

Listening: 📻 #3, p. 209

"What Color Goes Where?" Have students listen and write the colors on page 12.

EXPAND THE LESSON
Discussion Questions

1. What are the colors of your native country's flag? What do the colors mean?
2. What colors do you associate with Valentine's Day? Halloween?
3. What are good colors to paint a kitchen? a bedroom? a classroom?

Language Workout

△ Copy these sentences on the board and discuss their meanings.
1. That storm came *out of the blue.* The weather report said it would be sunny.
2. Shirley won the lottery. Her friends were *green with envy.*
3. They *rolled out the red carpet* for the president's visit.

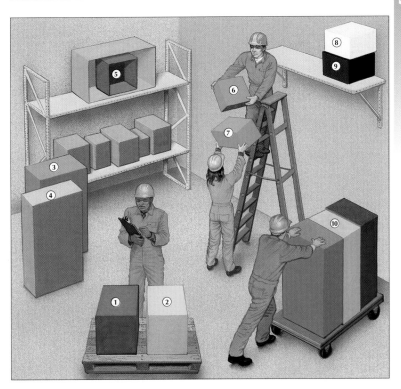

Prepositions

1. The red box is **next to** the yellow box, **on the left.**

2. The yellow box is **next to** the red box, **on the right.**

3. The turquoise box is **behind** the gray box.

4. The gray box is **in front of** the turquoise box.

5. The dark blue box is **in** the beige box.

6. The green box is **above** the orange box.

7. The orange box is **below** the green box.

8. The white box is **on** the black box.

9. The black box is **under** the white box.

10. The pink box is **between** the purple box and the brown box.

More vocabulary
near: in the same area
*The white box is **near** the black box.*

far from: not near
*The red box is **far from** the black box.*

13

Workbooks, p. 13
Classic Classroom Activities, Unit 1
Related Dictionary Pages
• Colors, p. 12
• Prepositions of Motion, p. 105

TOPIC NOTES

In the U.S., people on the East Coast tend to say *stand **on** line,* while people on the West Coast say *stand **in** line.*

TEACHING TIPS
Related vocabulary

beside	near*
inside	outside
in the center	on top of
over*	beneath
in back of	to the rear
facing	across *

Usage: *above/over* and *below/under* are sometimes used interchangeably. *Over* actually indicates something traveling above or spanning across something else: *The airplane is over land right now. The bridge is over the river.* Under can also indicate that something is beneath and concealed by something else. *The snake is under the rock.*

Pronunciation: Stress
Stress falls on the most important words or the newest information in a sentence. Say these sentences and have students identify the stressed information:

*The **purple** box is on the **gray** box.*
*The **purple** box is on the gray box.*
*The purple box is **on** the gray box.*
*The purple box is on the **gray** box.*

INTRODUCE THE TOPIC

Bring in a box. Move it into different locations around the room: on students' desks, above their heads, or under their chairs. Comment on what you're doing as you do it: *Nope, not next to the door. No, no, I don't like it above your head. Hmmm, maybe in front of Julio. Ummm, I think it looks good under Olga's desk.*

TEACH THE NEW WORDS

Act out and give a series of commands using students' school supplies. *I put the pencil on my book. Put the pencil on your book. I put the pencil in my book. Put the pencil in your book. Etc.*

PROVIDE PRACTICE
Chalkboard Activities

△ Draw a box on the board and have students come up and draw an X on the box, under the box, in the box, etc.

Conversations

△ Put models on the board and practice. Make appropriate substitutions.

A: I can't find the [white] box.
B: It's over there, <u>on the black box.</u>
A: Oh, I see it now.
  (All responses are based on the picture.)

A: Excuse me, where's [room 7]?
B: It's <u>next to</u> [the library].
A: <u>Next to</u> what?
B: [The library].
A: Thanks.
  (All responses are based on your school.)

Interview Questions

1. Where's your desk? pencil? book?
2. Do you have a TV? Where is it?

Listening: 🔲 #3, p. 209
"What Color Goes Where?" Have students write the prepositions they hear.

EXPAND THE LESSON
Drawing Dictation

1. Have partners sit so that one faces the board and the other doesn't.
2. Put one of these drawings on the board:

3. The students facing the drawing describe it, so their partners can draw it.
4. Students check their work, change seats, and work on the next drawing.

Workbooks, pp. 14 –15
Classic Classroom Activities, Unit 1
Related Dictionary Pages
- Personal Information, p. 4
- Weather, p. 10
- The Calendar, pp. 18–19
- Mathematics, p. 118
- Weights and Measures, p. 57

TOPIC NOTES

In the U.S., some people consider 3 and 7 to be lucky numbers and 13 to be unlucky. Many hotels and office buildings do not have a 13th floor.

The U.S. uses the customary, or English, system of measurement, which uses inches, feet, yards, and miles for distance, as well as the metric system, which uses millimeters, centimeters, and kilometers.

Cardinal numbers are used for counting and telling how many. *George has 3 brothers.*

Ordinal numbers tell the number in a series or the rank of something. *Carmen lives on the 3rd floor. Hilda was the 3rd person to finish the puzzle.*

TEACHING TIPS
Related Vocabulary

single	a dozen
a couple	a few
some	many
several	most
infinity	none

Pronunciation: These numbers sound alike: *13 / 30, 14 / 40, 15 / 50, 16 / 60, 17 / 70, 18 / 80, 19 / 90.* Point out that *"-ty"* is pronounced *"-dy"* in the numbers 20, 30, 40, etc., and is unstressed.

 Review classroom objects so that students can talk about "how many" there are of each.

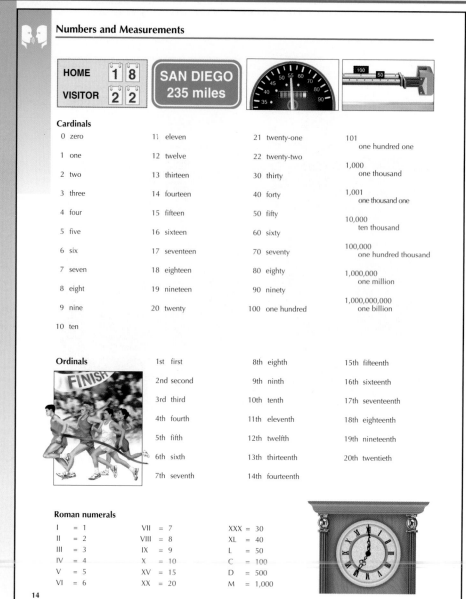

Numbers and Measurements

HOME 1 8
VISITOR 2 2

SAN DIEGO 235 miles

Cardinals

0 zero	11 eleven	21 twenty-one	101 one hundred one	
1 one	12 twelve	22 twenty-two		
2 two	13 thirteen	30 thirty	1,000 one thousand	
3 three	14 fourteen	40 forty	1,001 one thousand one	
4 four	15 fifteen	50 fifty		
5 five	16 sixteen	60 sixty	10,000 ten thousand	
6 six	17 seventeen	70 seventy	100,000 one hundred thousand	
7 seven	18 eighteen	80 eighty	1,000,000 one million	
8 eight	19 nineteen	90 ninety		
9 nine	20 twenty	100 one hundred	1,000,000,000 one billion	
10 ten				

Ordinals

1st first	8th eighth	15th fifteenth
2nd second	9th ninth	16th sixteenth
3rd third	10th tenth	17th seventeenth
4th fourth	11th eleventh	18th eighteenth
5th fifth	12th twelfth	19th nineteenth
6th sixth	13th thirteenth	20th twentieth
7th seventh	14th fourteenth	

Roman numerals

I	= 1	VII	= 7	XXX	= 30
II	= 2	VIII	= 8	XL	= 40
III	= 3	IX	= 9	L	= 50
IV	= 4	X	= 10	C	= 100
V	= 5	XV	= 15	D	= 500
VI	= 6	XX	= 20	M	= 1,000

14

INTRODUCE THE TOPIC

Talk about the pictures at the top of the page. *Look at the first picture. What sport is this? Who is winning? Look at the third picture. How fast is the car going?*

Ask students about people in the classroom, by questioning *How many… ? How many women are in class today? How many men? What percentage are men? How many walked to school today?*

Bring in documents with numbers on them: driver's license, Social Security card, etc. Talk about why it's important to remember these numbers.

TEACH THE NEW WORDS

Have students repeat the numbers as you say them in order. Say them out of order and have students point to them on the pages.

PROVIDE PRACTICE
Chalkboard Activities

△ Have students write words for the numbers:

2 _two_	15 _____	20 _____
7 _____	80 _____	26 _____

△ Have students write the Arabic equivalent:

III = *3*　　　**XVII =**　　　**XI =**

△ Draw a measuring stick on the board that goes to 7 feet. Mark it in inches and feet on one side, and meters on the other. Have students come up and measure their height.

7ft — 2m
6ft
5ft
4ft — 1m
3ft

Conversations

△ Put models on the board and practice. Make appropriate substitutions.

A: How many *[windows]* are in this classroom?
B: Wait a minute. Let me count them. There are *[three]*.

A: How many days are in a *[week]*?
B: *[Seven]*.

A: How did the game go?
B: We won—*[seven to three]*.

A: What a great sale!
B: Yes, the pants are *[30%]* off and the shoes are *[50%]* off!

A: How do your friends come to school?
B: *[Half]* take the bus, *[a quarter]* walk, and *[a quarter]* are in a car pool.

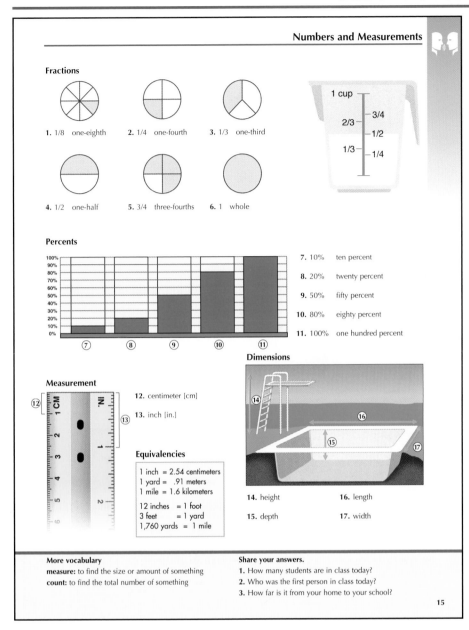

Numbers and Measurements

Fractions

1. 1/8 one-eighth
2. 1/4 one-fourth
3. 1/3 one-third
4. 1/2 one-half
5. 3/4 three-fourths
6. 1 whole

1 cup
3/4
2/3
1/2
1/3
1/4

Percents

7. 10% ten percent
8. 20% twenty percent
9. 50% fifty percent
10. 80% eighty percent
11. 100% one hundred percent

Measurement

12. centimeter [cm]
13. inch [in.]

Equivalencies

1 inch	= 2.54 centimeters
1 yard	= .91 meters
1 mile	= 1.6 kilometers
12 inches	= 1 foot
3 feet	= 1 yard
1,760 yards	= 1 mile

Dimensions

14. height
15. depth
16. length
17. width

More vocabulary
measure: to find the size or amount of something
count: to find the total number of something

Share your answers.
1. How many students are in class today?
2. Who was the first person in class today?
3. How far is it from your home to your school?

15

9. *My brother got a ticket. He was driving over **80** miles an hour.*

10. *It's very hot today, over **90**.*

EXPAND THE LESSON

Discussion Questions

1. Most countries use the metric system. The U.S. uses the customary, or English, system that was started in England 800 years ago. Do you think the U.S. should use the metric system exclusively? Why or why not?

2. The number 13 is considered unlucky in the U.S. Do you believe in lucky and unlucky numbers? What numbers are special to you? Why?

Information, Please

1. Get a list of students' birthdays.

2. Call roll by using numbers: for example, 10/21 for October 21. Speak at a normal speed.

3. Students say, "here" or "present" when their birthday is read.

Show Me

1. Bring in 12 items (beans, pennies, paper clips, etc.) for every student. Give commands beginning with numbers. *Show me 8. Show me 12.* Speak at a natural speed. Repeat the commands 5–7 times.

2. Students take the number of items and place them on the top of their desks. Walk around to check.

3. Continue with fractions and percentages. *Show me one half of the beans. Show me 25% of the beans.*

Language Workout

△ Copy these sentences on the board and discuss their meanings.

1. Sam always knows when it's going to rain. He has a *sixth sense* about that.

2. Frank likes basketball and baseball about the same. *It's six of one, half a dozen of the other.*

3. Frank's a great friend. He's *one in a million.*

GAMES

Number Bingo

1. Have students make a grid that is five rows across and five rows down and fill it in with numbers from 1 to 100.

2. Call out numbers randomly. Students circle numbers as you say them.

3. The game ends when one student has five in any row, vertically, horizontally, or diagonally, and calls out "Bingo!"

4. Continue playing until five students have gotten Bingo.

Interview Questions

1. How many brothers do you have?
2. How many sisters do you have?
3. What position are you in your family? (E.g., the first son, the second daughter, the third child, etc.)
4. What year where you born?
5. What is your ZIP code?
6. How far do you travel to school?
7. What percentage of the people in this class speak your native language?
8. Do you have a lucky number? What is it?
19. Do you have an unlucky number? What is it?
10. What is your height in feet and inches? What is your height in centimeters?

Listening: Listen and Write

△ Have students write the numbers in these sentences as you say them.

1. *The baby is so big! He weighs **13** pounds.*
2. *My grandmother is having a birthday! She's turning **70**.*
3. *My son just graduated from high school. He's **18**, you know.*
4. *Today is our anniversary. We've been married **16** years.*
5. *How much is the coffee? It's only **50** cents and it's delicious!*
6. *Slow down! The speed limit is **60** around here.*
7. *Helen, my daughter, thinks **30** is old. I think it's young!*
8. *Turn right! Turn right! That's Highway **15**.*

Workbooks, p. 16–17
Classic Classroom Activities, Unit 1
Related Dictionary Pages
- Numbers and Measurements, pp. 14–15
- Daily Routines, pp. 26–27

TOPIC NOTES

In the U.S., the expression "to watch the clock" typifies an attitude towards time. Children learn to tell time at an early age. Almost everyone wears a watch and checks it often to "keep track" of the time. People without watches will commonly ask, "Do you have the time?"

Early and **late** are time concepts which are very different from one society to the next. Arriving 30 minutes late for a business meeting may or may not have negative consequences depending on what culture or country one is in. In the U.S., being early or **on time** is expected for interviews, meetings, work, and school. Social engagements are more flexible, allowing people to arrive after the stated arrival time for get-togethers and celebrations.

TEACHING TIPS
Related Vocabulary

tardy	9:00 A.M. sharp
overtime	9:00 on the dot
time and a half	deadline
alarm clock	timetable
wristwatch*	digital clock
stopwatch	clock in/out

Usage: We say *in the morning, afternoon,* or *evening.* We say *at night.*

Pronunciation: Times on the hour are pronounced with a schwa [ə]: *1:00* is pronounced *one-[ə]-clock,* but *1:05* is pronounced *one-[ō]-five.*

Time

1. second   2. minute   3. hour   A.M.   P.M.

4. 1:00
one o'clock

5. 1:05
one-oh-five
five after one

6. 1:10
one-ten
ten after one

7. 1:15
one-fifteen
a quarter after one

8. 1:20
one-twenty
twenty after one

9. 1:25
one twenty-five
twenty-five after one

10. 1:30
one-thirty
half past one

11. 1:35
one thirty-five
twenty-five to two

12. 1:40
one-forty
twenty to two

13. 1:45
one forty-five
a quarter to two

14. 1:50
one-fifty
ten to two

15. 1:55
one fifty-five
five to two

Talk about the time.
What time is it? It's 10:00 a.m.
What time do you wake up on weekdays? At 6:30 a.m.
What time do you wake up on weekends? At 9:30 a.m.

Share your answers.
1. How many hours a day do you study English?
2. You are meeting friends at 1:00. How long will you wait for them if they are late?

16

INTRODUCE THE TOPIC

Act out your typical day, announcing activities and times. *It's 7:00 A.M.—time to get out of bed and start the day. Oh, no, it's already 8:15. I'd better hurry or I'll be late for work.*

Bring in a clock with movable hands or draw one on the board. Point to and say the time using alternative words. *Class starts at 6:30 P.M. That's half past six.*

Talk about U.S. time differences as you point to the areas on a large U.S. map. *It's 12:00 noon eastern time in New York. In Los Angeles, it's 9:00 A.M. Pacific time.*

TEACH THE NEW WORDS

Ask students to identify the numbers of the pictures on page 16 based on your descriptions: *Class begins at 1:10. (#6) At the tone, the time will be 1:55. (#15)*

PROVIDE PRACTICE
Chalkboard Activities

△ Have students write the numbers for the corresponding times:

half past one	*1:30*
a quarter to five	____

△ Have students write the words for the corresponding times:

1:10	*one ten or ten after one*
3:55	_____

Conversations

△ Put models on the board and practice. Make appropriate substitutions.

A: Excuse me. What time is it?
B: It's *one o'clock.*
   6. one-ten 7. one-fifteen 8. one-twenty
   9. one twenty-five, etc.

A: Do you have the time?
B: It's *one-thirty.*
A: I'm sorry. What did you say?
B: It's *half past one.*
   7. one-fifteen/7. a quarter after one
   13. one forty-five/13. a quarter to two
   14. one-fifty/14. ten to two, etc.

A. Have a great time in *[Hawaii].*
B. Thanks, but I'm not leaving today. I'm leaving tomorrow *morning.*
   17. noon 18. afternoon 19. evening
   20. night

A: Why are you calling at this time of day?
B: I'm so sorry. I forgot you're on *eastern time.*
   26. Pacific time 27. mountain time
   28. central time

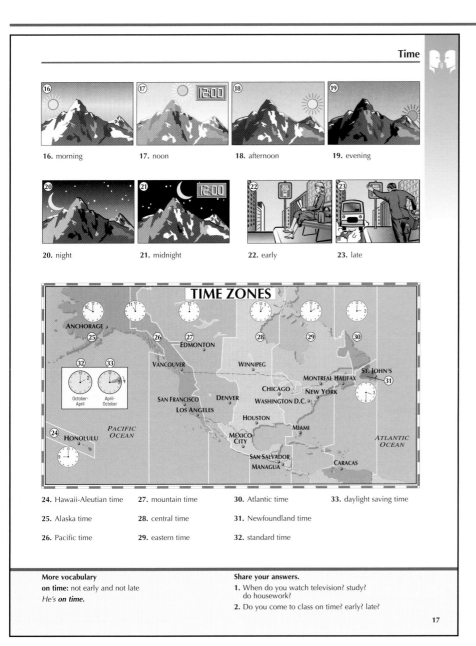

Time

16. morning   17. noon   18. afternoon   19. evening

20. night   21. midnight   22. early   23. late

TIME ZONES

ANCHORAGE

EDMONTON

VANCOUVER   WINNIPEG

October-April   April-October

SAN FRANCISCO   DENVER   CHICAGO   MONTREAL HALIFAX   ST. JOHN'S
LOS ANGELES   WASHINGTON D.C.   NEW YORK

HOUSTON

HONOLULU   PACIFIC OCEAN   MIAMI   ATLANTIC OCEAN

MEXICO CITY

SAN SALVADOR   CARACAS
MANAGUA

24. Hawaii-Aleutian time   27. mountain time   30. Atlantic time   33. daylight saving time

25. Alaska time   28. central time   31. Newfoundland time

26. Pacific time   29. eastern time   32. standard time

More vocabulary
on time: not early and not late
He's **on time.**

Share your answers.
1. When do you watch television? study?
   do housework?
2. Do you come to class on time? early? late?

17

Interview Questions

1. Do you go to bed early or late?
2. What activities do you do in the morning? in the evening?
3. How much time do you study English at home every day?
4. What time is it in your native country right now?
5. Are you usually early or late for class?
6. At what time do you prefer to work?
7. At what time do you prefer to relax?
8. What's your favorite time of day?

Listening: Listen and Write

△ Have students write the time in numbers as you read each sentence.
1. *At the tone, Pacific standard time will be* **one thirty-five.**
2. *At the tone, central standard time will be* **seven-eighteen and fifty seconds.**

3. *You've reached the Department of Motor Vehicles. Our offices open at* **eight-thirty A.M.** *Mondays through Fridays.*
4. *Let's see the* **five-fifteen** *movie. We only pay $5.00 for two tickets!*
5. *Hurry in for Val-Mart's Anniversary Sale! Stores open at* **nine A.M.**
6. *We're calling to confirm your appointment for September 3rd at* **three-thirty P.M.**
7. *Turn your clocks back one hour after* **midnight.**
8. *The next bus arrives at* **ten-ten A.M.**
9. *She fell asleep before the* **eleven o'clock** *news.*
10. *It's* **a quarter to six**—*hurry or we'll be late for class!*

EXPAND THE LESSON
Problem Solving
△ Have students brainstorm solutions. *Sasha's boss often tells her to stay late and work extra hours. Sasha wants to take some night classes and needs a more regular work schedule. She doesn't want to lose her job. What can she do?*

Discussion Questions
1. How much time does it take to travel across your native country?
2. New Year's Eve is celebrated at midnight. When are some other holidays celebrated?

Drawing Activity
1. Bring in white paper plates, grommet clips, scissors, and construction paper.
2. Have each student make a clock, writing numbers on the paper plate and attaching construction-paper hour and minute hands with the clip.
3. Call out several different times, asking students to set their clocks. Show the correct time on a large clock face on the board.
4. Have students, in pairs, take turns positioning the hands on their clocks and directing their partners to do the same. *The time is now 1:15.*
5. Pairs verify accuracy by comparing their clock faces after each turn.

Language Workout
△ Copy these sentences on the board and discuss their meanings.
1. *Take your time* and you won't make any mistakes.
2. *Long time no see!* How are you?
3. Leonardo Da Vinci was *ahead of his time.*
4. Stop *giving me a hard time* about my room—I'll clean it later!
5. I've got some *time to kill.* How about going shopping?
6. The last time I saw George he was a baby, now he's graduating from high school. My—how *time flies!*
7. This factory is open *around the clock,* so we have three eight-hour shifts.

GAMES
Team Quiz
1. Divide the class into two teams.
2. Distribute copies of newspaper TV listings.
3. Have each student write a question such as *What's on Channel…at…?*
4. Teams alternate asking and answering questions based on the handout. If teams answer correctly, they get a point.

Unit 1   The Calendar   page 18

Workbooks, pp. 18–19
Classic Classroom Activities, Unit 1
Related Dictionary Pages
- Personal Information, p. 4
- Numbers and Measurements, pp. 14–15
- Time, pp. 16–17
- Holidays, p. 168
- A Party, p. 169

TOPIC NOTES

In the U.S., many schools close or have limited programs in the **summer.** Historically, this allowed children and teenagers to help with farming. Where schools are overcrowded, some schools have year-round programs where **vacation** time falls throughout the year.

📁 The U.S. uses the Gregorian calendar. Other calendars used in different parts of the world are the Chinese calendar, the Hebrew calendar, and the Islamic calendar.

TEACHING TIPS
Related Vocabulary

decade	always
century	sometimes
millennium	usually
turn of the century	
the day before yesterday	
the day after tomorrow	

Pronunciation: The /th/ sound
Review *Thursday* (vs. *Tuesday*), *month, birthday, three, third, thirteen,* and *thirty.*

💡 Review ordinal numbers on page 14 so that students can talk about dates: *Yesterday was [the fourth]. I'm going to go to the… on [the sixth].*

💡 Bring in a calendar for this year and have students mark their birthdays. Have a monthly birthday party.

The Calendar

Days of the week

1. Sunday
2. Monday
3. Tuesday
4. Wednesday
5. Thursday
6. Friday
7. Saturday
8. year
9. month
10. day
11. week
12. weekdays
13. weekend
14. date
15. today
16. tomorrow
17. yesterday
18. last week
19. this week
20. next week
21. every day
22. once a week
23. twice a week
24. three times a week

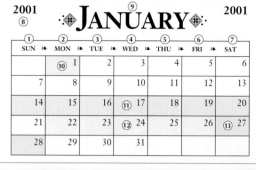

Talk about the calendar.
What's today's date? It's <u>March 10th</u>.
What day is it? It's <u>Tuesday</u>.
What day was yesterday? It was <u>Monday</u>.

Share your answers.
1. How often do you come to school?
2. How long have you been in this school?

18

INTRODUCE THE TOPIC

Ask students to look at page 18 and tell you if they have the same type of calendar in their country or a different one.

Draw a calendar for the week on the board. Talk about your schedule. *On Monday I have an appointment with the doctor. Tuesday is my mother's birthday. Wednesday I see the dentist. Thursday…* Etc.

TEACH THE NEW WORDS

Have students repeat the days of the week and months of the year as you say them in order. Establish one day as "today." Have students tell you the days for yesterday, tomorrow, etc.

Talk about the seasons, telling students what months are in each season.

PROVIDE PRACTICE
Chalkboard Activities

△ Have students categorize the months:

Summer	Fall	Winter	Spring
August	*October*	*January*	*April*

△ Have students say the day of the week that comes before and after the day you name:

Wednesday **Thursday** *Friday*

Conversation

△ Put models on the board and practice. Make appropriate substitutions.

A: What day is it?
B: Today? It's *[Sunday]*.
A: Of course! Yesterday was *[Saturday]*.

A: Nice seeing you again!
B: You, too. Have a great <u>day</u>!

8. year 9. month 11. week 13. weekend

A: When is your trip?
B: Not until next *fall*.

37. spring 38. summer 40. winter

Interview Questions

1. What is your favorite day of the week? Why?
2. What is your favorite season? Why?
3. How often do you study English?
4. How often do you go to the market?
5. How often do you go to a park?
6. Do you study on the weekends?
7. In what month is your birthday?
8. Which do you like more, weekends or weekdays? Why?
9. How long have you been in the U.S.?
10. Do you celebrate any religious holidays? When?

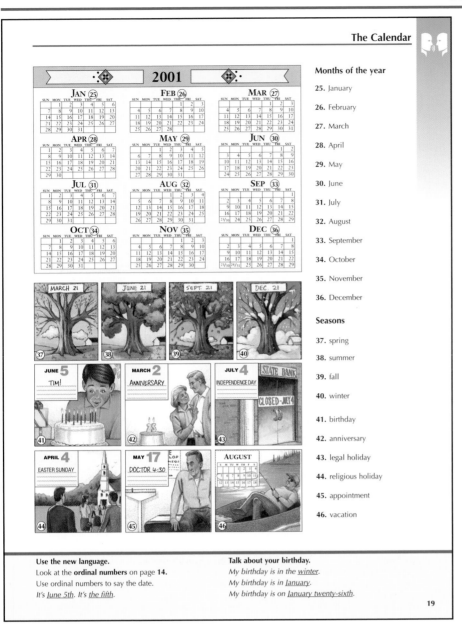

The Calendar

Months of the year

25. January

26. February

27. March

28. April

29. May

30. June

31. July

32. August

33. September

34. October

35. November

36. December

Seasons

37. spring

38. summer

39. fall

40. winter

41. birthday

42. anniversary

43. legal holiday

44. religious holiday

45. appointment

46. vacation

Use the new language.
Look at the **ordinal numbers** on page **14**.
Use ordinal numbers to say the date.
It's June 5th. It's the fifth.

Talk about your birthday.
My birthday is in the winter.
My birthday is in January.
My birthday is on January twenty-sixth.

19

Listening: Listen and Write

△ Have students write the dates in these sentences as you say them.

1. **May 4th** *would be a good day for the party. What do you think?*

2. *When is Thanksgiving this year?* **November 27th,** *I think.*

3. *School starts on* **September 8th** *this year. See you in two weeks!*

4. *My vacation begins* **July 9th.** *I can't wait!*

5. *I'm sorry; Tuesday is not good for me. I have a dentist appointment on* **February 11th.**

6. *We've set the wedding date. It's* **March 12th!** *Put it on your calendar!*

7. *I won't be in school tomorrow.* **January 6th** *is a religious holiday for me.*

EXPAND THE LESSON
Problem Solving

△ Have students brainstorm solutions.

1. *Phil made plans with two girls for the same day. What can he do?*

2. *Ken always forgets his wife Barbara's birthday. She is angry with him. How can he remember important dates?*

Discussion Questions

1. Some people like to do the same things on the same day of the week: market on Monday, cleaning on Tuesday, errands on Wednesday, etc. How about you? Do you like to do the same things on the same day each week?

2. What do you think of year-round schools? Vacations in these schools are at different times and not necessarily in the summer. Do you like this? Why or why not?

Student-to-Student Dictation

1. Pair students and have them write down a list of 6–8 important dates (birthday, the day they came to the U.S., etc.).

2. Student A dictates his list to Student B while Student B writes.

3. Student B dictates her list to Student A.

4. When both students have finished, they compare lists and talk about why these dates are important.

Silent Drill

1. Each student needs four sheets of paper, 5-1/2" by 8-1/2". (Cut notebook paper in half.)

2. Have students write one of the following phrases, large and dark, on each sheet: *every day, once a week, twice a week, three times a week.*

3. Choose a class mathematician to count and record the students' responses.

4. Act out and ask *How often do you exercise, watch TV, study English?* etc.

5. Students hold up their answers. For "never," they don't hold up anything. The class mathematician reports the numbers to the class.

Language Workout

△ Copy these sentences on the board and discuss their meanings.

1. I really miss my friend Hong. I haven't seen him in *a month of Sundays.*

2. Amos and Delia are getting married. He's 60 and she's 35. *It's a real May-December marriage.*

GAMES
Classroom Hunt

1. Write each day of the week (7), each month of the year (12) and each season (4) on separate index cards. [If you have more than 23 students, write different years on cards to make up the difference (1998, 1999, etc.)]

2. Hand out the index cards.

3. Have students walk around the room to find their same category. When they find all the people in their category, they arrange themselves in order.

4. The game ends when a group finds all the students in that category.

An Important Date

1. Have students write an important date in their lives and their name on a slip of paper and put it into a box or hat.

2. Pull out a slip of paper and put the information on the board. Have the class guess why this date is important. *Is this your anniversary? Is this your child's birthday? Etc.*

Unit 1 Money   page 20

Workbooks, p. 20
Classic Classroom Activities, Unit 1
Related Dictionary Pages
- Numbers and Measurements, pp. 14–15
- Shopping, p. 21
- A Bank, p. 97

TOPIC NOTES

In the U.S., many people use **checks, credit cards,** and bank cards to pay for goods and services. People who do not have personal checking accounts and must mail money usually buy **money orders** at the U.S. Post Office and other outlets.

Coins are made out of metal and are worth a dollar or less. **Bills** are made of paper and are worth a dollar or more.

TEACHING TIPS
Related Vocabulary

change*	debt
loan	gambling
owe	bank*
spend	purse*
save*	wallet*
hide*	exchange rate

- ☼ Review pages 14–15, *Numbers,* so that students can talk about different amounts of money.
- ☼ Bring in play money so that students can practice asking for and giving change.
- ☼ Bring samples of checks, credit cards, and money orders to class. Talk about how to get each one and how they are used.
- ☼ Credit cards may be new for some students. Talk about credit card theft and how to avoid it.

Money

Coins

1. $.01 = 1¢
a penny/1 cent

2. $.05 = 5¢
a nickel/5 cents

3. $.10 = 10¢
a dime/10 cents

4. $.25 = 25¢
a quarter/25 cents

5. $.50 = 50¢
a half dollar

6. $1.00
a silver dollar

Bills

7. $1.00
a dollar

8. $5.00
five dollars

9. $10.00
ten dollars

10. $20.00
twenty dollars

11. $50.00
fifty dollars

12. $100.00
one hundred dollars

Ways to pay

13. cash
14. personal check
15. credit card
16. money order
17. traveler's check

More vocabulary
borrow: to get money from someone and return it later
lend: to give money to someone and get it back later
pay back: to return the money that you borrowed

Other ways to talk about money:
a dollar bill or *a one*   *a ten-dollar bill* or *a ten*
a five-dollar bill or *a five*   *a twenty-dollar bill* or *a twenty*

20

INTRODUCE THE TOPIC

Show students real coins and bills. Ask them to name the coins and bills that they know. Ask questions to ascertain prior knowledge. Supply the answers if students don't know them. *How many quarters are in a dollar? How much is a dime?*

Walk around the room asking for change for a dollar. Comment on the process as you go. *Do you have change for a dollar? Oh, no, I see you only have two quarters. I'll ask someone else. Thanks, anyway.*

TEACH THE NEW WORDS

Ask students to point to the picture as you talk about the words. *This is worth 25¢. It's a quarter (#4). I use this for my car payment. It's a personal check (#14).*

PROVIDE PRACTICE
Chalkboard Activities

△ Have students call out equivalents:

Quarter	Dollar
25 pennies	*10 dimes*
2 dimes and a nickel	*4 quarters*

△ Write the following on the board and have students tell different ways to pay for them:

newspaper	**coffee**	**rent**
shoes	**books**	**car**
mortgage	**pencil**	**movie**
eyeglasses	**bus fare**	

Conversation

△ Put models on the board and practice. Make appropriate substitutions.

A: Excuse me. Do you have change for *$1.00?*
B: Sure. Here are *[four quarters].*
  8. $5.00 9. $10.00 10. $20.00 11. $50.00

A: I need to go to the bank.
B: What for?
A: I need some *personal checks.*
  13. cash 17. traveler's checks

Interview Questions

1. Do you try to save a certain amount of money every week?
2. Do you use a bank?
3. Do you have a credit card?

Listening: Listen and Write

△ Have students write the amounts as you say them.

1. $4.50	**3.** 75¢	**5.** $16
2. $5.07	**4.** $90	**6.** $4.35

EXPAND THE LESSON
Discussion Question

Do you think it's a good idea to play the lottery? Why or why not?

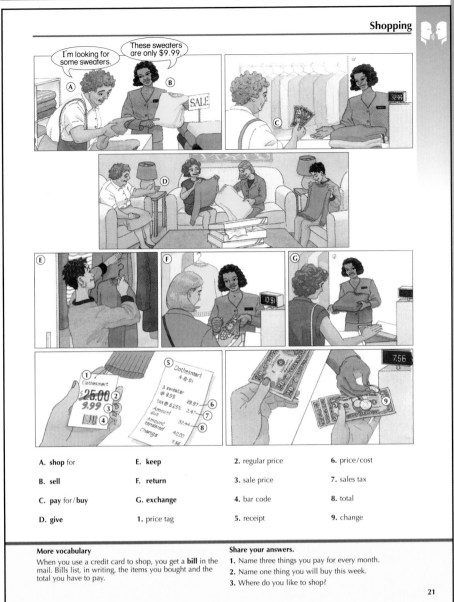

Shopping

I'm looking for some sweaters.

These sweaters are only $9.99.

A. shop for
B. sell
C. pay for / buy
D. give
E. keep
F. return
G. exchange
1. price tag
2. regular price
3. sale price
4. bar code
5. receipt
6. price/cost
7. sales tax
8. total
9. change

More vocabulary
When you use a credit card to shop, you get a **bill** in the mail. Bills list, in writing, the items you bought and the total you have to pay.

Share your answers.
1. Name three things you pay for every month.
2. Name one thing you will buy this week.
3. Where do you like to shop?

21

Workbooks, p. 21
Classic Classroom Activities, Unit 1
Related Dictionary Pages
• Money, p. 20
• The Market, pp. 54–55
• Clothing I–III, pp. 64–67

TOPIC NOTES

In the U.S., shoppers can purchase items with credit cards, cash, or checks. Many states add **sales tax** to the price of specific items (e.g., clothing, furniture, gifts). This tax isn't listed on the **price tag,** but is added to the **cost** when the item is purchased. Food products are usually not taxed.

Return or **exchange** policies vary from store to store. Many stores will only allow the shopper to return an item for credit towards another purchase in the same store.

A **receipt** is the customer's proof of purchase and is required for returns in many stores.

TEACHING TIPS
Related Vocabulary

salesclerk*   bargain
cash register*   clearance
department*   customer service
purchase   wrong size
credit slip   wrong color
display   shoplifting

☼ Review different amounts of money (e.g., 50¢, $1.50, $10.00, $150.00) on the board before teaching this topic.

☼ Collect newspaper ads, or ads from grocery, department, or electronics stores. Have students compare prices at different stores.

INTRODUCE THE TOPIC

Survey students to discover their favorite place, day, and time to shop. Graph the results on the board. (According to statistics, U.S. shoppers prefer Saturday.)

TEACH THE NEW WORDS

Tell students what you want to do as you act out each panel on the page. *I want to buy some sweaters.* Students can repeat the language they hear.

Ask students a series of yes/no questions about #1–9. *Is #3 the sale price?* (yes) *Is the total $20.00?* (no)

PROVIDE PRACTICE
Chalkboard Activities

△ Have students categorize vocabulary for the things you see on the following:

Price Tags	Receipts	Both
bar code	*tax*	*price*

Conversations

△ Put models on the board and practice. Make appropriate substitutions.

A: I'd like to *pay for* this [sweater].
B: I can help you at this register.
  C. buy F. return G. exchange

A: Would you help me? I can't find the *regular price* on this price tag.
B: Let's see. Here it is.
  3. sale price 4. bar code 6. price

A: What's this amount on the receipt?
B: That's the *price*.
  6. cost 7. sales tax 8. total

Interview Questions

1. What did you buy this week? Was it on sale? Are you happy with it?
2. Does it bother you to return something to the store?

Listening: 🔊 #4, p. 209
"Who's Saying What?" Have students listen and point to the person on the page they think is speaking.

EXPAND THE LESSON
Problem Solving

△ Have students brainstorm solutions. *You buy a sweater on sale. When you get home you see that the receipt shows you paid the regular price. What can you do?*

Language Workout

△ Put these sentences on the board and discuss their meanings.
1. He made a mistake and now he's going to *pay for it.*
2. He went to jail for 33 years. That was *too high a price to pay* for stealing a TV.

Workbooks, p. 22
Classic Classroom Activities, Unit 2
Related Dictionary Pages
• Describing Hair, p. 23
• Life Events, pp. 28–29

TOPIC NOTES

In the U.S., physically challenged adults and children receive federal government protection to ensure equal access to jobs, housing and education.

A **senior citizen** is a person over the age of 55. Seniors receive special benefits from the government. They often pay less for public and private services.

A *minor* is a person below the age of 18 or 21. Minors must have adult consent to get married and receive medical treatment.

Louis Braille (1809–1852), a **blind** teacher, invented the Braille system of writing for the blind. Braille, as the writing is called, is widely used today.

TEACHING TIPS
Related Vocabulary

infant	pretty
newborn	handsome
kid	beautiful
adolescent	skinny
handicapped/disabled	fat/obese
mature	guy
sign language	lady
Braille	

Spelling: Irregular plurals
man—men, woman—women, child—children, baby—babies

⚠ Most adults usually avoid asking direct questions about age and weight. However, talking about losing weight is common.

Age and Physical Description

1. children	4. 6-year-old boy	7. 13-year-old boy	10. woman
2. baby	5. 10-year-old girl	8. 19-year-old girl	11. man
3. toddler	6. teenagers	9. adults	12. senior citizen

13. young	17. average height	21. average weight	25. physically challenged
14. middle-aged	18. short	22. thin/slim	26. sight impaired/blind
15. elderly	19. pregnant	23. attractive	27. hearing impaired/deaf
16. tall	20. heavyset	24. cute	

Talk about yourself and your teacher.
I am young, average height, and average weight. My teacher is a middle-aged, tall, thin man.

Use the new language.
Turn to **Hobbies and Games,** pages 162–163. Describe each person on the page.
He's a heavy-set, short, senior citizen.

22

INTRODUCE THE TOPIC

Show two photos or drawings and ask students to pick the correct one based on your description.

Tell about several U.S. presidents using vocabulary from this page. *Franklin Roosevelt was physically challenged when he was elected president. John Kennedy was young and attractive.*

TEACH THE NEW WORDS

Ask students random questions about the pictures. *Is #3 a baby or a toddler?* (toddler) *Is person #16 tall or short?* (tall)

PROVIDE PRACTICE
Chalkboard Activities

△ Have students call out the people appropriate to each category:

Elementary School	**Adult School**
6-year-old boy	*19-year-old woman*

Conversations

△ Put models on the board and practice. Make appropriate substitutions.

A: Tell me about *[Mr. Nye].*
B: Well, he's *young* and *thin.*
  14. middle-aged/16. tall
  15. elderly/17. average height
  23. attractive/18. short

A: Here's *[ten dollars]* for two tickets.
B: Sorry, *teenagers* have to pay full price.
  1. children 9. adults 12. senior citizens

Interview Questions

1. Which three words best describe you?
2. Which three words describe your teacher?
3. Do girls and boys act the same way or are they different? In what ways?

Listening: ▭ #5, p. 209

"Hollywood Starrs" Students listen and point to the people on page 22 as they are described.

EXPAND THE LESSON
Problem Solving

△ Have students brainstorm solutions. *A friend of yours is tall and very slim. She thinks she is overweight and is always on a diet. How can you help?*

Language Workout

△ Copy these sentences on the board and discuss their meanings.
1. Look at Joe in his uniform. He's *all grown up.*
2. Don't be such a baby! *Act your age!*
3. My grandma is 85 and still *young at heart.*

Describing Hair

1. short hair
2. shoulder-length hair
3. long hair
4. part
5. mustache
6. beard
7. sideburns

8. bangs
9. straight hair
10. wavy hair
11. curly hair
12. bald
13. gray hair
14. red hair

15. black hair
16. blond hair
17. brown hair
18. brush
19. scissors
20. blow dryer
21. rollers

22. comb
A. cut hair
B. perm hair
C. set hair
D. color hair / **dye** hair

More vocabulary
hair stylist: a person who cuts, sets, and perms hair
hair salon: the place where a hair stylist works

Talk about your hair.
My hair is *long*, *straight*, and *brown*.
I have *long*, *straight*, *brown* hair.
When I was a child my hair was *short*, *curly*, and *blond*.

23

Workbooks, p. 23
Classic Classroom Activities, Unit 2
Related Dictionary Pages
• Colors, p. 12
• Age and Physical Description, p. 22
• Personal Hygiene, p. 76

TOPIC NOTES

In the U.S., men and women spend over 5 billion dollars a year in beauty parlors and barbershops. Trends in cutting, styling, and coloring hair are constantly changing. Hair grooming rituals have fueled a huge market for hair-care products.

Bangs, sideburns, and **beards** can be *trimmed* as opposed to cut.

Bald means having little or no hair. Losing hair is referred to as *going bald* or *balding*.

📁 Many parents save a lock of hair from their baby's first haircut.

TEACHING TIPS
Related Vocabulary

braid	fine hair
bun	coarse hair
pigtails	brunette
ponytail	auburn
wigs	white-haired
hairpiece	silver-haired

🔆 Bring the vocabulary on this page to life by acting out an appointment between a hair stylist (yourself) and a volunteer client. Bring in props (blow dryer, a smock, scissors) and "demonstrate your skills." *Your long black hair looks great. Do you want me to cut your bangs?*

⚠ Use this page to discuss the social and hygienic implications of grooming hair in public and of sharing combs.

INTRODUCE THE TOPIC

Bring in magazine pictures of current hair styles. Have students raise their hands if their hair matches in either color or style. *Who has brown hair?*

Talk about a recent appointment at a hair salon. *Last week, I got my hair permed. It used to be straight. Now my hair is curly.*

TEACH THE NEW WORDS

Ask students a series of *or* questions about the pictures. *Look at #1. Does the woman have long or short hair?* (short) *Look at the cart on the left. Is there a comb or a hair dryer on top of the cart?* (comb)

PROVIDE PRACTICE
Chalkboard Activities

△ Have students categorize vocabulary:

Length	Type	Color
short	straight	brown

Conversations

△ Put models on the board and practice. Make appropriate substitutions.
A: Your new hairstyle looks great!
B: It's OK, but I really like *long hair*.
　1. short hair **2.** shoulder-length hair
　7. sideburns **8.** bangs **9.** straight hair
　10. wavy hair **11.** curly hair
A: What do you charge to *cut hair*?
B: [Twenty-five dollars.]
A: Really? I think I'll do it myself.
　B. perm hair **C. set** hair **D. color** hair

Interview Questions

1. Who cuts your hair?
2. Do you like long or short hair for women? for men?

Listening: 📼 #8, p. 210

"Trends Hair Salon" Students listen and make checks on their papers for hair colors and styles.

EXPAND THE LESSON
Discussion Questions

1. What is the most unusual hairstyle you have ever seen?
2. What jobs might require workers to change their hairstyle? Do you think this is fair?

Language Workout

△ Copy these sentences on the board and discuss their meanings.
1. My vacation was a *hair-raising* experience.
2. I'm so worried about my new job, it's *making me gray*.

Unit 2   Family   page 24

Workbooks, pp. 24–25
Classic Classroom Activities, Unit 2
Related Dictionary Pages
- Everyday Conversation, p. 8
- Age and Physical Description, p. 22
- Life Events, pp. 28–29

TOPIC NOTES

In the U.S., family consists of people related by blood or marriage. Parents and siblings are considered our *immediate* family.

Step refers to relationships that are formed when a **parent** marries a second time. *John is my stepfather; he is my mother's second husband.*

Half refers to siblings who share one parent but not the other.

Affectionate words for **mother** are *mom, mommy, mama,* and *ma.* For **father** people use *dad, daddy, pop, papa,* and *pa.*

TEACHING TIPS
Related Vocabulary

generation	siblings
adoption	arranged marriage
mate	extended family
spouse	bachelor
lover	ex-wife / ex-husband
annulment	separation
nuclear family	blended family

Spelling: Irregular plural: *wife—wives.*

- ☼ Review page 22, *Age and Physical Description,* so that students can describe members of their family.
- ☼ Review possessives, e.g., *Mary's sister, Tom's mother,* so that students can introduce family members.

- ⚠ For immigrant students, talking about their families can be painful if they are separated from them.

Family

Tom Lee's Family

1. grandparents — Min, Lu
2. grandmother
3. grandfather
4. parents — Rose, Chang
5. mother
6. father
Tom
7. (Min and Lu's) grandson
Lily
8. sister
9. brother — Alex
Helen
10. aunt
Daniel
11. uncle
Emily
12. cousin
Berta, Mario
13. mother-in-law
14. father-in-law
Ana Garcia's Family
Ana
Marta
15. sister-in-law
Carlos
16. brother-in-law
Tito
19. husband
20. (Tito's) wife
Alice
17. niece
Eddie
18. nephew
Sara
21. daughter
Felix
22. son

More vocabulary
Lily and Emily are Min and Lu's **granddaughters.**
Daniel is Min and Lu's **son-in-law.**
Ana is Berta and Mario's **daughter-in-law.**

Share your answers.
1. How many brothers and sisters do you have?
2. What number son or daughter are you?
3. Do you have any children?

24

INTRODUCE THE TOPIC

Bring in a picture of your family and tell students who everyone is. *This is my son. His name is Alex. He is fourteen years old.*

Ask students to bring in a picture of one person in their family. Have them tell the class who the person is and their relationship.

Draw a family tree on the board. Place yourself on it. Continue to add names and tell students about each person.

TEACH THE NEW WORDS

Ask students to point to the correct person based on your description. *Look at Tom Lee's family. Point to Tom. He is a boy with straight hair. He is next to Lily, his sister.*

PROVIDE PRACTICE
Chalkboard Activities

△ Have students categorize the vocabulary:

Male	**Female**	**Male or Female**
father	mother	cousin

△ Have students call out contrasting relationships for each term listed:

sister	*brother*
aunt	
mother	
grandmother	

△ Draw a circle. Put "Ana" in the middle. Write the names of the family members on the outside. Have students take turns writing the relationship of these persons to Ana inside the circle.

Conversations

△ Put models on the board and practice. Make appropriate substitutions.

A: This is my *sister*. Her name is *[Ellen]*.
B: Nice to meet you, *[Ellen]*.
   2. grandmother 5. mother 10. aunt

A: What a great picture! Which one is your *brother*?
B: He's the one on the left.
   3. grandfather 6. father 7. grandson 11. uncle

A: How's the family?
B: Good. My *cousin* got divorced and is now remarried. He has a stepson.
   14. father-in-law 22. son

Family

Lisa Smith's Family

23. married

24. divorced

Carol   Dan

Lisa

25. single mother

26. single father

27. remarried

Rick   Carol

Dan   Sue

Rick   Carol

Lisa

Dan   Sue

28. stepfather

31. stepmother

David   Mary

Kim   Bill

29. half brother   30. half sister

32. stepsister   33. stepbrother

More vocabulary
Carol is Dan's **former wife**.
Sue is Dan's **wife**.
Dan is Carol's **former husband**.

Rick is Carol's **husband**.
Lisa is the **stepdaughter** of both Rick and Sue.

25

Interview Questions

1. How many brothers and sisters do you have?
2. What position are you in your family? oldest? youngest?
3. Do you have any children? How many?
4. Are you an uncle or aunt? How many nieces and nephews do you have?
5. What is the most common age for men and women to marry in your culture?
6. Is divorce common in your country? Do people remarry?
7. Who helps single parents take care of their children in your country?

Listening: 📼 #7, p. 210

"Family Is Family!" Students point to different members of the families of Tom Lee, Ana Garcia, and Lisa Smith.

EXPAND THE LESSON
Problem Solving

△ Have students brainstorm solutions.
A 25-year-old woman wants to marry a man her parents don't approve of. What should she do? Why?

Discussion Questions

1. What is considered a large family in your country? a small family?
2. An arranged marriage is one where the parents decide who will marry their daughter or son. Do arranged marriages exist in your country? What do you think about them?
3. How is life in the U.S. beneficial for families? How do families suffer?

Language Workout

△ Copy these sentences on the board and discuss their meanings.
1. My teenager and I argue a lot. It must be the *generation gap*.
2. Everyone in my friend's family has blue eyes. It *runs in the family*.
3. My cousin is a single mom. She is the *head of the household* for her family.

My Favorite Relative

△ Write the following incomplete sentences on the board and discuss ways to complete them:
My favorite relative is…
She/He is wonderful because…
She/He lives…

We Are Family!

1. Make ten large placards with vocabulary from the page: *wife, husband, mother, father,* etc.
2. Choose one person to be the wife. Give her the "wife" placard. Have her choose a husband. Give him the "husband" placard.
3. Continue giving out placards until you have created a large "class family."
4. Have students take turns introducing the members of their family.
5. Repeat with a different set of students.

GAMES
Chair Line-up

1. Have students draw pictures or bring in photos of their families.
2. Line up two long rows of chairs facing each other at the front of the class, and have students sit holding their pictures.
3. For one minute, each student explains to his or her partner who everyone is in the picture and where they live, and also gives any description they can.
4. After two minutes, the students in the row on the left move down one chair. With new partners, the students share again.

Team Quiz: Who Is…?

1. Divide the class into two teams. Have each student write a question starting with *Who is…?* based on pages 24–25, *Family. Who is Lily's brother? Who is Carlos's father?* Etc.
2. Students on each team take turns reading their questions in order to stump the other team. If a team answers correctly, they get a point.
3. The game ends when one team gets 10 points.

Unit 2   Daily Routines   page 26

Workbooks, pp. 26–27
Classic Classroom Activities, Unit 2
Related Dictionary Pages
• Time, pp. 16–17
• Personal Hygiene, pp. 76–77
• Places to Go, p. 152

TOPIC NOTES

In the U.S., people generally have very busy daily routines or schedules. Usually their time to **relax** is in the evening and on the weekends. These days, people spend more of their leisure time using a computer, doing housework, and watching videos and less time **watching TV** and doing crafts.

Pick up children has two meanings: 1. to get children from school or daycare and bring them home. 2. to lift children from a place like the ground or a bed.

📁 61% of women today say they have less free time than in 1990, and 44% of men say that they have less free time.

TEACHING TIPS
Related Vocabulary

schedule	spare time
free time	hobbies*
errands	housework*
car pool	workaholic
chores	

Pronunciation: read, read
When teaching the past tense, point out the change in pronunciation of *read* from [rēd] in the present tense to [rĕd] in the past tense.

🔆 Review pages 16–17, *Time*. Write digital times on the board and have students tell you what time it is.

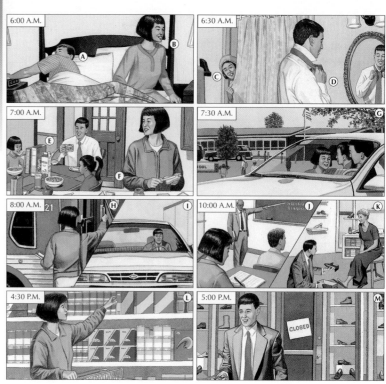

Daily Routines

A. **wake** up
B. **get** up
C. **take** a shower
D. **get** dressed
E. **eat** breakfast
F. **make** lunch
G. **take** the children to school
H. **take** the bus to school
I. **drive** to work / **go** to work
J. **be** in school
K. **work**
L. **go** to the market
M. **leave** work

Grammar point: 3rd person singular
For **he** and **she**, we add **-s** or **-es** to the verb.
He/She wakes up.
He/She watches TV.

These verbs are different (irregular):
be   *He/She is in school at 10:00 a.m.*
have   *He/She has dinner at 6:30 p.m.*

26

INTRODUCE THE TOPIC

Demonstrate your daily routine. Pretend you are waking up, taking a shower, etc. Speak as you do the actions: *It's 6:00 A.M. I'm waking up. I'm tired. It's 6:30. I'm finally taking a shower.*

Ask students to look at the dictionary page and tell you which actions they do seven days a week, five days a week, etc.

Show a picture of a famous person and describe a typical day. *The president gets up at 5:00 A.M. He reads four newspapers and eats breakfast.* Use body language to help explain the meaning.

TEACH THE NEW WORDS

Ask students a series of yes/no questions about the pictures. *Does the man get dressed at 7:00 A.M.?* (no) *Does the woman go to the market at 4:30?* (yes)

PROVIDE PRACTICE
Chalkboard Activities

△ Have students categorize vocabulary:

Monday–Friday	Saturday
go to work	go to the market

△ Have students brainstorm the daily routine for each of these:
a cat
a 7-year-old boy
a teenager
a mother with children
a police officer

△ Write six activities from these pages on the board. Ask students how long they spend doing each activity.
How much time do you spend watching TV?
How much time do you spend eating breakfast?

Conversations

△ Put models on the board and practice. Make appropriate substitutions.

A: Who in your house likes to *make lunch*?
B: Usually I do. Sometimes my [husband] does.
   G. take the children to school L. go to the market N. clean the house O. pick up the children P. cook dinner

A: Hi! What are you up to?
B: Right now, I'm *making breakfast*.
A: OK, call me back when you're free.
   D. getting dressed E. eating breakfast F. making lunch K. working

A: What are you doing after work?
B: I'm so busy today. First I'm picking up the kids, and then I'm *going to the market*.
A: Wow, you are busy!
   N. cleaning the house P. cooking dinner T. doing homework W. exercising

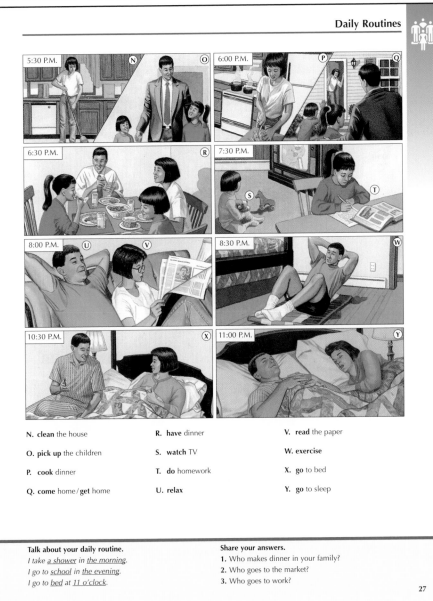

Daily Routines

N. **clean** the house

O. **pick up** the children

P. **cook** dinner

Q. **come** home / **get** home

R. **have** dinner

S. **watch** TV

T. **do** homework

U. **relax**

V. **read** the paper

W. **exercise**

X. **go** to bed

Y. **go** to sleep

Talk about your daily routine.
I take a shower in the morning.
I go to school in the evening.
I go to bed at 11 o'clock.

Share your answers.
1. Who makes dinner in your family?
2. Who goes to the market?
3. Who goes to work?

27

Interview Questions

1. What time do you wake up? go to school? go to work? eat dinner? go to bed?
2. What do you do in the morning? afternoon? evening?
3. Who makes breakfast in your home?
4. Who cleans the house? Who goes to the market? Who goes to school?
5. Is your daily routine the same every day? How does it change on the weekends?
6. What do you do in your free time?
7. Do you have a hard time getting up? going to sleep? going to work?
8. What do you do when you get home?

Listening: 🔊 **#8, p. 211**

"Welcome To Our House." Students write the times that correspond to the activities as they are described.

EXPAND THE LESSON

Problem Solving

△ Have students brainstorm solutions.

1. *Jan is 17 and in high school. She wants to sleep late and hang out with friends on the weekends. Her parents want her to get a job. What should Jan do?*
2. *Jakov has a full-time job and is learning English at night. He has no time for exercise, but his doctor says it is very important. What can he do?*

Discussion Questions

1. Who has more free time: a mother with three children, a busy lawyer, or an owner of a small market?
2. The average work week in the United States is 40 hours per week. Is this the same in your country?
3. About one in three Americans has problems going to sleep. Do you?

Chair Line-up

1. Ask each student to draw a clockface and write their daily routine next to each hour.
2. Line up two long rows of chairs facing each other at the front of the class, and have students sit holding their pictures.
3. For 1 minute, facing students explain their daily routines to each other.
4. After 2 minutes the students in the left row only move down one chair. Now with new partners, students share information again.

Language Workout

△ Copy these sentences on the board and discuss their meanings.

1. Carla has to *make time* to practice the piano.
2. My husband is always up by 5:00 A.M. We call him the *early bird* in the family.
3. I don't go to sleep until 2:00 or 3:00 in the morning. I'm the *night owl*.

GAMES

Charades

1. Write the verbs A–Y on slips of paper and put them into a box or hat.
2. Divide students into two teams.
3. Students take turns picking a word and acting it out for their own team.
4. Teams get a point for each word they guess correctly.
5. The game ends when all the slips are gone.

Class Go-Around: Charlie's Life

1. Begin by saying *Yesterday Charlie woke up at 6:00*.
2. The first volunteer continues by repeating the sentence and adding another action. *Charlie woke up at 6:00 and took a shower at 6:30*.
3. The next student volunteer continues the chain, adding another action and time.
4. Stop after the tenth student and begin the game again.

What the President Really Does!

1. Divide students into groups of three or four.
2. Have each group choose a famous person and write that person's daily routine without revealing the name. *... wakes up at 5:00 A.M. and reads six newspapers. Then he takes a shower.*
3. Groups exchange papers and guess who the famous person is.

Workbooks, pp. 28–29
Classic Classroom Activities, Unit 2
Related Dictionary Pages
- Age and Physical Description, p. 22
- Family, pp. 24–25
- Feelings, pp. 30–31

TOPIC NOTES

In the U.S., many people formally acknowledge important life events by sending announcements to friends and family: when they **graduate** from school, **have a baby,** or **move** to a new address. Couples **get married** on their wedding day. It is common for them to first get engaged. Later, friends of the bride may host a *shower party,* and friends of the groom give a *bachelor party.*

📁 At a wedding ceremony, couples may exchange rings, which are placed on each other's fourth fingers. This tradition began in the third century B.C. in Greece, where it was believed that a vein of love ran from this finger directly to the heart.

TEACHING TIPS
Related Vocabulary

green card	fiancé / fiancée
permit	bride
temporary	groom
permanent	wedding
expire	enlist
renew	pass away

💡 Review pages 30–31, *Feelings,* so that students can express their emotions surrounding life events. *My son is graduating from college. I am very proud.*

⚠ Do not ask students to show personal documents such as passports. Substitute realia or drawings.

Life Events

A. **be** born

B. **start** school

C. **immigrate**

D. **graduate**

E. **learn** to drive

F. **join** the army

G. **get** a job

H. **become** a citizen

I. **rent** an apartment

J. **go** to college

K. **fall** in love

L. **get** married

Grammar point: past tense

				These verbs are different (irregular):		
start		immigrate		be	— was	have — had
learn		graduate		get	— got	buy — bought
join	+ed	move	+d	become	— became	
rent		retire		go	— went	
28 travel		die		fall	— fell	

INTRODUCE THE TOPIC

Describe several life events for a famous person. Draw a time line and speak as you sequence the events. *This is the story of Gloria Estefan. She was born on Sept. 7, 1957. Etc.*

Bring in authentic realia such as a passport, driver's license, diploma. Talk about the procedure for obtaining each document. *In order to get my driver's license I took three tests—vision, written, and driving test. Now all I need is a car!*

TEACH THE NEW WORDS

Describe random pictures on pages 28–29. Ask students to give the letter of the life event you're describing. *It's 1949. He's raising his hand as he listens to the judge. He's becoming a citizen.* (H) *It's 1971. He's buying a house.* (O)

PROVIDE PRACTICE
Chalkboard Activities

△ Have students categorize vocabulary:

Age Limit	No Age Limit
join the army	*fall in love*

△ Have students tell you the order in which these things usually happen:

_____	**start school**
_____	**get married**
_____	**be born**
_1_	**have a baby**
_____	**graduate**

△ Have students brainstorm the situations where they would need a…

birth certificate	*enter school*
driver's license	*cash a check*

Conversations

△ Put models on the board and practice. Make appropriate substitutions.

A: Congratulations! I hear you are going to *join the army.*

B: Thanks. I'm really excited.

> E. learn to drive H. become a citizen
> J. go to college L. get married

A: Could I see some identification, please?

B: OK, here's a copy of my *birth certificate.*

A: Sorry, I need to see the original.

> 3. Resident Alien card 4. driver's license
> 5. Social Security card 6. Certificate of Naturalization 9. passport

A: I'm going to *graduate* next month. I'm kind of nervous.

B: I know just how you feel. I *graduated* last year!

> F. join the army G. get a job I. rent an apartment M. have a baby O. buy a house P. move

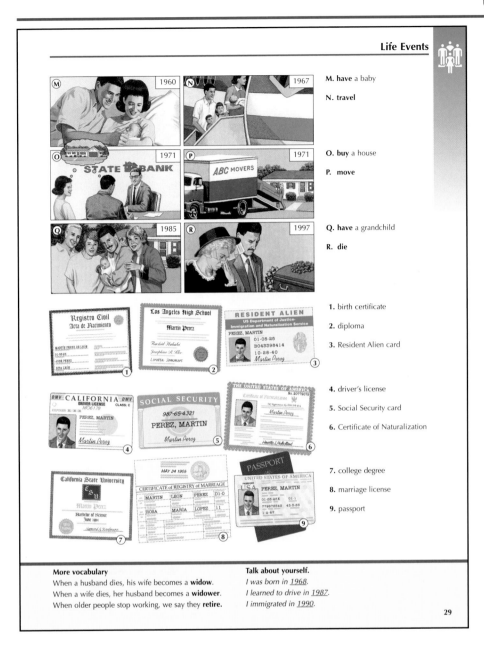

Life Events

M. **have** a baby

N. travel

O. **buy** a house

P. move

Q. **have** a grandchild

R. die

1. birth certificate

2. diploma

3. Resident Alien card

4. driver's license

5. Social Security card

6. Certificate of Naturalization

7. college degree

8. marriage license

9. passport

More vocabulary
When a husband dies, his wife becomes a **widow**.
When a wife dies, her husband becomes a **widower**.
When older people stop working, we say they **retire**.

Talk about yourself.
I was born in 1968.
I learned to drive in 1987.
I immigrated in 1990.

29

Interview Questions

1. Where were you born?
2. When did you immigrate to this country?
3. When did you start coming to this school?
4. Are you renting an apartment? by yourself or with others?
5. Did you go to college in your country?
6. Do you remember the first time you fell in love?
7. Do you want to get married?
8. Do you want to have a baby?
9. Do you want to move?
10. Where would you like to travel?

Listening: 🔊 #9, p. 211

"Sweet Memories" Students listen and point to the pictures as they are described by Grandma Rosa.

EXPAND THE LESSON
Problem Solving

△ Have students brainstorm solutions.
1. *A son wants to rent an apartment close to the community college, but his parents want him to save money and live at home. What should he do?*
2. *A divorced 38-year-old woman and a 32-year-old man are in love and plan to get married. The woman's teenage son is upset. What should they do?*

Discussion Questions

1. In your opinion, do most immigrants want to become citizens of their new country? Why or why not?
2. Many people marry more than once. How are first and second marriages different?
3. At what age do workers retire in your country? What is the best age to retire?

Language Workout

△ Put these sentences on the board and discuss their meanings.
1. Sam can buy anything he wants. He was *born with a silver spoon in his mouth.*
2. When Romeo met Juliet, it was *love at first sight.*
3. Robert and Diane fell in love in May. They *tied the knot* last week.

GAMES
Charades

1. Write the verbs A–R on slips of paper and put them into a box or hat.
2. Divide the class into two teams.
3. Students take turns picking a word and acting it out in front of their own teams.
4. Teams get a point for each word they guess correctly.
5. The game ends when all the slips are gone.

Class-Go-Around

1. Begin by making a statement such as *In 1978 Mark joined the army.*
2. The first volunteer repeats the sentence and adds an event. *In 1978 Mark joined the army, and in 1979 he got married.*
3. The next student volunteer continues, adding to the chain.
4. Stop after the tenth student and begin the game again.

Definition Bingo

1. Have students fold a blank sheet of paper into 16 squares. Show students the different rows on the paper: horizontal, vertical, and diagonal.
2. Dictate 16 life events and have students write them in random order on their pages, one item per square, until all the squares are filled.
3. Tell students they will be circling different words on their papers, as they hear you define them. Explain that when they get four circled words in a row, they shout "Bingo!"
4. Give a sample definition. *You meet your teacher and classmates on the first day.* Make sure all students have circled the words *start school* on their papers.
5. Call out definitions until one student gets four in a row. Check the student's work, and write his or her name on the board. Instruct him or her to try to get another set in a row and continue the game.
6. Continue playing until five players have gotten four in a row.

Workbooks, pp. 30–31
Classic Classroom Activities, Unit 2
Related Dictionary Pages
• Family, pp. 24–25
• Life Events, pp. 28–29

TOPIC NOTES

In the U.S., the usual response to the greeting *How are you?* or *How are you feeling?* is *Fine.* Between friends, the response can be more specific: *I'm tired.*

Feelings can be divided into two groups: physical states (**cold, hungry, thirsty,** etc.) and states of mind (**calm, happy, angry,** etc.) Some words, such as **tired** or **comfortable,** can fall into both groups.

📁 In a survey of 3,000 U.S. men and women, the three things they feared most were speaking before a group (41%), heights (32%), and insects/bugs (22%).

TEACHING TIPS
Related Vocabulary

feel*	be*
disappointed	depressed
emotions	emotional
shiver	yawn
drink*	eat*
cry*	smile*

Usage: We use the verb *to be* with the vocabulary of feelings more often than the verb *to feel,* e.g., *I'm cold* rather than *I feel cold.*

🔆 Review the following words to help students better discuss the pictures: *man, woman, girl, boy, brother, husband, wife, mother, daughter,* and *family.*

⚠ Some cultures discourage the discussion of romantic love in mixed gender groups.

Feelings

1. hot
2. thirsty
3. sleepy
4. cold
5. hungry
6. full
7. comfortable
8. uncomfortable
9. disgusted
10. calm
11. nervous
12. in pain
13. worried
14. sick
15. well
16. relieved
17. hurt
18. lonely
19. in love

More vocabulary
furious: very angry
terrified: very scared
overjoyed: very happy

exhausted: very tired
starving: very hungry
humiliated: very embarrassed

Talk about your feelings.
I feel happy when I see my friends.
I feel homesick when I think about my family.

30

INTRODUCE THE TOPIC

Act out the facial expressions and body language for some of these feelings as you name them: *I'm angry (…happy, sad, bored, surprised, proud,* and *scared).*

Describe different situations that evoke specific feelings. *The bus was late. How do you feel? There's a gift on your desk. How do you feel?* Etc.

Make up and tell a story about one of the picture sequences. Students listen with their books closed.

TEACH THE NEW WORDS

Describe the different pictures on the pages and have students identify the pictures you're talking about. *He doesn't like being up high. He's scared.* (#24) *Her stomach hurts. She's in pain.* (#12)

PROVIDE PRACTICE
Chalkboard Activity

△ Have students categorize vocabulary:

1. Physical	**Emotional**
hungry	*sad*

2.

homesick	*relieved*

Conversations

△ Put models on the board and practice. Make appropriate substitutions.

A: You look <u>uncomfortable</u>. What's up?
B: Nothing, really. I'm *[fine]*.
　9. disgusted 13. worried 14. sick 17. hurt
　26. bored 33. tired

A: How are you? Are you still <u>hungry</u>?
B: No, not anymore.
　1. hot 2. thirsty 3. sleepy 4. cold
　12. in pain

A: Do you have a minute? I'm really <u>nervous</u>.
B: I'm sorry to hear that. Let's go talk about it.
　17. hurt 20. sad 21. homesick 27. confused
　28. frustrated 29. angry 30. upset

A: How did she feel when he asked her to marry him?
B: She was <u>calm</u>, but she said yes.
　11. nervous 24. scared 25. embarrassed
　31. surprised

A: I'm so <u>proud</u>! My daughter had twins!
B: That's wonderful news! How are the new parents?
A: They're <u>tired</u> but happy.
　23. excited/3. sleepy
　32. happy/16. relieved
　33. tired/31. surprised

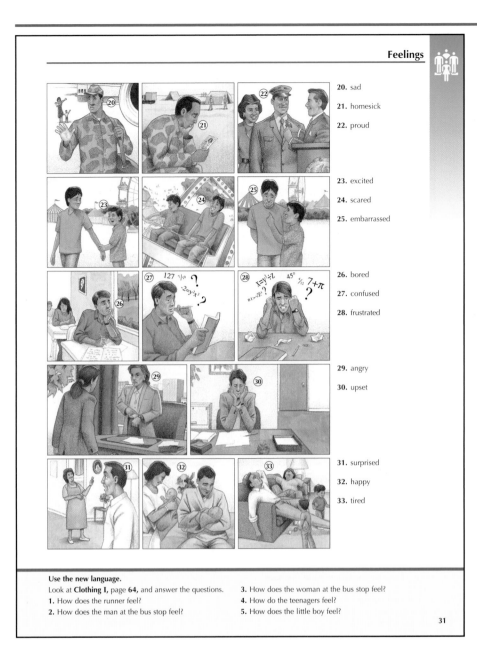

Feelings

20. sad
21. homesick
22. proud

23. excited
24. scared
25. embarrassed

26. bored
27. confused
28. frustrated

29. angry
30. upset

31. surprised
32. happy
33. tired

Use the new language.
Look at **Clothing I,** page **64,** and answer the questions.
1. How does the runner feel?
2. How does the man at the bus stop feel?
3. How does the woman at the bus stop feel?
4. How do the teenagers feel?
5. How does the little boy feel?

31

Discussion Question

Are there differences in the way people show their feelings in your culture compared with the U.S.? What are they?

Language Workout

△ Put these sentences on the board and discuss their meanings.
1. He's going to marry Norma. He's *head-over-heels in love.*
2. Dick forgot Eliza's birthday, and boy, *is his face red!*
3. I just said good-bye to my friend and I *feel blue.*

Drawing Activity

1. Have students draw a picture depicting one of their happiest moments.
2. Students label their pictures with information about the time, place, and people depicted in the picture. *This picture shows my sister and me at the beach last summer. I feel happy when I recall this time.*

GAMES
Charades

1. Write words 1–33 from pages 30–31 on slips of paper and put them into a box or hat.
2. Divide the class into team A and team B.
3. Team members take turns picking a word from the hat and acting it out for their teams.
4. Teams get a point for each word they guess correctly.
5. The game ends when all the slips are gone.

Variation: Instead of having students act out emotions, have them draw different expressions or situations on the board in order to help team members guess the emotion.

Spell Check

1. Divide the class into two teams.
2. Give teams 10 minutes to study the spelling of the words on pages 30–31.
3. Have teams line up on either side of the room.
4. Give the first student on each team a word from the pages and have them write it on the board.
5. Team members who spell the word correctly sit down and earn a point for their team.
6. Team members who make a mistake go to the end of the line, so that they can have another chance.
7. The game ends when all the team members of one team are seated.

Interview Questions

1. What do you do when you're angry?
2. Do you know anyone who is in love?
3. What scares you?
4. Are you ever bored in school? When?
5. Which school subjects confuse you?
6. Can you remember the last time you were happily surprised?
7. What do you do when you are nervous?
8. What makes you feel worried?
9. What do you do when you feel homesick?
10. Can you remember the last time you felt proud? What happened?

Listening: 🔊 #10, p. 212

"How Do They Feel?" Students point to the pictures as they hear various people talk about their feelings.

EXPAND THE LESSON
Problem Solving

△ Have students brainstorm solutions.
1. *A coworker is always late to work and the boss says that he will fire her if she is late again. What can she do?*
2. *A student is very confused in her English class, but she is uncomfortable asking questions in the classroom. What can she do?*
3. *Sam and Tom want to ride a high, fast roller coaster. Joe is afraid but embarrassed to say how he feels. What can he do?*

Workbooks, pp. 32–33
Classic Classroom Activities, Unit 2
Related Dictionary Pages
• Life Events, pp. 28–29
• Types of Schools, p. 112

TOPIC NOTES

In the U.S., students usually have graduation **ceremonies** when they finish high school or college. At the end of the graduation ceremony, students move the tassels on their **caps** from the right to the left.

The **valedictorian** is the **graduate** with the highest grade point average (GPA).

⚠ People in the U.S. hug and kiss friends, but not people they have just met.

TEACHING TIPS
Related Vocabulary

bachelor's degree*	award ceremony
master's degree*	scholarship
doctorate*	SAT
graduating class	GED

Grammar: *be* + [verb]-*ing*
Model the present continuous of the verbs on these pages: *What's he doing in this picture? He's graduating.* Note that when adding -*ing*, the silent *e* is dropped (*dance—dancing*), and the letter *g* is doubled in the word *hug* (*hug—hugging*).

🔅 Review the different schools on page 112 to help students identify which graduations are important in their cultures.

🔅 Act out a graduation ceremony. Call students forward by their full names to receive diplomas (rolled up scratch paper), have them shake hands with people sitting in the front row of the classroom, and sit down again.

A Graduation

The Ceremony

1. graduating class	5. podium	9. guest speaker	**B. applaud / clap**
2. gown	6. graduate	10. audience	**C. cry**
3. cap	7. diploma	11. photographer	**D. take** a picture
4. stage	8. valedictorian	**A. graduate**	**E. give** a speech

Talk about what the people in the pictures are doing.

She is	taking a picture. / giving a speech. / smiling. / laughing.	He is	making a toast. / clapping.	They are	graduating. / hugging. / kissing. / applauding.

32

INTRODUCE THE TOPIC

Ask students to tell you which school graduations are special in their culture.

Describe one of your own graduation ceremonies, and if possible, show a photo of yourself in a cap and gown.

TEACH THE NEW WORDS

Ask students a series of *yes/no* questions about the pictures: *Is the photographer wearing a cap and gown?* (no) *Is the guest speaker speaking?* (no) *Is the valedictorian a woman?* (yes)

PROVIDE PRACTICE
Chalkboard Activities

△ Have students categorize vocabulary:

People	Objects	Actions
photographer	*stage*	*cry*

△ Have students sequence actions:

_____ **Hear your name.**
_____ **Listen to the guest speaker.**
_____ **Go to a party.**
_____ **Walk on stage.**
__1__ **Sit in the audience.**
_____ **Get a diploma.**
_____ **Smile at the photographer.**

Conversations

△ Put models on the board and practice. Make appropriate substitutions.

A: My *[son, Jack,]* is graduating today.
B: Congratulations! You must be proud!
A: Where is the <u>*photographer*</u>?
B. *[She's]* near the *[stage]*.
   6. graduate 8. valedictorian
   9. guest speaker

A: We're having a party to celebrate *[Sara's]* graduation from *[college]*.
B: Will you have a <u>*DJ*</u>?
   12. caterer 13. buffet 16. dance floor

Interview Questions

1. Do people give graduation gifts in your culture? What kind of gifts?
2. Do you like to dance at parties?
3. Do you like to make speeches?
4. What's a common toast in your culture?
5. Name the last person you applauded.
6. Do you like to take pictures?
7. What makes you cry?
8. What makes you laugh?
9. Do you want to have a party on the last day of class?

A Graduation

The Party

CONGRATULATIONS GRADUATES!

12. caterer	15. banner	18. gifts	H. laugh
13. buffet	16. dance floor	F. kiss	I. make a toast
14. guests	17. DJ (disc jockey)	G. hug	J. dance

Share your answers.
1. Did you ever go to a graduation? Whose?
2. Did you ever give a speech? Where?
3. Did you ever hear a great speaker? Where?
4. Did you ever go to a graduation party?
5. What do you like to eat at parties?
6. Do you like to dance at parties?

33

Listening: Interactive Dictation
△ Have students close their books. Dictate the sentences below, speaking naturally and encouraging students to ask for clarification. *(Who? They're doing what?)*
1. *A young woman is graduating.*
2. *Two graduates are dancing.*
3. *The photographer is taking a picture.*
4. *The valedictorian is smiling.*
5. *The guests are toasting the graduates.*
6. *The guest speaker is making a speech.*
7. *The caterer is standing behind the table.*
8. *A woman is kissing her daughter.*
9. *A father is hugging his son.*
10. *Three friends are laughing.*

EXPAND THE LESSON
Problem Solving
△ Have students brainstorm solutions.
1. *Two friends of yours are graduating on the same day and you are invited to both ceremonies. What will you do?*
2. *Your 15-year-old friend wants to stop going to school. What can you say to him?*

Discussion Questions
1. Some students decide not to attend their graduation ceremonies. Are ceremonies important? Why or why not?
2. Some teenagers get a new car as a graduation gift. Do you think this is a good idea? Why or why not?
3. Some people in the U.S. hug and kiss good friends in public. Are you comfortable with this custom?

Drawing Activity
1. Show students a diploma. Put the following language on the board, inserting real information for the words in parentheses, and discuss its meaning: *This is to certify that* (first name, last name) *has completed* (name of class). *Witnessed on this date, the* (ordinal number) *of* (month) *in the year* (year). (name of teacher or principal)
2. Give students 8 1/2" x 11" sheets of paper and have them design a diploma for their class using the language above or language of their own.
3. Reproduce the students' favorite design for use on the last day of class.

Speeches
Note: This activity works best during the last few weeks of a course.
1. Write the following incomplete sentences on the board and brainstorm ways to complete them:

   This is a … day for me.
   I'd like to thank…
   One thing I enjoyed in this class was when we…
   I will always remember the time I…
   I plan to … in the future.

2. Help students with the pronunciation of these phrases by tapping out the rhythm and/or using your hand to indicate rising and falling intonation.
3. Give each student a 3" x 5" card on which to write a short speech using the phrases from the board and adding their own ideas.
4. Have students practice their speeches with partners or in groups.
5. Students can memorize the words or use their cards to give their speeches in front of the class.

GAMES
Questions Only!
1. Divide students into groups of 4–8 and have each group choose a recorder.
2. Have students look at page 33 and come up with as many questions as they can about the scene. *(Where is the DJ?)*
3. Recorders write their groups' questions on the board.
4. The group with the most correct questions wins.

Variation: Have the recorders read their groups' questions aloud.
Variation: Have students take turns quizzing you with their questions.

Workbooks, p. 34
Classic Classroom Activities, Unit 3
Related Dictionary Pages
• Finding a Home, p. 35
• Places to Go, p. 152

TOPIC NOTES

In the U.S., owning one's own home has been called "the American dream." In 1992, 64% of the people did live in places—**houses, farms, ranches, condominiums, mobile homes,** etc.—that they owned themselves. Of the remainder, almost 3 million farm workers moved from place to place to harvest crops.

Nursing homes are for people who need medical care and **shelters** are for people who cannot pay for other types of housing. Homelessness continues to be a problem. Over 40% of homeless adults have children.

📁 In the U.S. in any one year, 34% of the people who rent their homes move, compared with 9% of the people who live in their own houses.

TEACHING TIPS
Related Vocabulary

duplex	homeless
triplex	residence
hotel*	refugee camp
penthouse	condo
mansion	

Usage: We say *I live in an apartment, in a college dormitory, in a mobile home,* and *in a shelter.* We say *I live on a farm,* and *on a ranch.*

💡 Review the verbs *live, move,* and *stay* in the present and past tense so that students can talk about where they have lived.

Places to Live

1. the city/an urban area   2. the suburbs   3. a small town   4. the country/a rural area

5. apartment building   6. house   7. townhouse

8. mobile home   9. college dormitory   10. shelter

11. nursing home   12. ranch   13. farm

More vocabulary
duplex house: a house divided into two homes
condominium: an apartment building where each apartment is owned separately
co-op: an apartment building owned by the residents

Share your answers.
1. Do you like where you live?
2. Where did you live in your country?
3. What types of housing are there near your school?

34

INTRODUCE THE TOPIC

Point out the different cities, suburbs, small towns, and country regions that are closest to your school. Talk about the size and population of these places and interesting things to see in each one.

Ask students questions about the homes in their area, such as *What kind of homes are on Central Street?*

Talk about places where you have lived. Tell students how long you stayed there and why you moved. Draw pictures on the board to represent each place.

TEACH THE NEW WORDS

Ask students a series of *yes/no* questions about the pictures. *Do students live in a college dormitory?* (yes) *Do people have horses in a townhouse?* (no)

PROVIDE PRACTICE
Chalkboard Activities

△ Have students categorize vocabulary:

Big City	**Suburbs**	**Small Town**
[local city]	[local suburb]	[local town]

Conversations

△ Put models on the board and practice. Make appropriate substitutions.

A: I heard you are moving!
B: Yes, we're moving to *the suburbs*.
   1. the city 3. a small town 4. the country

A: Where do you live?
B: I live in a *house* on [Dory Avenue].
   5. an apartment building 7. a townhouse
   8. a mobile home 11. a nursing home

A: My daughter is not living at home.
B: Really? Where does she live?
A: She just moved to a(n) *apartment* with a friend.
   7. townhouse 9. college dormitory 13. farm

Interview Questions

1. What kind of housing is most common in your native city?

2. Tell different places you have lived. How long did you live there?

Listening: 🔊 #11, p. 212

"Looking To Buy" Students write the number of each type of place the Realtor describes.

EXPAND THE LESSON
Problem Solving

△ Have students brainstorm solutions.
Liz and Sal are married. Sal just got a job in the city, but Liz likes living in a small town. What can they do?

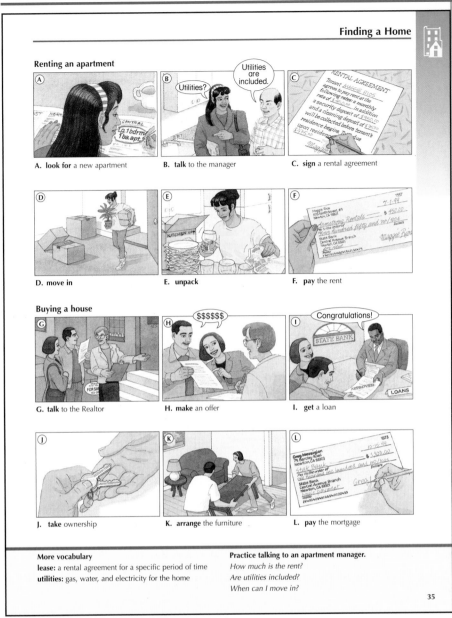

Finding a Home

Renting an apartment

A. **look for** a new apartment

B. **talk** to the manager

C. **sign** a rental agreement

D. **move in**

E. **unpack**

F. **pay** the rent

Buying a house

G. **talk** to the Realtor

H. **make** an offer

I. **get** a loan

J. **take** ownership

K. **arrange** the furniture

L. **pay** the mortgage

More vocabulary
lease: a rental agreement for a specific period of time
utilities: gas, water, and electricity for the home

Practice talking to an apartment manager.
How much is the rent?
Are utilities included?
When can I move in?

35

Workbooks, p. 35
Classic Classroom Activities, Unit 3
Related Dictionary Pages
• Places to Live, p. 34
• Apartments, pp. 36–37
• A House, p. 38
• A Yard, p. 39

TOPIC NOTES

In the U.S., The Federal Fair Housing Law prohibits housing discrimination based on race, color, religion, sex, national origin, and familial or handicap status.

An **apartment manager** or a *superintendent* usually lives on the property and handles the rental process for the owner of the building.

A **lease** is a contract that most renters sign. The renters promise to stay in the apartment for a specific amount of time. If the renters break the lease, they usually have to pay the landlord additional money.

TEACHING TIPS
Related Vocabulary

classified ads	accept an offer
superintendent	move out
landlady	realty office
put a house up for sale	escrow

☼ Review typical abbreviations found in classified ads: *bdrm, ba, nr, eve, /mo, inclu, excel, gd,* etc.

☼ Bring in local classified ads. Have students look through the ads on a scavenger hunt for one-bedroom apartments near transportation, three-bedroom houses for rent, studio apartments under $400, etc.

INTRODUCING THE TOPIC

Ask students about their housing. *How many of you are now in the same home (or apartment) you were in last year? How many of you want to be in a new home next year?*

Tell a story about your experience renting or buying a home. Pretend to forget some of the target vocabulary (leaving a sentence open-ended while pretending to think of the word). See if any students can supply the missing word. *I was 18 when I rented my first apartment. I talked to the...*

TEACH THE NEW WORDS

Describe each panel on the page, using the target language more than once. *This woman is looking for a new apartment. She's looking in the newspaper for a two-bedroom apartment.*

PROVIDE PRACTICE
Chalkboard Activities

△ Have students categorize vocabulary:

Actions	Paperwork	People
sign	lease	manager

Conversations

△ Put models on the board and practice. Make appropriate substitutions.

A: Have you found a new place yet?
B: Yes, I found one last week. I just have to *talk to the manager*.
   C. sign a rental agreement D. move in
   E. unpack F. pay the rent J. take ownership
   L. pay the mortgage

A: Do you want to help me *look for a new apartment*?
B: Sure. Just don't ask me to help you *pay the rent*.
   D. move in/H. make an offer
   G. talk to the Realtor/K. arrange the furniture

Interview Questions

1. Do you pay rent or a mortgage?
2. Which is harder, moving in or moving out?
3. Do you like arranging furniture?
4. How many homes have you lived in?

Listening: 🔊 #11, p. 212

"Looking To Buy" Students listen to a Realtor describe her day and write the letter of the action that's described.

EXPAND THE LESSON
Language Workout

△ Put these sentences on the board and discuss their meanings.
   1. Their house went *on the market* last month, but they only got one offer.
   2. She has to *break the lease* because her new job is in another state.

Workbooks, pp. 36–37
Classic Classroom Activities, Unit 3
Related Dictionary Pages
• Finding a Home, p. 35
• Household Problems and Repairs,
  pp. 48–49

TOPIC NOTES

In the U.S., some regions use the number of bedrooms to describe apartments: *a two-bedroom apartment.* Other areas use the total number of rooms including the bedrooms, kitchen, dining room and living room when talking about apartments: *a five-room apartment.*

TEACHING TIPS
Related Vocabulary

location	rent*
single	one-bedroom
furnished	unfurnished
vacancy	no vacancy
utilities*	security deposit
rules	roommate
buzzer	pets*

Usage: On the West Coast, apartment buildings have *managers* who are in charge of maintenance and general care of the building. On the East Coast, this person is called the *superintendent* or *"super."*

☼ Review *There is...* and *There are...* to enable students to talk about the features of an apartment building. *There is a laundry room in the basement. There are trash chutes on every floor.*

☼ Bring in classified ads for apartment rentals in order to teach abbreviations used to describe apartments: bd, kit, ba, air. cond., etc.

Apartments

1. first floor	**6.** playground	**11.** vacancy sign
2. second floor	**7.** fire escape	**12.** manager/superintendent
3. third floor	**8.** intercom/speaker	**13.** security gate
4. fourth floor	**9.** security system	**14.** storage locker
5. roof garden	**10.** doorman	**15.** parking space

More vocabulary
rec room: a short way of saying **recreation room**
basement: the area below the street level of an apartment or a house

Talk about where you live.
I live in Apartment 3 near the entrance.
I live in Apartment 11 on the second floor near the fire escape.

36

INTRODUCE THE TOPIC

Talk about the apartments in the picture. Describe their features, the tenants, and the tenants' actions. Ask questions and answer them yourself if students can't. *Look at the tall apartment building on page 36. How many floors does it have? That's right—four. See the roof garden on the top? (#5) What do you think people are growing? Look at the apartment building on page 37. See the swimming pool? (#16) How many people are swimming?*

Tell students you have to move and you're looking for a new apartment. Bring in the classified ads and read some of the descriptions. *Here's one—"2-bedroom, 2-bath, air conditioning, near schools, elevator, no pets." What do you think? I have a dog. Do you think I can have my dog there?*

TEACH THE NEW WORDS

Describe the pictures and have students point to the items. *Look at the staircase on the side of building. People don't use it unless there is a fire. It's called a fire escape. (#7) Look at the man at the front door. He checks everyone going in and coming out. He's called the doorman. (#10)*

PROVIDE PRACTICE
Chalkboard Activities

△ Have students categorize vocabulary:

Indoors	Outdoors
garage	pool

△ Write the following abbreviations on the board and have students guess their meanings: **bd, ba, ac, sec. bldg, excel cond., rec. rm., elev., htd pool**

Conversations

△ Put models on the board and practice. Make appropriate substitutions.

A: I'm interested in your two-bedroom apartment. Does it have a *laundry room?*
B: Yes, it does. And we have a *[pool].*
A: Can I see the apartment?
B: Of course.
   balcony, recreation room

A: Hello. My name is Carlos. I'm on the *first floor.* How about you?
B: I'm in *[206]* on the second floor.
   2. second floor 3. third floor 4. fourth floor

A: I can't find my key!
B: Maybe you left it in the *rec room.*
   5. roof garden 18. courtyard 34. elevator

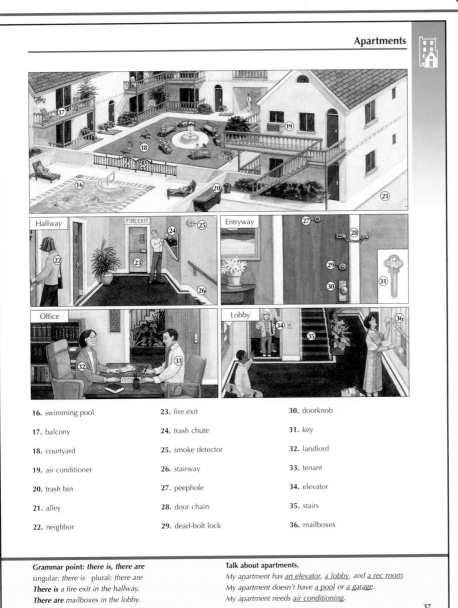

Apartments

16. swimming pool	23. fire exit	30. doorknob
17. balcony	24. trash chute	31. key
18. courtyard	25. smoke detector	32. landlord
19. air conditioner	26. stairway	33. tenant
20. trash bin	27. peephole	34. elevator
21. alley	28. door chain	35. stairs
22. neighbor	29. dead-bolt lock	36. mailboxes

Grammar point: *there is, there are*
singular: *there is* plural: *there are*
There is a fire exit in the hallway.
There are mailboxes in the lobby.

Talk about apartments.
My apartment has *an elevator, a lobby,* and *a rec room.*
My apartment doesn't have *a pool* or *a garage.*
My apartment needs *air conditioning.*

37

Interview Questions

1. Do you live in an apartment? Do you have friends who live in an apartment?
2. When you look for an apartment, what is the most important feature?
3. When you look for an apartment, which is the least important feature?
4. In a four-story apartment building, which floor would you like to live on?
5. Do you like neighbors who are friendly? What about noisy? How about quiet?

Listening: 📼 #12, p. 212

"The Case Of The Missing Wallet" Students point to the features of two different apartment buildings as they are described.

EXPAND THE LESSON

Problem Solving

△ Have students brainstorm solutions.
1. *Julio has a cat and can't find an apartment building in his price range that takes animals. What can he do?*
2. *Spartok has to go to work at 5:00 A.M. His neighbors are very noisy and play loud music until midnight. What can he do?*

Discussion Questions

1. Besides rent that you can afford, what else is important when you look for an apartment?
2. It is important to think of safety when living in an apartment. What are some safety tips that you know of?

Writing Activity

1. Have students imagine they are the landlord of an expensive apartment building. Have them write a classified ad for one apartment.
2. Have volunteers describe their apartment and how wonderful it is.

GAMES

A–Z Brainstorm

1. Divide students into groups of 3–4.
2. Have students study pages 36–37 for two minutes, then close their books.
3. Each group chooses a recorder. The recorder writes the letters A–Z on the left side of his or her paper.
4. As the rest of the group calls out the words, the recorder writes them down next to the letter the word begins with.
5. Call time after 5 minutes. The group with the most correct words wins.

Backwards Dictionary

1. Divide students into two teams.
2. Give definitions or descriptions of the vocabulary words to one team at a time and have them guess what the word is. *It's outside the building. You climb down it in case of a fire. It has two rails to hold onto. What is it?* (fire escape) *It's on the door of your apartment. You look through it to see who is at your door. It's very small.* (peephole)
3. The team with the most correct answers wins.

Class Go-Around: Celia Lost the Rent Check!

1. Begin by saying *Celia lost the rent check. She looked in the elevator.*
2. The first student volunteer repeats the sentences and adds another place. *Celia lost the rent check. She looked in the elevator* and *in the hallway.*
3. The next student volunteer continues the chain, adding another place.
4. Stop after ten students and begin the game again.

Questions Only!

1. Divide students into groups of 4–8 and have each group choose a recorder.
2. Have students look at pages 36–37 and come up with as many questions as possible about the scene, e.g., *How many people are in the pool?*
3. Recorders write their groups' questions on the board.
4. The group with the most correct questions wins.

Workbooks, p. 38
Classic Classroom Activities, Unit 3
Related Dictionary Pages
- Places to Live, p. 34
- Finding a Home, p. 35
- A Yard, p. 39

TOPIC NOTES

In the U.S., the median sale price for a single-family house in 1970 was $23,400. By 1996 the median price was $113,800.

A **storm door,** made of wood or metal, is hung outside the normal door for protection against severe weather.

A **screen door** is hung outside the front or back door and is made of wire mesh, allowing air, but not insects, to come into the home.

A **fence** is usually made of wood, chain link, or wrought iron. Walls of brick or concrete block are also used to separate houses.

A **mailbox** can be mounted on a pole or fence near the sidewalk, or on the outside of the house in the front. Some front doors have mail slots.

TEACHING TIPS
Related Vocabulary

attic	bathroom*
basement*	bedroom*
two-story	living room*
split level	porch
kitchen*	mudroom

 Although many students may not be in a financial position to buy a home, you can use the vocabulary in this topic to talk about the homes they grew up in or about the homes in your city or town.

A House

1. floor plan
2. backyard
3. fence
4. mailbox
5. driveway
6. garage
7. garage door
8. screen door
9. porch light
10. doorbell
11. front door
12. storm door
13. steps
14. front walk
15. front yard
16. deck
17. window
18. shutter
19. gutter
20. roof
21. chimney
22. TV antenna

More vocabulary
two-story house: a house with two floors
downstairs: the bottom floor
upstairs: the part of a house above the bottom floor

Share your answers.
1. What do you like about this house?
2. What's something you don't like about the house?
3. Describe the perfect house.

38

INTRODUCE THE TOPIC

Draw a house on the board as you talk about it. *This house has a large front door and two…two… what are they? Oh yes, windows. Two windows next to the door.*

Have students name the features of a house as you write them on the board. Compare their lists with page 38.

TEACH THE NEW WORDS

Ask students a series of *or* questions about the picture. *Is #16 the deck or the porch?* (deck) *Is it in the front yard or the backyard?* (backyard)

PROVIDE PRACTICE
Chalkboard Activity

△ Have students categorize vocabulary:

In Front	In Back	On the Roof
doorbell	*deck*	*chimney*

Conversations

△ Put models on the board and practice. Make appropriate substitutions.

A: I need someone to fix my *chimney*. It looks terrible.
B: Don't worry. I have the number of a good handyman.
  7. garage door, 8. screen door, 20. roof

A: Here's the floor plan of my new house and a photo I took from the *driveway*.
B: Looks nice, but what's this?
A: That's the *gutter*.
  13. steps/3. fence
  14. front walk/9. porch light
  15. front yard/12. storm door
  16. deck/22. TV antenna

Interview Questions

1. Which do you like better, a house with or without a fence?
2. Do you prefer using the front or the back door to come into a house?

Listening: 🔊 #13, p. 213

"I love my home." Students listen to Chuck describe his home and point to the items they hear described.

EXPAND THE LESSON
Problem Solving

△ Have students brainstorm solutions. *Every week kids from Norma's neighborhood write on the fences and walls of her house. She keeps painting over the writing, but she's angry. What can she do?*

Discussion Questions

1. What's different about the house on page 38 from the houses in your area? From those in your native country?
2. Describe your idea of the perfect home. What is it made of? How many stories does it have? Where is it located?

A Yard

1. hedge	8. sprinkler	15. pruning shears	22. lawn mower
2. hammock	9. hose	16. wheelbarrow	A. **weed** the flower bed
3. garbage can	10. compost pile	17. watering can	B. **water** the plants
4. leaf blower	11. rake	18. flowerpot	C. **mow** the lawn
5. patio furniture	12. hedge clippers	19. flower	D. **plant** a tree
6. patio	13. shovel	20. bush	E. **trim** the hedge
7. barbecue grill	14. trowel	21. lawn	F. **rake** the leaves

Talk about your yard and gardening.
I like to plant trees.
I don't like to weed.
I like/don't like to work in the yard/garden.

Share your answers.
1. What flowers, trees, or plants do you see in the picture? (Look at **Trees, Plants, and Flowers**, pages **128–129** for help.)
2. Do you ever use a barbecue grill to cook?

39

Workbooks, p. 39
Classic Classroom Activities, Unit 3
Related Dictionary Pages
- A House, p. 38
- Trees and Plants, p. 128
- Flowers, p. 129
- The Park and Playground, p. 153

TOPIC NOTES

In the U.S., home gardening is very popular. People grow vegetables and flowers in their backyards. During warm weather, people eat and entertain there.

A **compost pile** is an area in the yard where a family puts fruit and vegetable peels, lawn clippings, and yard waste. The mixture becomes fertilizer as it decomposes.

Some urban areas provide only one **garbage can** per household. In this way only trash that can't be composted or recycled gets thrown away.

TEACHING TIPS
Related Vocabulary

garden* (v/n)	work gloves
prune (v)	charcoal (briquets)
fertilize	gardener*
fertilizer	landscape designer
yard work	seedlings

💡 Help students research the best types of plants for your climate. Start seedlings inside the classroom and chart their growth.

💡 Check with your administrator to see if there is an area on campus you can beautify. Students can divide the necessary tasks: weeding, trimming, raking, planting, and watering.

INTRODUCE THE TOPIC

Talk about the yard work you do on a regular basis. Demonstrate the action as you say it. *Sometimes I mow the lawn in my backyard. I like to plant roses.*

Ask students about their experience with gardens. *How many of you have a yard or a garden? Does anybody have any flower pots? A patio?* Draw on the board or show magazine pictures to make the questions comprehensible.

TEACH THE NEW WORDS

Describe the yard on page 39 and have students point to each item as you talk about it. *This yard has a green lawn. (#21) My lawn doesn't look this good! The lawn mower, on the left, cuts the grass. (#22)*

PROVIDE PRACTICE
Chalkboard Activities

△ Have students categorize vocabulary:

Plants	Equipment	Actions
flower	*rake*	*mow*

Conversations

△ Put models on the board and practice. Make appropriate substitutions.

A: Get the <u>hose</u> for me, please.
B: If you want, I'll [water the plants].
A: Thanks so much!

   11. **rake** 12. **hedge clippers** 13. **shovel**
   22. **lawn mower**

Interview Questions

1. Does your house have a yard? a flower bed? a patio? a hedge?
2. Do you like yard work? What kind is the hardest? the easiest?

Listening: 📼 #13, p. 213

"I love my home." Students listen to Chuck describe his yard and point to what they hear described.

EXPAND THE LESSON
Drawing Activity: Landscape Design

1. Elicit items found in a yard or garden such as a pool, swing set, bench, etc.
2. List students' words on the board and encourage them to look up any new words in their dictionaries.
3. Ask students to design the ideal garden or yard. Students can use pages 128–129 (Trees and Plants; Flowers) for reference.
4. Students then label the elements of their design and share their pictures.

Unit 3   A Kitchen   page 40

Workbooks, p. 40
Classic Classroom Activities, Unit 3
Related Dictionary Pages
- Housework, p. 46
- Food Preparation, p. 58
- Kitchen Utensils, p. 59

TOPIC NOTES

In the U.S., kitchens vary in size from small functional cooking areas to large multipurpose rooms combining eating and entertainment areas.

Microwave ovens and **food processors** are two examples of time-saving kitchen appliances. Many kitchens have modern appliances; however, busy schedules often mean that people cook less and eat out more often.

Although the technology behind microwave cooking was invented in 1940, it wasn't until 1952 that the first microwave was available for domestic use. Electromagnetic energy agitates food molecules, providing sufficient heat for cooking.

TEACHING TIPS
Related Vocabulary

juicer	garbage pail
coffee grinder	trash compactor
range	pressure cooker
water purifier	waffle iron
ice tray	pantry
pot holder*	cupboard

Grammar: Agent nouns
Point out that the endings *-er* and *-or* sometimes indicate agent nouns. Words like *refrigerator*, *freezer* and *toaster* come from the verbs *refrigerate*, *freeze* and *toast*.

A Kitchen

1. cabinet	8. shelf	15. toaster oven	22. counter
2. paper towels	9. refrigerator	16. pot	23. drawer
3. dish drainer	10. freezer	17. teakettle	24. pan
4. dishwasher	11. coffeemaker	18. stove	25. electric mixer
5. garbage disposal	12. blender	19. burner	26. food processor
6. sink	13. microwave oven	20. oven	27. cutting board
7. toaster	14. electric can opener	21. broiler	

Talk about the location of kitchen items.
The toaster oven is on the counter near the stove.
The microwave is above the stove.

Share your answers.
1. Do you have a garbage disposal? a dishwasher? a microwave?
2. Do you eat in the kitchen?

40

INTRODUCE THE TOPIC

Ask students to cover the words at the bottom of the page and call out those they already know.

Describe the kitchen in your home, drawing a simple plan of the area as you speak. *I have a large **sink** and my **microwave** is above the **stove**.*

TEACH THE NEW WORDS

Describe various kitchen items and have students identify the number or name of the picture. *This is a large appliance that keeps food cold.* (refrigerator) *Put your wet plates and cups in this.* (dish drainer)

PROVIDE PRACTICE
Chalkboard Activities

△ Have students categorize vocabulary:

1. Noisy Things   **Quiet Things**
blender   *shelf*

2. Uses Heat   **Doesn't Use Heat**
toaster   *can opener*

Conversations

△ Put models on the board and practice. Make appropriate substitutions.

A: Where did you put the *[chicken]*?
B: It's in the *pot*.
   **10. freezer 13. microwave 20. oven
   21. broiler**

A: This *[plate]* is broken.
B: Don't put it in the *sink*!
   1. cabinet 3. dish drainer 4. dishwasher

A: *[Shears]* is having an appliance sale.
B: Great! I want to buy a new *refrigerator.*
   **5. garbage disposal 7. toaster
   11. coffeemaker 12. blender
   14. electric can opener 15. toaster oven**

Interview Questions

1. What foods do you always have in your refrigerator?
2. What kitchen items do you use?
3. Do you ever leave dirty pots and pans in the sink?

Listening: Definitions

△ Have students write the number of the item as you describe it. E.g.:
1. *You use this to clean up spills. (#2)*
2. *This appliance combines foods at different speeds. (#25)* Etc.

EXPAND THE LESSON
Discussion Questions

1. What kitchen appliances are most useful?
2. What safety tips help prevent accidents in the kitchen?

40

A Dining Area

1. china cabinet
2. set of dishes
3. platter
4. ceiling fan
5. light fixture
6. serving dish
7. candle

8. candlestick
9. vase
10. tray
11. teapot
12. sugar bowl
13. creamer
14. saltshaker

15. pepper shaker
16. dining room chair
17. dining room table
18. tablecloth
19. napkin
20. place mat
21. fork

22. knife
23. spoon
24. plate
25. bowl
26. glass
27. coffee cup
28. mug

Practice asking for things in the dining room.
Please pass the platter.
May I have the creamer?
Could I have a fork, please?

Share your answers.
1. What are the women in the picture saying?
2. In your home, where do you eat?
3. Do you like to make dinner for your friends?

41

Workbooks, p. 41
Classic Classroom Activities, Unit 3
Related Dictionary Pages
• A Kitchen, p. 40
• A Restaurant, pp. 62–63

TOPIC NOTES

In the U.S., some homes have separate dining rooms, while others have a dining area that is a part of the kitchen or living room.

China refers to high-quality ceramic dishware that is fired twice. In some homes there are two **sets of dishes,** one for every day and one for special occasions. The everyday dishes are usually kept in the kitchen cabinets, while the special-occasion dishes may be kept in a separate **china cabinet.**

TEACHING TIPS
Related Vocabulary

chandelier	hot pad
coffee pot	hutch
buffet	wine glass*
silverware	napkin ring
trivet	salad bowl

Grammar: Compound nouns
Point out items that have two or more words, such as *china cabinet, ceiling fan, light fixture,* or *coffee cup.* Show students that the plural marker *-s* should be added only to the last word: *coffee cups.*

To help students discuss the dining scene, teach the following: the verbs *eat* and *drink*, page 60, and *pour*, page 62; the prepositions *on, next to, between,* and *in*, page 13.

INTRODUCE THE TOPIC

Bring in silverware, a cloth napkin, and a china plate. Have students guess what room of the house they will be studying.

Describe the dining area in your home, drawing a simple plan of the area as you speak.

TEACH THE NEW WORDS

Ask students a series of *yes/no* questions about the large picture. *Is the woman holding a fork?* (no) *Is the older woman in front of the china cabinet?* (no) *Is the tablecloth on the table?* (yes)

PROVIDE PRACTICE
Chalkboard Activities

△ Have students categorize vocabulary:

Furniture	**Dishware**	**Other**
china cabinet	*platter*	*napkin*

Conversations

△ Put models on the board and practice. Make appropriate substitutions.

A: I can't find the *serving dish!*
B: Relax! It's on the dining room table, near the *[teapot].*
A: RELAX?!! I can't relax. Our guests will be here any minute!

   3. platter 9. vase 14. saltshaker 15. pepper shaker 27. coffee cups

A: Would you please pass me that *plate?*
B: Certainly.

   12. sugar bowl 13. creamer 21. fork 22. knife 23. spoon 28. mug

A: What great looking *candlesticks!*
B: Thanks. They were a wedding gift.

   7. candles 19. napkins 20. place mats

Interview Questions

1. What color are your dishes?
2. Do you like to use candles?

Listening: Definitions

△ Have students write the word they hear being defined. *This cloth covers the dining room table.* (tablecloth) *This has sugar in it.* (sugar bowl) Etc.

GAME
Questions Only!

1. Divide students into groups of 4–8 and have each group choose a recorder.
2. Have students look at page 41 and come up with as many questions as they can about the scene. E.g.: *Where's the tray?*
3. Recorders write their group's questions on the board.
4. The group with the most correct questions wins.

Workbooks, p. 42
Classic Classroom Activities, Unit 3
Related Dictionary Pages
- Describing Things, p. 11
- Colors, p. 12
- Prepositions, p. 13
- Housework, p. 46

TOPIC NOTES

In the U.S., the living room is a gathering place for family and friends. Larger homes may have both a living room for formal entertaining and a family room or den for everyday activities. Small homes and apartments may feature a living room/dining room combination.

Wall units range from simple shelves to elaborate entertainment units that hold **televisions, stereos,** and numerous knickknacks. They can be freestanding or built into the wall.

TEACHING TIPS
Related Vocabulary

recessed lighting
curtain rod
ottoman
recliner
area rug*

picture*
TV tray table
upholstery
slipcovers
room divider

Grammar: Compound Nouns
Point out the following compound nouns. *coffee table, floor lamp, wall unit, bookcase, lightbulb,* and *fireplace*. Note that there are one word and two word compuonds.

💡 Review page 11, *Describing Things,* and page 12, *Colors,* so students can talk about the picture as well as their own home furnishings.

A Living Room

1. bookcase	8. mantel	15. floor lamp	22. magazine holder
2. basket	9. fireplace	16. drapes	23. coffee table
3. track lighting	10. fire	17. window	24. armchair / easy chair
4. lightbulb	11. fire screen	18. plant	25. love seat
5. ceiling	12. logs	19. sofa / couch	26. TV (television)
6. wall	13. wall unit	20. throw pillow	27. carpet
7. painting	14. stereo system	21. end table	

Use the new language.
Look at **Colors,** page 12, and describe this room.
There is a gray sofa and a gray armchair.

Talk about your living room.
In my living room I have a sofa, two chairs, and a coffee table.
I don't have a fireplace or a wall unit.

42

INTRODUCE THE TOPIC

Describe the living room in your home, drawing a simple plan of the area as you speak. *My blue sofa is under the window. It's very comfortable. My coffee table is right in front of the sofa.*

Bring in magazine or newspaper ads showing living room furnishings. Survey students to see if they own a similar item.

TEACH THE NEW WORDS

Ask students a series of *yes/no* questions about the picture on page 42. *Is the woman sitting in the armchair?* (yes) *Are there books in the wall unit?* (no)

PROVIDE PRACTICE
Chalkboard Activities

△ Have students categorize vocabulary:

Furniture
bookcase

Electrical Items
track lighting

△ Have students call out words to complete the activities.

Dust the ...	Hang a ...
Watch ...	Open the ...
Sit on the ...	Turn on the ...

Conversations

△ Put models on the board and practice. Make appropriate substitutions.

A: Where do you want the *end table*?
B: Put it near the *[floor lamp]*.
> 19. sofa 23. coffee table 24. armchair
> 25. love seat

A: Boy, this *carpet* is in bad shape.
B: Yeah, but we can't fix it now. We don't have the money.
> 3. track lighting 13. wall unit
> 14. stereo system 26. TV

Interview Questions

1. How much time do you spend in your living room every day ?

2. What would you like to buy for your living room? Why?

Listening: 📼 **#14, p. 213**
"A Moving Decision" Students cover up the living room scene and write the numbers of the words they hear.

EXPAND THE LESSON
Drawing Activity

1. Pairs of students choose any ten items from the living room page.

2. Using blank paper and a manila folder barrier, each partner designs a room containing these items. Upon completion, students compare their living rooms and talk about similarities and differences.

A Bathroom

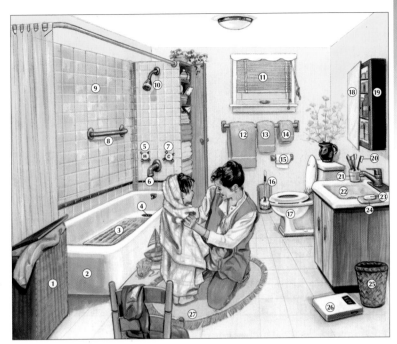

1. hamper	**8.** towel rack	**15.** toilet paper	**22.** sink
2. bathtub	**9.** tile	**16.** toilet brush	**23.** soap
3. rubber mat	**10.** showerhead	**17.** toilet	**24.** soap dish
4. drain	**11.** (mini)blinds	**18.** mirror	**25.** wastebasket
5. hot water	**12.** bath towel	**19.** medicine cabinet	**26.** scale
6. faucet	**13.** hand towel	**20.** toothbrush	**27.** bath mat
7. cold water	**14.** washcloth	**21.** toothbrush holder	

More vocabulary
half bath: a bathroom without a shower or bathtub
linen closet: a closet or cabinet for towels and sheets
stall shower: a shower without a bathtub

Share your answers.
1. Do you turn off the water when you brush your teeth? wash your hair? shave?
2. Does your bathroom have a bathtub or a stall shower?

43

Workbooks, p. 43
Classic Classroom Activities, Unit 3
Related Dictionary Pages
• Household Problems and Repairs, p. 49
• Personal Hygiene, pp. 76–77

TOPIC NOTES

In the U.S., the bathroom is the one room where privacy prevails. English reflects a sense of modesty and contains numerous euphemisms for the universal need to use the "rest room." Bathrooms in homes vary from simple toilet facilities to elaborate ones complete with indoor spas and whirlpool tubs.

Medicine cabinets hold a vast array of personal items, including medicines and health and beauty products.

TEACHING TIPS
Related Vocabulary

toilet seat cover	bath toy
loofah sponge	soap dispenser
shower curtain	face cloth
shower curtain rings	vanity

☼ Introduce the vocabulary on pages 76–77, *Personal Hygiene,* so that students can talk about everyday bathroom routines such as taking a shower or bath, washing hair, and brushing teeth.

⚠ Be aware of cultural taboos inherent in discussing bathroom habits. However, the vocabulary on this page can be used to stimulate discussions around water conservation, grooming habits, safety issues (such as toilet locks for children), and plumbing problems.

INTRODUCE THE TOPIC

Describe the bathroom on page 43, leaving some sentences open-ended as though you'd forgotten the words. *Look at the little girl—you can hardly see her under that large…* (bath towel). See if students can supply the missing word(s).

Demonstrate some actions in the bathroom. Pretend you are opening the medicine cabinet, singing in the shower, stepping on the scale, etc. Speak as you do the actions. *Hmm, where did I put the aspirin?* Or, *Oh no, it's time to go on a diet!*

TEACH THE NEW WORDS

Give various information as you repeat each word. *Item #1 is a hamper. You put dirty clothes in a hamper. Hampers are made of wicker or plastic.*

PROVIDE PRACTICE
Chalkboard Activities

△ Have students categorize vocabulary:

1. Wet Things	**Dry Things**
hot water	miniblinds

2. Stationary	**Moveable**
bathtub	hamper

Conversations

△ Put models on the board and practice. Make appropriate substitutions.

A: What happened to your *[ring]*?
B: I think it fell in the *hamper*.
> **2.** bathtub **4.** drain **24.** soap dish
> **25.** wastebasket

A: Have you seen my *[toothbrush]*?
B: No. Did you look near the *sink*?
> **6.** faucet **14.** washcloth **18.** mirror
> **19.** medicine cabinet **21.** toothbrush holder
> **23.** soap

Listening: Interactive Dictation

△ Have students close their books. Dictate questions about page 43. Speak naturally and encourage students to ask for clarification *(Where is the what? Who is doing what?).* Have students in pairs check their work and then write the answers. E.g.:
1. *Where's the mirror?*
2. *What's in the hamper?*
3. *Where's the soap?* Etc.

EXPAND THE LESSON
Problem Solving

△ Have students brainstorm solutions. *Sue has a large family but only one bathroom. Everybody fights to get in first. The hot water runs out when she takes a shower. What can she do?*

43

Workbooks, p. 44
Classic Classroom Activities, Unit 3
Related Dictionary Pages
- Describing Things, p. 11
- Colors, p. 12
- Prepositions, p. 13
- Housework, p. 46

TOPIC NOTES

In the U.S., bedrooms are designed for privacy, intimacy, relaxation, and recuperation from illness. Apartments and houses may have one or more bedrooms of varying sizes. Master bedrooms are larger in size and usually contain an attached bathroom and/or dressing area.

Beds can be defined by their size (twin, full/double, queen, king) or style (bunk, trundle, day, water, four-poster, canopy).

"Sleep tight and don't let the bed bugs bite" is an expression from long ago describing the actual danger of sleeping on a mattress. Organic stuffings such as straw, leaves, and pine needles mildewed and rotted, nurturing bedbugs, mice, and even rats!

TEACHING TIPS
Related Vocabulary

light socket	armoire
bedding	hope chest
footboard	cot
pillow sham	hospital bed*
electric blanket	sofa/convertible bed
quilt	mattress cover

Pronunciation: Short vowel sounds
Help students hear and produce short vowel sounds by indicating consonant-vowel-consonant patterns in words such as *lamp* [lămp], *bed* [bĕd], *clock* [klŏk], and *rug* [rŭg].

A Bedroom

1. mirror	8. bed	15. headboard	22. dust ruffle
2. dresser / bureau	9. pillow	16. clock radio	23. rug
3. drawer	10. pillowcase	17. lamp	24. floor
4. closet	11. bedspread	18. lampshade	25. mattress
5. curtains	12. blanket	19. light switch	26. box spring
6. window shade	13. flat sheet	20. outlet	27. bed frame
7. photograph	14. fitted sheet	21. night table	

Use the new language.
Describe this room. (See **Describing Things**, page 11, for help.)
I see a soft pillow and a beautiful bedspread.

Share your answers.
1. What is your favorite thing in your bedroom?
2. Do you have a clock in your bedroom? Where is it?
3. Do you have a mirror in your bedroom? Where is it?

44

INTRODUCE THE TOPIC

Bring in magazine pictures showing popular styles of bedding and bedroom furnishings. Talk about the pictures as you show them. *It's very cold now—should I buy this blanket? Well, these flannel sheets look warm. Maybe I'll buy pillowcases to match the sheets.*

TEACH THE NEW WORDS

Ask students a series of yes/no questions about the picture. *Is the woman looking under the bed?* (yes) *Are the curtains closed?* (no) *Is the cat near the outlet?* (no)

PROVIDE PRACTICE
Chalkboard Activities

△ Have students categorize vocabulary:

Bedding	**Electrical Items**
pillow	*outlet*

Conversations

△ Put models on the board and practice. Make appropriate substitutions.

A: When are you going to make the bed?
B: Later. I'm washing the *bedspread* now.
   10. pillowcase 12. blanket 13. flat sheet
   14. fitted sheet 22. dust ruffle
B: Do you like the new *mirror*?
A: Yes, I do, but why don't we move it *[near the dresser?]*
   7. photograph 16. clock radio 17. lamp
   23. rug

Interview Questions

1. What kind of bed do you have?
2. Do you prefer a soft or hard mattress?
3. What side of the bed do you usually sleep on?
4. Where do you keep your clothes?
5. What's under your bed?

Listening: 🔊 #15, p. 214

"The Lost Slipper" Students listen and point to the bedroom items on page 44.

EXPAND THE LESSON
Discussion Questions

1. What do you think the expression "to get up on the wrong side of the bed" means?
2. Many people believe that dreams are important. What's your opinion? Have you ever had a dream come true? What was it?
3. We usually wake up to buzzers, bells, or music. What's the best way to wake up?

A Children's Bedroom

1. bunk bed	**7.** bumper pad	**13.** diaper pail	**19.** cradle
2. comforter	**8.** chest of drawers	**14.** dollhouse	**20.** coloring book
3. night-light	**9.** baby monitor	**15.** blocks	**21.** crayons
4. mobile	**10.** teddy bear	**16.** ball	**22.** puzzle
5. wallpaper	**11.** smoke detector	**17.** picture book	**23.** stuffed animals
6. crib	**12.** changing table	**18.** doll	**24.** toy chest

Talk about where items are in the room.
The dollhouse is near the coloring book.
The teddy bear is on the chest of drawers.

Share your answers.
1. Do you think this is a good room for children? Why?
2. What toys did you play with when you were a child?
3. What children's stories do you know?

45

Workbooks, p. 45
Classic Classroom Activities, Unit 3
Related Dictionary Pages
• A Bedroom, p. 44
• Childcare Center, pp. 94–95
• Hobbies and Games, pp. 162–163

TOPIC NOTES

In the U.S., brothers and sisters often share a bedroom. Babies sometimes sleep in the parents' room for the first few months and then are moved into a separate bedroom.

All children's furniture should be inspected for safety. **Toy chests** should have safety lids that lock into position and **bunk beds** should have guard rails.

A **bunk bed** is two twin beds built so that one is on top of the other.

TEACHING TIPS
Related Vocabulary

bassinet	mural
youth bed	wall hanging
guard rail	ladder*
balloon	toy cars and trucks
action figure*	puppet
pillow*	blanket*

🔆 Review names of family members—*mother, father,* etc.—and various age designations—*baby, toddler, children,* etc.—so students can talk about where these people sleep. (See pages 22, 24, and 25.)

🔆 Bring in items from around the house that babies and children play with that are not toys (pots, cans, etc.) Talk about which ones are safe.

🔆 Have a day when students bring in toys from their countries. Talk about toys that have lasting value.

INTRODUCE THE TOPIC

Ask students to tell you what kinds of furniture and toys they would expect to see in a child's bedroom.

Bring in different kinds of children's books and/or toys and talk about them with students.

TEACH THE NEW WORDS

Ask students a series of *or* questions about the pictures. *Is the little boy holding a ball or a block?* (a ball) *Does the little girl sleep in the bunk bed or the crib?* (the bunk bed)

PROVIDE PRACTICE
Chalkboard Activities

△ Have students categorize vocabulary:

Furniture	**Bedding**	**Toys**
bunk bed	comforter	blocks

Conversations

△ Put models on the board and practice. Make appropriate substitutions.

A: I think it's time to pick up this room!
B: What's the matter?
A: There are *puzzles* everywhere!
> **16.** balls **17.** picture books **18.** dolls
> **21.** crayons **23.** stuffed animals

A: Tina's baby shower is next week!
B: I know. I bought the baby a *mobile*.
A: OK. I'll get her something different.
> **3.** night-light **12.** changing table **19.** cradle
> **24.** toy chest

A: Where should we put the *crib*?
B: How about [*next to the door*]?
> **1.** bunk beds **8.** chest of drawers
> **12.** changing table **13.** diaper pail

Interview Questions

1. What was your favorite toy? Who gave it to you?

2. Do you have cribs like this one in your native country?

Listening: Listen and Draw

△ Have students draw a picture of the furniture and toys as you say them. *1) draw a ball 2) draw a dollhouse.* Etc.

EXPAND THE LESSON
Discussion Questions

1. Some children in the U.S. have many toys. They have lots of stuffed animals, dolls, etc. What do you think about this?

2. Do you think it's possible for a child to have too many toys?

3. Should children have their own rooms? Why or why not?

Workbooks, p. 46
Classic Classroom Activities, Unit 3
Related Dictionary Pages
• Cleaning Supplies, 47
• all rooms of the house, pp. 40–45

TOPIC NOTES

In the U.S., many appliances are available that help people clean their homes, such as vacuum cleaners and dishwashers. Even so, most people say they spend the same amount of time cleaning their homes as their parents did.

Wash usually means to use soap when you clean something. **Clean** means to remove the dirt whether you use soap or not.

TEACHING TIPS
Related Vocabulary

straighten up	neat*
arrange*	dirty*
wax (v)	messy*
defrost	dusty
disinfect	spot
clean (adj)	stain*

Grammar: Irregular verbs
sweep—swept, make—made, put—put, take out—took out.

🔅 Review vocabulary students will be using in the phrases on page 46: *window, carpet, counter, sheets, garbage,* etc.

🔅 Bring in items from page 47, Cleaning Supplies, as prompts for open-ended statements. Hold up a rag and say *I use this to…* (dust).

🔅 Bring in recyclable items (cans, plastic bottles, etc.) and talk about local recycling centers.

Housework

A. **dust** the furniture
B. **recycle** the newspapers
C. **clean** the oven
D. **wash** the windows
E. **sweep** the floor
F. **empty** the wastebasket

G. **make** the bed
H. **put away** the toys
I. **vacuum** the carpet
J. **mop** the floor
K. **polish** the furniture
L. **scrub** the floor

M. **wash** the dishes
N. **dry** the dishes
O. **wipe** the counter
P. **change** the sheets
Q. **take out** the garbage

Talk about yourself.
I wash the dishes every day.
I change the sheets every week.
I never dry the dishes.

Share your answers.
1. Who does the housework in your family?
2. What is your favorite cleaning job?
3. What is your least favorite cleaning job?

46

INTRODUCE THE TOPIC

Act out sweeping the floor, washing the dishes, cleaning the oven, etc. Speak as you do the actions. *My floor is dirty so I'm sweeping it. I have so many dishes from dinner. I'm washing them now. Just look at my oven. I just cleaned it a month ago!*

Bring in various cleaning supplies. Tell students you are going to talk about what you can do with them. *This is oven cleaner. I use it to clean the oven. This is furniture polish and these are rags. I use these items to polish the furniture.*

TEACH THE NEW WORDS

Ask students to identify the letter of the picture based on your description. *His windows are dirty. He washes his windows every week.* (D)

PROVIDE PRACTICE
Chalkboard Activities

△ Have students brainstorm the cleaning chores in each of these rooms:

Kitchen	Bedroom	Bathroom
wipe counters	*make beds*	*scrub floors*

△ Have students brainstorm vocabulary:

Clean	Put Away	Recycle
windows	*food*	*cans*

Conversations

△ Put models on the board and practice. Make appropriate substitutions.

A: I have so much to do!
B: How can I help?
A: Could you *dust the furniture*?

B. recycle the newspapers E. sweep the floors F. empty the wastebaskets
G. make the beds

A: I'll split the housework with you. I'll *clean the oven*.
B: Thanks, I'll wash the dishes.

J. mop the floor K. polish the furniture
L. scrub the floor N. dry the dishes
O. wipe the counter P. change the sheets

Interview Questions

1. What cleaning chores do you do every day? once a week? never?
2. What is your least favorite chore?

Listening: 📻 #16, p. 214

"And His House Got Very Clean!" Students pantomime the actions as they listen to the chores in this song.

EXPAND THE LESSON
Discussion Question

Every family divides housework differently. Who does cleaning chores in your home? How do you get family members to help?

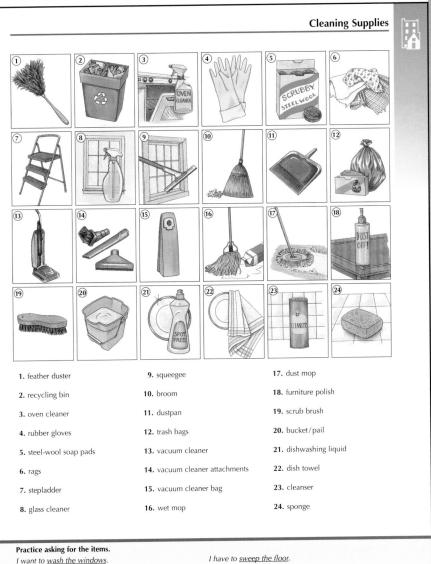

Cleaning Supplies

1. feather duster
2. recycling bin
3. oven cleaner
4. rubber gloves
5. steel-wool soap pads
6. rags
7. stepladder
8. glass cleaner

9. squeegee
10. broom
11. dustpan
12. trash bags
13. vacuum cleaner
14. vacuum cleaner attachments
15. vacuum cleaner bag
16. wet mop

17. dust mop
18. furniture polish
19. scrub brush
20. bucket / pail
21. dishwashing liquid
22. dish towel
23. cleanser
24. sponge

Practice asking for the items.
I want to <u>wash the windows</u>.
Please hand me <u>the squeegee</u>.

I have to <u>sweep the floor</u>.
Can you get me <u>the broom</u>, please?

47

Workbooks, p. 47
Classic Classroom Activities, Unit 3
Related Dictionary Pages
• Housework, p. 46
• all rooms of the house, pp. 40–45

TOPIC NOTES

In the U.S., many different types of stores carry cleaning supplies: markets, hardware stores, discount stores, and large warehouse stores that carry these items in bulk.

Nonpolluting products are often identified as biodegradable or environmentally safe.

TEACHING TIPS
Related Vocabulary

wax	dust
dirt	grease
mildew	scum
scrubber	ammonia
bleach*	baking soda
vinegar	poisonous

☼ Review vocabulary from page 46, *Housework,* so that students can talk about what the cleaning supplies on this page are used for. All the cleaning supplies needed for the housework tasks on page 46 are depicted on this page.

☼ Many cleaning supplies are dangerous and/or poisonous. Teaching a lesson on warning labels and the symbols on them can help students prevent accidents. Storage and disposal should be discussed also.

☼ Talk about natural cleaners such as lemon, vinegar, and baking soda that people have used for a long time.

INTRODUCE THE TOPIC

Bring in some of the cleaning supplies on this page. Take an informal class survey of the items students have in their homes.

Ask students to cover the words at the bottom of the page and call out the words they already know.

TEACH THE NEW WORDS

Ask students to identify pictures by number as you describe them. *This is used to reach high places. It folds up. It has two steps. It's called a stepladder.* (#7)

PROVIDE PRACTICE
Chalkboard Activities

△ Have students categorize vocabulary:

Dangerous for Children
oven cleaner

OK for Children with Supervision
vacuum cleaner

△ Have students brainstorm the supplies for each of these:

mop the floor	*mop, bucket*
dry the dishes	
scrub the floor	
clean the oven	

Conversations

△ Put models on the board and practice. Make appropriate substitutions.

A: Excuse me. I'm looking for a <u>broom</u>.
B: We don't have one. Try *[Jon's]* across the street.
   1. feather duster 7. stepladder 9. squeegee
   11. dustpan 16. wet mop 17. dust mop

A: Where are the <u>rags</u>?
B: In the closet. Why?
A: Today is my day to clean!
   4. rubber gloves 12. trash bags
   14. vacuum cleaner attachments

Interview Questions

1. What cleaning supplies are the most important? the least important?

2. What do you use to clean the floor? to wipe the counter? to wash the dishes?

Listening: 💿 **#16, p. 214**

"And His House Got Very Clean!" Students point to the cleaning supplies as they listen to this song.

EXPAND THE LESSON
Discussion Questions

1. Sometimes people find unusual ways to clean things. Do you know of any products that are cheaper or better than those in the stores? What are they?

2. Many cleaning products are dangerous and small children are good climbers. Discuss good places to keep dangerous products out of children's reach.

Unit 3   Household Problems and Repairs   page 48

Workbooks, pp. 48–49
Classic Classroom Activities, Unit 3
Related Dictionary Pages
- Tools and building supplies, pp. 150–151
- places around the home and rooms in the house, pp. 36–45

TOPIC NOTES

In the U.S., many people take care of their own household problems. They are called "do-it-yourselfers." Other homeowners call on **repair persons.** Renters call their manager or landlord to take care of repairs.

A **locksmith** has to have a special license to repair locks.

Exterminators work with dangerous chemicals and must be licensed in most states.

Stopped up and **overflowing** describe similar problems. If a drain pipe is stopped up, it means the water won't drain and the sink may overflow.

TEACHING TIPS
Related Vocabulary

gas leak	trap
water leak	handyman
gas valve	contractor
water valve	insured
jack of all trades	time and materials
licensed and bonded	guarantee

- Review vocabulary needed to discuss the verbs on these pages: *furnace, water heater, roof, window, lock, wall, steps, toilet, faucet, sink,* and *pipes.*

- Bring in various tools that are used to remedy household problems, e.g., a hammer, a saw, a wrench, and pesticide. Talk about what they are used for.

Household Problems and Repairs

1. The water heater is **not working**.
2. The power is **out**.
3. The roof is **leaking**.
4. The wall is **cracked**.
5. The window is **broken**.
6. The lock is **broken**.
7. The steps are **broken**.
8. roofer
9. electrician
10. repair person
11. locksmith
12. carpenter
13. fuse box
14. gas meter

Use the new language.
Look at **Tools and Building Supplies,** pages **150–151.**
Name the tools you use for household repairs.

I use a hammer and nails to fix a broken step.
I use a wrench to repair a dripping faucet.

48

INTRODUCE THE TOPIC

Tell students a story about a recent housing problem you have had. *Last week my sink was stopped up. I couldn't wash my dishes! I called the plumber. He wanted $60 to come to my house. When he came, it took him 30 minutes to fix it.*

Go around the classroom looking for repairs. Talk as you hunt. *Oh, look at the ceiling. It has a crack. It is going to leak.* (Turn off the lights.) *Oh, no! The power is out. I need an electrician.*

Ask students to look at pages 48 and 49. Talk about the house, the people working on it, and what kind of condition it is in. *Look at this house. How old do you think it is? It has a lot of problems. How many people are working on the house?*

TEACH THE NEW WORDS

Ask students to identify pictures by number as you describe them. *Someone hit a ball through the window. There is a broken window. (#5) This is a pest that lives in the basement or in the attic. It's bigger than a mouse and eats garbage. It's a rat. (#27)*

PROVIDE PRACTICE
Chalkboard Activities

- Have students prioritize these problems. What should the landlord fix first? (You can expand the list.)

____ no heat	____ frozen pipes
____ stopped up sink	____ broken steps
____ mice	____ broken window

- Have students categorize vocabulary:

Kitchen
leaking pipes

Bathroom
stopped up toilet

Outside
broken lock

- Write six problems from pages 48–49 on the board. Ask students how long they think it would take to fix each. E.g.:

The wall is cracked.	*2 hours*
The window is broken.	_____

Conversations

- Put models on the board and practice. Make appropriate substitutions.

A: Uh oh, *the furnace is broken!*
B: Can you fix it yourself?
A: I think so—with some help!

1. the water heater is not working
2. the power is out
3. the roof is leaking
5. the window is broken
6. the lock is broken

A: Hello. Can you send a plumber right away? *My toilet is stopped up.*
B: I'm sorry. All our plumbers are out. We'll have to call you back.

16. The faucet is dripping 17. The sink is overflowing 19. The pipes are frozen

48

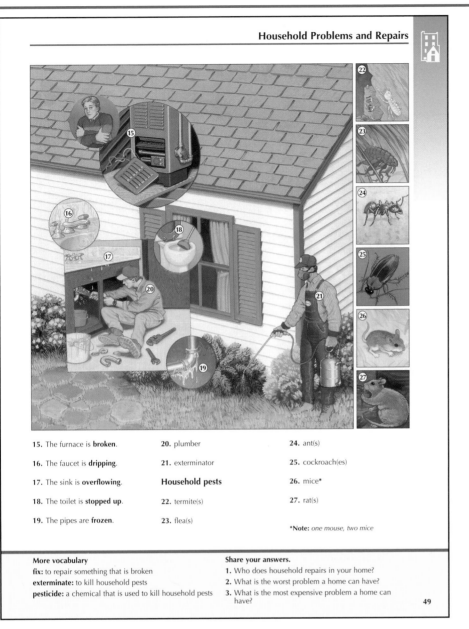

Household Problems and Repairs

15. The furnace is **broken**.

16. The faucet is **dripping**.

17. The sink is **overflowing**.

18. The toilet is **stopped up**.

19. The pipes are **frozen**.

20. plumber

21. exterminator

Household pests

22. termite(s)

23. flea(s)

24. ant(s)

25. cockroach(es)

26. mice*

27. rat(s)

*Note: *one mouse, two mice*

More vocabulary
fix: to repair something that is broken
exterminate: to kill household pests
pesticide: a chemical that is used to kill household pests

Share your answers.
1. Who does household repairs in your home?
2. What is the worst problem a home can have?
3. What is the most expensive problem a home can have?

49

A: Hello. No-Pests Exterminators.
B: This is [Marika Fisher]. I live in [Norwood]. I've got <u>cockroaches</u> in my kitchen! When can you come?
A: I think we can be there in a couple of hours. What's your address?
B: [1314 Polk St.]
A: Will someone be home?
B: Of course. Thanks very much.
  23. termites 24. ants 26. mice

Interview Questions

1. What repairs can you do yourself?
2. What repairs cost the most?
3. What are some typical problems in an apartment?
4. What are some typical problems in a house?

Listening: 📼 #17, p. 215

"One House, Many Problems" Students point to household problems as they are described.

EXPAND THE LESSON
Problem Solving

△ Have students brainstorm solutions.
An apartment renter has cockroaches. He has tried everything and can't get rid of them. What can the renter do?

Discussion Questions

1. What can an apartment renter do if a landlord won't fix a problem?
2. What can a homeowner do if repairs are done poorly by a repair person? by a spouse?
3. Discuss the cost of repairs in your area. What prices seem fair for different problems on this page?

---

4. Many Americans like to do repairs themselves. What are the advantages and disadvantages of this?
5. Do you know how to turn off the water, electricity, and gas in your home? What are some reasons to turn them off?

Language Workout

△ Copy these sentences on the board and discuss their meanings.
1. Oscar said he was going to work right now, but I don't believe him. *I smell a rat!*
2. You'll like your new neighbor. He's *as quiet as a mouse.*

Question Brainstorm

1. Students work in groups of 3–4.
2. Tell students you've been busy working on your house.
3. Have each group choose a recorder and brainstorm a list of questions that they can ask you about your house. *Do you have a leaking roof? Is your power out? Do you have cockroaches?* etc.
4. Have the recorder of each group ask you some of the questions.

GAMES
Charades

1. Write different household problems on slips of paper and put them into a box or hat.
2. Divide students into two teams.
3. Students take turns picking a problem and acting out fixing it for their own team.
4. Teams get a point for each problem they guess correctly.
5. The game ends when all the slips are gone.

Class Go-Around: Karen's House Needs a Lot of Work!

1. Begin by saying *Karen's house needs a lot of work. <u>The roof is leaking</u>.*
2. The first volunteer repeats the sentence and adds another problem. *Karen's house needs a lot of work. <u>The roof is leaking</u> and <u>her house has ants</u>.*
3. The next student volunteer continues the chain, adding another problem.
4. Stop after the tenth student and begin the game again.

Workbooks, p. 50
Classic Classroom Activities, Unit 4
Related Dictionary Pages
• Colors, p. 12
• Vegetables, p. 51
• The Market, pp. 54–55
• Food Preparation, p. 58
• Kitchen Utensils, p. 59

TOPIC NOTES

In the U.S., a variety of fresh fruits are available year-round from local farm stands, "greengrocers," and supermarkets. Fruits are a staple item in salads, pastries, (pies, cakes, breads) drinks, (juices, sodas, "smoothies") ice cream, jams, and jellies. Fruits and vegetables are referred to as "produce."

Rotten fruit is decayed, decomposed, and not fit to eat. When **rotten** is used to describe people or situations it means foul or horrible. *My new schedule is rotten. I never have a day off!*

TEACHING TIPS
Related Vocabulary

nectarines	organic
cranberries	pulp
blackberries	seeds*
figs	stem
kiwis	core
skin*	pit*

Usage: The article *a* refers to a single item, piece, or slice. *Pack a fruit.* When referring collectively to food, drop the article. *Fruit is a healthy snack.*

Spelling: Plurals
Words with *-y* endings change to *-ies, strawberry—strawberries;* words with *-ch/-sh* endings change to *-es peach—peaches.*

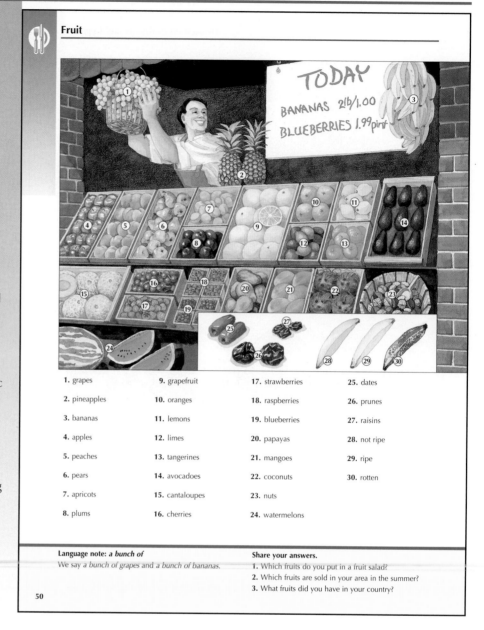

Fruit

TODAY
BANANAS 2lb/1.00
BLUEBERRIES 1.99/pint

1. grapes	**9.** grapefruit	**17.** strawberries	**25.** dates
2. pineapples	**10.** oranges	**18.** raspberries	**26.** prunes
3. bananas	**11.** lemons	**19.** blueberries	**27.** raisins
4. apples	**12.** limes	**20.** papayas	**28.** not ripe
5. peaches	**13.** tangerines	**21.** mangoes	**29.** ripe
6. pears	**14.** avocadoes	**22.** coconuts	**30.** rotten
7. apricots	**15.** cantaloupes	**23.** nuts	
8. plums	**16.** cherries	**24.** watermelons	

Language note: a bunch of
We say *a bunch of grapes* and *a bunch of bananas.*

Share your answers.
1. Which fruits do you put in a fruit salad?
2. Which fruits are sold in your area in the summer?
3. What fruits did you have in your country?

50

INTRODUCE THE TOPIC

Bring in a variety of fruits. Plastic realia or large pictures may be substituted. Arrange them randomly on a table, asking students to name the ones they know. Talk about each fruit. *Grapes are easy to eat. I like both red and green ones.*

Ask questions about the fruit you have displayed. *Do you have oranges in your refrigerator? Do you drink apple juice? Do you put lemon in your tea?*

TEACH THE NEW WORDS

Ask a series of *or* questions about the fruits on page 50. *Look at #5. Are they pears or peaches?* (peaches) *Now look at #11. Are they limes or lemons?* (lemons)

PRACTICE
Chalkboard Activities

△ Have students categorize vocabulary:

Have Pits	**Have Seeds**
peaches	*apples*

Conversations

△ Put models on the board and practice. Make appropriate substitutions.

A: Do you have any *grapes?*
B: I think so. Look in the *[fruit bowl].*
   1. grapes **2.** pineapples **3.** bananas
   4. apples **10.** oranges

A: Let's put some *bananas* in this *[cereal].*
B: We can't. They're *not ripe.*
   5. peaches/30. rotten
   17. strawberries/28. not ripe
   18. raspberries/28. not ripe

A: What's for dessert?
B: How about some *pears?*
   7. apricots **8.** plums **16.** cherries **23.** nuts

Interview Questions

1. What's your favorite fruit?
2. Which fruit juice do you like?
3. Which fruits do you buy raw? canned? frozen? dried?

Listening: 📼 #18, p. 215

"Eating The Alphabet—A To Z" Students look at the word list and write the number of the fruit they hear.

EXPAND THE LESSON
Language Workout

△ Put these sentences on the board and have students guess their meanings.
1. The brakes on my car are bad. *I bought a lemon.*
2. My sister won the lottery—our family really *went bananas.*
3. Play soccer in the rain? Are you *nuts?*

Vegetables

1. lettuce

9. celery

17. scallions

25. string beans

2. cabbage

10. parsley

18. eggplants

26. mushrooms

3. carrots

11. spinach

19. peas

27. corn

4. zucchini

12. cucumbers

20. artichokes

28. onions

5. radishes

13. squash

21. potatoes

29. garlic

6. beets

14. turnips

22. yams

7. sweet peppers

15. broccoli

23. tomatoes

8. chili peppers

16. cauliflower

24. asparagus

Language note: *a bunch of, a head of*

We say *a bunch of carrots, a bunch of celery,* and *a bunch of spinach.*

We say *a head of lettuce, a head of cabbage,* and *a head of cauliflower.*

Share your answers.

1. Which vegetables do you eat raw? cooked?
2. Which vegetables need to be in the refrigerator?
3. Which vegetables don't need to be in the refrigerator?

51

Workbooks, p. 51
Classic Classroom Activities, Unit 4
Related Dictionary Pages
- Colors, p. 12
- Fruit, p. 50
- The Market, pp. 54–55
- Food Preparation, p. 58
- Kitchen Utensils, p. 59

TOPIC NOTES

In the U.S., vegetable consumption is up. Americans are eating more raw and cooked vegetables as part of a healthy diet and to reduce the risks for heart disease and cancer.

Tomatoes and **eggplants** are really fruit, but they are most often referred to as vegetables.

In 1994, 7% of Americans said they were vegetarians. Vegetarians include a variety of vegetables as well as fruits and grains in their diet.

📁 Cooked yams, sweet corn, and baked potatoes have the highest amount of sugar among common vegetables.

TEACHING TIPS
Related Vocabulary

iceberg lettuce	pumpkin
bok choy cabbage	cob
cherry tomatoes	cilantro
plum tomatoes	spuds
acorn squash	lima beans
butternut squash	rind

Grammar: Partitives
We can count these vegetables by adding partitives: two asparagus *spears,* three *cloves* of garlic, two celery *stalks,* and two lettuce *leaves.*

INTRODUCE THE TOPIC

Bring in a variety of vegetables. (Plastic realia or pictures may be substituted.) Arrange them randomly on a table, asking students to name the ones they know. Talk about each vegetable. *These are delicious raw. They taste great in a salad. They are orange-colored.* (carrots)

Ask questions about the vegetables you have displayed. *Do you have lettuce in your refrigerator? Do you drink carrot juice? Which vegetables do you buy frozen?*

TEACH THE NEW WORDS

Ask a series of *or* questions about the vegetables on page 51. *Look at #5. Are they beets or radishes?* (radishes) *Now look at #21. Are they potatoes or tomatoes?* (potatoes)

PROVIDE PRACTICE
Chalkboard Activities

△ Have students categorize vocabulary:

1. Green — celery
Red — radishes
Other Color — corn

2. Peel — carrots
Don't Peel — lettuce

Conversations

△ Put models on the board and practice. Make appropriate substitutions.

A: Do you have any *lettuce*?
B: I think so. Look in the *[refrigerator]*.
  2. cabbage **3.** carrots **4.** zucchini
  5. radishes **9.** celery

A: These <u>beets</u> taste yucky!
B: Don't you know they're good for you?
A: I don't care. I want *[cake]* instead.
  11. spinach **13.** squash **14.** turnips
  19. peas **25.** string beans **26.** mushrooms

Interview Questions

1. Do you have a vegetable garden?
2. How do you cook vegetables?
3. Which vegetables are grown in your native country?

Listening: 📼 #18, p. 215

"Eating The Alphabet—A To Z" Students look at the word list and write the vegetable they hear.

EXPAND THE LESSON
Language Workout

△ Copy these sentences on the board and have students guess their meanings.
  1. Mario and Lupe are so much alike, they're *like two peas in a pod.*
  2. That joke is so old that it's really *corny.*

Unit 4   Meat and Poultry   page 52

Workbooks, p. 52
Classic Classroom Activities, Unit 4
Related Dictionary Pages
• Weights and Measures, p. 57
• Food Preparation, p. 58

TOPIC NOTES

In the U.S., people buy meat and poultry in supermarkets, markets, and small butcher shops. It comes **fresh, frozen,** canned, raw, cooked and dried.

Pork, lamb, turkey, chicken and **beef** come as ground meat.

In American slang, **chicken** means "coward" and is derogatory. *He won't go on the roller coaster. He's chicken.*

The most popular meat in the U.S. is beef, but chicken and turkey are becoming more popular as people are watching their weight and fat intake.

TEACHING TIPS
Related Vocabulary

fresh*	cow*
frozen*	spare ribs
cut-up	sirloin
whole*	hamburger*
white meat	hot dog*
dark meat	red meat
pig*	vegetarian

Spelling: Silent letters
In *thigh,* gh is silent. In *lamb,* the b is silent.

Bring in food ads, flyers from markets, and recipe books with pictures as resource materials. Students can look through them before class and during breaks.

Review or expose students to the words *pounds, ounces,* and *weigh* so that they can talk about amounts.

Meat and Poultry

Beef
1. roast beef
2. steak
3. stewing beef
4. ground beef

5. beef ribs
6. veal cutlets
7. liver
8. tripe

Pork
9. ham
10. pork chops
11. bacon
12. sausage

Lamb
13. lamb shanks
14. leg of lamb
15. lamb chops

16. chicken	19. breasts	22. drumsticks	24. **raw** chicken
17. turkey	20. wings	23. gizzards	25. **cooked** chicken
18. duck	21. thighs		

More vocabulary
vegetarian: a person who doesn't eat meat
Meat and poultry without bones are called **boneless**.
Poultry without skin is called **skinless**.

Share your answers.
1. What kind of meat do you eat most often?
2. What kind of meat do you use in soup?
3. What part of the chicken do you like the most?

52

INTRODUCE THE TOPIC

Talk about cooking dinner for your family. Tell students about which meats and poultry different family members like and don't like. *I like to eat a lot of poultry, but my children like ground meat, like hamburgers.*

Bring in food ads from local markets. Talk about the specials for the week in meat and poultry. *Look, here at Ted's, whole chicken is only 89¢ a pound.*

TEACH THE NEW WORDS

Ask students to identify the number of the particular item on page 52 you are describing. *You make hamburgers or meatloaf with this. It comes from a cow. It's called ground beef. (#4) This comes in strips. You usually fry it. It comes from a pig. It's called bacon. (#11)*

PROVIDE PRACTICE
Chalkboard Activities

△ Have students brainstorm possibilities:

For Soup	For Grilling	For Frying
chicken	steak	bacon

Conversations

△ Put models on the board and practice. Make appropriate substitutions.

A: How much is the *steak* today?
B: It's *[$2.49]* a pound. How much do you want?
A: *[Two]* pounds, please.
   3. stewing beef 4. ground beef 7. liver
   8. tripe
A: All right. The chicken is cut up. Tell me what part you want.
B: I want *thighs*.
A: Here you go.
B: Thanks.
   19. breasts 20. wings 22. drumsticks

Interview Questions

1. Do you buy meat fresh, frozen or already cooked?
2. What kind of meat do you cook for special holidays?

Listening: #19, p. 216

"Mary's Restaurant" Students point to meat and poultry items they hear.

EXPAND THE LESSON
Discussion Question

Some people eat a lot of meat; some people never do. Are meat and poultry a big part of your diet? Why or why not?

Language Workout

△ Copy this sentence on the board and discuss its meaning.
   I work six days a week to *bring home the bacon.*

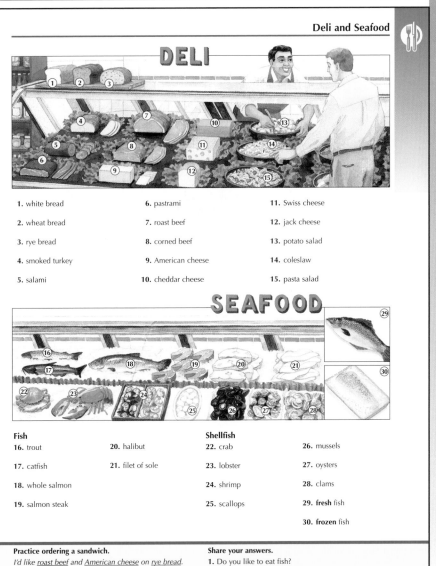

Deli and Seafood

DELI

1. white bread

2. wheat bread

3. rye bread

4. smoked turkey

5. salami

6. pastrami

7. roast beef

8. corned beef

9. American cheese

10. cheddar cheese

11. Swiss cheese

12. jack cheese

13. potato salad

14. coleslaw

15. pasta salad

SEAFOOD

Fish

16. trout

17. catfish

18. whole salmon

19. salmon steak

20. halibut

21. filet of sole

Shellfish

22. crab

23. lobster

24. shrimp

25. scallops

26. mussels

27. oysters

28. clams

29. fresh fish

30. frozen fish

Practice ordering a sandwich.

I'd like _roast beef_ and _American cheese_ on _rye bread_.

Tell what you want on it.

Please put _tomato, lettuce, onions,_ and _mustard_ on it.

Share your answers.

1. Do you like to eat fish?

2. Do you buy fresh or frozen fish?

53

Workbooks, p. 53

Classic Classroom Activities, Unit 4

Related Dictionary Pages

• Weights and Measures, p. 57

• Fast Food, p. 60

TOPIC NOTES

In the U.S., there are many delicatessen-style restaurants with deli counters. Some markets have deli counters too.

Fish and **seafood** are becoming more popular these days because many Americans are eating less red meat (beef, pork, and lamb).

Fish is sold at markets, seafood stores, and sometimes in refrigerated trucks that go door-to-door.

Deli is informal for _delicatessen_, a store selling prepared delicacies such as cooked meats and salads.

TEACHING TIPS

Related Vocabulary

on the half shell	mayonnaise*
smoked	lettuce*
slices	onion*
roll*	ketchup*
tomato*	pickle
mustard*	

Pronunciation: Final -s sounds

There is a final /s/ sound in _scallops_. There is a final /z/ sound in _cheese, oysters,_ and _clams._

☼ Expose students to the words _pounds, ounces, slices,_ and _pieces_ so that they can order at a deli or seafood counter.

☼ Have students draw a picture of their favorite sandwich and label everything that's in it. Then students can use the picture to practice ordering the sandwich at a deli.

INTRODUCE THE TOPIC

Bring in a deli sandwich and talk about what's in it.

Ask students to cover the seafood words, look at the pictures, and call out the numbers of the kinds of seafood that are popular in their native countries.

TEACH THE NEW WORDS

Ask students a series of _yes/no_ questions about the pictures. _Is #7 meat?_ (yes) _Is it chicken?_ (no) _Is it roast beef?_ (yes) _Is #23 lobster?_ (yes)

PROVIDE PRACTICE

Chalkboard Activities

△ Have students brainstorm a list of seafood in your area:

Fresh	Frozen	Canned
trout	_halibut_	_salmon_

△ Have students "build" a sandwich on the board and label it. Start with a slice of bread.

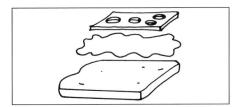

Conversations

△ Put models on the board and practice. Make appropriate substitutions.

A: I'd like a pound of _mussels_.

B: Sure. We also have fresh _trout_ today.

A: No thanks.

25. scallops/17. catfish

27. oysters/20. halibut

28. clams/22. crab

A: What's in your sandwich? It looks great.

B: _Salami_ and [Swiss cheese].

4. smoked turkey 6. pastrami 7. roast beef

8. corned beef

Interview Questions

1. Are there delicatessens in your country? What do they sell?

2. Do you eat fish? What kind?

Listening: 📼 #20, p. 216

"You're Next!" Students write down the items each person orders at a deli and seafood counter.

EXPAND THE LESSON

Language Workout

△ Copy this text on the board and discuss its meaning:

I don't know what's wrong with Stu today. He's a real _crab_!

Workbooks, pp. 54–55
Classic Classroom Activities, Unit 4
Related Dictionary Pages
- Prepositions, p. 13
- food pp. 50–53
- Containers and Packaged Foods, p. 56
- Weights and Measures, p. 57

TOPIC NOTES

In the U.S., many people shop at large markets called supermarkets. Usually these markets are chains with stores all over one area of the country.

TEACHING TIPS
Related Vocabulary

grocery store	paper towels*
supermarket	sandwich bags
groceries	wax paper
English muffins	napkins*
corn chips	low-fat products
tortillas	international foods
vinegar	brand name

Grammar: Count vs. Non-count
Help students learn which foods are not countable by having them identify the words in the wordlist without the plural -s marker and those with it. Liquid, grains, dairy products, and meat are usually not countable. Packages or weights of these products are countable, however. (*Some cheese* vs. *two packages of cheese. Some chicken* vs. *three pounds of chicken.*)

Pronunciation: Stress
Produce is fresh vegetables and fruit.
Pro**duce** means to make or manufacture.

💡 Create a shopping list in class. Have pairs of students go to a local supermarket and record the prices of each item on the list.

 The Market

1. bottle return	3. shopping cart	6. baked goods	9. dairy section
2. meat and poultry section	4. canned goods	7. shopping basket	10. pet food
	5. aisle	8. manager	11. produce section

24. soup	28. rice	32. cake	36. butter
25. tuna	29. bread	33. yogurt	37. sour cream
26. beans	30. rolls	34. eggs	38. cheese
27. spaghetti	31. cookies	35. milk	39. margarine

54

INTRODUCE THE TOPIC

Ask students to name markets in the area and talk about which language they use at their market.

Bring in a paper or plastic grocery bag filled with 8–10 different foods that students have previously learned. Have students guess what foods are in the bag. Give clues about the general type of food and the color. *It's a fruit. It's red.*

Show the class grocery ads from three or four different markets. Choose three common market items that are featured in all the ads, e.g., chicken, grapes, and milk. Compare the prices of the items at the different stores and ask students to compare these prices with what they usually pay.

TEACH THE NEW WORDS

Ask students information questions about the sections of the market, the names of market workers, and the food items on the page. *I'm in the canned food section. What kinds of food do I see?* (canned soup, tuna) *There aren't any more shopping baskets. What can I use?* (a shopping cart)

PROVIDE PRACTICE
Chalkboard Activities

△ Have students categorize vocabulary:

Dairy	milk
Canned Goods	soup
Frozen Foods	ice cream
Baked Goods	bread
Groceries	plastic wrap
Snacks	candy
Market Sections	dairy
Market Workers	checker

Conversations

△ Put models on the board and practice. Make appropriate substitutions.

A: Oh, no! We're out of *soup.*
B: Don't worry. I'll run to the market and get some. Anything else?
A: We need some *cookies,* too.
B: Let's make a list before I go.
　　26. beans/32. cake
　　27. spaghetti/33. yogurt
　　28. rice/34. eggs

A: I'm looking for the [tuna].
B: Check [aisle 3] in *canned goods.*
A: Thanks.
　　6. baked goods 9. the dairy section
　　10. pet food 11. produce section
　　12. frozen foods 15. beverages

A: Where I can find the *gum*?
B: I think it's on [aisle 4], but let me ask the manager. I'm new.
　　40. potato chips 43. frozen vegetables
　　44. ice cream 45. flour 46. spices, etc.

The Market

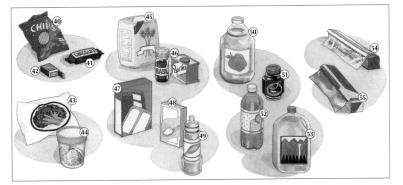

12. frozen foods	15. beverages	18. cash register	21. bagger
13. baking products	16. snack foods	19. checker	22. paper bag
14. paper products	17. checkstand	20. line	23. plastic bag

40. potato chips	44. ice cream	48. sugar	52. soda
41. candy bar	45. flour	49. oil	53. bottled water
42. gum	46. spices	50. apple juice	54. plastic wrap
43. frozen vegetables	47. cake mix	51. instant coffee	55. aluminum foil

55

Interview Questions
1. Which markets do you go to?
2. What language do you speak at the market?
3. How long does it take you to shop?
4. In your family, who goes to the market the most?
5. What's your favorite canned food?
6. What's your favorite snack food?
7. What three food items are always on your shopping list?
8. What's one food item you never buy?
9. Do you return your glass bottles to the market?

Listening: 💿 #21, p. 216
"Where Are The Pretzels?" Students listen and write the section of the market each customer is in.

EXPAND THE LESSON
Problem Solving
△ Have students brainstorm solutions. *The market Sam always goes to stopped carrying his favorite brand of spaghetti. What can Sam do?*

Discussion Question
What would you do if you were in the canned goods section and you saw someone putting a can of soup into his coat pocket?

Who's Coming to Dinner?
1. Divide students into small groups of 4–6
2. Have students think of and name an interesting person they'd like to invite to dinner.

3. Write the following sample language on the board: *We need some… Why don't we pick up some… We should buy some…*
4. Tell students to plan the menu and a shopping list for their dinner.
5. Have students share their menus with the class.

GAMES
Class Go-Around: A Shopping Trip
1. Begin by saying *I'm going to the market to buy some eggs.*
2. The first student volunteer repeats the sentence and adds another item. *I'm going to the market to buy some eggs and some potato chips.*
3. The next student volunteer continues the chain, adding another item.
4. Stop after the tenth student and begin the game again.

Spell Check
1. Divide the class into two teams.
2. Give teams 10 minutes to study the spelling of the words on pages 54–55.
3. Have teams line up on either side of the room.
4. Give the first student on each team a word from the pages and have him/her write it on the board.
5. Team members who spell the word correctly sit down and earn a point for their team.
6. Team members who make a mistake go to the end of the line so that they can have another chance.
7. The game ends when all the team members of one team are seated.

Word Links
1. Divide the class into teams A and B.
2. Have students study the words on pages 54–55 for 2 minutes and then close their books.
3. Write the word *produce* horizontally on the board.
4. Have a volunteer from team A come up and write a connecting word vertically, using any letter in the word *produce*.

p r o d u c e
a
i
r
y

5. A volunteer from team B then comes up and links to either the first or the second word on the board.
6. Play continues until students run out of words or board space.

Unit 4   Containers and Packaged Foods   page 56

Workbooks, p. 56
Classic Classroom Activities, Unit 4
Related Dictionary Pages
- Numbers and Measurements, pp. 14–15
- The Market, pp. 54–55
- Weights and Measures, p. 57

TOPIC NOTES

In the U.S., consumables and nonconsumables are sold in a variety of metal, glass, and plastic containers. Through voluntary and mandatory regulation, information such as unit pricing, expiration date, and nutritional value is provided on most packages and containers.

Containers and **cartons** are commonly identified by the quantity of dry or liquid ingredients they hold, e.g., a quart of milk, a pint of cottage cheese.

TEACHING TIPS
Related Vocabulary

stick	redeemable
tub	recyclable
aerosol	bulk
pump	twist-off
spray	childproof
bar	pop-top

Pronunciation: Reduced sounds
In phrases such as *a bottle of soda,* the word *of* is often pronounced [ə].

☼ Review or show common sizes of containers (pint, quart, gallon), common weight measures (ounces, pounds, liters), and equivalencies (16 ounces = 1 pound).

Containers and Packaged Foods

1. bottle
2. jar
3. can
4. carton
5. container
6. box
7. bag
8. package
9. six-pack
10. loaf
11. roll
12. tube

13. a bottle of soda
14. a jar of jam
15. a can of soup
16. a carton of eggs

17. a container of cottage cheese
18. a box of cereal
19. a bag of flour
20. a package of cookies

21. a six-pack of soda
22. a loaf of bread
23. a roll of paper towels
24. a tube of toothpaste

Grammar point: How much? How many?
Some foods can be counted: *one apple, two apples.*
How many apples do you need? I need **two** apples.

Some foods cannot be counted, like liquids, grains, spices, or dairy foods. For these, count containers: *one box of rice, two boxes of rice.*
How much rice do you need? I need **two boxes.**

56

INTRODUCE THE TOPIC

Bring in a variety of containers or pictures. Talk about the items they contain and survey students to see if they have similar items at home. *Here's a jar of peanut butter. Do you have jars at your home? What's in them?*

Tell a story about unpacking your groceries. Say the types of containers and packages for the various items as you "put everything away." *First, I put the carton of eggs in the refrigerator so they'll stay fresh. I usually buy two packages of cookies. I love cookies!*

TEACH THE NEW WORDS

Ask students a series of *or* questions about pictures 1–24. *Is #3 a carton or a can?* (can)

PROVIDE PRACTICE
Chalkboard Activities

△ Have students categorize vocabulary:

1. Holds Solids   **Holds Liquids**
box   *can*

2. Plastic	Paper	Glass
bottle	*bag*	*jar*

Conversations

△ Put models on the board and practice. Make appropriate substitutions.

A: I'm going to *[Jon's]* Market. Do you need anything?

B: Yes. Could you pick up *a bottle of soda?*
    16. a carton of eggs 19. a bag of flour 20. a package of cookies 22. a loaf of bread etc.

A: We're almost out of *[Choco cereal].*

B: How many *boxes* should I buy?

A: Get *[two].* I have a coupon for them.
    1. bottles 2. jars 3. cans 4. cartons
    5. containers 7. bags 8. packages etc.

Interview Questions

1. Name three containers you have in your refrigerator.

2. What size containers do you usually buy—small, medium, or large? Why?

3. What containers do you recycle?

Listening: 🔊 #21, p. 216
"Where Are The Pretzels?" Students listen and write the containers they hear.

EXPAND THE LESSON
Problem Solving

△ Have students brainstorm solutions. *You have saved a variety of glass jars, plastic containers, and paper boxes. Your community doesn't recycle. How can you re-use these containers? Think of as many creative ways as possible.*

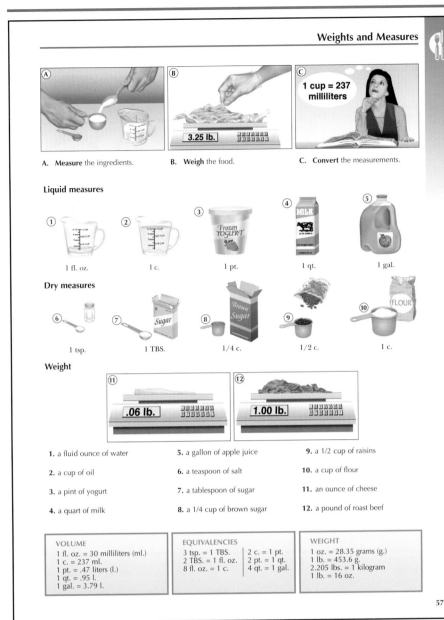

Weights and Measures

A. **Measure** the ingredients.

B. **Weigh** the food.

C. **Convert** the measurements.

1 cup = 237 milliliters

3.25 lb.

Liquid measures

1 fl. oz.   1 c.   1 pt.   1 qt.   1 gal.

Dry measures

1 tsp.   1 TBS.   1/4 c.   1/2 c.   1 c.

Weight

.06 lb.   1.00 lb.

1. a fluid ounce of water
2. a cup of oil
3. a pint of yogurt
4. a quart of milk
5. a gallon of apple juice
6. a teaspoon of salt
7. a tablespoon of sugar
8. a 1/4 cup of brown sugar
9. a 1/2 cup of raisins
10. a cup of flour
11. an ounce of cheese
12. a pound of roast beef

VOLUME
1 fl. oz. = 30 milliliters (ml.)
1 c. = 237 ml.
1 pt. = .47 liters (l.)
1 qt. = .95 l.
1 gal. = 3.79 l.

EQUIVALENCIES
3 tsp. = 1 TBS.   2 c. = 1 pt.
2 TBS. = 1 fl. oz.   2 pt. = 1 qt.
8 fl. oz. = 1 c.   4 qt. = 1 gal.

WEIGHT
1 oz. = 28.35 grams (g.)
1 lb. = 453.6 g.
2.205 lbs. = 1 kilogram
1 lb. = 16 oz.

57

Workbooks, p. 57
Classic Classroom Activities, Unit 4
Related Dictionary Pages
• Numbers and Measurements, pp. 14–15
• The Market, pp. 54–55

TOPIC NOTES

In the U.S., both the International System (modernized metric) and the Customary U.S. Weights and Measures appear on packaged foods and newer LED scales.

📁 The U.S. Metric Conversion Act was signed on December 23, 1975, declaring a national policy of encouraging the voluntary use of the metric system.

TEACHING TIPS

Related Vocabulary

measuring spoons	liquid
measuring cups	solid
scale*	recipe
kilograms	ingredients*

Pronunciation: Reduced sounds
In phrases such as *a cup of flour,* the word *of* is often pronounced [ə].

Usage: When a recipe talks about ingredients, the words *a* and *one* are often interchangeable. These two sentences mean the same thing:
Use one cup of flour.
Use a cup of flour.

💡 As a culminating activity, have students follow a simple (no-bake) recipe to prepare foods like fruit salad, horchata, or gazpacho.

INTRODUCE THE TOPIC

Bring in various measuring cups and spoons. Distribute the items to students and have students line up from the smallest measurement to the largest.

Show students a box of dry cereal and ask them to predict how many cups of cereal are in the box. Write the predictions on the board and then have volunteers come up and measure out the contents.

TEACH THE NEW WORDS

Ask students *or* questions about the pictures on the page. *Is #3 a gallon or a pint?* (pint) *Is #6 a teaspoon or a tablespoon?* (teaspoon) *Does #12 weigh a pound or an ounce?* (pound)

PROVIDE PRACTICE

Chalkboard Activities

△ Have students categorize vocabulary:

Dry Measure	**Liquid Measure**
flour	*oil*

Conversations

△ Put models on the board and practice. Make appropriate substitutions.

A: Could I borrow <u>a teaspoon of salt</u>?
B: Sure, here you go.
   7. a tablespoon of sugar 8. a 1/4 cup of brown sugar 9. a 1/2 cup of raisins, etc.

A: This recipe calls for a <u>*cup of oil*</u>!
B: Wow, <u>*8 ounces*</u>! That's a lot!
   3. a pint of yogurt/2 cups
   4. a quart of milk/4 cups
   5. a gallon of apple juice/16 cups

A: How much is *[one fluid ounce]* of *[oil]*?
B: That's *[30 milliliters]*.
   (Students use volume chart.)

Interview Questions

1. Do you prefer to measure using the U.S. or the metric system?
2. How much flour is there in your kitchen? How much milk?
3. What do you buy that comes by the pint? By the quart? By the gallon?

Listening: 📼 #22, p. 217

"Chef Klaus" Students listen and write the measurements in Chef Klaus's recipe.

EXPAND THE LESSON

Language Workout

△ Copy these sentences on the board and discuss their meanings.
1. *Ounce for ounce,* orange juice gives you more vitamin C than apple juice.
2. *Pound for pound,* ground chicken has less fat than ground meat.

Workbooks, p. 58
Classic Classroom Activities, Unit 4
Related Dictionary Pages
• Meat and Poultry, p. 52
• Deli and Seafood, p. 53
• The Market, pp. 54–55
• Kitchen Utensils, p. 59

TOPIC NOTES

In the U.S., more and more people are cooking by steaming, broiling, and roasting rather than by frying and sautéing. The former do not require oil, margarine, or vegetable shortening. Frying and sautéing both use oil or fat.

Casseroles, baked one-dish meals, are popular because they are inexpensive and easy to prepare.

TEACHING TIPS
Related Vocabulary

dice	whip (v)
poach	mash
marinate	cover
mince	shred

Grammar: Agent nouns
The verbs *beat, steam, grate, mix, peel, fry, broil,* and *roast* can all be turned into nouns by adding the suffix *-er*. Something that beats eggs is a *beater*. Something that grates cheese is a *grater*.

- ☀ Review the food vocabulary needed to discuss the phrases on the page: *eggs, celery, pan, onions,* etc.

- ☀ As a culminating activity, have students share recipes from their cultures. Duplicate and bind the recipes to create a class cookbook.

Food Preparation

Scrambled eggs

A. **Break** 3 eggs.
B. **Beat** well.
C. **Grease** the pan.
D. **Pour** the eggs into the pan.
E. **Stir.**
F. **Cook** until done.

Vegetable casserole

G. **Chop** the onions.
H. **Sauté** the onions.
I. **Steam** the broccoli.
J. **Grate** the cheese.
K. **Mix** the ingredients.
L. **Bake** at 350° for 45 minutes.

Chicken soup

M. **Cut up** the chicken.
N. **Peel** the carrots.
O. **Slice** the carrots.
P. **Boil** the chicken.
Q. **Add** the vegetables.
R. **Simmer** for 1 hour.

Five ways to cook chicken

S. fry   T. barbecue / grill   U. roast   V. broil   W. stir-fry

Talk about the way you prepare these foods.
I *fry* eggs.
I *bake* potatoes.

Share your answers.
1. What are popular ways in your country to make rice? vegetables? meat?
2. What is your favorite way to cook chicken?

58

INTRODUCE THE TOPIC

Act out the first sequence, scrambling eggs. Explain as you act out each step.
Bring in magazine pictures of casseroles, soups, and chicken dishes. Ask the class to name the dishes they know how to prepare.

TEACH THE NEW WORDS

Present a "cooking show" for students, featuring each of the three recipes and the five ways to cook chicken. Talk about how you are preparing each dish as you act out the steps. Once in a while, ask students to look at their dictionary "cookbooks" and tell you one step.

PROVIDE PRACTICE
Chalkboard Activities

△ Have students categorize vocabulary:

Ways to Cut	**Ways to Cook**
chop	steam

Conversations

△ Put models on the board and practice. Make appropriate substitutions.

A: Look at the recipe for <u>scrambled eggs</u>. What do I do first?
B: You have to <u>break 3 eggs</u>.
  vegetable casserole/ G. chop the onions
  chicken soup/ N. peel the carrots
A: Please *break 3 eggs.*
B: *[Break]* what? Oh, *[eggs].*
  G. chop the onions H. sauté the onions
  I. steam the broccoli
A: I'm going to go fry the chicken.
B: Why don't you <u>broil</u> it instead?
A: That's a good idea.
  T. barbecue U. roast W. stir-fry

Interview Questions

1. Who prepares your meals? What dishes can you prepare?
2. Do you prefer vegetable or chicken casseroles?
3. Do you prefer vegetable or chicken soup?

Listening: 🔊 #22, p. 217

"Chef Klaus" Have students listen and take notes on Chef Klaus's recipes.

EXPAND THE LESSON
Drawing Activity

1. Have students in small groups choose a magazine picture of a prepared dish.
2. The group discusses how the dish is prepared and then writes and illustrates a step-by-step recipe for the dish.

Kitchen Utensils

1. can opener	**8.** double boiler	**16.** paring knife	**24.** lid
2. grater	**9.** wooden spoon	**17.** colander	**25.** saucepan
3. plastic storage container	**10.** garlic press	**18.** kitchen timer	**26.** cake pan
	11. casserole dish	**19.** spatula	**27.** cookie sheet
4. steamer	**12.** carving knife	**20.** eggbeater	**28.** pie pan
5. frying pan	**13.** roasting pan	**21.** whisk	**29.** pot holders
6. pot	**14.** roasting rack	**22.** strainer	**30.** rolling pin
7. ladle	**15.** vegetable peeler	**23.** tongs	**31.** mixing bowl

Talk about how to use the utensils.
You use a peeler to peel potatoes.
You use a pot to cook soup.

Use the new language.
Look at **Food Preparation**, page **58**.
Name the different utensils you see.

59

Workbooks, p. 59
Classic Classroom Activities, Unit 4
Related Dictionary Pages
• A Kitchen, p. 40
• Weights and Measures, p. 57
• Food Preparation, p. 58

TOPIC NOTES

In the U.S., a wide assortment of cooking utensils are marketed for home or commercial use, varying from multipurpose items such as **pots** and **pans** to gadgets such as **whisks** that perform specialized tasks.

Plastic storage containers come in numerous shapes and sizes for pantry and refrigerator use. They are most commonly used for storing leftovers.

 In 1958, France unveiled the first nonstick **frying pan** with Teflon, a material named the "most slippery substance on earth." Besides cooking utensils, Teflon is used on heart valves, space suits, and the Statue of Liberty!

TEACHING TIPS
Related Vocabulary

baster	bundt pan
tea strainer	stock pot
flour sifter	wok
cookie cutters	ice cube tray
muffin tin	gadget
cooling rack	corkscrew

☼ Review food preparation verbs and food vocabulary. Provide context with TPR or actual cooking demonstrations.

INTRODUCE THE TOPIC

Bring in some of the cooking utensils on this page. Take an informal class survey asking students which of the items they have in their kitchens.

Act out the preparation of a holiday meal. Talk about the utensils that you need to prepare the food items. *My turkey is ready for the roasting pan. Let's set the kitchen timer for four hours. I'd better sharpen this carving knife.*

TEACH THE NEW WORDS

Say each word several times in different contexts. Have students point to each item as you describe it. *Item #4 is a steamer. You use it to cook foods with hot water. Steamers heat food above the water.*

PROVIDE PRACTICE
Chalkboard Activities

△ Have students categorize vocabulary:

Cook Food	**Prepare Food**
steamer	grater

Conversations

△ Put models on the board and practice. Make appropriate substitutions.

A: Can you hand me the *can opener*?
B: In a minute. I'm *[using it]*.
  2. grater 15. vegetable peeler
  20. eggbeater 22. strainer

A: Can I borrow your *cake pan*?
B: Why?
A: I'm baking *[a chocolate cake]*.
  27. cookie sheet 28. pie pan
  30. rolling pin 31. mixing bowl

Interview Questions

1. What cooking utensils do you frequently use?
2. Do you prefer metal, wood, or plastic cooking utensils? Why?
3. What utensils can a five-year-old use safely?

Listening: Definitions

△ Give students definitions and have them write the number of the item on a separate piece of paper. *You grate cheese with this. (#2) You cover a pot with this. (#24)*

EXPAND THE LESSON
Problem Solving

△ Have students brainstorm solutions. *You are planning an overnight camping trip. You can take five cooking utensils. Which ones will you take? Why?*

Workbooks, p. 60
Classic Classroom Activities, Unit 4
Related Dictionary Pages
• Containers and Packaged Foods, p. 56
• A Coffee Shop Menu, p. 61
• A Restaurant, pp. 62–63

TOPIC NOTES

In the U.S., fast food is available at multinational restaurant chains, small ethnic eateries and push-cart vendors. Fast food implies menu items that are quickly prepared, reasonably priced, and rapidly eaten. Changing consumer tastes have influenced fast-food restaurants to expand menu items and offer healthier alternatives.

In 1852, the frankfurter became popular in Frankfurt, Germany. Its sausage shape resembled a butcher's pet dachshund. In U.S. baseball stadiums, vendors later coined the phrase "Get your red-hot dog."

TEACHING TIPS
Related Vocabulary

to go	sub sandwich
for here	chicken bowl
drive-thru	refill
take-out	pastry
hold the mayo	dispenser
extra ketchup	tray

Spelling: *Doughnut* is also spelled *donut*. Another spelling for *ketchup* is *catsup*.

Bring in fast-food take-out menus. Have one student place an order while another student checks off the items and asks for clarification. *Did you say two hamburgers or three?*

Fast Food

1. hamburger	8. green salad	15. doughnut	22. sugar substitute
2. french fries	9. taco	16. salad bar	23. ketchup
3. cheeseburger	10. nachos	17. lettuce	24. mustard
4. soda	11. frozen yogurt	18. salad dressing	25. mayonnaise
5. iced tea	12. milk shake	19. booth	26. relish
6. hot dog	13. counter	20. straw	A. eat
7. pizza	14. muffin	21. sugar	B. drink

More vocabulary
donut: doughnut (spelling variation)
condiments: relish, mustard, ketchup, mayonnaise, etc.

Share your answers.
1. What would you order at this restaurant?
2. Which fast foods are popular in your country?
3. How often do you eat fast food? Why?

60

INTRODUCE THE TOPIC

Ask students to cover the words at the bottom of the page and name the words they already know.

Tell a story about the grand opening of a fast-food restaurant. *Did you hear about the new Burger Barn? The double hamburgers are only 99¢! The salad bar has hot and cold foods—even frozen yogurt!*

TEACH THE NEW WORDS

Say each word several times in different contexts. Have students point to the correct pictures as you describe them. *A taco is a folded, fried tortilla stuffed with meat, chicken, or fish. Tacos are delicious—add some cheese, lettuce, or tomatoes on top!* (#9)

PROVIDE PRACTICE
Chalkboard Activities

△ Have students categorize vocabulary:

Hot Foods	Cold Foods	Non-food
pizza	green salad	counter

Conversations

△ Put models on the board and practice. Make appropriate substitutions.

A: I'll have a *hamburger*—no, make it two *[hamburgers]*.
B: Anything to drink?
A: Oh, yeah—a large *soda*, please.

  3. cheeseburger/5. iced tea
  6. hot dog/12. milk shake
  7. pizza/4. soda
  9. taco/5. iced tea

A: I'm going to the salad bar.
B: While you're up, could you get me a packet of *ketchup*?

  21. sugar 22. sugar substitute 24. mustard
  25. mayonnaise

Listening: Interactive Dictation

△ Have students close their books. Dictate fast food orders. Speak naturally and encourage students to ask for clarification. (*Did you say mustard or mayo on the hot dogs?*) Then, have student volunteers write the orders on the board and have the class check spelling using page 60.
1. *I'll have a double hamburger, small fries, and a medium iced tea.*
2. *Give me two hot dogs with mustard and relish, a green salad, and a chocolate milk shake.*

EXPAND THE LESSON
Discussion Questions

1. What fast-food menu items do you think are "junk food"? Why?
2. Why do you think fast-food restaurants are popular with children, teenagers, and senior citizens?

A Coffee Shop Menu

Breakfast

Lunch

Dinner

Desserts   **B**everages

1. scrambled eggs	**8.** grilled cheese sandwich	**14.** baked potato	**21.** pie
2. sausage	**9.** chef's salad	**15.** pasta	**22.** coffee
3. toast	**10.** soup of the day	**16.** garlic bread	**23.** decaf coffee
4. waffles		**17.** fried fish	**24.** tea
5. syrup	**11.** mashed potatoes	**18.** rice pilaf	
6. pancakes	**12.** roast chicken	**19.** cake	
7. bacon	**13.** steak	**20.** pudding	

Practice ordering from the menu.
I'd like a grilled cheese sandwich and some soup.
I'll have the chef's salad and a cup of decaf coffee.

Use the new language.
Look at **Fruit**, page **50**.
Order a slice of pie using the different fruit flavors.
Please give me a slice of apple pie.

61

Workbooks, p. 61
Classic Classroom Activities, Unit 4
Related Dictionary Pages
• Deli and Seafood, p. 53
• Fast Food, p. 60
• A Restaurant, pp. 62–63

TOPIC NOTES
In the U.S., coffee shops, diners, and cafeterias offer relatively standard menu items. Regional differences may appear in some food items and prices. "Home Cooking," "Breakfast Served All Day," and "Blue Plate Special" are common coffee shop lingo.

Pasta, made from rice and bean flour, was an Asian, not Italian, creation. Explorers Marco and Maffeo Polo returned from China in 1300 with the original noodle recipes.

TEACHING TIPS
Related Vocabulary

omelet	supper
eggs over easy	entree
sunnyside up	side order
home fries	appetizer
hash browns	fruit cup
hot cakes	a la mode
brunch	

Pronunciation: Reduced *and*
The connector word *and* is reduced to *'n*: *hamburger 'n fries, cream 'n sugar.*

Bring in copies of coffee shop menus and practice giving and taking orders.

INTRODUCE THE TOPIC
Describe a recent meal at your local coffee shop. Ask students to guess if you ordered breakfast, lunch, or dinner.

Ask students to name types of toast or soup on a coffee shop menu (e.g., wheat, white, or rye toast; tomato or split pea soup).

TEACH THE NEW WORDS
Act out the role of server as you describe "today's specials" on the menu. Have students point as you describe each food item. *Our soup of the day is chicken noodle. (#10) You can order a cup or a bowl of soup. Do you want dessert? We have chocolate, lemon, or angel food cake. (#19) We bake all our cakes here.*

PROVIDE PRACTICE
Chalkboard Activities
△ Have students categorize vocabulary:

Meat Items	**Non-meat Items**
sausage	*toast*

Conversations
△ Put models on the board and practice. Make appropriate substitutions.

A: Would you like to see a menu?
B: No, I'll have scrambled eggs.
A: Coming right up. Glass of water?
B: No thanks. I'll have a cup of coffee.
   2. sausage/23. decaf coffee
   3. toast/24. tea
   4. waffles/23. decaf coffee
   6. pancakes/24. tea

A: This grilled cheese sandwich is cold.
B: Would you like me to reheat it?
A: No, I'd like a [tuna sandwich] instead.
   12. roast chicken 13. steak
   14. baked potato 15. pasta

Listening: Interactive Dictation
△ Have students close their books. Dictate orders from the coffee shop menu. Speak naturally and encourage students to ask for clarification. (*Did you say white or wheat toast?*) Have student volunteers write the orders on the board and have the class check spelling using page 61.
  1. *I'll have two scrambled eggs with sausage, wheat toast, and a cup of decaf.*
  2. *I'd like the roast chicken, baked potato, no butter on it, and tea with lemon. Wait, give me a side of pasta instead of the potato. Thanks.*

EXPAND THE LESSON
Problem Solving
△ Have students brainstorm solutions. *You are opening a coffee shop in your neighborhood. What items would you include on a breakfast or lunch menu?*

Workbooks, pp. 62–63
Classic Classroom Activities, Unit 4
Related Dictionary Pages
- Prepositions, p. 13
- Fast Food, p. 60
- A Coffee Shop Menu, p. 61

TOPIC NOTES

In the U.S., there are different kinds of restaurants: fast food, family-style, diner, coffee shop, food counter, cafeteria-style, gourmet, and ethnic. The family-style restaurant is usually less expensive than the gourmet restaurant. Ethnic restaurants serve foods from different nationalities. For example, a Chinese restaurant serves Chinese food.

📁 The restaurant industry employed 6.5 million people in 1996. The only industry with more workers is health services, with 8.1 million workers.

TEACHING TIPS
Related Vocabulary

eating out	fine dining
maitre d'	gratuity
cashier*	service
utensils*	pitcher
bar	tablecloth*
bartender	nonsmoking section

Usage: The words *waiter* and *waitress* are being replaced by the word *server* because this word can be used for both men and women.

💡 Have students use the foods from page 60, *Fast Food,* and page 61, *A Coffee Shop Menu,* to create a menu for the restaurant shown on pages 62–63.

A Restaurant

1. hostess
2. dining room
3. menu
4. server/waiter
5. patron/diner

A. **set** the table
B. **seat** the customer
C. **pour** the water
D. **order** from the menu
E. **take** the order
F. **serve** the meal
G. **clear** the table
H. **carry** the tray
I. **pay** the check
J. **leave** a tip

More vocabulary
eat out: to go to a restaurant to eat
take out: to buy food at a restaurant and take it home to eat

Practice giving commands.
Please set the table.
I'd like you to clear the table.
It's time to serve the meal.

62

INTRODUCE THE TOPIC

Demonstrate some of the service vocabulary on the pages by seating students as they come in, asking them if they would like some water, and serving them water when they say yes.

Ask students to name restaurants in the area and tell you whether they are expensive or inexpensive.

Bring in different dish, glass, and silverware items (paper and plastic are fine) and ask students to name as many items as they can.

TEACH THE NEW WORDS

Create a "restaurant table" in the front of the class. Use TPR commands to guide students through the target vocabulary. *Seat the customer. Pour the ice water.*

PROVIDE PRACTICE
Chalkboard Activities

△ Have students categorize vocabulary:

Actions	People	Things
seat	customer	menu

△ Have students sequence the actions.

_____	**take the order**
_____	**clear the dishes**
_____	**serve the food**
_1_	**seat the customer**
_____	**pour the water**
_____	**give the customer the menu**
_____	**carry the dessert tray**

Conversations

△ Put models on the board and practice. Make appropriate substitutions.

A: Excuse me, but I need a *water glass*.
B: Oh, I'll get you one right away!
  21. cup 22. saucer 23. napkin, etc.

A: Hi, I'm the new *hostess*. What should I do?
B: *Seat the customer* over there first. Then I'll show you where everything is.
  4. server/F. serve the meal
  9. busperson/G. clear the table

A: This is how you set the table: put the *[napkin]* next to the plate, the *[knife]* on the right, the *[fork]* on the left.
B: Put it where?
A: *[Napkin]* next to the plate, *[knife]* on the right, *[fork]* on the left.
B: OK, let me try.

Interview Questions

1. How often do you go to restaurants? Every week? Twice a month? Never?
2. Do you have any friends who work in restaurants? What do they do there?
3. How do you set the table at home?

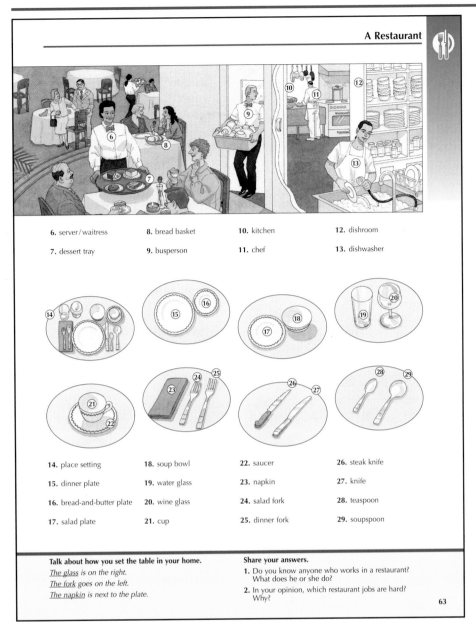

A Restaurant

6. server / waitress   8. bread basket   10. kitchen   12. dishroom

7. dessert tray   9. busperson   11. chef   13. dishwasher

14. place setting   18. soup bowl   22. saucer   26. steak knife

15. dinner plate   19. water glass   23. napkin   27. knife

16. bread-and-butter plate   20. wine glass   24. salad fork   28. teaspoon

17. salad plate   21. cup   25. dinner fork   29. soupspoon

Talk about how you set the table in your home.

The glass is on the right.

The fork goes on the left.

The napkin is next to the plate.

Share your answers.

1. Do you know anyone who works in a restaurant? What does he or she do?

2. In your opinion, which restaurant jobs are hard? Why?

63

Listening: Interactive Dictation

△ Have students close their books. Dictate these questions about pages 62–63. Speak naturally and encourage students to ask for clarification. *(Where is who? Who is doing what?)* Have students check their work and then work in pairs to write the answers.

1. *What is the hostess doing?*

2. *What is the busperson clearing?*

3. *What are the customers looking at?*

4. *What is on the dessert tray?*

5. *Where is the bread basket?*

6. *Where is the dishwasher?*

7. *Where is the chef?*

8. *Who is paying the bill?*

9. *Who is pouring the water?*

10. *How many people are working at this restaurant?*

EXPAND THE LESSON

Problem Solving

△ Have students brainstorm solutions.

1. *You are in an expensive restaurant but the service is terrible. What can you do?*

2. *You work in a restaurant and a customer is rude to you. What are some things you can say to the customer?*

Discussion Questions

1. The typical tip is 15% of the bill. When do you think you should give more? Less?

2. In many cities it is not possible to smoke in restaurants. Do you agree with this law? Why or why not?

Secret Setup

1. Draw two simple but different place settings:

2. Photocopy half a class set of each drawing.

3. Pair students and identify an "A" and "B" in each pair.

4. Give the pairs a manila folder to set up between them as a blind.

5. Have the "B" partners take out scratch paper and a pencil.

6. Give all the "A" partners the first place-setting drawing and instruct them not to show it to the "B" partners.

7. Have all "A" partners use their drawings to guide the "B's" in drawing a matching picture.

8. Partners can follow this model dialogue to create matching pictures:
   A: Put the plate in the center.
   B: Where?
   A: In the center.

9. When both partners' drawings "match," have the partners switch roles, and give the "B's" the second place-setting picture.

Variation: Students can manipulate realia: plastic cutlery, paper plates, etc., to create matching place settings.

GAMES

Charades

1. Write the verbs A–J on slips of paper and put them into a box or hat.

2. Divide the class into two teams.

3. Team members take turns picking a word and acting it out for their team.

4. Teams get a point for each word they guess correctly.

5. The game ends when all the slips are gone.

Questions Only!

1. Divide students into groups of 4–8 and have each group choose a recorder.

2. Have students look at pages 62–63 and come up with as many questions as they can about the scene. *Where is the busperson going?*

3. Recorders write their groups' questions on the board.

4. The group with the most correct questions wins.

Variation 1: Have the recorders read their groups' questions aloud.

Variation 2: Have teams quiz each other with their questions.

Unit 5   Clothing I   page 64

Workbooks, pp. 64–65
Classic Classroom Activities, Unit 5
Related Dictionary Pages
- Colors, p. 12
- Clothing II–III, pp. 66–67
- Describing Clothes, pp. 70–71

TOPIC NOTES

In the U.S., there are three general categories for clothing worn outside the home: casual wear, formal wear, and work or business clothes. Employers, restaurants, and schools often have dress codes that tell people what kind of clothes they have to wear.

A **split skirt** is also called a *skort* or *culottes*.

📁 Women are responsible for 68.6% of the total purchases of men's clothes.

TEACHING TIPS

Related Vocabulary

hat*	flannel shirt
shoes*	formal* wear
socks*	casual* wear
glasses*	dress code
belt*	attire

💡 Review the vocabulary from page 12, *Colors,* to help students discriminate among the various clothing items in the picture.

💡 Bring in half a class set of clothing catalogs or sales circulars from department stores. Have students, in pairs, search through the catalogs for specific items of clothing and note the colors, sizes, and prices of the items.

Clothing I

1. three-piece suit	6. sports coat	11. pullover sweater
2. suit	7. turtleneck	12. T-shirt
3. dress	8. slacks/pants	13. shorts
4. shirt	9. blouse	14. sweatshirt
5. jeans	10. skirt	15. sweatpants

More vocabulary:
outfit: clothes that look nice together
When clothes are popular, they are **in fashion**.

Talk about what you're wearing today and what you wore yesterday.
I'm wearing a gray sweater, a red T-shirt, and blue jeans.
Yesterday I wore a green pullover sweater, a white shirt, and black slacks.

64

INTRODUCE THE TOPIC

Describe the clothing you're wearing, mentioning each item several times while commenting on the color and material of each piece. *Do you like my shirt? My blue shirt is made of cotton. This is my favorite shirt.*

Ask students to brainstorm a list of clothing items while you record the items on the board. Working from the list, ask students to stand if they are wearing a particular item. *Everyone wearing pants stand up. Everyone wearing a T-shirt stand up.*

Bring in several large magazine pictures of models in very fashionable clothing and place one at each corner of the room. Ask students to stand near the picture they like best and exchange names with the students in their corner.

TEACH THE NEW WORDS

Describe each person in the scene. Have students point to the clothing items as you describe them. *Look at the businessman on the left. He's waiting for the bus. He's in a three-piece suit. The three-piece suit is gray and white. The suit has a pair of pants, a jacket, and a vest. The woman next to him is looking at the movie line. She's wearing a blue suit and a pink blouse. Her suit has a skirt and a jacket. They're the same color.* Etc.

PROVIDE PRACTICE
Chalkboard Activities

△ Have students categorize vocabulary:

Women	Men	Both
skirt	sports coat	T-shirt

Conversations

△ Put models on the board and practice. Make appropriate substitutions.

A: You can't wear those to work!
B: What's wrong with them? I always wear *jeans* to work!
    13. shorts 15. sweatpants 21. overalls

A: I want to buy a new *suit*.
B: I'll take you to the mall. They're having a sale on *[suits]*.
    7. turtleneck 11. pullover sweater 12. T-shirt
    14. sweatshirt 27. cardigan sweater

A: I'm looking for a *dress* for my mom.
B: Here's a nice *[dress]*, and it's marked down 50% today.
A: What a bargain! I'll take it!
    9. blouse 10. skirt 18. jumper 22. tunic
    24. vest 25. split skirt

Clothing I

16. jumpsuit	**21.** overalls	**26.** sports shirt
17. uniform	**22.** tunic	**27.** cardigan sweater
18. jumper	**23.** leggings	**28.** tuxedo
19. maternity dress	**24.** vest	**29.** evening gown
20. knit shirt	**25.** split skirt	

Use the new language.
Look at **A Graduation**, pages **32–33**.
Name the clothes you see.
The man at the podium is wearing a suit.

Share your answers.
1. Which clothes in this picture are in fashion now?
2. Who is the best-dressed person in this line? Why?
3. What do you wear when you go to the movies?

65

Interview Questions

1. What's your favorite thing to wear?
2. Do you like to wear sweaters?
3. Do you prefer wearing slacks or jeans?
4. Do you prefer wearing T-shirts or knit shirts?
5. Which person in the picture has the best outfit? Why?
6. Which person in the picture has the worst outfit? Why?
7. Which of these outfits could you wear to work?
8. What clothes do you wear to relax in?
9. Have you ever worn a tuxedo or gown? Where did you wear it?

Listening: ▭ #23, p. 217
"The Movie Line" Students listen and point to the people as they are described.

EXPAND THE LESSON
Problem Solving

△ Have students brainstorm solutions.

1. *Miguel is going on a business trip to Canada. Because he has so many papers to bring, he can only take three items of clothing and his pajamas. How should he decide what to take?*

2. *Anna's best friend has asked her to be the maid of honor at her wedding. The gown for the maid of honor is very formal and very expensive. Anna does not have money in her budget for that kind of dress. What can Anna do in this situation?*

Discussion Questions

1. Psychologists advise U.S. parents they should not criticize their teens' clothing choices unless they are unhealthy or unsafe. Is this good advice? Why or why not?

2. Some people think looking at someone's clothes tells you what kind of person that person is. Do you agree or disagree? Why?

GAMES
Definition Bingo

1. Have students fold a blank sheet of paper into 16 squares.
2. Dictate 16 clothing items (that students are wearing) and have students write the items in random order on their papers.
3. Tell students they will be circling different words on their papers, as they hear you define them. Explain that, when they get four circled words in a row (horizontally, vertically, or diagonally), they shout "Bingo!"
4. Give a sample definition. *This is something you wear when you are cold. Juan is wearing a green one today.* Make sure all the students have circled the correct word on their papers.
5. Call out definitions until one student gets Bingo.
6. Continue playing until five players have gotten Bingo.

Who Is It?

1. Have a student volunteer step out of the room, while the class decides on one person who will be "it."
2. Once the class has decided, the volunteer comes in and asks a series of *yes/no* questions about the mystery person, focusing on the person's clothing. *Is the mystery person a man?* (no) *Is she wearing a sweater?* (no) *Is she wearing a blue dress?* (yes) *Is she Fatima?* (yes).
3. Have another volunteer step out of the room and continue the game for three more rounds.

Memory Game

1. Divide the class into two teams.
2. Have students study the scene on pages 64–65.
3. Alternately quiz the teams by making *true/false* statements about the scene. Students respond. *The man at the bus stop is wearing a sweater.* (false) *There are three children in the movie line.* (true)
4. Correct answers get one point.
5. The game ends after 15 statements.

Workbooks, p. 66
Classic Classroom Activities, Unit 5
Related Dictionary Pages
- Colors, p. 12
- The Calendar, pp. 18–19
- Describing Clothes, pp. 70–71

TOPIC NOTES

In the U.S., many men and women are comfortable wearing **bathing suits** in public places (pools, beaches, and parks).

A **raincoat** is any coat that is waterproof and meant to protect the wearer from the rain.

A **trench coat** is a belted, rainproof coat, cut in a military style.

⚠ Students may be very uncomfortable with the depiction of the women in the fourth picture. It may be helpful to discuss the cultural acceptance of such dress in the U.S. and elicit students' views on appropriate dress for men, women, and children.

TEACHING TIPS

Related Vocabulary

rain hat	chilly
down jacket	rainy
fur coat	windy*
fake fur	sunny*

☀ Review different types of materials (wool, cotton, leather, and nylon, p. 70, *Describing Clothes*) and weather conditions (windy, freezing, sunny, p. 10, *Weather*) so that students will be better able to discuss the clothing on page 66.

Clothing II

1. hat	5. gloves	8. parka	12. earmuffs
2. overcoat	6. cap	9. mittens	13. down vest
3. leather jacket	7. jacket	10. ski cap	14. ski mask
4. wool scarf/muffler		11. tights	15. down jacket

16. umbrella	20. trench coat	24. windbreaker
17. raincoat	21. sunglasses	25. cover-up
18. poncho	22. swimming trunks	26. swimsuit/bathing suit
19. rain boots	23. straw hat	27. baseball cap

Use the new language.
Look at **Weather,** page 10.
Name the clothing for each weather condition.
Wear *a jacket* when it's *windy*.

Share your answers.
1. Which is better in the rain, an umbrella or a poncho?
2. Which is better in the cold, a parka or a down jacket?
3. Do you have more summer clothes or winter clothes?

INTRODUCE THE TOPIC

Ask students to brainstorm a list of all the outerwear words they know. Circle all the words that are represented in the classroom.

Bring in examples of different outerwear and draw symbols for sun, wind, snow, and rain on the board. Ask student volunteers to put on the clothing and stand beneath the correct symbol.

TEACH THE NEW WORDS

Ask students a series of *or* questions. *It's a sunny day. Should I wear the windbreaker or the overcoat?* (windbreaker) *It's freezing. Should I wear my down vest or my poncho?* (down vest) *It's raining. Should I wear my trench coat or my leather jacket?* (trench coat)

PROVIDE PRACTICE
Chalkboard Activities

△ Have students categorize vocabulary:

Hands	Body	Legs/Feet	Head/Neck
mittens	parka	tights	hat

Conversations

△ Put models on the board and practice. Make appropriate substitutions.

A: It's freezing outside! Put on your <u>mittens</u>.
B: Relax! I'm already wearing [them].
   4. wool scarf 10. ski cap 11. tights
   12. earmuffs 13. down vest
   14. ski mask 15. down jacket

A: You're soaking wet! Didn't you take your <u>poncho</u>?
B: No, I didn't. But at least I took my <u>hat</u>!
   16. umbrella/7. jacket
   17. raincoat/19. rain boots
   20. trenchcoat/6. cap

Interview Questions

1. Do you prefer a poncho or a raincoat?
2. Do you prefer a cap or a hat?
3. Do you prefer gloves or mittens?
4. What cold-weather clothes do you have at home?

Listening: 🔊 #24, p. 217
"Outdoor Fashion" Students listen to people looking at a fashion magazine. They write the number of the clothing item.

EXPAND THE LESSON
Drawing Activity

1. Have students draw themselves dressed for both their favorite and least favorite weather conditions.

2. Divide the students into pairs and have the partners ask and answer questions about their pictures.

Clothing III

1. leotard	3. bike shorts	4. pajamas	7. blanket sleeper
2. tank top		5. nightgown	8. bathrobe
		6. slippers	9. nightshirt

10. undershirt	16. (bikini) panties	22. full slip
11. long underwear	17. briefs / underpants	23. half slip
12. boxer shorts	18. girdle	24. knee-highs
13. briefs	19. garter belt	25. kneesocks
14. athletic supporter / jockstrap	20. bra	26. stockings
15. socks	21. camisole	27. pantyhose

More vocabulary
lingerie: underwear or sleepwear for women
loungewear: clothing (sometimes sleepwear) people wear around the home

Share your answers.
1. What do you wear when you exercise?
2. What kind of clothing do you wear for sleeping?

67

Workbooks, p. 67
Classic Classroom Activities, Unit 5
Related Dictionary Pages
• Colors, p. 12
• Clothing I–II, pp. 64–66
• Describing Clothes, pp. 70–71

TOPIC NOTES

In the U.S., as staying fit becomes more and more popular, people are wearing exercise gear outside the home and gym. T-shirts, sweatpants, and sweatshirts are also popular exercise gear and/or sleepwear.

Underwear for women is also called **lingerie.** Female friends give each other lingerie as gifts. However, a man rarely gives this kind of gift to a woman, unless they are married.

A camisole is a short feminine undergarment that covers the upper body, but not the arms or upper chest. The top of the camisole may be meant to be seen under sweaters or blouses.

⚠ Be wary of using ads featuring female models dressed in revealing sleepwear, exercise gear, and underwear as visual aids. While common in U.S. print media, students may find these ads offensive.

TEACHING TIPS

Related Vocabulary

lingerie	bodystocking
hose	long johns
brassiere	

Spelling: Plurals with no singlular form *Pantyhose* (like *jeans* and *shorts*) has no singular form, and takes a plural verb. *Those pantyhose are torn.*

INTRODUCE THE TOPIC

Ask students what they wear when they exercise and sleep.

Talk about underwear such as corsets, pantaloons, and longjohns, comparing them with underwear today.

TEACH THE NEW WORDS

Describe the scenes, emphasizing the vocabulary, as students point to the appropriate pictures. *This family is exercising together. The woman is wearing a leotard, a turquoise leotard. (#1)*

Ask students to chorally repeat words 10–27 as they point to each item.

PROVIDE PRACTICE

Chalkboard Activities

△ Have students categorize vocabulary:

| **Outside** | **At Home Only** |
| *leotard* | *nightgown* |

Conversations

△ Put models on the board and practice. Make appropriate substitutions.

A: It's time to go to bed.
B: Aw, *[Mom]!*
A: No arguments! Put on your <u>nightgown</u> and slippers now!
  4. pajamas 8. bathrobe 9. nightshirt

A: How much is this <u>girdle?</u>
B: It's on sale for $18.99. <u>Knee-highs</u> are on sale too, if you're interested.
  19. garter belt/25. kneesocks
  20. bra/26. stockings
  21. camisole/27. pantyhose
  22. full slip/25. kneesocks

Interview Questions

1. What kind of slippers do you wear?
2. What do you like to wear when you exercise?

Listening: Checklist

1. Have students make checklists with the three headings *Men, Women, Both.*
2. Randomly say underwear clothing items, #10–12 and #14–27, while students make a check under the appropriate column.
3. Have students tell you their tallies and discuss them.
4. Repeat the activity until all tallies are accurate.

EXPAND THE LESSON

Discussion Questions

1. Do you think it is appropriate to wear exercise wear in public? Why or why not?
2. Is giving underwear as a gift ever appropriate in your culture?

Unit 5   Shoes and Accessories   page 68

Workbooks, pp. 68–69
Classic Classroom Activities, Unit 5
Related Dictionary Pages
• Describing Things, p. 11
• Colors, p. 12
• Clothing I and II, pp. 64–66
• Describing Clothes, pp. 70–71

TOPIC NOTES

In the U.S., shoes and accessories are selected by men and women on the basis of both function and style. Current fashion trends often dictate varieties in color, fabric, and price.

Shoes and clothing accessories, by design both ornamental and decorative, have been worn throughout history to indicate social status.

📁 The oldest shoe, discovered in an Egyptian tomb and dated 2000 B.C., is a sandal.

TEACHING TIPS
Related Vocabulary

pocketbook	gemstones
pendant	birthstones
brooch	shoehorn
clutch bag	sneakers
cummerbund	tie clip
costume jewelry	cufflinks
fine jewelry	shawl

Pronunciation: Reduced syllables
The number of syllables in a word is determined by the number of vowel sounds. The dropped *e* reduces *bracelet* to two syllables. [brās'lət]

💡 Bring in jewelry and accessories (realia or pictures) to show varieties of bracelets (ankle, I.D. bangle, friendship), hats (panama, beret, cowboy, visor), and earrings (stud, hoop, drop).

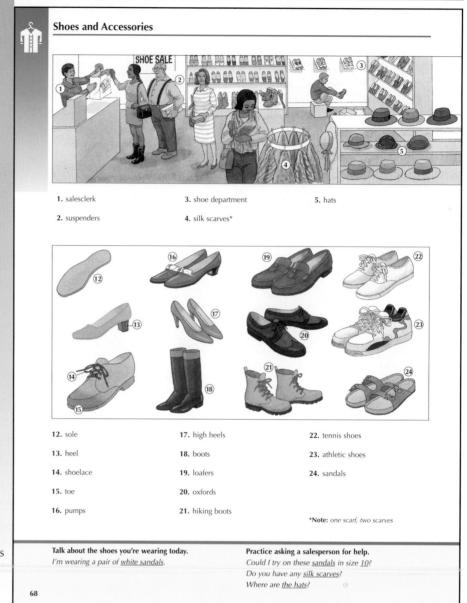

Shoes and Accessories

1. salesclerk
2. suspenders
3. shoe department
4. silk scarves*
5. hats

12. sole
13. heel
14. shoelace
15. toe
16. pumps
17. high heels
18. boots
19. loafers
20. oxfords
21. hiking boots
22. tennis shoes
23. athletic shoes
24. sandals

Note: one scarf, two scarves

Talk about the shoes you're wearing today.
I'm wearing a pair of white sandals.

Practice asking a salesperson for help.
Could I try on these sandals in size 10?
Do you have any silk scarves?
Where are the hats?

68

INTRODUCE THE TOPIC

Tell a story about your next vacation. Describe your plans and talk about what shoes you need. *My hotel is on the beach. I'd better pack my sandals. I'm bringing my tennis racket, so I'll need tennis shoes.*

Act out the role of salesclerk as you show, or pretend to show, some fine jewelry items. *This gorgeous sterling silver chain is 50% off. Here, try it on.*

TEACH THE NEW WORDS

Ask students to call out the number of each picture as you describe it. *Look at page 68. These silk scarves will look so nice around my neck. They come in many beautiful colors. This one feels soft.* (#4)

PROVIDE PRACTICE
Chalkboard Activities

△ Have students categorize vocabulary:

1. Carry It — **Wear It**
wallet — suspenders

2. Casual — **Formal** — **Both**
sandals — bow tie — pin

Conversations

△ Put models on the board and practice. Make appropriate substitutions.

A: How do those *high heels* feel?
B: Not so good. *[The heel hurts].*
   16. pumps 18. boots 19. loafers 20. oxfords
   21. hiking boots 22. tennis shoes
   23. athletic shoes 24. sandals

A: I'm looking for a special gift.
B: How about a gold *chain*?
A: It's very *[elegant]*. How much is it?
   33. locket 34. wristwatch 35. bracelet
   36. pin 39. ring

A: There's no price tag on these *silk scarves*.
B: Why don't you ask the salesclerk?
A: OK, let's bring *[this brown scarf]* with us.
   2. suspenders 5. hats 6. purses
   9. necklaces 10. ties 11. belts

Interview Questions

1. What type of shoe do you wear most often?
2. Do you prefer gold or silver jewelry?
3. Where is a good place to buy shoes?
4. What kind of jewelry did you buy recently?
5. Do you wear a watch every day? How often do you check the time?
6. Do you own any formal or "dressy" jewelry? When do you wear it?
7. What kind of earrings look good on women? on men?

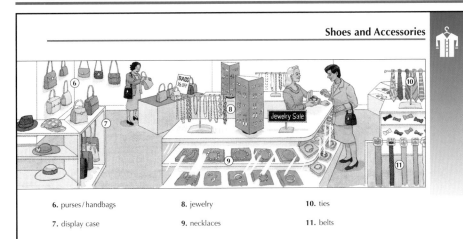

Shoes and Accessories

6. purses/handbags   8. jewelry   10. ties

7. display case   9. necklaces   11. belts

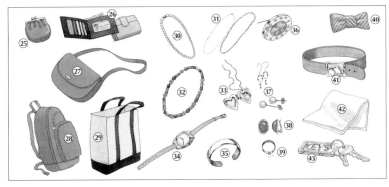

25. change purse   30. string of pearls   35. bracelet   40. bow tie

26. wallet   31. chain   36. pin   41. belt buckle

27. shoulder bag   32. beads   37. pierced earrings   42. handkerchief

28. backpack/bookbag   33. locket   38. clip-on earrings   43. key chain

29. tote bag   34. (wrist)watch   39. ring

Share your answers.

1. Which of these accessories are usually worn by women? by men?

2. Which of these do you wear every day?

3. Which of these would you wear to a job interview? Why?

4. Which accessory would you like to receive as a present? Why?

69

Language Workout

△ Copy these sentences on the board and discuss their meanings.

1. Poor Luis lost his job after one day. His boss just *gave him the boot.*

2. When the economy is bad, everyone has to *tighten their belts.*

3. Saul is living with his wife, sister, and mother-in-law. *Put yourself in his shoes.* How would you feel?

4. Marta is a full-time secretary, takes care of four children, and manages her apartment building. She *wears many hats.*

GAMES

Scavenger Hunt

1. Post a list of ten shoes or accessories that students can find within the classroom: a black leather wallet, a blue denim backpack, a gold charm bracelet, a pair of clip-on earrings, etc.

2. Group students in fours and have a recorder in each group copy the list.

3. Have students look up any new words in their dictionaries.

4. Groups try to find as many items on the list as possible from within their own group by asking and answering the question *Do you have…?*

5. Compare the results of the scavenger hunt with the whole class.

6. Discuss which items were the easiest, the most difficult, or impossible to find.

Option: You can give students a new list and have them search for items at home.

What's Missing?

△ Students identify missing objects in a picture or display.

1. Set up a table in the front of the class with various accessories.

2. Students have 30 seconds to study the display. They then close their eyes.

3. Remove 3–5 objects.

4. Students try to name which items are missing.

Class Go-Around: A Shopping Trip

1. Begin by saying *I'm going to [J.C. Nickles] because they're having a sale on belts.*

2. The first volunteer repeats the sentence and adds another item. *I'm going to [J.C. Nickles] because they're having a sale on belts and ties.*

3. The next volunteer continues the chain by adding another item.

4. Stop after the tenth item or when a student makes a mistake, and begin the game again.

Listening: Checklist

1. Have students make checklists with the headings *Men, Women, Both.*

2. Read a store inventory list of shoes and accessories, while students make a check under the appropriate column.
   *14-karat gold heart-shaped locket
   engraved gold wedding ring
   round pearl clip-on earrings
   waterproof sports watch
   silk print bow tie
   red patent leather pumps, size 7
   brown loafers, size 13
   canvas floral tote bag
   imported 16-inch pearl necklace
   sterling silver belt buckle*

3. Have students tell you their tallies. (Correct tallies are *Men* 5, *Women* 8, *Both* 3.)

EXPAND THE LESSON

Discussion Questions

1. What can you do to protect your backpack or handbag from theft?

2. Do you own a favorite piece of jewelry? Describe it.

3. An heirloom is special jewelry that is passed from one family member to another. Do you have any?

Problem Solving

△ Have students brainstorm solutions.

1. *You find a wallet on the street with $100.00 and a credit card, but no identification. What do you do?*

2. *You gave your fiancée an expensive diamond engagement ring, but the wedding is canceled. She refuses to return the ring. What can you do?*

Workbooks, pp. 70–71
Classic Classroom Activities, Unit 5
Related Dictionary Pages
• Colors, p. 12
• Clothing I–III, pp. 64–67

TOPIC NOTES

In the U.S., clothing **sizes** usually conform to the following numbering system.

Misses (average women) sizes 2–14
Women (larger women) sizes 16–24
Junior (young women) sizes 1–13
Girls sizes 7–14
Boys sizes 8–20
Toddler sizes: 2T–4T
Baby sizes: Newborn–2 years

Men buy pants by waist size and inseam length, jackets by chest size, and dress shirts by neck size and sleeve length.

TEACHING TIPS
Related Vocabulary

petite	husky
fad	slim
stylish	chic
spot	in style
tear	native dress

Pronunciation: Final /t/ sound
Practice the final sound in *striped* and *checked*.

Grammar: Order of adjectives
The order of adjectives used when describing clothes is by: color, pattern, then material. *I want a red striped cotton blouse.*

☼ Review page 12, *Colors*, so that students can describe the clothes and patterns by color.

☼ Review clothing items that are used as examples on pages 70–71: *sweater, shirt, shoes, skirt, dress, blouse, jacket, pants, tie,* and *heels.*

Describing Clothes

Sizes

1. extra small   2. small   3. medium   4. large   5. extra large

Patterns

6. solid green   8. polka-dotted   10. print   12. floral
7. striped   9. plaid   11. checked   13. paisley

Types of material

14. **wool** sweater   16. **cotton** T-shirt   18. **leather** boots
15. **silk** scarf   17. **linen** jacket   19. **nylon** stockings*

Problems

20. too small   22. stain   24. broken zipper
21. too big   23. rip / tear   25. missing button

*Note: Nylon, polyester, rayon, and plastic are synthetic materials.

70

INTRODUCE THE TOPIC

Walk around the room and describe the clothes that students are wearing. *Jorge, I see you are wearing a long-sleeved shirt today. It's a solid blue. Afra, I like your turtleneck sweater.*

Show students an example of a clothing problem, something with a stain or tear. Tell how it happened. *See the stain? I spilled coffee on this sweater. Did you ever do that?*

Bring in clothes that depict some of the vocabulary, e.g., high heels and low heels, a wide tie and a narrow one. Ask *or* questions. *Are these high or low heels? Is this a wide or narrow tie?*

TEACH THE NEW WORDS

Ask students to identify the number of a particular picture based on your description. Use clothing in the classroom as additional examples. *Look at Yee Wan's shirt. It has two colors. The colors go up and down. It is striped.* (#7)

PROVIDE PRACTICE
Chalkboard Activities

△ Have students categorize vocabulary:

1. **Every Day**	**Holidays**
low heels	*high heels*

2. **Cold weather**	**Hot Weather**
heavy jacket	*sleeveless shirt*

△ Tape to the chalkboard three or four large pictures of clothes from fashion ads. Choose a variety of sizes, fabric, styles and patterns. Space them far apart. Have students come to the board and write as many descriptive words as they can next to the pictures.

△ Write the following words on the board. Have students come up and write the opposites.

fancy	*plain*	**long**
old		**wide**
casual		**tight**
heavy		**high**

Conversations

△ Put models on the board and practice. Make appropriate substitutions.

A: Do you like the styles in the stores?
B: Not really. Everything is *striped* and long.
  8. polka dotted 9. plaid 10. print
  11. checked 12. floral 13. paisley
A: I hate to tell you this, but your [shirt] has a *rip*.

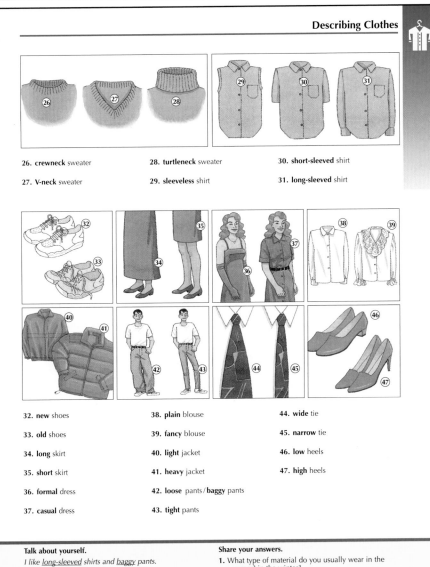

Describing Clothes

26. **crewneck** sweater

27. **V-neck** sweater

28. **turtleneck** sweater

29. **sleeveless** shirt

30. **short-sleeved** shirt

31. **long-sleeved** shirt

32. **new** shoes

33. **old** shoes

34. **long** skirt

35. **short** skirt

36. **formal** dress

37. **casual** dress

38. **plain** blouse

39. **fancy** blouse

40. **light** jacket

41. **heavy** jacket

42. **loose** pants / **baggy** pants

43. **tight** pants

44. **wide** tie

45. **narrow** tie

46. **low** heels

47. **high** heels

Talk about yourself.
I like long-sleeved shirts and baggy pants.
I like short skirts and high heels.
I usually wear plain clothes.

Share your answers.
1. What type of material do you usually wear in the summer? in the winter?
2. What patterns do you see around you?
3. Are you wearing casual or formal clothes?

71

B: Oh, thanks for telling me! I'm going to go take care of it right now.
A: Don't worry. It hardly shows.
  **22. stain 24. broken zipper
  25. missing button**

A: Do like this blouse?
B: It's too *formal* for me, but it looks great on you!
  37. casual 38. plain 39. fancy

Interview Questions

1. What are your favorite patterns?
2. What fabrics do you like to wear in the summer? in the spring? in the winter?
3. Do you like long- or short-sleeved shirts in the summer?
4. Do you like to wear formal clothes?
5. Do you wear mostly natural fabrics like cotton and wool, or synthetics?

Listening: Listen and Write

△ Have students draw ten one-inch squares and number them 1-10. Students follow your directions to fill in the squares.

1. *Write the abbreviation for extra large in square 1.*
2. *Put the abbreviation for small in square 2.*
3. *Put the abbreviation for medium in square 3.*
4. *Put the abbreviation for large in square 4.*
5. *Put the abbreviation for extra small in square 5.*
6. *Make square 6 striped.*
7. *Make square 7 solid.*
8. *Make square 8 polka-dot.*
9. *Make square 9 floral.*
10. *Make square 10 checked.*

EXPAND THE LESSON
Problem Solving
△ Have students brainstorm solutions.
1. *Dory is going to a wedding. Her dress has a big stain. Her other dress is too big. What can she do?*
2. *Pedro, who is 15 years old, likes to wear baggy pants, but his parents don't like them. He tells them that all the other boys at school wear them. What can they do?*

Discussion Questions
1. Not everyone can afford to buy expensive clothes. What are some ways to get the clothes you like without spending more money than you want?
2. Some people hate to wear formal or fancy clothes. Other people think it's exciting and fun. What about you? Do you like to wear formal clothes?
3. Most people have favorite styles—long sleeves, high heels, wide ties. What are some of your favorite styles?

GAME
Chair Line-Up
1. Have students draw a picture of themselves on a special occasion.
2. Line up two long rows of chairs facing each other at the front of the class, and have students sit holding their pictures.
3. For one minute students take turns describing what they are wearing in the pictures and why the day is special.
4. After two minutes the students in the row on the left move down one chair. With new partners, the students share again.

Variation: Students do not draw a picture but take turns describing what the other person is wearing.

Language Workout
△ Copy this text on the board and discuss its meaning.
I saw Gilbert sneaking into Joan's office. He has something *up his sleeve* and I don't know what it is.

Class Go-Around: A Bad Clothes Day!
1. Begin by saying *Yesterday Dave had a bad clothes day! His shirt was too big.*
2. The first volunteer repeats the sentence and adds another clothing problem. *Yesterday Dave had a bad clothes day! His shirt was too big and his jacket was too long.*
3. The next student volunteer continues the chain, adding another problem.
4. Stop after the tenth student and repeat the game.

Unit 5　Doing the Laundry　page 72

Workbooks, p. 72
Classic Classroom Activities, Unit 5
Related Dictionary Pages
- Clothing I–III, pages 64–67
- Describing Clothes, pp. 70–71

TOPIC NOTES

In the U.S., all clothes sold must have a care label telling how to clean the item and what fabric it is made of.

People sometimes go to Laundromats to do their laundry. Prices vary for using the washing machines, and some places offer free drying.

The use of gas or electric dryers is very common, but hanging clothes on a clothesline is obviously more economical and environmentally sound.

TEACHING TIPS

Related Vocabulary

wash(v)*	dry (v)*
rinse cycle	spin cycle
gentle	permanent press
starch	press
delicate	pre-soak
air dry	dry cleaners*
shrink	wash and wear

- Bring in clothing items so that students can practice reading laundry labels.
- Draw copies of real washing machine knobs and dryer knobs, and explain the meaning of the terms *hot, cold, delicate, rinse, spin, air dry,* etc.
- ⚠ Some students may not have any experience doing the laundry. You can begin the discussion by establishing who does laundry in the household.

Doing the Laundry

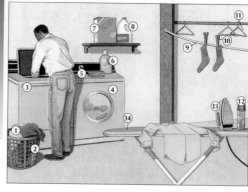

1. laundry	6. fabric softener	11. hanger	16. **clean** T-shirt
2. laundry basket	7. laundry detergent	12. spray starch	17. **wet** T-shirt
3. washer	8. bleach	13. iron	18. **dry** T-shirt
4. dryer	9. clothesline	14. ironing board	19. **wrinkled** shirt
5. dryer sheets	10. clothespin	15. **dirty** T-shirt	20. **ironed** shirt

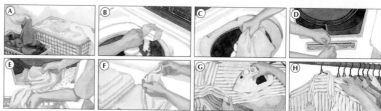

A. **Sort** the laundry.	D. **Clean** the lint trap.	G. **Iron** the clothes.
B. **Add** the detergent.	E. **Unload** the dryer.	H. **Hang up** the clothes.
C. **Load** the washer.	F. **Fold** the laundry.	

More vocabulary
dry cleaners: a business that cleans clothes using chemicals, not water and detergent

- 🔲 wash in cold water only
- 🔲 line dry
- ⬛ no bleach
- ⭕ dry-clean only, do not wash

72

INTRODUCE THE TOPIC

Bring in detergent, dryer sheets, bottles of softener, bleach, and spray starch. Take an informal class survey asking students which of the items they have in their homes.

Act out the sequence of doing the laundry, beginning with sorting the clothes. Speak as you do the actions. *I have a lot of dirty clothes. These socks are white—they go in this pile. This shirt is brown—it goes in this pile. I'll start with the light clothes. First I add the detergent.*

TEACH THE NEW WORDS

Ask students a series of *or* questions about the pictures. *Is #3 a washer or a dryer?* (a washer) *Is # 18 wet or dry?* (dry)

PROVIDE PRACTICE
Chalkboard Activities

△ Bring in clothing items and have students categorize them according to washing instructions:

Wash & Dry	Wash Only	Dry-clean
cotton shirt	*sweatshirt*	*wool pants*

Conversations

△ Put models on the board and practice. Make appropriate substitutions.

A: My pants are _dirty_.
B: You can't wear them until they are _clean_.

　17. wet/18. dry
　19. wrinkled/20. ironed

A: Rats! I forgot to buy _laundry detergent_.
B: Here, use some of mine. I bought it at a discount store.

　5. dryer sheets 6. fabric softener 8. bleach
　12. spray starch

Interview Questions

1. Do you go to the laundromat?
2. Do you dry clothes in a clothes dryer or on a clothesline?
3. Do you iron clothes? What items do you iron?

Listening: Listen and Write

△ Have students look in their picture dictionaries and write the letters of the phrases as you say them. E.g.:
1. *Iron the clothes.* (G)
2. *Fold the laundry.* (F) Etc.

EXPAND THE LESSON
Discussion Question

Laundry costs can be high. What are some ways to keep laundry costs down?

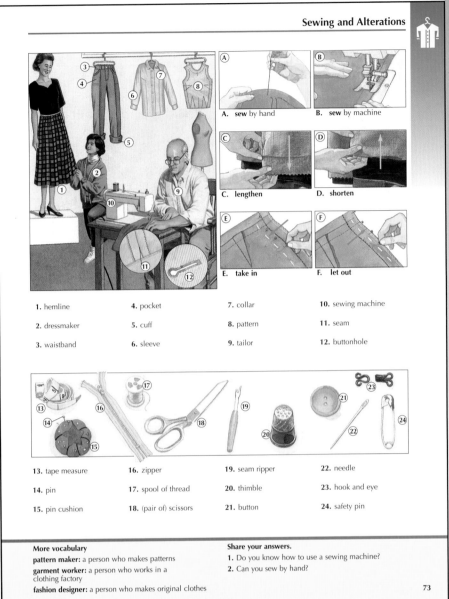

Sewing and Alterations

A. **sew** by hand
B. **sew** by machine
C. lengthen
D. shorten
E. take in
F. let out

1. hemline	4. pocket	7. collar	10. sewing machine
2. dressmaker	5. cuff	8. pattern	11. seam
3. waistband	6. sleeve	9. tailor	12. buttonhole

13. tape measure	16. zipper	19. seam ripper	22. needle
14. pin	17. spool of thread	20. thimble	23. hook and eye
15. pin cushion	18. (pair of) scissors	21. button	24. safety pin

More vocabulary
pattern maker: a person who makes patterns
garment worker: a person who works in a clothing factory
fashion designer: a person who makes original clothes

Share your answers.
1. Do you know how to use a sewing machine?
2. Can you sew by hand?

73

Workbooks, p. 73
Classic Classroom Activities, Unit 5
Related Dictionary Pages
• Clothing I–II, pages 64–66
• Describing Clothes, pp. 70–71

TOPIC NOTES

In the U.S., some people take their clothes to a tailor or dressmaker to be altered. Others own their own **sewing machines** or **sew by hand.** Many people use sewing machines to do home crafts such as quilting.

A **tailor** is generally a maker of men's clothes, especially suits, jackets, and pants, while a **dressmaker** is a maker of women's clothing, although women can have suits and/or jackets made by a tailor as well.

People first began to sew over 17,000 years ago, using bone needles. The first practical sewing machine was invented by Elias Howe in 1846.

TEACHING TIPS
Related Vocabulary

stitch	pin (v)
baste	button (v)
gather	made-to-order
hem	the garment industry
measure*	sweatshop
cut*	

- Review articles of clothing on pages 64–67 so that students can talk about clothes that need alterations.

- Review clothing problems from page 70, *Describing Clothes*. Talk about how you might fix the clothes that are too small or too big.

- Talk about the different kinds of jobs in sewing and alterations.

INTRODUCE THE TOPIC

Bring in some of the sewing supplies on this page. Take an informal class survey asking students which of the items they have used before.

Explain to students what alterations are. Ask students what the difference is between sewing a dress and altering a dress.

Present a problem to students. Bring in two pairs of pants—one too short and too tight, one too loose and too long. Have students tell you what the problem is.

TEACH THE NEW WORDS

Act out and give a series of commands using the pictures on the page and items in class. *Touch a button. Touch the sleeve. Point to the dressmaker on the page.*

PROVIDE PRACTICE
Chalkboard Activities

△ Draw simple clothing on the board and have students label the parts:

Conversations

△ Put models on the board and practice. Make appropriate substitutions.

A: Hi, Sam. Do you have time to *let out* my pants?
B: Sure. They will be ready by Friday.
  C. lengthen D. shorten E. take in

A: I need to fix this *[tear]*. Can you get me a *needle?*
  14. pin 15. pin cushion 17. spool of thread

Interview Questions

1. What items on this page do you have at home?

2. What sewing repairs on this page can you do yourself? What do you do if you can't?

Listening: Listen and Draw

△ Have students draw a picture of the sewing tools and accessories as you say them: *1. Draw a zipper. 2. Draw a pin.* Etc.

EXPAND THE LESSON
Discussion Questions

1. Fewer Americans are learning to sew. What do you think about this?

2. Which clothes are more expensive to alter, men's or women's? Why?

3. Do you know anyone who has a job sewing clothes? What do they say about their job?

Workbooks, pp. 74–75
Classic Classroom Activities, Unit 6
Related Dictionary Pages
• Personal Hygiene, pp. 76–77
• Symptoms and Injuries, p. 78
• Illnesses and Medical Conditions, p. 79

TOPIC NOTES

In the U.S., people have different levels of comfort when talking about the human body. Talking about internal and external organs is not taboo but can make some people uncomfortable, especially in mixed groups of men and women.

⚠ If you have students who do not feel comfortable talking about certain parts of the body, not all the vocabulary has to be discussed.

🗀 The human body is 65% water. The **heart** beats about 100,000 times each day. The human body gradually replaces its outermost layer of **skin** every 15–30 days.

TEACHING TIPS
Related Vocabulary

earlobe	ovaries
temple	egg*
nostril	vagina
torso	penis
nipple	testicles
uterus	sperm

Pronunciation: Silent letters
knee: The *k* is silent.
thigh: The *gh* is silent.
muscle: The *c* is silent.

🔅 Bring in puppets or dolls to use in demonstrating parts of the body.

🔅 Bring in pictures of athletes, dancers, and children for students to label.

The Body

1. head	**7.** foot	**13.** chest
2. neck	**8.** hand	**14.** breast
3. abdomen	**9.** arm	**15.** elbow
4. waist	**10.** shoulder	**16.** thigh
5. hip	**11.** back	**17.** knee
6. leg	**12.** buttocks	**18.** calf

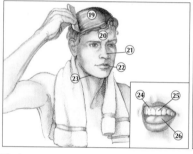 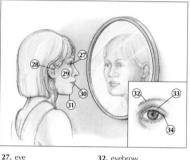

The face			
19. hair	**23.** jaw	**27.** eye	**32.** eyebrow
20. forehead	**24.** gums	**28.** ear	**33.** eyelid
21. nose	**25.** teeth	**29.** cheek	**34.** eyelashes
22. mouth	**26.** tongue	**30.** lip	
		31. chin	

74

INTRODUCE THE TOPIC

Ask students to look at the dictionary pages and while covering the words call out the parts of the body they already know.

Demonstrate a series of stretching exercises and talk as you are doing them. *Every morning I like to stretch. I put my hands over my head. I touch my toes.*

TEACH THE NEW WORDS

Ask students to point to the pictures based on your description. *These are used for breathing. They are inside your chest. They are called lungs. (#37) This is what you think with. It's inside your head. It's called a brain. (#35)*

Ask students a series of *or* questions about the pictures. *Is #10 a shoulder or an arm?* (a shoulder) *Is #38 a heart or a brain?* (a heart)

PROVIDE PRACTICE
Chalkboard Activities

△ Have students categorize vocabulary:

1. One	**Two**	**Ten**
head	*lungs*	*toes*

2. Head	**Body**	**Arm**	**Leg**
ear	*back*	*hand*	*foot*

△ Draw a large outline of a body. Have students come to the board and write the parts of the body on the outline.

Conversations

△ Put models on the board and practice. Make appropriate substitutions.

A: I want the doctor to look at my <u>neck</u>.
B: Why?
A: It hurts a little.
   3. abdomen 5. hip 6. leg 7. foot 8. hand, etc.

A: The doctor wants to check my <u>lungs</u>.
B: Is everything OK?
A: I hope so.
   38. heart 39. liver 40. gallbladder
   41. stomach 42. intestines

A: Can you <u>smell</u> the garlic in the soup?
B: No, I can't <u>smell</u> it.
   A. see D. taste

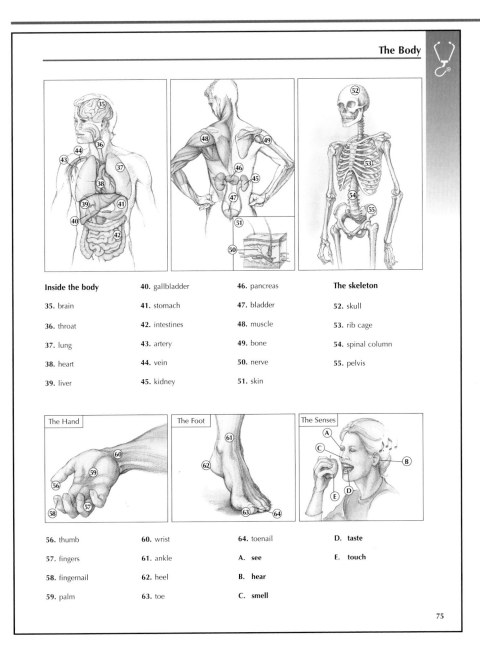

The Body

Inside the body

35. brain
36. throat
37. lung
38. heart
39. liver

40. gallbladder
41. stomach
42. intestines
43. artery
44. vein
45. kidney

46. pancreas
47. bladder
48. muscle
49. bone
50. nerve
51. skin

The skeleton

52. skull
53. rib cage
54. spinal column
55. pelvis

The Hand

56. thumb
57. fingers
58. fingernail
59. palm

60. wrist
61. ankle
62. heel
63. toe

The Foot

64. toenail
A. see
B. hear
C. smell

The Senses

D. taste
E. touch

75

Interview Questions

1. On what part of the body do you wear jewelry?
2. On what part of the body have you ever had an X ray?
3. What part of the body do children usually injure?

Listening: Total Physical Response

△ Have students follow these commands as you say them. (Add to these if you like.)
Touch your arm.
Touch your leg.
Touch your chin.
Touch your knee with your thumb.
Touch your mouth with your finger.
Touch your neck.
Touch your right cheek.
Touch your stomach.
Put two hands on your waist.
Put one hand on each ear.

EXPAND THE LESSON
Discussion Questions

1. Many people are thinking about their bodies more. They exercise and eat healthy food. Do you do this also? Why or why not?
2. The body part that is the most often injured at work is the back. What can you do to avoid injuring your back?

Extraterrestrial!

1. Divide students into pairs.
2. Have each student draw a picture of a being from outer space, e.g., a head with three eyes, two mouths, and one ear, and a body with five legs, each leg with two feet.
3. After each student has drawn an extraterrestrial, the students take turns describing their beings to their partners. The partner has to draw

without looking at the original drawing.

4. The activity ends when both partners have had a chance at describing and drawing.

Language Workout

△ Copy these sentences on the board and discuss their meanings.

1. Henry can't fix anything. He's *all thumbs.*
2. Mandy wanted to buy some new boots but they cost *an arm and a leg.*
3. Ken and his brother argue all the time. They never *see eye to eye* on anything.
4. Emily has a *big heart.* She will always help out a friend.
5. Leo told his sister her clothes were ugly. He always *puts his foot in his mouth.*

GAMES
Backward Dictionary

1. Divide students into two teams.
2. Give definitions or descriptions of the vocabulary words to one team at a time and have each team guess what the word is. *They hold the body up. Sometimes they get broken. They show up in X rays. What are they?* (bones) *It surrounds your whole body. Sometimes it gets wet. Sometimes it is itchy. What is it?* (skin) *You use these to walk with. You wear shoes on them. Each one has ten toes.* (feet)
3. The team with the most correct answers wins.

Word Bingo

1. Have students make a grid that is five rows across and five rows down and fill it in random order with 25 words from pages 74–75.
2. Call out vocabulary words randomly. Students circle the words as you say them.
3. The games ends when one student has five in any row, vertically, horizontally, or diagonally and calls out "Bingo!"
4. Continue playing until five students have gotten Bingo.

Variation: Have students draw the various parts of the body, one in each square.

Scrambled Words

1. Have students number their papers 1–10.
2. Spell out loud ten vocabulary words in scrambled order, e.g., *k-e-n-c* (neck) and *l-r-v-e-i* (liver).
3. Students unscramble the words.
4. The game ends when one student has unscrambled all the words.

Workbooks, pp. 76–77
Classic Classroom Activities, Unit 6
Related Dictionary Pages
• Describing Hair, p. 23
• Daily Routines, pp. 26–27
• The Body, pp. 74–75

TOPIC NOTES

In the U.S., people consider it common to **shower** or **bathe** every day or almost every day. Most people **use deodorant** every day and many people use **sunscreen** regularly to protect their skin against ultraviolet rays. Most men **shave** facial hair, and most women shave unwanted body hair.

TEACHING TIPS
Related Vocabulary

antiperspirant	nail file
lip gloss	acrylic nails
facial	pedicure
manicure	hairstyle
orange stick	liquid soap

Grammar: Possessive adjectives
Teach possessive adjectives *my, your, his, her, our, your* (plural), and *their* for use with verbs E–K and N–P. Teach *myself, herself,* and *himself* to use with the reflexive verb *shave* (M).

☼ Review the appropriate parts of the body and face on pages 74–75 so that students can talk about how they use these products.

☼ Americans, in general, use a lot of water for personal hygiene. Talk about ways to conserve water.

Personal Hygiene

A. **take** a shower   B. **bathe/take** a bath   C. **use** deodorant   D. **put on** sunscreen

1. shower cap	4. deodorant	7. body lotion
2. soap	5. perfume/cologne	8. moisturizer
3. bath powder/talcum powder	6. sunscreen	

E. **wash**...hair   F. **rinse**...hair   G. **comb**...hair   H. **dry**...hair   I. **brush**...hair

9. shampoo	12. hair spray	15. curling iron	18. barrette
10. conditioner	13. comb	16. blow dryer	19. bobby pins
11. hair gel	14. brush	17. hair clip	

76

INTRODUCE THE TOPIC

Act out a morning routine: taking a shower, washing hair, etc. Talk about what you are doing and the products you are using. *I like to take a shower in the morning. I use a good shampoo that you can use every day.*

Bring in different types of personal hygiene items. Have students help you categorize them by where they are used: face, hair, mouth, hands, or body.

Talk about the hairstyling supplies on this page. Take an informal class survey asking students which of the items they use.

Ask students to look at the dictionary page and tell you the words they already know. Write them on the board as they say them. Use them as the first words you teach.

TEACH THE NEW WORDS

Ask students to identify the number or letter of the picture based on your description. *You do this to get clean. Water comes out above you. You take a shower in the morning.* (A) *I do this to get my hair clean. I wash my hair three times a week.* (E) *You use this when you wash your hands or in a bath. Soap makes you clean.* (#2)

PROVIDE PRACTICE
Chalkboard Activities

△ Draw an outline of a body or a very large face on the board. Have students come up and write the appropriate products next to where they are used.

△ Have students categorize vocabulary:

Take a Shower	**Style Hair**	**Shave**
soap	brush	razor

Put on Makeup	**Do Nails**	**Brush Teeth**
lipstick	nail polish	toothbrush

Conversations

△ Put models on the board and practice. Make appropriate substitutions.

A: I'm all out of <u>sunscreen</u>.
B: Already?
A: Well, I use it every day.

    **5. perfume 7. body lotion 8. moisturizer
9. shampoo 21. toothpaste 22. dental floss
23. mouthwash**

A: I need to get up earlier.
B: Why?
A: It takes me a long time to <u>take a shower</u>.

    **B. take a bath E. wash my hair H. dry my
hair M. shave P. put on my makeup**

Personal Hygiene

J. brush…teeth   K. floss…teeth   L. gargle   M. shave

20. toothbrush
21. toothpaste
22. dental floss

23. mouthwash
24. electric shaver
25. razor

26. razor blade
27. shaving cream
28. aftershave

N. cut…nails   O. polish…nails   P. put on…makeup

29. nail clipper
30. emery board
31. nail polish
32. nail polish remover

33. eyebrow pencil
34. eye shadow
35. eyeliner
36. blush / rouge

37. lipstick
38. mascara
39. face powder
40. foundation

More vocabulary
A product without perfume or scent is **unscented**.
A product that is better for people with allergies is **hypoallergenic**.

Share your answers.
1. What is your morning routine if you stay home? if you go out?
2. Do women in your culture wear makeup? How old are they when they begin to use it?

77

Interview Questions
1. Do you prefer to take a shower or a bath?
2. Do you prefer to shower in the morning or in the evening?
3. What do you use to style your hair?
4. How old do you think children should be when they can take a shower alone?
5. What do you think is the most essential item on this page?
6. Do you buy most of these items in the market, at a drugstore, or at a discount store?

Listening: ▭ #25, p. 218
"Morning With The Simms Family"
Students point to the actions and personal hygiene products they hear as the Simms family gets ready for the day.

EXPAND THE LESSON
Problem Solving
△ Have students brainstorm solutions.
1. *Kate is 15 years old and has two sisters. Every morning they all fight over time in the bathroom. What can they do?*
2. *Loofa likes to wear a lot of makeup. Her husband likes Loofa better when she only wears lipstick. What should Loofa do?*

Discussion Questions
1. Some young women in the U.S. start to wear lipstick when they are 12 years old. Others are not allowed to until they are 14 or 15 or older. At what age do you think a young woman can start wearing lipstick? What about eye makeup?

2. Some men hate to shave. Do you think most men should shave every day? Do you like mustaches and/or beards on men?

GAMES
Classroom Hunt
1. Write each verb (A–P) and each product (1–40) on separate index cards. If you have fewer than 56 students, delete some of the products in each category so that each student has one card.
2. Have students walk around the room and form groups of one verb together with all its products.
3. The game ends when all the groups' members find each other.

A–Z Brainstorm
1. Divide students into groups of 4 or 5.
2. Have students study the products on pages 76–77 for two minutes and then close their books.
3. Each group chooses one leader and one recorder. The leader (with book open) says a verb *(brush…teeth)*. The others call out the products one uses *(toothbrush, toothpaste)*.
4. The recorder writes down the vocabulary words as the rest of the group calls them out.
5. Call time after 5 minutes. The group with the most correct words wins.

Class Go-Around: Carol Clean!
1. Begin by saying *Yesterday Carol Clean woke up and took a shower.*
2. The first student volunteer repeats the sentences and adds another action. *Carol Clean woke up, took a shower, and used deodorant.*
3. The next student volunteer continues the chain, adding another action.
4. Stop after ten students and begin the game again.

Guess What!
1. Bring in personal hygiene products in small paper bags, one for each pair of students in your class. (Do not bring in sharp objects!) Number each bag on the outside.
2. Group students in pairs and distribute the bags. Have each pair guess the object by feeling the outside of the bag. Have students exchange bags until all pairs have a turn.
3. Have students keep a list of their guesses for each bag on a separate piece of paper.
4. The game ends when all pairs have guessed and you reveal what is inside each bag.

Workbooks, p. 78
Classic Classroom Activities, Unit 6
Related Dictionary Pages
• The Body, pp. 74–75
• Illnesses and Medical Conditions, p. 79
• Health Care, pp. 80–81
• Medical Emergencies, p. 82
• First Aid, p. 83

TOPIC NOTES

In the U.S., minor ailments and injuries account for a large percentage of doctor visits. Although these ailments are usually not life threatening, they account for many work and school absences.

Migraines are severe headaches. Their exact cause is unknown. Although there is no known cure, there are many ways to treat them.

TEACHING TIPS
Related Vocabulary

pain*	diarrhea
muscle cramps	constipation
sprained muscle	bee sting
stiff neck	black eye
dislocated bone	scrape
laryngitis	wart

Usage: *Cut* and *cough* are both verbs and nouns. *She cut her finger. That's a deep cut. He coughed all last night. He has a terrible cough.*

⚠ Explain to students that the greeting "How are you?" does not require a detailed medical response.

🔅 Page 78 and page 79 can be taught in conjunction with *Health Care,* pages 80 and 81.

Symptoms and Injuries

1. headache	**6.** sore throat	**A.** cough
2. toothache	**7.** nasal congestion	**B.** sneeze
3. earache	**8.** fever/temperature	**C.** feel dizzy
4. stomachache	**9.** chills	**D.** feel nauseous
5. backache	**10.** rash	**E.** throw up/vomit

11. insect bite	**14.** sunburn	**17.** bloody nose
12. bruise	**15.** blister	**18.** sprained ankle
13. cut	**16.** swollen finger	

Use the new language.
Look at **Health Care,** pages **80–81.**
Tell what medication or treatment you would use for each health problem.

Share your answers.
1. For which problems would you go to a doctor? use medication? do nothing?
2. What do you do for a sunburn? for a headache?

78

INTRODUCE THE TOPIC

Talk about your "numerous" aches and pains. Pause before you identify the symptom or injury to see if students can guess it. *Oh, my head really hurts. I have pain above my eyes. This is a terrible…* (headache).

Bring in different items from your medicine cabinet and have students help you choose the best treatment for each symptom or injury. *I have a sore throat. Should I gargle with this liquid? What's best for a fever? Should I take aspirin or nonaspirin?*

TEACH THE NEW WORDS

Ask students a series of *or* questions about the pictures. *Look at #4. Does he have a stomachache or a backache?* (stomachache) *Look at picture C. Does she feel dizzy? Is she throwing up?* (feel dizzy)

PROVIDE PRACTICE
Chalkboard Activities

△ Have students categorize vocabulary:

1. Visible	**Not Visible**
blister	headache

2. Symptom	**Injury**
chills	cut

Conversations

△ Put models on the board and practice. Make appropriate substitutions.

A: What's the matter?
B: I don't feel well. I have a(n) <u>headache</u>.
A: Sorry to hear that.

  2. toothache 3. earache 4. stomachache
  5. backache 6. sore throat 8. fever

A: Look at my <u>swollen finger</u>.
B: Oh, too bad, *[put it on ice]*.
A: Thanks for the advice.

  11. insect bite 12. bruise 13. cut etc.

Interview Questions

1. How are you feeling now?
2. What can you take for a stomachache?
3. Have you ever had a bloody nose? a sprained ankle?
4. What makes you sneeze? cough?

Listening: 📼 #26, p. 218

"Ben Knows Best" Students listen and point to the symptoms and injuries on page 78 that are mentioned.

EXPAND THE LESSON
Discussion Questions

1. Some people talk constantly or exaggerate stories about their health ailments. Why do they do this?
2. Coughing and sneezing spread disease. How can you protect yourself and others from contagious germs?

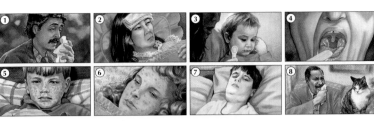

Illnesses and Medical Conditions

Common illnesses and childhood diseases

1. cold
2. flu
3. ear infection
4. strep throat
5. measles
6. chicken pox
7. mumps
8. allergies

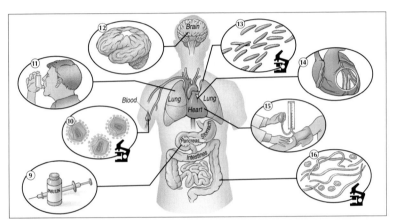

Medical conditions and serious diseases

9. diabetes
10. HIV (human immunodeficiency virus)
11. asthma
12. brain cancer
13. TB (tuberculosis)
14. heart disease
15. high blood pressure
16. intestinal parasites

More vocabulary

AIDS (acquired immunodeficiency syndrome): a medical condition that results from contracting the HIV virus

influenza: flu

hypertension: high blood pressure

infectious disease: a disease that is spread through air or water

Share your answers.

Which diseases on this page are infectious?   79

Workbooks, p. 79
Classic Classroom Activities, Unit 6
Related Dictionary Pages
• The Body, pp. 74–75
• Symptoms and Injuries, p. 78
• Health Care, pp. 80–81
• Medical Emergencies, p. 82
• First Aid, p. 83

TOPIC NOTES

In the U.S., new and improved drug therapies, vaccines , technologies and surgical procedures have done much to improve health care. Most consumers rely on traditional "Western medicine" for the diagnosis and treatment of illness. However, there is growing acceptance of alternative, even ancient healing approaches.

Flu, like the common cold, is a virus that spreads rapidly in schools and in the workplace.

The World Health Organization estimates that 17 million people worldwide have been infected with HIV. By the year 2000, an estimated 30 to 40 million people will have been infected.

TEACHING TIPS
Related Vocabulary

pneumonia	benign
hepatitis	contagious
bronchitis	radiation
appendicitis	chemotherapy
heart attack	stroke
arthritis	antibiotics

Pick one disease that your class wants to learn more about. Check the phone book to find a community clinic that will send a speaker to your class.

⚠ Respect confidentiality and privacy when discussing medical conditions.

INTRODUCE THE TOPIC

Describe pictures on the page as you use the target language several times. *Look at #3. The boy has an ear infection. His ear hurts. Ear infections are not contagious. He needs antibiotics to get well.*

Tell a story about your experience with a common illness or medical condition. *My grandfather has diabetes. His pancreas doesn't produce insulin. My family helps him watch his diet. He can't eat many sweet foods.*

TEACH THE NEW WORDS

Ask students a series of *or* questions about the pictures. *Look at #5. Does the boy have measles or mumps?* (measles) *Look at #16. Do parasites develop in the lungs or intestines?* (intestines)

PROVIDE PRACTICE
Chalkboard Activities

△ Have students categorize vocabulary:

1. **Visible**	**Not Visible**
measles	*asthma*

2. **Vaccine**	**No Vaccine**
chicken pox	*tuberculosis*

Conversations

△ Put models on the board and practice. Make appropriate substitutions.

A: ABC School. Can I help you?
B: Yes, this is *[José Ortega's mom]. [José]* is sick with *a cold* today.
  2. the flu 3. an ear infection 4. strep throat 5. the measles 6. chicken pox

A: Dr. *[Weiss]*, do I have *asthma*?
B: Your test result is negative, but let's run another test to make sure.
  9. diabetes 12. brain cancer 13. TB 16. intestinal parasites, etc.

Interview Questions

1. Which childhood illnesses did you have?
2. Is there a history of cancer or heart disease in your family?

Listening: Listen and Write

△ Have students write the number, e.g.:

1. *Pain, fever and dizziness are signs of an ear infection.* (#3)
2. *Diabetes is not a contagious disease.* (#9) Etc.

EXPAND THE LESSON
Problem Solving

△ Have students brainstorm solutions. *Eva, age 14, has a serious disease. Her parents' religion forbids medical treatment. The doctors say she could die without treatment. Who should decide for Mona?*

Unit 6 Health Care page 80

Workbooks, pp. 80–81
Classic Classroom Activities, Unit 6
Related Dictionary Pages
• The Body, pp. 74–75
• Symptoms and Injuries, p. 78
• Illnesses and Medical Conditions, p. 79
• Medical Emergencies, p. 82
• First Aid, p. 83

TOPIC NOTES

In the U.S., Americans annually spend more than 30 billion dollars for pharmaceutical and health-care products. There are more than half a million **over-the-counter** items to prevent and treat specific conditions and maintain health.

TEACHING TIPS

Related Vocabulary

ice pack*	homeopathic medication
refill	inoculation/shot
inhaler	creme/salve
decongestant	optician*
brand name	nutritionist
generic	child-proof
time-release	side effect

Grammar: Word Endings *-ist, -logy*
The suffixes *-ist* and *-logy* indicate nouns. The suffix *-ist* "a person who is skilled in— or works at—". The suffix *-logy* is Latin, and means "the science of." *A pharmacist understands pharmacology, the science of drugs.*

- Review cardinal numbers and page 57, *Weights and Measures,* to help students discuss typical dosages of liquid medicines. Bring in realia to help students read drug labels.
- Review page 78, *Symptoms and Injuries,* and page 79, *Illnesses and Medical Conditions,* so that students can talk about various treatments.

Health Care

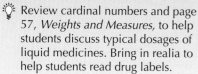

1. crutches	9. pharmacy	A. **Get** bed rest.
2. humidifier	10. pharmacist	B. **Drink** fluids.
3. heating pad	11. prescription medication	C. **Change** your diet.
4. air purifier	12. over-the-counter medication	D. **Exercise.**
5. walker	13. prescription	E. **Get** an injection.
6. wheelchair	14. prescription label	F. **Take** medicine.
7. cane	15. warning label	
8. sling		

More vocabulary
dosage: how much medicine you take and how many times a day you take it
expiration date: the last day the medicine can be used

treatment: something you do to get better
Staying in bed, drinking fluids, and getting physical therapy are treatments.
An injection that stops a person from getting a serious disease is called **an immunization** or **a vaccination.**

80

INTRODUCE THE TOPIC

Bring in a variety of medications and health care products from your medicine cabinet. Ask students to identify as many items as they can. Talk about the symptoms and/or illnesses that these items treat. *An antacid is used for an upset stomach or indigestion.*

Ask students to look at page 80, treatments A–F, and give reasons for recommending each one. *Get bed rest if you have the flu. Take medicine if you have an infection.*

TEACH THE NEW WORDS

Ask students a series of *or* questions about the health care pictures. *Is #5 a walker or wheelchair?* (walker)

PROVIDE PRACTICE

Chalkboard Activities

△ Have students categorize vocabulary:

1. External Use | **Internal Use**
heating pad | *cold tablets*

2. People | **Products**
optometrist | *eyeglasses*

Conversations

△ Put models on the board and practice. Make appropriate substitutions.

A: What kind of *walker* should I buy?
B: Talk to your *[orthopedist]. [He]* can advise you which one is best.
    1. crutches 6. wheelchair 7. cane
    8. sling 31. brace

A: I need some *pain reliever.* Can you help me?
B: Look on aisle *[10].*
    17. cold tablets 18. antacid 19. vitamins
    20. cough syrup 21. throat lozenges
    22. eyedrops 23. nasal spray 24. ointment

Interview Questions

1. Where can you buy over-the-counter medication? prescription medication?
2. Do you have a humidifier or air purifier in your home? If you do, why?
3. Where do you keep medications?
4. What kind of pain reliever do you prefer? Why?
5. Have you ever worn a cast? a sling?
6. Do you need eyeglasses or contact lenses? When do you wear them?
7. Have you ever gotten acupuncture? Why?
8. Have you ever gone to a chiropractor?

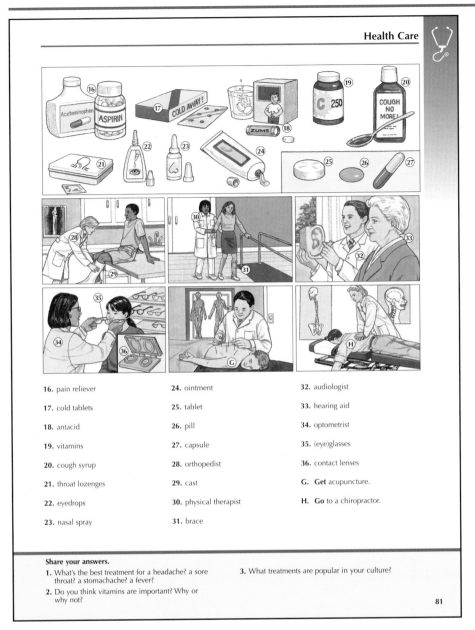

Health Care

16. pain reliever
17. cold tablets
18. antacid
19. vitamins
20. cough syrup
21. throat lozenges
22. eyedrops
23. nasal spray

24. ointment
25. tablet
26. pill
27. capsule
28. orthopedist
29. cast
30. physical therapist
31. brace

32. audiologist
33. hearing aid
34. optometrist
35. (eye)glasses
36. contact lenses
G. **Get** acupuncture.
H. **Go** to a chiropractor.

Share your answers.
1. What's the best treatment for a headache? a sore throat? a stomachache? a fever?
2. Do you think vitamins are important? Why or why not?
3. What treatments are popular in your culture?

81

Listening: 🔊 #26, p. 218

"Ben Knows Best" Students listen and point to the health care remedies.

EXPAND THE LESSON

Discussion Questions

1. Thousands of Americans need hospital treatment each year because they misuse medications. How can people use medicine safely?
2. What are some items that are important for a home medicine chest?
3. Do you prefer to use brand name or generic medications? Why?
4. In your opinion, how should government money for health care or medical research be spent?
5. What "alternative" treatments do you know that can be used instead of over-the-counter medicine?

6. You are organizing a community health fair. Look at pages 80–81. Which health-care professionals do you want to invite? What information would you like them to discuss?

Problem Solving

△ Have students brainstorm solutions. *Your four-year-old nephew has an ear infection and a bad cough. He refuses to swallow his cough syrup or pills. How can you get him to take his medicine?*

Language Workout

△ Copy these sentences on the board and discuss their meanings.
1. Buster hit Michael. Michael's brother gave Buster a black eye. Buster got *a taste of his own medicine.*

2. David's girlfriend gave back his engagement ring and started dating his best friend. *It was a bitter pill to swallow for David.*

Backward Dictionary

△ Give definitions or descriptions of the target vocabulary and have students guess what the word is. *It's made of plaster. You need it to heal a broken leg or arm. What is it?* (cast) *They're made of soft plastic. You put them in your eyes. They help you see better. What are they?* (contact lenses)

GAMES

Definition Bingo

1. Have students fold a blank sheet of paper into 16 squares. Show students the different rows on the paper: horizontal, vertical, and diagonal.
2. Dictate 16 health care words and have students write the items in random order on their pages, one item per square, until all the squares are filled.
3. Tell students they will be circling different words on their papers, as they hear you define them. Explain that when they get four circled words in a row, they shout "Bingo!"
4. Give a sample definition. *This helps keep the air clean.* Make sure all students have circled the word *air purifier* on their papers.
5. Call out definitions until one student gets four in a row. Check the student's work, and write his or her name on the board. Instruct him or her to try to get another set in a row and continue the game.
6. Continue playing until five players have gotten four in a row.

Class Go-Around: A Shopping Trip

1. Begin by saying, *I'm going to the pharmacy because I have to buy some eyedrops.*
2. The first volunteer repeats the sentence and adds another item. *I'm going to the pharmacy because I have to buy some eyedrops and cold tablets.*
3. The next student volunteer continues the chain by adding another item.
4. Stop after the tenth item or when a student makes a mistake, and begin the game again.

81

Workbooks, pp. 82
Classic Classroom Activities, Unit 6
Related Dictionary Pages
- The Body, pp. 74–75
- Emergencies and Natural Disasters, pp. 102–103
- Job Safety, p. 147

TOPIC NOTES

In the U.S., people with medical emergencies are usually taken to the emergency room in hospitals. In most places, it is possible to call 911 for a paramedic and an ambulance. Paramedics are able to administer first aid.

Some of the emergencies on this page, such as **having an allergic reaction, burning yourself, bleeding, or falling** can be minor problems that do not require medical attention. They are included here because in their extreme form they are life threatening. *Shock* has several meanings: as a medical condition, **to be in shock** is an acute state of physical collapse; whereas **to get an electric shock** is to receive a sudden charge of electricity through the body, which stimulates the nerves and contracts the muscles. Finally, *to be shocked* is also an emotional state.

TEACHING TIPS
Related Vocabulary

paramedic	ambulance*
wound	pain
miscarriage	puncture
seizure	coma
fracture	faint
heatstroke	hypothermia
snakebite	panic

💡 Review pages 74–75, *The Body,* so that students can describe medical emergencies if the need arises.

Medical Emergencies

A. **be** injured / **be** hurt
B. **be** unconscious
C. **be** in shock
D. **have** a heart attack
E. **have** an allergic reaction
F. **get** an electric shock

G. **get** frostbite
H. **burn** (your)self
I. **drown**
J. **swallow** poison
K. **overdose** on drugs
L. **choke**

M. **bleed**
N. **can't** breathe
O. **fall**
P. **break** a bone

Grammar point: past tense

burn	—	burned	choke	—	choked	bleed	—	bled
drown	—	drowned	be	—	was, were	can't	—	couldn't
swallow	—	swallowed	have	—	had	fall	—	fell
overdose	—	overdosed	get	—	got	break	—	broke

82

INTRODUCE THE TOPIC

Tell a story about a medical emergency you helped take care of, read about, or saw on TV. Talk about how it happened, what the outcome was, and what different people at the scene did.

Bring in detergent, a bottle of over-the-counter medication, such as aspirin, and a pair of scissors. Talk about the emergencies resulting from accidents with these items or their improper use.

TEACH THE NEW WORDS

Ask students to identify the number of a particular picture based on your description. *She stayed outside too long. Now she's so cold she can't feel her fingers. She got frostbite. (G) She climbed up on the washing machine and drank some bleach. She swallowed poison. (J)*

PROVIDE PRACTICE
Chalkboard Activities

△ Have students categorize vocabulary:

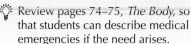

Emergency (Always)	Emergency (Sometimes)
be unconscious	*bleed*

Conversations

△ Put models on the board and practice. Make appropriate substitutions.

A: 9-1-1. What is the problem?
B: My friend *is injured*.
A: What is the address and telephone number?
B: *[738 1st Street, Torrey. 555-9545]*.
A: We'll send an ambulance right away.

B. is unconscious C. is in shock
D. is having a heart attack
E. is having an allergic reaction etc.

Interview Questions

1. What do you do if you burn yourself?
2. What do you do if you cut yourself with a knife?

Listening: 📼 #27, p. 219
"County Hospital, 4:00, Channel 14"
Students point to emergencies as they hear them described.

EXPAND THE LESSON
Discussion Questions

1. Many people have different ideas about what to do in an emergency. Where can you get good information about first aid?
2. What are some things you can do to prevent small children from drowning in a pool? On a boat? In the ocean?
3. Many people get hurt in their homes. What are some things you can do to make your home a safer place?

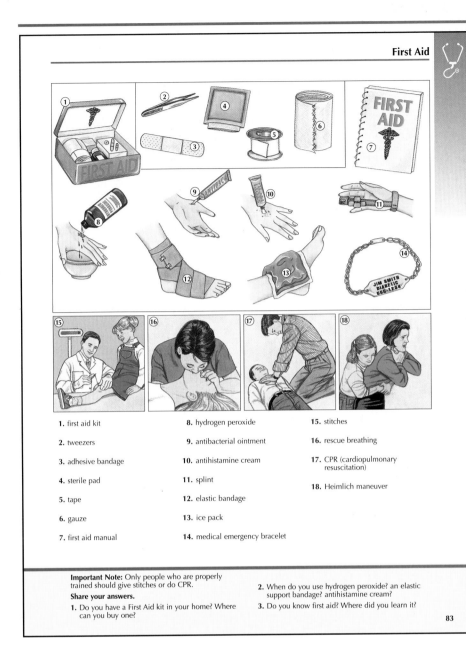

First Aid

1. first aid kit

2. tweezers

3. adhesive bandage

4. sterile pad

5. tape

6. gauze

7. first aid manual

8. hydrogen peroxide

9. antibacterial ointment

10. antihistamine cream

11. splint

12. elastic bandage

13. ice pack

14. medical emergency bracelet

15. stitches

16. rescue breathing

17. CPR (cardiopulmonary resuscitation)

18. Heimlich maneuver

Important Note: Only people who are properly trained should give stitches or do CPR.

Share your answers.

1. Do you have a First Aid kit in your home? Where can you buy one?

2. When do you use hydrogen peroxide? an elastic support bandage? antihistamine cream?

3. Do you know first aid? Where did you learn it?

83

Workbooks, p. 83
Classic Classroom Activities, Unit 6
Related Dictionary Pages
• The Body, pp. 74–75
• Symptoms and Injuries, p. 78
• Illnesses and Medical Conditions, p. 79
• Medical Emergencies, p. 82

TOPIC NOTES

In the U.S., 911 is the universal telephone number for emergency aid. Operators can call for ambulances, firefighters, and the police department.

First aid is help you give victims of a medical emergency until they can receive medical attention. A **first aid kit** should be kept closed and out of the reach of children.

The **Heimlich maneuver** is given when a person is choking and can no longer cough or breathe.

Cardiopulmonary resuscitation, or **CPR,** is a combination of chest compression and mouth-to-mouth resuscitation, and requires training. It is given when a person's heart has stopped beating.

Rescue breathing (mouth-to-mouth resuscitation or artificial respiration) is given when someone has stopped breathing.

TEACHING TIPS
Related Vocabulary

iodine	alcohol
syrup of ipecac	Epsom salts
boric acid	smelling salts
to save a life	
internal use only	
external/topical use only	

⚠ Students may not know what a particular product is used for. Teaching how to read warning labels is a worthwhile follow-up lesson.

INTRODUCE THE TOPIC

Ask students to look at the dictionary page and name the items they have in their homes.

Tell students a story about a time you used one of the items on this page. Talk about the injury or medical problem and how you took care of it.

Act out how a person removes a splinter. Speak as you do the actions. *I have a little piece of wood in my finger. I'm going to take it out with tweezers.*

TEACH THE NEW WORDS

Ask students to identify the number of a particular picture based on your description. *You use this if you have a cut. It doesn't burn. It's hydrogen peroxide. (#8) You use this if you sprained or broke a finger. The finger can't move when you use it. It's a splint. (#11)*

PROVIDE PRACTICE
Chalkboard Activities

△ Draw a large outline of a body. Have students write the first aid item on the board on the area of the body where it is used.

Conversations

△ Put models on the board and practice. Make appropriate substitutions.

A: Excuse me, where can I find *tape*?
B: On aisle 6, *[near the back]*.
A: Thanks for your help.
> **6. gauze 8. hydrogen peroxide
> 9. antibacterial ointment 10. antihistamine cream**

A: I really want to learn how to do *the Heimlich maneuver*.
B: Why?
A: It saved my friend's life!
> **16. rescue breathing 17. CPR**

Interview Questions

1. Do you have a first aid kit? Where do you keep it? What's in it?
2. What do you usually put on a small cut?
3. What do you put on an insect bite?

Listening: 🔊 #27, p. 219
"County Hospital, 4:00, Channel 14"
Students point to first aid items or procedures as they hear them named.

EXPAND THE LESSON
Discussion Questions

1. A medical emergency ID bracelet tells medical personnel about serious medical conditions. What are some reasons to wear one?
2. What are some good reasons to learn CPR and rescue breathing?

Workbooks, p. 84
Classic Classroom Activities, Unit 6
Related Dictionary Pages
• The Body, pp. 74–75
• Medical and Dental Exams, p. 85
• A Hospital, pp. 86–87

TOPIC NOTES

In the U.S., there are public and private clinics. Public clinics use federal money and generally charge less for services than private clinics.

Workers often receive health benefits through their companies. The company's Health Management Organization (HMO) may have its own clinics and doctors, or may pay part of the cost of private care.

The **doctor/physician** depicted on this page is a *primary care provider.* Primary care providers are general practitioners (GPs), that is, doctors who can treat most typical health problems.

TEACHING TIPS
Related Vocabulary

appointment	cleaning
health insurance	plaque
midwife	gum disease
dentures/false teeth	headgear
bridge	retainer

Pronunciation: The /th/ sound Demonstrate the /th/ sound in the words *stethoscope, thermometer,* and *orthodontist.* Contrast that sound with the /t/ sound present in the words *doctor, tartar,* and *dentist,* and the /sh/ sound in *patient* and *receptionist.*

🔅 Teach the medical clinic and medical exam sections, pages 84 and 85, before the dental clinic and dental exam sections.

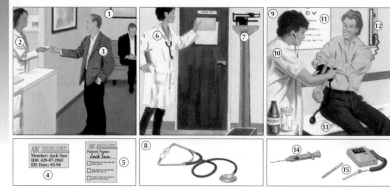

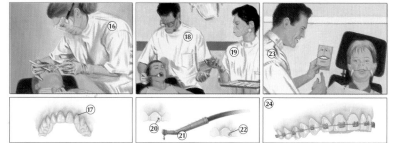

Clinics

Medical clinic

1. waiting room	**6.** doctor	**11.** eye chart
2. receptionist	**7.** scale	**12.** blood pressure gauge
3. patient	**8.** stethoscope	**13.** examination table
4. insurance card	**9.** examining room	**14.** syringe
5. insurance form	**10.** nurse	**15.** thermometer

Dental clinic

16. dental hygienist	**19.** dental assistant	**22.** filling
17. tartar	**20.** cavity	**23.** orthodontist
18. dentist	**21.** drill	**24.** braces

84

INTRODUCE THE TOPIC

Talk about the last time you went to a medical or dental clinic. Tell what happened to you, how long you waited, etc.

Ask questions about page 84. *How many people do you see?* (13) *How many people are working?* (7) *How many doctors do you see?* (3) *nurses?* (2)

TEACH THE NEW WORDS

Ask a series of *yes/no* questions about the scenes. *Is the receptionist in the examining room?* (no) *Is the doctor near the scale?* (yes), etc.

PROVIDE PRACTICE
Chalkboard Activities

△ Have students categorize vocabulary:

Clinic Personnel	**Equipment**
receptionist	*scale*

Conversations

△ Put models on the board and practice. Make appropriate substitutions.

A: Hi, I'm *[Ari Raz]*, a new patient.
B: Do you have an *insurance card*?
A: Yes, here it is.
  5. insurance form.

A: Where's the *stethoscope*?
B: It's in the examining room.
  12. blood pressure gauge 14. syringe
  15. thermometer

A: *[Pat]* really wants to be *a doctor*.
B: I know. It's all *[she]* talks about.
  10. a nurse 16. dental hygienist
  18. a dentist 19. a dental assistant
  23. an orthodontist

Interview Questions

1. Do you have medical insurance?
2. When did you last see a doctor?
3. How often do you see a dentist?
4. Have you ever had a cavity?
5. Have you ever had braces?

Listening: 📼 #28, p. 219

"The Patient Doctor" While a patient talks about an exam, students write the numbers of the words they hear.

Problem Solving

△ Have students brainstorm solutions.
  1. *It's 3:00, and Linda had a 2:00 doctor's appointment. She is still waiting and no one has given her an explanation. What can Linda do?*
  2. *Toshi has a cavity but he doesn't like his dentist. What advice would you give him?*

Discussion Question

Why do you think U.S. medical care is so expensive? How does it compare to medical care in your country?

Medical and Dental Exams

A. **make** an appointment
B. **check**...blood pressure
C. **take**...temperature
D. **listen** to...heart
E. **look** in...throat
F. **examine**...eyes
G. **draw**...blood
H. **get** an X ray

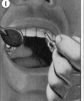
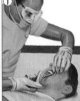

I. **clean**...teeth
J. **give**...a shot of anesthetic
K. **drill** a tooth
L. **fill** a cavity
M. **pull** a tooth

More vocabulary
get a checkup: to go for a medical exam
extract a tooth: to pull out a tooth

Share your answers.
1. What is the average cost of a medical exam in your area?
2. Some people are nervous at the dentist's office. What can they do to relax?

85

Workbooks, p. 85
Classic Classroom Activities, Unit 6
Related Dictionary Pages
• The Body, pp. 74–75
• A Hospital, pp. 86–87

TOPIC NOTES
In the U.S., the most common reason for seeing a doctor or dentist is for a general exam, or **check up.** This is because U.S. medicine stresses prevention and early treatment of serious illnesses. Check ups help doctors find health problems early, before they become difficult to treat.

After the doctor examines the patient, she may ask the patient to take several tests (X rays, blood tests, EKGs, MRIs, etc.). These tests are often expensive, and insurance does not always cover the cost.

📁 Prior to the use of anesthetic, most people were terrified to go to the dentist. In 1846, William Morton, an American, gave a public exhibition of the use of ether and dentists as well as surgeons began using anesthetics for their procedures.

TEACHING TIPS
Related Vocabulary

referral	cap a tooth
cancel	rinse* (mouth)
cancellation	perform a root canal

💡 Have students identify the people and medical equipment from page 84, *Clinics,* that also appear on page 85.

INTRODUCE THE TOPIC
Model making an appointment with a doctor or a dentist.

Draw a mock eye chart on the board or overhead and ask students to tell you what happens during an eye exam.

Ask questions about students' experiences at the dentist. *Have you ever had an anesthetic? Did the dentist ever pull a tooth? fill a cavity? were you relaxed? nervous? asleep?*

TEACH THE NEW WORDS
Act out one of the sequences with student volunteers playing the part of patients. *Do you want to make an appointment?* (yes) *OK, come in now. Sit on the examining table. First I will check your blood pressure. Great. Now I will listen to your heart. Sounds good. Etc.*

PROVIDE PRACTICE
Chalkboard Activities
△ Have students categorize vocabulary.

| Actions | Body Parts | Other |
| *make* | *heart* | *appointment* |

Conversations
△ Put models on the board and practice. Make appropriate substitutions.

A: Sit on the examining table, *[Mr. Raz].* I'm going to check your *blood pressure.*
B: Is everything OK?
A: Everything looks fine.
  C. take your temperature
  D. listen to your heart E. look in your throat
  F. examine your eyes
A: Just sit back, *[Ms. Chin].* I have to *clean your teeth* now.
B: Is it going to hurt?
A: Not too much.
  J. give you an anesthetic K. drill a tooth
  L. fill a cavity M. pull a tooth

Listening: 📼 #28, p. 219
"The Patient Doctor" While a patient talks about an exam, students point to the pictures as they are described.

EXPANDING THE LESSON
Charades
1. Write the phrases A–M on 13 separate slips of paper and put them in a hat or box.
2. Divide the class into two teams.
3. Students take turns picking a phrase and acting it out for their teams.
4. Teams get a point for each action they guess.
5. The game ends when all the slips are gone.

Unit 6   A Hospital   page 86

Workbooks, pp. 86–87
Classic Classroom Activities, Unit 6
Related Dictionary Pages
• The Body, pp. 74–75
• Clinics, p. 84
• Medical and Dental Exams, p. 85

TOPIC NOTES

In the U.S., people go to hospitals for medical emergencies, surgeries, outpatient testing and procedures, and health counseling. Physicians are usually affiliated with a hospital where they send their patients when necessary.

As technology improves and health care costs rise, hospital stays are getting shorter and shorter. Many surgeries that were in-patient in 1985 (e.g., gall bladder, appendectomy, and hysterectomy) are now regularly performed as outpatient surgeries.

Hospital staff includes doctors, **nurses, orderlies,** social workers, clerical workers, and accountants.

TEACHING TIPS
Related Vocabulary

specialist	billing department
general practitioner	operation/surgery
health-care worker	major surgery
social worker	routine procedure
ambulance	anesthesia
inpatient	outpatient

Usage: Point out that the nouns *nurse, doctor,* and *volunteer* can also be used as verbs.

☼ Review pages 74–75, *The Body,* so that students are able to talk about the specialists named on page 86.

A Hospital

Hospital staff

1. obstetrician	4. pediatrician	7. ophthalmologist
2. internist	5. radiologist	8. X-ray technician
3. cardiologist	6. psychiatrist	

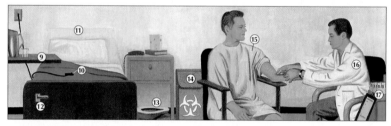

Patient's room

9. bed table	12. bed control	15. hospital gown
10. call button	13. bedpan	16. lab technician
11. hospital bed	14. medical waste disposal	17. blood work / blood test

More vocabulary

nurse practitioner: a nurse licensed to give medical exams

specialist: a doctor who only treats specific medical problems

gynecologist: a specialist who examines and treats women

nurse midwife: a nurse practitioner who examines pregnant women and delivers babies

86

INTRODUCE THE TOPIC

Talk about a hospital experience you've had, the type of doctor you had, and how long you stayed.

Ask questions about students' hospital experiences. *Have you ever stayed overnight at a hospital? Have you ever been in the emergency room? Etc.*

Bring in a picture of a new mother and father holding their infant in a hospital room. Discuss the situation with the students. *Where are they? What is happening? How do they feel?*

TEACH THE NEW WORDS

Ask students a series of *yes/no* questions about the hospital staff on pages 86–87. *Does the obstetrician work with pregnant women?* (yes) *Does the ophthalmologist examine the ears?* (no)

Describe the scenes, emphasizing the target vocabulary. *The bed table is on the left, near the bed. There's some water on the bed table.*

PROVIDE PRACTICE
Chalkboard Activities

△ Have students categorize vocabulary:

1. Medical Staff   **Nonmedical Staff**
    obstetrician   *volunteer*

2. Clothing   **Equipment**
    hospital gown   *vital signs monitor*

Conversations

△ Put models on the board and practice. Make appropriate substitutions.

A: [Ms. Garcia], I want you to see <u>an obstetrician</u>.
B: But you're my doctor!
A: You need to see a specialist.
    2. an internist 3. a cardiologist
    6. a psychiatrist

A: I need some help with this <u>call button</u>.
B: I'll be right there.
    9. bed table 11. hospital bed
    12. bed control 15. hospital gown

A: Who has the <u>medication tray</u> for this patient?
B: The <u>volunteer</u> does.
    17. blood work/16. lab technician
    20. medical charts/22. RN

A Hospital

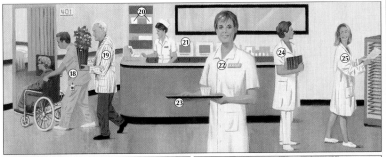

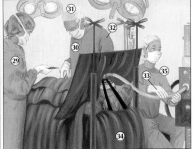

Nurse's station

18. orderly

19. volunteer

20. medical charts

21. vital signs monitor

22. RN (registered nurse)

23. medication tray

24. LPN (licensed practical nurse)/
    LVN (licensed vocational nurse)

25. dietician

Emergency room

26. emergency medical technician
    (EMT)

27. IV (intravenous drip)

28. stretcher/gurney

Operating room

29. surgical nurse

30. surgeon

31. surgical cap

32. surgical gown

33. latex gloves

34. operating table

35. anesthesiologist

Practice asking for the hospital staff.
Please get the nurse. I have a question for her.
Where's the anesthesiologist? I need to talk to her.
I'm looking for the lab technician. Have you seen him?

Share your answers.
1. Have you ever been to an emergency room? Who helped you?
2. Have you ever been in the hospital? How long did you stay?

87

Interview Questions

1. Is there a hospital in your neighborhood?
2. Have you ever been in an emergency room?
3. Have you ever worked in a hospital?
4. Which job would you want in this hospital?
5. Who is the most important person in this hospital? Why?

Listening: Interactive Dictation

△ Have students close their books. Dictate these hospital guidelines. Speak naturally and encourage students to ask for clarification. *(Who? They will what?)*

1. *Place all belongings on the bed table or in the closet.*
2. *Use the call button to call the nurse.*

3. *Use the bed control to raise or lower the hospital bed.*
4. *Wear your hospital gown while you are in your room.*
5. *You will get your medication tray every four hours.*
6. *The lab technician will draw blood every day.*
7. *The anesthesiologist will talk to you before the operation.*
8. *The surgeon will talk to you after the operation.*

EXPANDING THE LESSON
Problem Solving

△ Have students brainstorm solutions.

1. *Grace Alvarez' baby was born in the hospital on Monday. The hospital wants to send her home after 24 hours. Grace is very tired and wants to stay one more day. What should she do?*

2. *Karl Simms is afraid of hospitals. His doctor just told him he has to have his gall bladder removed. This is a simple operation, but Karl doesn't want it because he is too scared to go to the hospital. What advice would you give to Karl?*

Discussion Questions

1. How long do you think someone should stay in the hospital if they have a routine operation? a major operation?
2. What are the benefits of a national health care system? What are the benefits of a private health care system?
3. What are some ways you would improve hospital health care?
4. What qualities should people have if they want to be health care professionals?

Writing Activity

△ Have students imagine they are new volunteers at a hospital. Have them write a letter to a friend describing who and what they saw on their first day there.

GAMES
Definition Bingo

1. Have students fold a blank sheet of paper into 16 squares.
2. Dictate 16 hospital items and have students write the items in random order on their papers.
3. Tell students they will be circling different words on their papers, as they hear you define them. Explain that when they get four circled words in a row (horizontally, vertically, or diagonally), they shout "Bingo!"
4. Give a sample definition. *This doctor works with patients who have heart disease.* Make sure all students have circled the word *cardiologist* on their papers.
5. Call out definitions until one student gets Bingo.
6. Continue playing until five players have gotten Bingo.

Questions Only!

1. Divide students into groups of 4–8 and have each group choose a recorder.
2. Have students look at pages 86–87 and come up with as many questions as they can about the scenes. *(Who is wearing a surgical gown?)*
3. Recorders write their groups' questions on the board.
4. The group with the most correct questions wins.

Unit 7   City Streets   page 88

Workbooks, pp. 88–89
Classic Classroom Activities, Unit 7
Related Dictionary Pages
- Prepositions, p. 13
- An Intersection, pp. 90–91
- A Mall, pp. 92–93
- Prepositions of Motion, p. 105

TOPIC NOTES

In the U.S., during the 70s and 80s, many cities had serious financial problems. Independently owned businesses closed and homeless populations moved onto city streets. In the 90s, renovation of these downtown areas began, with new housing, new performing arts centers, and new businesses coming into the cities.

A **church,** a **synagogue,** and a **mosque** are also called *houses of worship.*

Many people go to **health clubs** before or after work for daily exercise.

TEACHING TIPS
Related Vocabulary

street*	around the corner*
intersection*	between*
across*	turn left/right*
next to*	go up/down the street

Usage: We say *go to the library, go to the coffeeshop,* etc. However, for church, synagogue, school, and city hall, we drop the article *the:*
go to church, go to school, etc.
Note: We say *go downtown.*

Arrange classroom aisles to create "city streets." Write different city locations on pieces of paper and put them on students' desks. Have student volunteers walk through the "city," following your directions to specific locations.

City Streets

1. fire station	6. church	11. movie theater
2. coffee shop	7. hospital	12. gas station
3. bank	8. park	13. furniture store
4. car dealership	9. synagogue	14. hardware store
5. hotel	10. theater	15. barber shop

More vocabulary
skyscraper: a very tall office building
downtown/city center: the area in a city with the city hall, courts, and businesses

Practice giving your destination.
I'm going to go downtown.
I have to go to the post office.

88

INTRODUCE THE TOPIC

Ask questions about the city the students live in or near. *Do we live in a large city or a small city? Is this school downtown? Do you like to go downtown? What do you do there? Is it OK to walk around the city at night?*

Invite students to name the different businesses or locations they know in their city or town. List their ideas on the board and have them tell you which ones are near the school.

Bring in pictures of four different city skylines: for example, San Francisco, Paris, New York, and Seoul. Have students try to guess the identities of the cities.

Talk about your most recent experience in the nearest city, or describe a typical trip downtown.

TEACH THE NEW WORDS

Describe each location in the city, emphasizing the target vocabulary. *The motel is on Main Street, at the end of the street. You can sleep here if you are visiting the city. The courthouse is next to city hall. They are both government buildings. The courthouse is where judges and lawyers work.*

Say each word and have students repeat the word and point to the correct picture.

PROVIDE PRACTICE
Chalkboard Activity

△ Have students categorize vocabulary:

Government	**House of Worship**
post office	synagogue
Service Business	**Other Business**
motel	office building

Conversations

△ Put models on the board and practice. Make appropriate substitutions.

A: Excuse me, is there a *motel* near here?
B: Yes, there is. It's on *[Main].*
  2. coffee shop 24. office building, etc.

A: Where are you going?
B: First I'm going to the *post office;* then I'm going to the *barber shop.*
A: Wait. I'll come too!
  14. hardware store/8. park
  16. bakery/20. market
  28. library/3. bank, etc.

A: How do I get to the *hotel* from here?
B: We're at the corner of Main and 1st. *[Go straight on Main.]* The *hotel* is on Main. You can't miss it!
  7. hospital 19. police station 21. health club, etc.

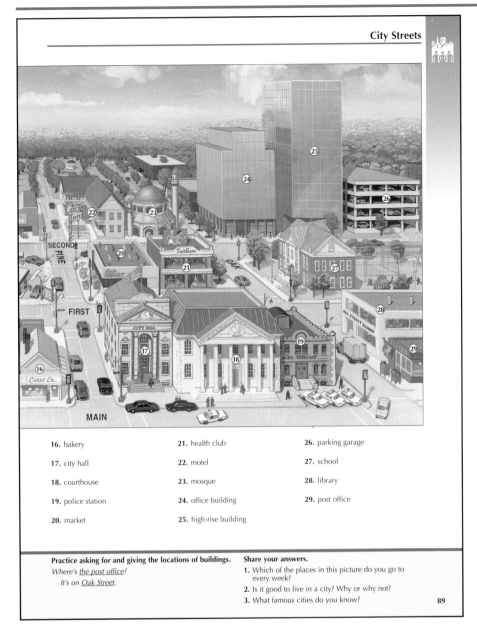

City Streets

16. bakery
17. city hall
18. courthouse
19. police station
20. market
21. health club
22. motel
23. mosque
24. office building
25. high-rise building
26. parking garage
27. school
28. library
29. post office

Practice asking for and giving the locations of buildings.
Where's the post office?
*   It's on Oak Street.*

Share your answers.
1. Which of the places in this picture do you go to every week?
2. Is it good to live in a city? Why or why not?
3. What famous cities do you know?

89

Interview Questions
1. Name three cities you know.
2. Do you like to go downtown?
3. Where do you go when you go downtown?
4. Which of these places do you go to every week?
5. Is there a park near your home? What street is it on?
6. In your opinion, what's the best park in the city?
7. In your opinion, what's the best market in the city? What street is it on?

Listening: 🔊 #29 p. 220
"Where Ya' Goin'?" Have students listen to people talking about places downtown. Students point to the place that is being described.

EXPAND THE LESSON
Problem Solving
△ Have students brainstorm solutions.
1. *Misha moved to Chicago a month ago from a small town in Armenia. He only goes out to work and to go to school. Where can he go to start making friends?*
2. *Fiona has jury duty. She doesn't live downtown and doesn't know how to get to the courthouse. How could she get directions?*

Discussion Questions
1. Urban planners decide how cities should look. What changes do you think they need to make in your city or a city near your home?
2. In many cities, homeless people sleep on the street and in parks. What can we do about homelessness?

Drawing Activity
Note: You will need construction paper, tape, scissors, and markers.
1. Elicit a list of places in the city from students. Write the places on the board as students call them out.
2. Demonstrate how to construct a model of one of these places using the materials above.

3. Ask each student to choose a different place from the list on the chalkboard and construct it.
4. Once students have completed construction, they show their buildings to the class: *This is (a/the) _____. People come here to _____.*

GAMES
Memory Game
1. Divide the class into two teams.
2. Have students study the scene on pages 88–89 for two minutes and close their books.
3. Alternately quiz the teams with true/false statements about the scene. *The motel is on Main Street.* (false) *There are children at school.* (true)
4. Correct answers get one point.
5. The game ends after 15 statements.

Definition Relay
Note: You will need two bells.
1. Divide the class into two teams.
2. Assign each team a different bell.
3. The first person on each team gets the team bell.
4. Make a statement about a place in the city, but don't name the place. *This is where I go to buy a car.*
5. The first person to think of the answer rings the bell and names the vocabulary item. *A car dealership!*
6. Teams get a point for each correct answer.
7. Bells are passed to the next team member who responds to another statement about a different place.
8. The game ends when one team has 10 points.

Unit 7   An Intersection   page 90

Workbooks, pp. 90–91
Classic Classroom Activities, Unit 7
Related Dictionary Pages
• City Streets, pp. 88–89
• A Mall, pp. 92–93
• Places to Go, p. 152

TOPIC NOTES

In the U.S., many new immigrants become small-business owners. They open up shops similar to the ones depicted here. Small businesses employ the second largest number of workers in the country next to service businesses such as hotels.

Convenience stores are small markets that sell food, over-the-counter medication, drinks, grocery items, and sometimes beer. They usually open early and close late.

TEACHING TIPS

Related Vocabulary

video arcade	party store
fabric store	art supply store
buy*/get*	small business

- ☀ Review *buy* and *go to* to be able to talk about doing errands.

- ☀ Review the directions *next to, across from,* and *around the corner.* Talk about where various stores and places are located on pages 90–91.

- ☀ Bring in a telephone book. Have students look up the names of similar small businesses in your area. Brainstorm a list of questions about prices, available services, etc. Have students call or visit these places and report the information to the class.

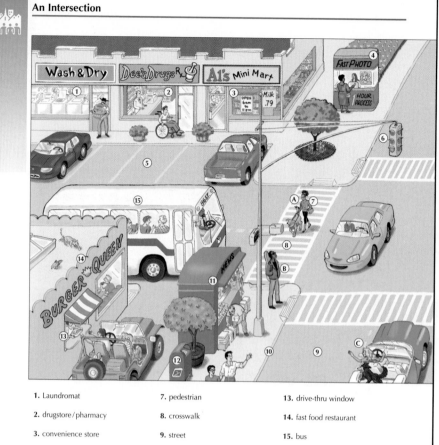

An Intersection

1. Laundromat	7. pedestrian	13. drive-thru window
2. drugstore/pharmacy	8. crosswalk	14. fast food restaurant
3. convenience store	9. street	15. bus
4. photo shop	10. curb	A. **cross** the street
5. parking space	11. newsstand	B. **wait** for the light
6. traffic light	12. mailbox	C. **drive** a car

More vocabulary
neighborhood: the area close to your home
do errands: to make a short trip from your home to buy or pick up something

Talk about where to buy things.
You can buy newspapers at a newsstand.
You can buy donuts at a donut shop.
You can buy food at a convenience store.

90

INTRODUCE THE TOPIC

Name and describe the stores and other vocabulary words in the picture. Talk about the people and what they are doing. Ask questions and answer them yourself if students can't. *Look at the Laundromat on page 90. What are people doing there? That's right—washing their clothes. Look at the woman going into the drugstore. Maybe she has a headache and needs some aspirin. What do you think?*

Write on the board a few stores in your area that are similar to the ones on this page: a nearby Laundromat, a donut shop, or fast food restaurant. Ask students if they know these places.

Ask students to cover the word list, look at the pictures, and name the items and places they know.

TEACH THE NEW WORDS

Ask students to identify the number of a particular picture based on your description. *This store has many different things—soda, magazines, milk, laundry detergent, cans of soup. It's a convenience store.* (#3)

PROVIDE PRACTICE

Chalkboard Activities

△ Have students categorize vocabulary:

Products	Services	Both
convenience store	Laundromat	pharmacy

△ Draw a large intersection on the chalkboard. Have students come up and draw different vocabulary items from the page including street lights, stores, signs, etc.

Conversations

△ Put models on the board and practice. Make appropriate substitutions.

A: Why don't you come with me to the *Laundromat*?
B: No, thanks. I just want to relax today.
   2. drugstore 11. newsstand 20. donut shop
   24. dry cleaners 25. nail salon, etc.

A: Excuse me. Do you know if I can *cross the street* here?
B: I think you can. There's no sign here that says not to.
   D. park the car E. ride a bicycle

A: I can't find a *parking space* anywhere!
B: I think there's one near the *[corner]*.
   12. mailbox 21. public telephone

90

An Intersection

16. bus stop	22. copy center / print shop	28. fire hydrant
17. corner	23. streetlight	29. sign
18. parking meter	24. dry cleaners	30. street vendor
19. motorcycle	25. nail salon	31. cart
20. donut shop	26. sidewalk	D. **park** the car
21. public telephone	27. garbage truck	E. **ride** a bicycle

Share your answers.

1. Do you like to do errands?
2. Do you always like to go to the same stores?
3. Which businesses in the picture are also in your neighborhood?
4. Do you know someone who has a small business? What kind?
5. What things can you buy from a street vendor?

91

Interview Questions

1. Do you use the Laundromat?
2. How often do you go to the drugstore?
3. Do you go to a convenience store? What do you buy there?
4. Is there a newsstand that sells newspapers in your language? Where?
5. Do you go to a copy center? What kinds of papers do you copy?
6. Where do you have photographs developed?
7. Do you eat in fast food restaurants?
8. Do you ever ride a bicycle? Where?

Listening: 📼 #30, p. 220

"Up and Down the Street" Students point to the place where they hear the people talking.

EXPAND THE LESSON

Discussion Questions

1. What are the benefits of having a convenience store in your neighborhood? What are the drawbacks?
2. What are the benefits of having street vendors in a neighborhood? What are the drawbacks? Do you buy from street vendors?

Drawing Activity

1. Give students a large sheet of paper (at least 11″ x 14″).
2. Have students work in pairs to make a map of an intersection near the school.
3. Have them label each store, a crosswalk, traffic light, curb, and sidewalk.
4. Post the maps so students can share what they have done.

Classroom Yellow Pages

1. Show students the yellow pages from a local phone book. Explain what kind of information the ads contain.
2. Have pairs of students write an ad for a real business near the school—a donut shop, laundromat, fast food restaurant, etc.
3. Have them find out the address, phone number, business hours, and products the business sells or services it provides.
4. Have each pair write up an ad that can be put on a bulletin board or photocopied.

Chair Lineup

1. Have students draw an intersection near the school. (See drawing activity above.)
2. Line up two long rows of chairs facing each other at the front of the class, and have students sit holding their pictures.
3. For one minute, students facing each other take turns explaining what intersection they are at and give any description they can.
4. After two minutes the students in the row on the left move down one chair. With new partners, the students share again.

GAMES

Questions Only!

1. Form groups of 4–6 students each and have each group choose a recorder.
2. Have students look at pages 90–91 and come up with as many questions as they can about the scene. *Who is crossing the intersection?*
3. Recorders write their groups' questions on the board.
4. The group with the most correct questions wins.

Where Am I Going?

1. Divide students into two teams.
2. Tell students they have to guess where you are going. Give them clues about what you need to buy or what you need to do. *I want a magazine on computers and a newspaper with want ads. Where am I going?*
3. Have each team take turns guessing where you are going. The activity ends when one team guesses correctly.

91

Unit 7   A Mall   page 92

Workbooks, pp. 92–93
Classic Classroom Activities, Unit 7
Related Dictionary Pages

- Prepositions, p. 13
- Shopping, p. 21
- Clothing, pp. 64–67
- Shoes and Accessories, pp. 68–69

TOPIC NOTES

In the U.S., shopping malls serve as major hubs of community activity. Malls may be indoor or outdoor facilities and usually include attached parking structures.

A **card store** is sometimes referred to as a stationery store. Besides greeting cards, card stores carry a variety of gifts and novelty items.

 The largest mall in the U.S. is the Mall of America in Minneapolis, MN. This megamall would fill 88 football fields, and contains Camp Snoopy, the world's largest indoor amusement park.

TEACHING TIPS
Related Vocabulary

elevator*	novelty store
parking structure	video arcade
window shopping	retail store
stroller rental	outlet store
kiosk	

- Review *Shopping*, page 21. Have the class act out buying, selling, returning, and exchanging items in various mall stores.

- Students brainstorm a list of items they'd find in a mall. Have them shop in a local mall by finding two prices for each item on the list.

A Mall

1. music store
2. jewelry store
3. candy store
4. bookstore
5. toy store
6. pet store
7. card store
8. optician
9. travel agency
10. shoe store
11. fountain
12. florist

More vocabulary
beauty shop: hair salon
men's store: a store that sells men's clothing
dress shop: a store that sells women's clothing

Talk about where you want to shop in this mall.
Let's go to the card store.
I need to buy a card for Maggie's birthday.

92

INTRODUCE THE TOPIC

Tell a story about your experience at the local shopping mall. *I enjoy shopping at the Galleria. Did you know they opened up a new department store? It's usually crowded on Saturday, so I go early. My favorite store is….*

Ask students to name types of stores in the area (e.g. jewelry, shoe, electronics) and tell you whether they are located in a shopping mall.

Write the names of several of the mall stores from pages 92–93 on the board. Talk about some things you need or want to buy. Ask students to identify the stores where these items might be found. *My mom's birthday is next week. I know she would really like a pair of earrings. What stores sell jewelry? My brother loves CDs. What stores do you think sell them?*

TEACH THE NEW WORDS

Ask students questions about various mall stores. *I need a new pair of sunglasses. Where is the optician?* (on the first floor, next to the card store) *A bookstore is a great place to buy a good mystery novel or a sports magazine. Is there a bookstore in this mall?* (yes)

PROVIDE PRACTICE
Chalkboard Activities

△ Have students categorize vocabulary:

$5 or less	**More than $5**
ice cream stand	*jewelry store*

△ Have students sequence the following actions:

_____	**Go into the video store.**
_____	**Look around.**
_1_	**Check the directory.**
_____	**Buy some blank tapes.**
_____	**Leave the video store.**

Conversations

△ Put models on the board and practice. Make appropriate substitutions.

A: Excuse me. Do you know where the *pet store* is?
B: I'm not sure. Why don't you check the directory?
   2. jewelry store 3. candy store
   4. bookstore 5. toy store 7. card store, etc.

A: I'm starving. Let's get some *[pizza]* at the *food court*.
B: OK. It's my treat.
   3. candy store 20. ice cream stand

A: The *music store* is having a grand opening.
B: Yeah, I hear they're giving *[free cassettes]* to the first 100 customers.
   2. jewelry store 5. toy store 7. card store
   10. shoe store 15. video store
   18. electronics store

A Mall

13. department store
14. food court
15. video store
16. hair salon
17. maternity shop
18. electronics store
19. directory
20. ice cream stand
21. escalator
22. information booth

Practice asking for and giving the location of different shops.

Where's the maternity shop?
  It's on the first floor, next to the hair salon.

Share your answers.
1. Do you like shopping malls? Why or why not?
2. Some people don't go to the mall to shop. Name some other things you can do in a mall.

93

Interview Questions

1. Is there a mall close to your home?
2. When do you have time to shop?
3. What department stores are in a shopping mall near your home?
4. Which foods do you like to eat in the food court?
5. Which store would you like to get a gift certificate from?
6. Do you buy clothes at a mall? Where?
7. Which stores on this page would you shop at often? seldomly?
8. Would you like to work at this mall? Which store would you choose?

Listening: 📻 #31 p. 220

"Shopping at the Mall" Students listen and point to the stores they hear described by a couple visiting a mall.

EXPAND THE LESSON
Problem Solving

△ Have students brainstorm solutions.
You are the manager of a music store in the mall. There is an increase in shoplifting in your store. What can you do?

Discussion Questions

1. Why do you think malls are such popular meeting spots for teens?
2. Which stores have good gifts for children? Which stores would teenagers like to receive a gift certificate from? Where would you shop for a gift for grandparents?
3. Which stores are most fun to "window-shop"?
4. What different kinds of jobs are available at shopping malls? What job would you like to have?

Language Workout

△ Put this sentence on the board and discuss its meaning:
When Joe goes into the video store, he's *like a kid in a candy store.*

GAMES
Definition Bingo

1. Have students fold a blank sheet of paper into 16 squares.
2. Dictate 16 shopping mall locations and have students write them in random order on their papers.
3. Tell students they will be circling different words on their papers as they hear you define them. Explain that when they get four circled words in a row (horizontally, vertically, or diagonally), they shout "Bingo!"
4. Give a sample definition. *This is a store where you can buy an airplane ticket.* Make sure all students have circled the words *travel agency* on their papers.
5. Call out definitions until one student gets Bingo.
6. Continue playing until five players have gotten Bingo.

Questions Only!

1. Divide students into groups of 4–8 and have each group choose a recorder.
2. Have students look at pages 92–93 and come up with as many questions as they can about the scenes. *Where's the maternity store? How many people are eating ice cream?* Etc.
3. Recorders write their group's questions on the board.
4. The group with the most correct questions wins.

Class Go-Around: A Shopping Trip

1. Begin by saying *When I go to the mall, I go to the pet store.*
2. The first student volunteer repeats the sentence and adds another item. *When I go to the mall, I go to the pet store and the video store.*
3. The next student volunteer continues the chain, adding another item.
4. Stop after the tenth student and begin the chain again.

Variation: For a challenge, choose one shopping mall location and have students chain items available only in that store.
E.g., *I'm going to the card store to buy a birthday card. I'm going to the card store to buy a birthday card and wrapping paper.*

Workbooks, pp. 94–95
Classic Classroom Activities, Unit 7
Related Dictionary Pages
• Age and Physical Description, p. 22
• A Children's Bedroom, p. 45
• The Park and Playground, p. 153

TOPIC NOTES

In the U.S., childcare centers enable parents to work while providing a nurturing environment for infants, toddlers, and preschool children. These centers may have public or private financial support. They are found in community centers, churches, schools, and offices.

Childcare workers are also employed in daycare centers, which are often smaller facilities or family homes.

Nurse a baby means to breastfeed a baby.
Cubby is short for *cubicle,* a storage bin which holds each child's personal belongings.

TEACHING TIPS
Related Vocabulary

sleep mat
security blanket
lunch box
childproof

sign-in sheet
circle time
potty trained
booster seat

Grammar: The verbs *get dressed* and *dress* are used interchangeably to mean put on clothing: *I dressed,* or *I got dressed.* When we refer to dressing someone else the verb takes an object pronoun: *I dressed him,* or *I got him dressed.*

⚠ There are strong cultural differences regarding topics such as nursing and child discipline. Use care in discussing them.

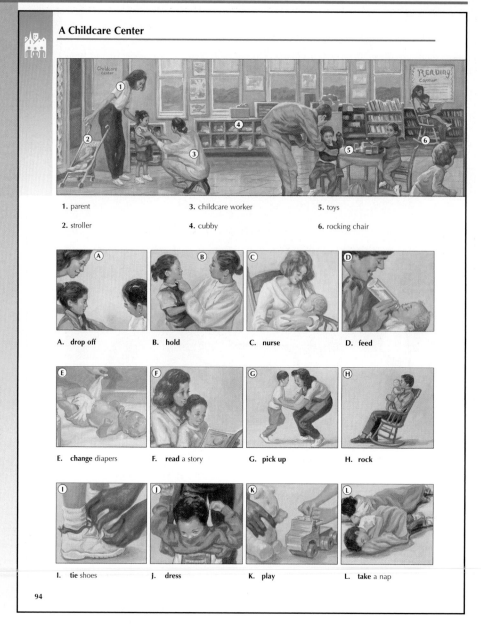

A Childcare Center

1. parent
2. stroller
3. childcare worker
4. cubby
5. toys
6. rocking chair

A. drop off
B. hold
C. nurse
D. feed

E. change diapers
F. read a story
G. pick up
H. rock

I. tie shoes
J. dress
K. play
L. take a nap

94

INTRODUCE THE TOPIC

Talk about childcare centers in your community. Identify some places that have infant, nursery, or preschool programs.

Describe a typical day for a two-year-old from the child's point of view. *Hi. My name's Tommy and I like my childcare worker, Marta. She helps me put stuff in my cubby and she always has neat toys for me to play with. Sometimes I miss my mom and I cry, but Marta tells me a funny story in the rocking chair.*

Ask students to brainstorm a list of items they might find in a childcare center. Discuss which items are needed to care for infants and toddlers and which ones can be used with older children.

TEACH THE NEW WORDS

Act out the role of a childcare worker, using a plastic baby doll and realia (bottle, baby food, etc.). Use TPR commands to guide students through the target vocabulary. Have the class repeat each command. *Look, Daniel is crying! He's hungry. Mai, please hold him for a minute. Luis, could you come to the front of the room and feed Daniel? Oh, it's easy. First, fill the bottle with formula. Don't forget to burp him when you are done. Put this cloth diaper on your shoulder…*

PROVIDE PRACTICE
Chalkboard Activity

△ Have students categorize vocabulary:

Feeding	Changing Diapers
bib	cloth diapers

Conversations

△ Put models on the board and practice. Make appropriate substitutions.

A: Oh, no! Angela is getting fussy!
B: Give her <u>some toys</u>. That will calm her down.
A: You're right. She stopped crying.

25. some formula 26. a bottle 28. some baby food 29. a pacifier 30. a teething ring 31. a rattle

A: Do I have to pack a lunch for [Sam]?
B: No, we provide meals. But please bring a supply of <u>wipes</u>.

20. disposable diapers 21. cloth diapers 22. diaper pins 24. training pants

A: How did you learn to <u>hold</u> a baby so well?
B: It's easy. My [sister] taught me.

D. feed E. change G. pick up H. rock J. dress

A Childcare Center

7. high chair   8. bib   9. changing table   10. potty seat

11. playpen	18. baby powder	25. formula
12. walker	19. disinfectant	26. bottle
13. car safety seat	20. disposable diapers	27. nipple
14. baby carrier	21. cloth diapers	28. baby food
15. baby backpack	22. diaper pins	29. pacifier
16. carriage	23. diaper pail	30. teething ring
17. wipes	24. training pants	31. rattle

95

Interview Questions

1. Were there any childcare centers in your hometown? Where?
2. Do you know anyone who uses a childcare center? Who?
3. Do you know how to change diapers?
4. If you were a childcare worker, what would you like to do with the kids?
5. Did you ever take care of a group of young children under age five? Was it fun?
6. Do you buy childcare supplies? Where?
7. What kind of toy do you think is good for a baby? for a toddler?

Listening: 🔊 #32, p. 221

"Rainbow Day Care" For page 94 students write the letter of the action as it is described. For page 95, they point to the childcare items.

EXPAND THE LESSON
Problem Solving

△ Have students brainstorm solutions. *Rose works full-time and drops off her six-month-old daughter, Molly, at a childcare center. Since she began daycare, Molly seems to get sick a lot. When Rose leaves work early to pick her up, her boss gets upset. What can Rose do?*

Discussion Questions

1. How can parents find a good childcare center?
2. What qualities do you think make a good childcare worker?
3. What is one question you would ask about a childcare center?
4. Which do you think are better, disposable diapers or cloth diapers?

5. Did you ever babysit or take care of children in your native country? What kind of experience was it?
6. What kinds of books or stories help children learn?
7. Did you ever have a special toy or "security blanket" that made you feel safe? When? What was it?
8. In your opinion, who should pay for childcare costs: government, private companies, or families?
9. Look at page 83, *First Aid*. What medical supplies do you think childcare centers need?
10. Who usually takes care of children for working mothers in your native country?

Language Workout

△ Copy this sentence on the board and discuss its meaning.
You want me to babysit the twins? Are you *off your rocker?* They're double trouble.

GAMES
Backwards Dictionary

1. Divide students into two teams.
2. Give definitions or descriptions of the vocabulary words to one team at a time and have the team guess what the word is. *This is a soft harness that a baby sits in. You wear it on your chest or back.* (baby carrier) *This is a folding chair with wheels, usually used for babies over six months old.* (stroller)
3. The team with the most correct answers wins.

Word Bingo

1. Have students make a grid that is five rows across and five rows down and fill it with 25 words from pages 94–95.
2. Call out vocabulary words at random. Students circle the words as you say them.
3. When one student has five in a row, vertically, horizontally, or diagonally and calls out "Bingo!"
4. Continue playing until five students have gotten Bingo.

Variation: Have students draw the various childcare items or actions.

Charades

1. Write verbs A–L on separate slips of paper and put them into a box or hat.
2. Divide the class into two teams.
3. Team members take turns picking a word and acting it out for their team.
4. Teams get a point for each word they guess correctly.
5. The game ends when all the slips are gone.

Workbooks, p. 96
Classic Classroom Activities, Unit 7
Related Dictionary Pages
- Personal Information, p. 4
- Numbers and Measurements, pp. 14–15

TOPIC NOTES

In the U.S., the post office handles over 160 billion pieces of mail per year. ZIP codes and machine sorting have increased the speed with which letters can be delivered.

Greeting cards fall into several different categories: birthday, wedding, new baby, anniversary, get well, sympathy, and "any occasion" cards.

⚠ Sympathy cards have been sent as birthday cards by nonnative speakers. Show students a variety of greeting cards and discuss the occasions associated with each.

TEACHING TIPS
Related Vocabulary

post office*	junk mail
postal worker*	book rate
money order*	scale*
change of address form	sort letters
roll/book/sheet of stamps	dead letter

⚠ Students may distrust the mail service. Many students may have received little personal or social mail in their native countries. In some countries, the only way to be sure a letter arrives at its destination is to pay for a courier.

💡 Send a short letter (with a few questions) to each student. Have students tell you when they get the letters. Encourage students to write back to you, answering your questions.

U.S. Mail

1. envelope
2. letter
3. postcard
4. greeting card
5. package

6. letter carrier
7. return address
8. mailing address
9. postmark
10. stamp/postage

Emily Rose
1543 Oak Lane
Springvale, CA 91254

SPRINGVALE
5-7-99
CA

USA

Alyson Shepard
249 Courtney Drive
Newton, NY 10043

11. certified mail
12. priority mail
13. air letter/aerogramme
14. ground post/parcel post
15. Express Mail/overnight mail

FRAGILE
EXPRESS

A. **address** a postcard
B. **send** it/**mail** it
C. **deliver** it
D. **receive** it

96

INTRODUCE THE TOPIC

Bring in a postcard, a greeting card, and other items presented on page 96. See how many items students can name.

Talk about a card or letter you received recently and how it made you feel.

TEACH THE NEW WORDS

Name each item (#1–15) and have students repeat the word(s) while pointing to the appropriate picture.

PROVIDE PRACTICE
Chalkboard Activity

△ Have students categorize vocabulary:

Things You See on a Postcard	Things You Do to a Postcard
a stamp	address it

Conversations

△ Put models on the board and practice. Make appropriate substitutions.

A: I'd like to send this package by _priority mail_.
B: Will there be anything else?
A: Yes, I need some stamps.

   11. certified mail 14. ground or parcel post
   15. Express mail

A: The letter carrier is almost here.
B: I know, I know. I just have to address this _envelope_.

   2. letter 3. postcard 4. greeting card
   5. package

Interview Questions

1. Do you send a lot of letters?
2. Whom do you write to?
3. What time is the mail delivered to your home?
4. What's your letter carrier's name?

Listening: Dictation

1. Give each student a blank envelope.
2. Dictate an interesting or imaginary mailing address. Have students write the address on their envelopes.
3. Speak naturally, giving the address once without interruptions.
4. Have students take turns asking for the information they did not hear.

EXPAND THE LESSON
Writing Activity

1. Write a simple model letter or greeting card for students to use in writing to a "pen pal" from another class.
2. Have students choose pen pals' names from a hat, then write their letters.
3. A student "letter carrier" can deliver the letters.

A Bank

1. teller
2. vault
3. ATM (automated teller machine)
4. security guard

5. passbook
6. savings account number
7. checkbook
8. checking account number
9. ATM card
10. monthly statement
11. balance
12. deposit slip
13. safe-deposit box

Using the ATM machine

A. **Insert** your ATM card.

B. **Enter** your PIN number.*

C. **Make** a deposit.

D. **Withdraw** cash.

E. **Transfer** funds.

F. **Remove** your ATM card.

*PIN: personal identification number

More vocabulary
overdrawn account: When there is not enough money in an account to pay a check, we say the account is overdrawn.

Share your answers.
1. Do you use a bank?
2. Do you use an ATM card?
3. Name some things you can put in a safe-deposit box.

97

Workbooks, p. 97
Classic Classroom Activities, Unit 7
Related Dictionary Pages
• Numbers and Measurements, p. 15
• Money, p. 20
• Shopping, p. 21

TOPIC NOTES

In the U.S., banks perform many services. They offer checking and savings accounts and provide loans and investment services.

ATMs (automated teller machines) are becoming very popular, and many people are now banking by computer.

TEACHING TIPS
Related Vocabulary

loan application	bank officer
withdrawal slip	bounced check
insufficient funds	signature*
save*	cash*
cashier's check	interest rates

☼ Review page 20, *Money*, so that students can talk about different bank transactions using the correct amounts.

☼ Bring in a checkbook, passbook, withdrawal and deposit slips, a monthly statement, etc., with account numbers deleted. Make copies of them so students can practice filling them out.

☼ Talk to students about various services and types of loans available at banks: credit cards; bank cards; home, automobile, or vacation loans.

☼ Some students may not be familiar with banking procedures. Discussing how banks work and what charges they can make to an account is a valuable lesson. Explain the difference between a *savings and loan* and a *commercial bank*.

INTRODUCE THE TOPIC

Bring in some bank forms, plastic bank cards, and credit cards. Take an informal class survey, asking students which of the banking services they have used.

Ask students to cover the word list, look at the pictures and name the items they know.

TEACH THE NEW WORDS

Ask students to identify the numbers or letters of particular pictures based on your description. *This is the book that tells you how much you have in your savings account. It's a passbook. (#5) This is what you get from the bank at the end of each month to tell you the balance. It's your monthly statement. (#10)*

PROVIDE PRACTICE
Chalkboard Activity

△ Have students sequence the following actions:

_____	**Withdraw** cash.
_____	**Remove** your ATM card.
_____	**Enter** your PIN number.
1	**Insert** your ATM card.

Conversations

△ Put models on the board and practice. Make appropriate substitutions.

A: I have a question about my *passbook*.
B: Sure, I think I can help you.

   7. **checkbook** 10. **monthly statement**
   11. **balance** 13. **safe-deposit box**

A: I'd like to *make a deposit*.
B: Sure. Just put in your PIN number first.

   D. **withdraw cash** E. **transfer funds**

Interview Questions

1. Do you know anyone who works in a bank? Is it a good job?
2. Which bank is close to your home?

Listening: Listen and Point

△ Have students point to the pictures as you say the target vocabulary words in the sentences. E.g.:

1. *This is a **vault**.*
2. *This man is a **security guard**.*
3. *This is your **balance**.* Etc.

EXPANSION
Discussion Question

More and more banks are encouraging customers to use ATMs. Someday banks may charge for coming in to speak to a teller. What do you think about ATMs? Do you use them? How can they be made safer to use?

Workbooks, p. 98
Classic Classroom Activities, Unit 7
Related Dictionary Pages
- City Streets, pp. 88–89
- Entertainment, pp. 166–167

TOPIC NOTES

In the U.S., the public library systems allow users to borrow **books, records,** and **audio** and **video cassettes.** Reference materials, CD-ROMs, periodicals, and **microfilm** are not usually loaned out, but can be used during library hours.

The **card catalog** is being replaced by the **online catalog** in many libraries. Using computers, library patrons can get information on books in all branches of their city library as well as other libraries state- and country-wide.

TEACHING TIPS
Related Vocabulary

Dewey Decimal System	patron
children's book	CD ROM disc*
novel	photocopier*
poetry	overdue fine
biography	dictionary*

💡 Pick up a class set of library card applications and help your students fill them out. Arrange for your class to tour a local library. Have students turn in their forms at that time.

💡 Have students check out some children's books from the library. Give students time to learn to read their books aloud. Call a nearby preschool and arrange to have your class read to the children.

A Library

1. reference librarian	7. magazine	13. videocassette	19. library card
2. reference desk	8. newspaper	14. CD (compact disc)	20. library book
3. atlas	9. online catalog	15. record	21. title
4. microfilm reader	10. card catalog	16. checkout desk	22. author
5. microfilm	11. media section	17. library clerk	
6. periodical section	12. audiocassette	18. encyclopedia	

More vocabulary
check a book out: to borrow a book from the library
nonfiction: real information, history or true stories
fiction: stories from the author's imagination

Share your answers.
1. Do you have a library card?
2. Do you prefer to buy books or borrow them from the library?

98

INTRODUCE THE TOPIC

Bring in your library card and show it to the class. Ask how many students have a card.

Ask students to name things they can find in a library. List their ideas on the board. Have students compare the word list on page 98 with their words.

TEACH THE NEW WORDS

Say each word several times in different contexts. Have students point to the picture as you say the word. *Here's an atlas. The atlas is #3. The atlas is a book with many maps.* Etc.

PROVIDE PRACTICE
Chalkboard Activity

△ Have students categorize vocabulary:

People	Reference Materials	Items to Check out
librarian	atlas	audio cassette

Conversations

△ Put models on the board and practice. Make appropriate substitutions.

A: Do you know where the *atlas* is?
B: No, I don't. You have to ask at the reference desk.
> **1. reference librarian 5. microfilm 18. encyclopedia**

A: I'd like to check out this *magazine*.
B: I'm sorry. It's reserved.
> **8. newspaper 12. audiocassette 13. videocassette**

Interview Questions

1. Do you like to go to the library?
2. Do you ever check out audiocassettes? How about videocassettes?
3. Do you prefer fiction or nonfiction?
4. What subjects do you like to read about?

Listening: "Say What?"

1. Give a "tour" of the library in the picture, but make mistakes. E.g.: *This is the Crescent City Library. You see the reference librarian on the left? She's helping someone with the encyclopedia.* (She's helping someone with the atlas.) Etc.

2. Have students raise their hands when they hear the mistake.

3. Call on volunteers and have them correct you.

EXPAND THE LESSON
Problem Solving

△ Have students brainstorm solutions. *Jayme returned ten books to the library that were three weeks late. She paid $10.50 in overdue fines. She checks out books for her kids, but can never find the books when they're due. What ideas do you have for Jayme?*

The Legal System

You have the right to remain silent…

Bail is set at $20,000.

A. **arrest** a suspect

1. police officer
2. handcuffs

B. **hire** a lawyer/**hire** an attorney

3. guard
4. defense attorney

C. **appear** in court

5. defendant
6. judge

D. **stand trial**

7. courtroom

8. jury
9. evidence

10. prosecuting attorney
11. witness

12. court reporter
13. bailiff

Guilty.

7 years.

E. **give** the verdict*

F. **sentence** the defendant

G. **go** to jail/**go** to prison

14. convict

H. **be released**

*Note: There are two possible verdicts, "guilty" and "not guilty."

Share your answers.

1. What are some differences between the legal system in the United States and the one in your country?

2. Do you want to be on a jury? Why or why not?

99

Workbooks, p. 99
Classic Classroom Activities, Unit 7
Related Dictionary Pages
• Crime, p. 100
• U.S. Government and Citizenship, p. 116

TOPIC NOTES

In the U.S., criminal law protects the rights of the defendant to: 1) be presumed innocent until proven guilty; 2) be appointed an attorney if he or she cannot afford one; 3) receive a fair trial by a jury of 12 peers; and 4) be able to appeal a jury's decision to a higher court.

⚠ Students may be used to different criminal procedures than those described on page 99. It is preferable that students bring up the differences, rather than the teacher. The legal systems in other countries may include closed courts, tribunals acting with or without juries, judges questioning witnesses, and witnesses being permitted to give testimony based on hearsay.

TEACHING TIPS
Related Vocabulary

misdemeanor	plea
felony	testimony
district attorney	fingerprints
grand jury	death penalty
indictment	penitentiary
juror	parole
Legal Aid Society	civil liberties

Usage: News reports often use the passive voice to describe a criminal proceeding. *The defendant was found guilty. He will be sentenced tomorrow. His motion for a new trial was denied.*

INTRODUCE THE TOPIC

Tell the story of the pictures on page 99 or of an infamous, internationally known trial. Intentionally pause in your story to see if students can fill in certain details, such as a name, a date, or a crime.

TEACH THE NEW WORDS

Ask students a series of *or* questions about the target vocabulary. *Is the police officer putting handcuffs on the suspect or the attorney?* (the suspect) *Is the defendant going to hire the attorney or arrest him?* (hire him)

PROVIDE PRACTICE
Chalkboard Activity

△ Have students categorize vocabulary:

People	**Actions**	**Things**
suspect	arrest	handcuffs

Conversations

△ Put models on the board and practice. Make appropriate substitutions.

A: Did you see *[Max Sims]* on TV last night?

B: Who is *[he]*?

A: *[He's]* the *police officer* in that famous court case.

　4. defense attorney 5. defendant 6. judge
　10. prosecuting attorney 11. witness
　12. court reporter

A: What did the *police officer* say when the trial was over?

B: *[He]* said, "It was hard to *arrest the suspect.*"

　5. defendant/D. stand trial
　8. jury/E. give the verdict
　6. judge/F. sentence the defendant

Interview Questions

1. Do you know anyone who is a police officer? a lawyer? a court reporter?
2. Have you ever been a witness in a trial? When?

Listening: Listen and Point

△ Describe the pictures on page 99. Students listen and point to the correct picture. E.g.: *This picture shows the convict is on his bed, in jail.* (G) Etc.

EXPAND THE LESSON
Discussion Questions

1. What are good qualities in a judge? How about in a lawyer?
2. In some states, defendants can be sentenced to death for murder. Do you think there should be a death penalty? Why or why not?

Workbooks, p. 100
Classic Classroom Activities, Unit 7
Related Dictionary Pages
• Feelings, pp. 30–31
• The Legal System, p. 99
• Public Safety, p. 101

TOPIC NOTES

In the U.S., all types of crime continue to be major problems. Some people feel the high rate of crime is due to the glorification of violence in the media, drug use, the availability of firearms, and economic disparity.

TEACHING TIPS
Related Vocabulary

rape	stab
theft	holdup
carjacking	vandals
arson	weapon
felony	report (n)
misdemeanor	police*
kill	witness*

Usage: Talk about the different words used for criminals. E.g., people who sell drugs are *drug dealers*; people who commit vandalism are *vandals*. Other words are *drunk driver, mugger, robber, murderer, thief.*

- Review the words from *Feelings*, pages 30–31, such as *angry, embarrassed, upset,* so that students can talk about how crime victims feel.

- Follow up this lesson with one about *Public Safety*, page 101, and what students can do for their own safety.

⚠ If a student has been a crime victim, this may be a difficult topic. Explain to students that it is important to learn the language so they can get help or describe a crime to the police.

Crime

1. vandalism
2. gang violence
3. drunk driving
4. illegal drugs
5. mugging
6. burglary
7. assault
8. murder
9. gun

More vocabulary
commit a crime: to do something illegal
criminal: someone who commits a crime
victim: someone who is hurt or killed by someone else

Share your answers.
1. Is there too much crime on TV? in the movies?
2. Do you think people become criminals from watching crime on TV?

100

INTRODUCE THE TOPIC

Tell a story about a crime you have read about or heard about on TV. Describe the crime, the victim, and how it happened according to the source.

Ask students to look at page 100. Talk about which crimes they hear about most in their communities.

TEACH THE NEW WORDS

Ask students to identify the number of a particular picture based on your description. *One man is backed against the fence. The other man is going to hit him. We call this "assault." (#7) This man is grabbing the man's wallet and threatening him. We call this "mugging." (#5) Etc.*

PROVIDE PRACTICE
Chalkboard Activity

△ Have students categorize vocabulary:

A Problem Near Our School	Not A Problem Near Our School
vandalism	*mugging*

Conversations

△ Put models on the board and practice. Make appropriate substitutions.

A: Did you hear there was <u>a mugging</u> near our school?
B: Yes, wasn't it awful!
A: We really have to be careful!
   6. a burglary 7. an assault 8. a murder

A: There's a discussion at 8:00 P.M. on <u>gang violence</u> at the school tonight.
B: Let's go together. It's important.
   1. vandalism 3. drunk driving
   4. illegal drugs

Interview Questions

1. Is crime worse in this country or in your country?
2. Are you scared to go out at night?
3. Have you ever seen a crime happen?

Listening: 📼 #33, p. 221

"Officer Lopez Comes to Class." Students point to different crimes which the police officer talks about.

EXPAND THE LESSON
Discussion Questions

1. If you were the mayor of this city, what would you do to help prevent crime?
2. What are the qualities of a good police officer?

Public Safety

A. **Walk** with a friend.

B. **Stay** on well-lit streets.

C. **Hold** your purse close to your body.

D. **Protect** your wallet.

E. **Lock** your doors.

F. **Don't open** your door to strangers.

G. **Don't drink** and **drive.**

H. **Report** crimes to the police.

More vocabulary
Neighborhood Watch: a group of neighbors who watch for criminals in their neighborhood
designated drivers: people who don't drink alcoholic beverages so that they can drive drinkers home

Share your answers.
1. Do you feel safe in your neighborhood?
2. Look at the pictures. Which of these things do you do?
3. What other things do you do to stay safe?

101

Workbooks, p. 101
Classic Classroom Activities, Unit 7
Related Dictionary Pages
• Feelings, pp. 30–31
• The Legal System, p. 99
• Crime, p. 100

TOPIC NOTES

In the U.S., most people are safety conscious. They lock their doors and windows, carry their money safely, and travel with a companion. Police officers often come to public schools to teach about safety to both children and adults. Many cities have designated-driver programs to taxi people home who have been drinking while out at night.

TEACHING TIPS
Related Vocabulary

self-defense	security system
guard	buddy system
defend	description
protect	suspect*
suspicious	drunk
dangerous*	

☼ Review the words on the page that are part of the safety advice: *friend, well-lit street, purse, body, wallet, doors, strangers, crime,* and *police.*

☼ Review page 100, *Crime,* so that students can talk about what public safety advice might help prevent particular crimes.

☼ After you have taught page 101, invite a local police officer to come to class to talk about public safety.

☼ Have students generate a list of questions that a police officer might ask when making out a crime report. Talk about home safety and what precautions to take when traveling in the city.

INTRODUCE THE TOPIC

Ask students questions about safety precautions when they are at home. *How many of you lock your doors when you are home? How many of you look through a window to see who is at your door? How many of you keep your windows locked?*

Act out hiding your money in a wallet or purse. Ask students to tell you what you are doing and why you are doing it.

TEACH THE NEW WORDS

Ask students to identify the letter of a particular picture based on your description. *He just drank a few beers. His wife said "Don't drink and drive," so he's calling a taxi. (G) She just got paid and she knows people can come and take her purse. She knows she should hold her purse close to her body. (C)*

Chalkboard Activity

△ Have students complete these sentences in as many ways as they can.

Lock your _door_.
Protect your _____.
If you drink alcohol and need transportation, _____.
If you are a victim of a crime, _____.
If you want to protect yourself against a mugger, _____.

Conversations

△ Put models on the board and practice. Make appropriate substitutions.

A: What did you tell your daughter?
B: I told her, "No matter what, _walk with a friend_."

B. stay on well-lit streets C. hold your purse close to your body D. protect your wallet, etc.

Interview Questions

1. Do you lock your doors?
2. What do you do when a stranger comes to your door?
3. How do you protect your money?

Listening: 📼 #33, p. 221

"Officer Lopez Comes to Class." Students point to different public safety tips which the police officer talks about.

EXPAND THE LESSON
Problem Solving

△ Have students brainstorm solutions.
1. *Oscar's son drove the family car and came home drunk. What can Oscar do?*
2. *Sally saw someone steal her neighbor's TV. Sally is afraid to tell the police because she doesn't know what the police will do. What advice do you have for her?*

Workbooks, pp. 102–103
Classic Classroom Activities, Unit 7
Related Dictionary Pages
- Personal Information, p. 4
- Weather, p. 10
- Medical Emergencies, p. 82
- First Aid, p. 83
- Geography, p. 117
- Job Safety, p. 147

TOPIC NOTES

In the U.S., varied geography and climate account for widely ranging weather conditions. About 12,000 weather stations nationwide monitor conditions that lead to natural disasters such as **blizzards** and hurricanes. However, many disasters are caused not by "mother nature," but by human error, e.g., car crashes, **explosions**, **fires**.

Hurricanes and **tornadoes** are referred to as *cyclone storms*. Hurricanes develop over the ocean, traveling for several days. Tornadoes develop over land, usually last only an hour, and can have wind speeds over 85 miles per hour.

📁 Most earthquakes in the U.S. occur in Alaska, California, and Washington. Most tornados occur in Texas, Oklahoma, and Florida.

TEACHING TIPS
Related Vocabulary

collision	evacuate
Richter scale	arson
rockslide	bomb
avalanche	state of emergency

🔆 Review and practice telephone use during emergencies.

🔆 Use the First Aid and Survival Guide sections of the phone book to supplement your lesson.

Emergencies and Natural Disasters

1. lost child	**4.** explosion	**7.** fire
2. car accident	**5.** earthquake	**8.** firefighter
3. airplane crash	**6.** mudslide	**9.** fire truck

Practice reporting a fire.
This is <u>Lisa Broad</u>. There is a fire.
The address is <u>323 Oak Street</u>.
Please send someone quickly.

Share your answers.
1. Can you give directions to your home if there is a fire?
2. What information do you give to the other driver if you are in a car accident?

102

INTRODUCE THE TOPIC

Talk about a recent natural disaster or emergency that was covered by the media. *Did you hear about the fires in California? They started in the mountains. Over 200 homes burned. Some firefighters were seriously burned, too. Many roads and schools were closed.*

Ask students to name one or more natural disasters that occur in their native countries. Use *Geography*, page 117, to help students describe their countries. Provide an example. *Cholada, you're from India, aren't you? India has many rivers. When there is too much rain, do you have floods?*

Bring in a flashlight, a blanket, and a pen. Have students brainstorm other items that could be useful for emergencies or disasters.

TEACH THE NEW WORDS

Ask students to identify the number of a particular picture based on your description. *Flames and smoke are coming out the windows. People are using fire escapes to exit the building. (#7)*

PROVIDE PRACTICE
Chalkboard Activities

△ Have students categorize vocabulary: What causes these situations?

Nature	People	Both
earthquake	lost child	fire

△ Draw a large outline of a two-story house. Indicate the locations for a bedroom, kitchen and living room. Draw a stick figure smoking in bed. Have students come to the board and mark an X on other areas where a fire might start. Have students circle or draw exit areas.

Conversations

△ Put models on the board and practice. Make appropriate substitutions.

A: Did you hear about the <u>earthquake</u> in Hawaii?
B: No. We're going there [tomorrow] for vacation.
A: Vacation? Are you crazy?

6. mudslide 12. hurricane 15. tidal wave 16. flood

A: Hello, operator? I'm calling to report a <u>fire</u>.
B: What's your location?
A: [5645 Thunderbird Drive.]
B: We'll call an emergency crew immediately.

2. a car accident 3. an airplane crash 4. an explosion

Emergencies and Natural Disasters

10. drought

11. blizzard

12. hurricane

13. tornado

14. volcanic eruption

15. tidal wave

16. flood

17. search and rescue team

Share your answers.

1. Which disasters are common in your area? Which never happen?

2. What can you do to prepare for emergencies?

3. Do you have emergency numbers near your telephone?

4. What organizations will help you in an emergency?

103

Interview Questions

1. Have you ever had a car accident?

2. When you were a child, did you ever get lost? Where?

3. What things would you take from your home if you had just a few minutes to evacuate?

4. How long would it take you to evacuate your home in an emergency?

5. What kinds of emergency numbers do you keep near your phone?

Listening: Listen and Write

△ State the situations below. Students should write the number of the emergency or disaster that they hear.

1. *Scenic highway is closed due to a car accident in the left lane. Expect traffic delay on southbound routes.* (#2)

2. *Japan has reported a 5.0 earthquake, centered north of Kyoto.* (#5)

3. *The snowstorm continues, with blizzard conditions expected.* (#11)

4. *Farmers worry that the drought will affect their fruit crops.* (#10)

5. *Attention shoppers! Please look out for a lost child, last seen at the ice cream stand.* (#1)

6. *Hurricane Eliza is scheduled to hit the coast tomorrow morning. Expect high winds and coastal evacuation.* (#12)

7. *In the event of an airplane crash, your seat cushion can be used as a flotation device.* (#3)

8. *Heavy rains reported across the state are responsible for floods all over the inland valleys.* (#16)

EXPAND THE LESSON

Problem Solving

△ Have students brainstorm solutions. *You witness a car accident at a busy intersection. The driver at fault drives away. What can you do?*

Discussion Questions

1. What disasters happen most in your area? When do they happen most often?

2. How can you protect your family and possessions from fire? Make a list of things to buy and things to do around the home.

3. How can you prevent damage to your home before a flood or fire occurs?

4. What equipment do you see on a fire truck? How is it used?

5. What should you do if you wake up and smell smoke in your home?

6. Where are safe places to keep important papers and photographs in case of fire or earthquake?

7. There are many superstitions about disasters. Do you know stories that try to explain them?

Language Workout

△ Put these sentences on the board and discuss their meanings.

1. A *flood* of work orders just came in. Now I have to work overtime.

2. Why are you rushing? The movie starts in a half hour. *Where's the fire?*

Drawing Activity

1. Tell students they are going to be making posters for National Safety Week. Brainstorm slogans with the class that deal with prevention of fires or car accidents, e.g., "Don't Drink and Drive" or "Smokey the Bear Says..." List the suggestions on the board.

2. Divide students into groups of 4 and give each group posterboard, scratch paper, markers, magazines, scissors, and glue.

3. Tell groups they must work together to create a poster with a safety message about preventing either car accidents or fires.

4. Give students 10–15 minutes to come up with their slogan and plan their design, while you monitor and assist as needed.

5. Give students additional time to create their posters.

6. Have a volunteer from each group bring the finished poster to the front and show it to the class.

Workbooks, p. 104
Classic Classroom Activities, Unit 8
Related Dictionary Pages
• Time, pp. 16–17
• Money, p. 20
• Prepositions of Motion, p. 105
• Directions and Traffic Signs, p. 107

TOPIC NOTES

In the U.S., airlines now handle most long-distance passenger travel, while subway trains, buses, and taxis provide the majority of intracity service.

Train systems may run on the surface, underground, or on elevated tracks.

Subways, which are underground electric trains, may be called *metros*, or a local name such as *the T*. Mass transit routes, or lines, are identified by numbers, letters, colors, or a final destination.

📁 New York City has the longest city rail system in the U.S., with 492.9 miles of subway track.

TEACHING TIPS
Related Vocabulary

mass transit	trolley
express	commute
local	engineer
turnstile	captain
timetable	porter
railroad	peak hours
shuttle	board a bus

💡 Bring in bus, train, or subway schedules so that students can practice asking for information.

💡 Using a U.S. map, have students choose a travel destination, select a type of public transportation, and estimate cost and travel time.

✈ 🚊 **Public Transportation**

1. bus stop	7. passenger	13. train station	19. taxi stand
2. route	8. bus driver	14. ticket	20. taxi driver
3. schedule	9. subway	15. platform	21. meter
4. bus	10. track	16. conductor	22. taxi license
5. fare	11. token	17. train	23. ferry
6. transfer	12. fare card	18. taxi/cab	

More vocabulary
hail a taxi: to get a taxi driver's attention by raising your hand
miss the bus: to arrive at the bus stop late

Talk about how you and your friends come to school.
I take the bus to school.   *He drives to school.*
You take the train.   *She walks to school.*
We take the subway.   *They ride bikes.*

104

INTRODUCE THE TOPIC

Ask questions about public transportation in your area. *I don't have a car. I need to go downtown. What's the fastest way? How can I get a taxi? Where's the closest bus stop from this school?*

TEACH THE NEW WORDS

Say each word several times in different contexts. Have students repeat the target words and point to the correct picture. *Number 1 is a bus stop. Express and local buses stop at the curb, near this sign.*

PROVIDE PRACTICE
Chalkboard Activity

△ Have students categorize vocabulary:

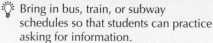

Hold a…	Take the…	Talk to a…
token	*bus*	*bus driver*

Conversations

△ Put models on the board and practice. Make appropriate substitutions.

A: How do you get to work?
B: I take *the train*. It's pretty convenient during the week.
  4. the bus 9. the subway 18. a taxi
  23. the ferry
A: Hurry up or we'll miss the bus! It's coming at *[7:55]*.
B: Oh, no! I can't find my *token!*
A: Don't worry. I have an extra one.
  6. transfer 12. fare card 14. ticket

Interview Questions

1. What public transportation do you use most?
2. How long is your commute each day? How much does it cost?
3. Is there a special place you like to sit on a train or bus? Why?

Listening: Definitions

△ Students open their books to page 104 and write the number of each item as you describe it. E.g.:

1. *Check the arrival time on this.* (#3)
2. *This machine records distance and cost of a cab trip.* (#21).
3. *This person drives the bus.* (#8)
4. *This carries you over the water.* (#23)
5. *This person collects your train ticket.* (#16) Etc.

EXPAND THE LESSON
Discussion Questions

1. When should you tip taxi drivers?
2. How would you improve transportation in your city?

Prepositions of Motion

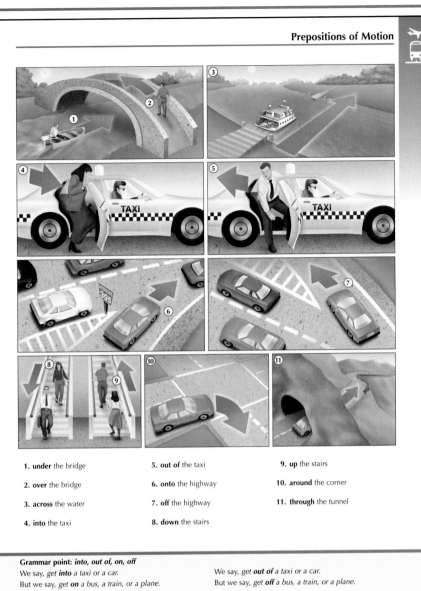

1. **under** the bridge

2. **over** the bridge

3. **across** the water

4. **into** the taxi

5. **out of** the taxi

6. **onto** the highway

7. **off** the highway

8. **down** the stairs

9. **up** the stairs

10. **around** the corner

11. **through** the tunnel

Grammar point: *into, out of, on, off*
We say, *get **into** a taxi or a car.*
But we say, *get **on** a bus, a train, or a plane.*

We say, *get **out of** a taxi or a car.*
But we say, *get **off** a bus, a train, or a plane.*

105

Workbooks, p. 105
Classic Classroom Activities, Unit 8
Related Dictionary Pages
• Prepositions, p. 13
• An Intersection, pp. 90–91
• Public Transportation, p. 104
• Cars and Trucks, p. 106
• Directions and Traffic Signs, p. 107

TOPIC NOTES

In the U.S., some prepositions vary colloquially. For example, in the Northeast, people stand *on line*, while they stand *in line* in the South and the West.

TEACHING TIPS
Related Vocabulary

throughout	toward
beneath	away from
by	past
along	up to

Usage: The preposition *into* is used interchangeably with *in* to describe going inside or getting involved with a situation. *Get **into/in** the car. Don't get **into/in** trouble.*

Grammar: Note that *down* can be a preposition. *He walked down the stairs.* The word *downstairs* is used as an adverb in *Take the elevator downstairs* and may also be used as an adjective, as in *He has a downstairs office.*

• Bring in manipulatives (magnets, toy blocks, toy cars) to demonstrate the vocabulary.

• Draw a picture on the board of a mountain with a tunnel, and a river next to it. Demonstrate <u>all</u> the prepositions: *He's next to the mountain. He's going through the mountain,* etc.

INTRODUCE THE TOPIC

Draw four squares on the board. Identify each square, e.g., a building, a radio, a fence, a pocket. Draw arrows showing the motion as you talk about each square. *Walk around the building. Take the batteries out of the radio. Climb over the fence. Put the money into your pocket.*

Tell a story about a trip using many prepositions of motion. *First, I got into the taxi. I looked through the window at the busy streets. Next, we drove onto a ferry boat. The ferry went under a bridge and across the water to an island. We drove off the ferry and around a corner…*

TEACH THE NEW WORDS

Ask a series of *yes/no* questions about the pictures. *Look at #4. Is the man getting out of the taxi?* (no)

PROVIDE PRACTICE
Chalkboard Activity

△ Draw a large rectangle to represent a park. Put in a tree, lake, bridge, and park bench. Have students come to the board and sketch in simple figures with arrows showing motion, e.g., a bird flying over the tree, a ball rolling under the bench, a man walking onto the bridge.

Conversations

△ Put models on the board and practice. Make appropriate substitutions.

A: Where's [George]?
B: We lost him when he rode <u>through</u> the park.
  3. across 4. into 5. out of

A: Do you know a good shortcut?
B: Yes, we just go <u>down</u> this way.
  9. up 10. around 11. through

Interview Questions

1. How do you get to school from your home? Describe your route.

2. Do you like going over high bridges? Through dark tunnels?

Listening: Listen and Write

△ Students open their books to page 105 and write the preposition on their paper as you say each sentence. E.g.:
1. *Get **onto** the highway at the light.*
2. *Hold the rail when you go **down** the stairs.* Etc.

EXPAND THE LESSON
Discussion Questions

1. Do you think it's bad luck to walk under a ladder? Would you walk under or around it?

2. What's the best way to get from school to the beach? What's another way?

Workbooks, p. 106
Classic Classroom Activities, Unit 8
Related Dictionary Pages
- Prepositions of Motion, p. 105
- Directions and Traffic Signs, p. 107
- Parts of a Car and Car Maintenance, pp. 108–109

TOPIC NOTES

In the U.S., 80% of the population travels by automobile. This has led to increased traffic congestion and air pollution in many cities. Government emission-control standards and engine modifications such as catalytic converters have helped reduce pollution, but "gridlock" and auto accidents are still major problems.

Pickup trucks are also referred to as *light trucks.*

TEACHING TIPS
Related Vocabulary

economy	flatbed truck
luxury	limousine
recreational vehicle	motorcycle*
sedan	jeep
hatchback	import
coupe	jackknife
catering truck	fender bender

Usage: Cars and trucks are described with adjectives in the following order: year, color, make, model; e.g., *'96 blue Toyota Camry sedan.*

Bring in classified ads or local circulars advertising new or used vehicles. Conduct a class search where students find the best price for a particular model car or truck.

Cars and Trucks

1. subcompact	6. sports car	10. minivan	15. tractor trailer/semi
2. compact	7. pickup truck	11. camper	16. cab
3. midsize car	8. station wagon	12. dump truck	17. trailer
4. full-size car	9. SUV (sports utility vehicle)	13. tow truck	
5. convertible		14. moving van	

More vocabulary
make: the name of the company that makes the car
model: the style of car

Share your answers.
1. What is your favorite kind of car?
2. What kind of car is good for a big family? for a single person?

106

INTRODUCE THE TOPIC

Ask students to name types of cars or trucks they see on the road every day. Take an informal survey of vehicles owned by students or their family members.

Tell a story about an accident on the highway. Describe the vehicles involved. *A long, low, fast blue sports car ran a stop sign and hit a big heavy-duty dump truck full of sand. The truck bed flipped up, dumped the sand, and blocked the highway. A tow truck arrived, and the driver used its big winch to lift the front of the car and pull it to the repair shop.*

TEACH THE NEW WORDS

Ask students a series of *or* questions about the cars and trucks depicted on the page. *Is #1 a compact or a subcompact car?* (subcompact) *Look at #6. Does this sports car seat two or six passengers?* (two)

PROVIDE PRACTICE
Chalkboard Activity

△ Have students categorize vocabulary:

1–4 Passengers	**More Than 4 Passengers**
subcompact	camper

Conversations

△ Put models on the board and practice. Make appropriate substitutions.

A: Welcome to AutoWorld. Can I help you?
B: Does this <u>convertible</u> come with [airbags]?
A: Yes, all our new models have them.
   6. sports car 7. pickup truck 8. station wagon 9. sports utility vehicle 10. minivan

A: Acme Transport needs drivers. Do you want to apply?
B: Sure. I can drive a <u>tow truck</u>.
   12. dump truck 14. moving van
   15. tractor trailer 17. trailer

Interview Questions

1. In your opinion, what's the best car? the best truck? Why?
2. Would you like to drive a semi? Why or why not?

Listening: Listen and Write

△ Students open their books to page 106 and write the number of the car or truck they hear in sentences you dictate. E.g.:
1. *Compact cars get good gas mileage.* (#2)
2. *Vacations are fun in a camper.* (#10) Etc.

EXPAND THE LESSON
Discussion Questions

1. Tractor trailers can "jackknife," and some sports utility vehicles can tip over at high speeds. What car or truck do you think is the safest? Why?
2. Should driving laws be the same for trucks and cars? Why or why not?

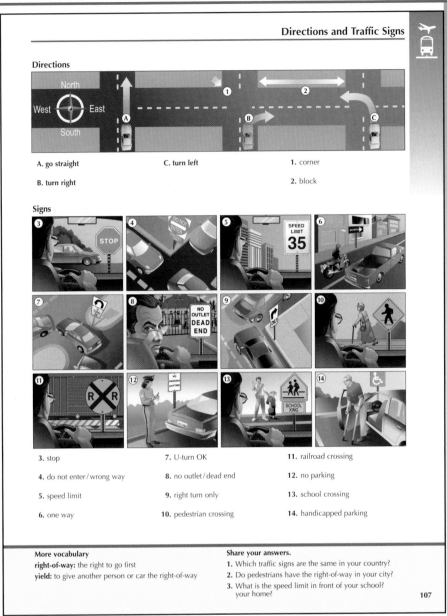

Directions and Traffic Signs

Directions

North
West ⊕ East
South

A. go straight

B. turn right

C. turn left

1. corner

2. block

Signs

3. stop

4. do not enter / wrong way

5. speed limit

6. one way

7. U-turn OK

8. no outlet / dead end

9. right turn only

10. pedestrian crossing

11. railroad crossing

12. no parking

13. school crossing

14. handicapped parking

More vocabulary
right-of-way: the right to go first
yield: to give another person or car the right-of-way

Share your answers.
1. Which traffic signs are the same in your country?
2. Do pedestrians have the right-of-way in your city?
3. What is the speed limit in front of your school? your home?

107

Workbooks, p. 107
Classic Classroom Activities, Unit 8
Related Dictionary Pages
• An Intersection, pp. 90–91
• Prepositions of Motion, p. 105

TOPIC NOTES

In the U.S., traffic signs vary from state to state, but most are similar to the signs depicted on this page.

Parking in a **handicapped parking** space requires a special permit issued by the Department of Motor Vehicles. Parking illegally can result in a heavy fine. Some communities have made it necessary to have parking permits to park in certain neighborhoods.

TEACHING TIPS
Related Vocabulary

no left turn   icy, chains required
passing prohibited   bicycle path
slippery when wet   falling rocks
two-way traffic   traffic ticket

Usage: When giving directions, many people use *go* instead of *turn. Go right at the light* is the same as *turn right at the light.*

- ☀ Create a map of the city nearest the school. Give directions to a place, but don't name it. Students guess the destination.

- ☀ After you have taught this page, invite a local police officer to class to talk about traffic laws and the meaning of various traffic signs.

- ☀ Write different examples of parking restrictions on the board so that students can learn about the various types of *no parking* signs.

INTRODUCE THE TOPIC

Draw a map on the board that shows your route from home to school. Tell students a story about how you come to school and include the directions.

Ask students to cover the word list, look at the pictures and name the traffic signs they know.

Talk about a time you or someone you know got a traffic ticket. Explain what you had done wrong or what sign you didn't see, and what the fine or outcome was.

TEACH THE NEW WORDS:

Ask students a series of *yes/no* questions about the pictures. *Is the car in picture A going straight?* (yes) *Is it OK to make a U-turn in #7?* (yes) *Is #11 a handicapped parking sign?* (no)

PROVIDE PRACTICE
Chalkboard Activity

△ Have students categorize vocabulary by the kind of sign:

Parking Information	Driving Information
no parking	*do not enter*

Conversations

△ Put models on the board and practice. Make appropriate substitutions.

A: Excuse me. How do I get to *[Ross Road]?*
B: *Go straight* at the light.
A: Thanks!
    B. Turn right C. Turn left
A: There was a *stop* sign back there.
B: Sorry, officer, I didn't see it.
A: Your driver's license, please.
    4. wrong way 5. speed limit
    6. one way 9. right turn only

Interview Question

Have you ever gotten a parking or traffic ticket? What did you do?

Listening: Interactive Dictation

△ Dictate directions from your school to a store in the area. Encourage students to ask for clarification. (*Where? On what street?*)

EXPAND THE LESSON
Discussion Question

What traffic laws are the most difficult for most people to follow?

Drawing Activity

1. Have students draw a map showing how to get from school to their home.
2. Have students in pairs take turns explaining how to get to their homes.
3. Students can repeat step 2 with new partners.

Workbooks, pp. 108–109
Classic Classroom Activities, Unit 8
Related Dictionary Pages
• Cars and Trucks, p. 106

TOPIC NOTES

In the U.S., cars come equipped with a **radio,** a **heater,** and **spare tire** as standard equipment, but cars have many other features that can be ordered.

For cars made after 1992, **air bags** on the driver's side are considered standard. Many gas stations used to do car repairs; however, *self-service* stations have become more common, and people take their cars to repair shops.

TEACHING TIPS
Related Vocabulary

armrest	transmission
headrest	alternator
defroster	vent
visor	service
antenna	mechanic
sunroof	repairs
fan belt	tune-up

- Explain the difference between car repair and standard maintenance.
- Review various makes and models of cars so that students can talk about which cars have good service records.
- Bring in various bills for car repairs. Explain to students the importance of estimates and what their signature means when having car repairs done. Talk about typical prices for various car services and repairs in your area.

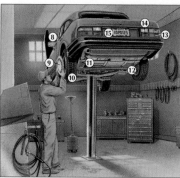

Parts of a Car and Car Maintenance

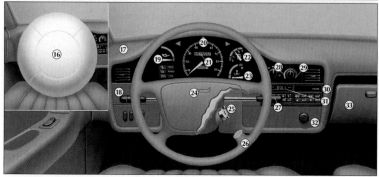

1. rearview mirror	10. tire	19. oil gauge	28. air conditioning
2. windshield	11. muffler	20. speedometer	29. heater
3. windshield wipers	12. gas tank	21. odometer	30. tape deck
4. turn signal	13. brake light	22. gas gauge	31. radio
5. headlight	14. taillight	23. temperature gauge	32. cigarette lighter
6. hood	15. license plate	24. horn	33. glove compartment
7. bumper	16. air bag	25. ignition	
8. sideview mirror	17. dashboard	26. steering wheel	
9. hubcap	18. turn signal	27. gearshift	

108

INTRODUCE THE TOPIC

Have students tell you the parts of a car. Write their words on the board and compare their list with the words on pages 108–109.

Tell a story about recent car repairs you have had. Talk about what the problem was, how much it cost to fix, and how long it took.

Take a survey of students in the class. Ask how many have cars, how many fix their cars themselves, and which cars seem to have the best repair records.

TEACH THE NEW WORDS

Ask students a series of *or* questions about the pictures. *Is #5 a headlight or a rearview mirror?* (headlight) *Is #15 a tire or a license plate?* (license plate)

PROVIDE PRACTICE
Chalkboard Activities

△ Have students categorize vocabulary:

1. On the Inside	On the Outside
dashboard	*taillight*

2. For Safety	For Enjoyment
seat belt	*radio*

△ Draw a simple picture of the side view or front view of a car. As you call out a car part, have students come to the board and draw it on the car.

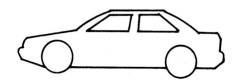

Conversations

△ Put models on the board and practice. Make appropriate substitutions.

A: Can I help you?
B: I'm having a problem with my *muffler*. Can you check it?
A: Sure. Just fill out this form.

> 20. speedometer 29. heater 44. emergency brake 45. clutch 46. brake pedal, etc.

A: What happened to your car?
B: Someone hit it in the parking lot and my *taillight* was damaged.
A: Oh, I'm sorry.

> 5. headlight 7. bumper 8. sideview mirror 15. license plate

A: I don't have my car today.
B: Why?
A: *The car needs oil* and it's at my mechanic's.

> 56. The radiator needs coolant,
> 57. The car needs a smog check
> 58. The battery needs recharging

Parts of a Car and Car Maintenance

34. lock	43. battery	52. jumper cables
35. front seat	44. emergency brake	53. spare tire
36. seat belt	45. clutch*	54. The car needs **gas**.
37. shoulder harness	46. brake pedal	55. The car needs **oil**.
38. backseat	47. accelerator/gas pedal	56. The radiator needs **coolant**.
39. child safety seat	48. stick shift	57. The car needs **a smog check**.
40. fuel injection system	49. trunk	58. The battery needs **recharging**.
41. engine	50. lug wrench	59. The tires need **air**.
42. radiator	51. jack	

*Note: Standard transmission cars have a clutch; automatic transmission cars do not.

109

Interview Questions

1. Can you drive a stick shift? How about an automatic?
2. Do you have a car?
3. Who repairs your car, you or a mechanic?
4. How often do you change the oil in your car? put air in the tires?
5. Do you know how to make simple car repairs?

Listening: Definitions

△ Have students write the car part they hear being defined. E.g.:
1. *This plays music.* (radio)
2. *This is on the passenger's side of the dashboard. You can open it and put maps inside.* (glove compartment) Etc.

EXPAND THE LESSON
Problem Solving

△ Have students brainstorm solutions.
1. *Thanh had his car fixed and the bill came to $100 more than the estimate. What can he do next time?*
2. *Kamal bought a used car. After he got it home, he realized the radiator was broken. What can he do? What are some things you can do to be sure a used car is a good one?*

Discussion Questions

1. A trunk can hold many things. What are some good items to keep in the trunk of your car in case of a flat tire? an accident? bad weather?
2. Car repairs can be very expensive. What are some ways to keep costs down? to be sure mechanics are doing a good job?

Language Workout

△ Copy these sentences on the board and discuss their meanings.
1. Jack always tells me how nice he is. He loves to *toot his own horn.*
2. Roger asks too many questions. He is *driving me up the wall.*
3. Alan was working 70 hours a week. He finally took off to *recharge his batteries.*

GAMES
Questions Only!

1. Give students a description of different parts of a car. E.g.: *This tells you how fast you are going.*
2. Have students guess what the word is and tell you in the form of a question. *(What is a speedometer?)*

One-Minute Study

1. Divide students into groups of 3–4. Each group chooses a recorder.
2. Have students look at pages 108–109 for one minute and close their books.
3. Recorders write down the vocabulary words as the group calls them out.
4. The activity ends after 10 minutes.

What Does It Do?

1. Divide students into two teams.
2. Call out a part of a car. Students from each team take turns telling what that part does.
   Teacher: *Brake.*
   Student: *It stops the car.*
3. The activity ends when one team has ten correct answers.

Problems! Problems!

1. Divide students into two teams.
2. Tell students a problem you are having. Students from each team take turns giving a solution. Each correct answer earns a point.
   Teacher: *The oil light is on!*
   Student: *The car needs oil.*
3. The activity ends when one team has ten points.

Picture Bingo

1. Have students make a grid that is five rows across and five rows down, and fill it in randomly with any 25 words from pages 108–109.
2. Call out vocabulary words randomly. Students circle the word as you say them.
3. The game ends when one student has five in any row, vertically, horizontally, or diagonally, and calls out "Bingo!"
4. Continue playing until five students have gotten Bingo.

Unit 8   An Airport   page 110

Workbooks, p. 110
Classic Classroom Activities, Unit 8
Related Dictionary Pages
• Life Events, pp. 28–29
• Public Transportation, p. 104
• A Plane Trip, p. 111

TOPIC NOTES

In the U.S., airports in Chicago, Dallas, Los Angeles, Atlanta, San Francisco, Denver, and Miami are on the list of the top ten busiest airports in the world! Chicago is the number one airport on that list.

⚠ Students may not know that the following items are not allowed on board U.S. airplanes: concealed weapons (including items such as scissors), knives, mace, pepper spray, lighter fluid, and heavy objects that are not packed securely. Also, smoking is not allowed during domestic flights.

TEACHING TIPS
Related Vocabulary

travel agent*	navigator
airline	runway
porter	propeller plane
claim check	landing gear
ticket counter	beverage cart
jetway	lavatory
air traffic controller	

Usage: *The plane/flight is on time* means that the plane is leaving or arriving on schedule. *The plane/flight is delayed* means the plane is late.

💡 Airline schedules are an excellent resource for pair work. Students can ask and answer questions such as *Where does flight 509 go? What time does it arrive there?*

An Airport

1. airline terminal	9. airplane	17. baggage claim area
2. airline representative	10. overhead compartment	18. carousel
3. check-in counter	11. cockpit	19. luggage carrier
4. arrival and departure monitors	12. pilot	20. customs
5. gate	13. flight attendant	21. customs officer
6. boarding area	14. oxygen mask	22. declaration form
7. control tower	15. airsickness bag	23. passenger
8. helicopter	16. tray table	

110

INTRODUCE THE TOPIC

Talk about a recent experience you had at the airport, using some of the target vocabulary in your story. *When I went to the boarding area, it was so crowded there were no seats.*

Find out how many of your students regularly go to the airport, and whether they usually go as passengers or to pick up or drop off their friends.

TEACH THE NEW WORDS

Describe each scene on the page, giving additional context to the target vocabulary. Have students point to the areas in each scene as you describe them. *This is a picture of a boarding area in an airline terminal. A boarding area is where you wait to board the plane. Usually there's a check-in counter in the boarding area.*

PROVIDE PRACTICE
Chalkboard Activity

△ Have students categorize vocabulary:

On a Plane	In an Airport
cockpit	*check-in counter*

Conversations

△ Put models on the board and practice. Make appropriate substitutions.

A: I have to park the car. Do you want to get out here?
B: Sure, where should I meet you?
A: Let's meet near the <u>check-in counter</u>.
   5. gate 17. baggage claim area
   18. carousel 20. customs

A: Excuse me. I'm having trouble with this <u>overhead compartment</u>.
B: Here, let me help.
A: That would be great. Thanks.
   16. tray table 19. luggage carrier
   22. declaration form

Interview Questions

1. Have you ever flown on a plane? Where did you go?
2. How often do you go to the airport?
3. Do you know any pilots? Have you ever been in the cockpit of a plane?

Listening: 📼 **#34, p. 222**
"LAX to SFO" Students listen to different travelers describing their experiences and point to the correct items.

EXPAND THE LESSON
Problem Solving

△ Have students brainstorm solutions. *Ruth just found out that her luggage is lost. It's 11:00 P.M. and she's at the airport in jeans and a sweater. She only has $15.00. She has a job interview at 8:00 A.M. tomorrow. What can she do?*

110

A Plane Trip ✈

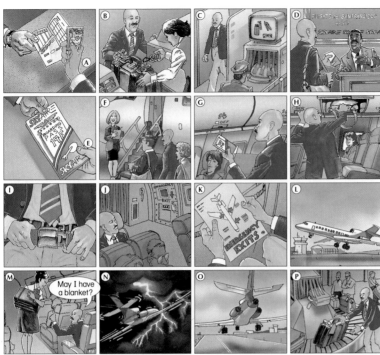

A. **buy** your ticket

B. **check** your bags

C. **go through** security

D. **check in** at the gate

E. **get** your boarding pass

F. **board** the plane

G. **find** your seat

H. **stow** your carry-on bag

I. **fasten** your seat belt

J. **look for** the emergency exit

K. **look at** the emergency card

L. **take off / leave**

M. **request** a blanket

N. **experience** turbulence

O. **land / arrive**

P. **claim** your baggage

More vocabulary

destination: the place the passenger is going

departure time: the time the plane takes off

arrival time: the time the plane lands

direct flight: a plane trip between two cities with no stops

stopover: a stop before reaching the destination, sometimes to change planes

111

Workbooks, p. 111
Classic Classroom Activities, Unit 8
Related Dictionary Pages
• Life Events, pp. 28–29
• Public Transportation, p. 104
• An Airport, p. 110

TOPIC NOTES

In the U.S., 288 million passengers flew on U.S. planes in 1980. By 1994, that figure was up to 509 million. The figure is expected to double by 2010.

Carry-on bags must fit under the seat in front of the passenger or in the overhead compartment.

Stow your bags or *put away your bags* is a commonly-used expression when traveling by plane, boat, or ship.

TEACHING TIPS
Related Vocabulary

travel agent*	departures*
curbside check-in	flotation device
sky cap	aisle*
flight number	plane crash*
arrivals*	security*

Usage: We use *look at* when we have the object or person in view. We use *look for* when we can't see the objects or people and want to find them.

💡 To give students communicative practice, have them use the target vocabulary as the basis for a plane trip role play. Assign passenger and crew roles as well as the emotional state of each. (See pp. 30–31, *Feelings,* for ideas.) Have the class suggest language to be used during the role play and write the ideas on the board for the actors to use.

INTRODUCE THE TOPIC

Bring in a suitcase and a plane ticket and have students guess the topic of the lesson.

Ask students to brainstorm places in the world they'd like to travel to. List their ideas on the board and use the information throughout the lesson.

TEACH THE NEW WORDS

Act out each part of a plane trip, describing what you're doing as you do it. *First, I buy my ticket. Next, I check my bags.* Now, direct student volunteers through each action and ask the class, *What do they do next?*

PROVIDE PRACTICE
Chalkboard Activity

△ Have students categorize vocabulary:

In the Airport
buy your ticket

On the Plane
find your seat

Conversations

△ Put models on the board and practice. Make appropriate substitutions.

A: Where do I *buy my ticket*?
B: Over there. See the sign?

    B. check my bag D. check in E. get my boarding pass F. board the plane P. claim my baggage

A: We'll be taking off in a few minutes. Please *find your seat.*
B: Do you think we'll experience turbulence?
A: No, I don't think so.

    H. stow your carry-on bag I. fasten your seat belt K. look at the emergency card

Interview Questions

1. Do you go on many plane trips?
2. Do you like to fly? Why or why not?
3. Have you ever experienced turbulence? When?

4. Where do you like to sit in a plane: on the aisle or at the window? in the front, middle, or back?

Listening 📻 #34 p. 222

"LAX to SFO" Students listen to different travelers describing their experiences and write the letter of the action they hear described.

GAMES
Charades

1. Write the verbs A–P on slips of paper and put them into a box or hat.
2. Divide the class into two teams.
3. Students take turns picking a word and acting it out for their team.
4. Teams get a point for each word they guess correctly.
5. The game ends when all the slips are gone.

Workbooks, p. 112
Classic Classroom Activities, Unit 9
Related Dictionary Pages
- School, p. 5
- A Graduation, pp. 32–33

TOPIC NOTES

In the U.S., most children begin school in kindergarten at age 5 and get their high school diplomas at 17 or 18. Many children attend preschool at age 3.

Public schools are free of charge to all children. Taxes collected by local, state, and federal governments support these schools.

Private schools accept students who meet the school requirements and can pay the tuition. Some schools offer scholarships to families in need.

Parochial schools offer religious instruction in addition to academic curriculum. These schools sometimes have separate instruction for boys and girls.

TEACHING TIPS
Related Vocabulary

first grade, etc.	tuition
subject	test scores
major	SAT
course	boarding school
dean	campus
principal*	scholarship

⚠ Some students may not have completed elementary, middle, or high school in their countries. Avoid asking questions in front of the whole class about an individual student's level of education.

Types of Schools

1. public school

2. private school

3. parochial school

4. preschool

5. elementary school

6. middle school/ junior high school

7. high school

8. adult school

9. vocational school / trade school

10. college/university

Note: In the U.S. most children begin school at age 5 (in kindergarten) and graduate from high school at 17 or 18.

More vocabulary
When students graduate from a college or university they receive a **degree**:
Bachelor's degree—usually 4 years of study
Master's degree—an additional 1–3 years of study

Doctorate—an additional 3–5 years of study
community college: a two-year college where students can get an Associate of Arts degree.
graduate school: a school in a university where students study for their master's and doctorates.

112

INTRODUCE THE TOPIC

Draw a flow chart starting with preschool and moving through high school, then branching out to adult school, vocational/trade school, and college/university. Using this chart, discuss the educational system with the class.

Ask students to name all the schools they know in the area and classify them by referring to the chart above.

TEACH THE NEW WORDS

Describe each type of school in consecutive order. Next, give the same descriptions in random order and have students identify the school they hear described: *This is a school that anyone can go to. You don't pay the school, but you pay taxes to help the schools.* (public school)

PROVIDE PRACTICE
Chalkboard Activity

△ Have students sequence the schools:

_____	**high school**
_____	**college**
_1_	**preschool**
_____	**community college**
_____	**middle school**
_____	**elementary school**

Conversations

△ Put models on the board and practice. Make appropriate substitutions.

A: I hear *[Joe]* is going to *preschool!*
B: Yes, *[he]* started in September.
   5. elementary school 6. middle school 7. high school, etc.

A. Does Emily like her school?
B: Yes, she loves going to a *public school.*
   2. private school 3. parochial school

Interview Questions

1. Would you rather learn English at an adult school or at a university?
2. Would you rather teach at a preschool or at a middle school?

Listening: Question Dictation

△ Dictate questions about the topic, speaking naturally and encouraging students to ask for clarification. *(What school?)* E.g.:
1. *When do children start preschool?*
2. *What do high school students study?*
3. *What classes can you take in vocational or trade school?* Etc.

Once the questions are written, students can write the answers.

EXPAND THE LESSON
Discussion Question

Which is better for children, public school or private school? Why?

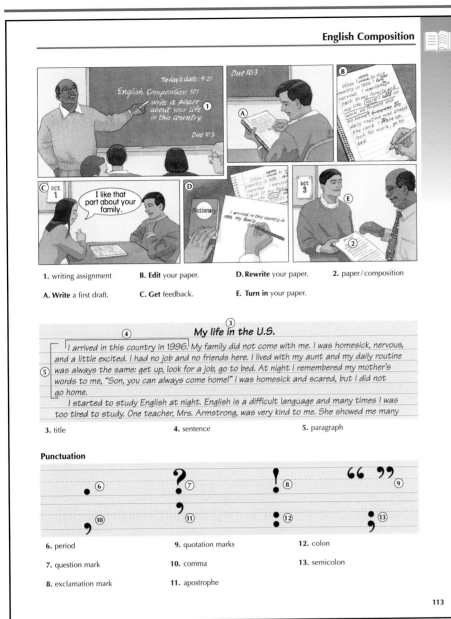

English Composition

1. writing assignment
B. **Edit** your paper.
D. **Rewrite** your paper.
2. paper / composition

A. **Write** a first draft.
C. **Get** feedback.
E. **Turn in** your paper.

My life in the U.S.

I arrived in this country in 1996. My family did not come with me. I was homesick, nervous, and a little excited. I had no job and no friends here. I lived with my aunt and my daily routine was always the same: get up, look for a job, go to bed. At night I remembered my mother's words to me, "Son, you can always come home!" I was homesick and scared, but I did not go home.

I started to study English at night. English is a difficult language and many times I was too tired to study. One teacher, Mrs. Armstrong, was very kind to me. She showed me many

3. title
4. sentence
5. paragraph

Punctuation

6. period
9. quotation marks
12. colon

7. question mark
10. comma
13. semicolon

8. exclamation mark
11. apostrophe

113

Workbooks, p. 113
Classic Classroom Activities, Unit 9
Related Dictionary Pages
- Studying, pp. 6–7
- More School Subjects, p. 121

TOPIC NOTES

In the U.S., schools are teaching writing as a process, emphasizing the editing procedure of **first draft,** rewrite, and final draft.

Feedback, or "constructive criticism," is what the reader (a student or teacher) responds to the writer, orally or in writing, about the ideas presented in the composition.

⚠ Students who have developed an intermediate level of fluency are often frustrated by their inability to communicate accurately in writing. Assure students that all writers, native and nonnative speakers alike, go through the writing process depicted on page 113.

TEACHING TIPS
Related Vocabulary

correct (v)	parts of speech
hand in	noun
essay	verb
report	adjective
research paper	preposition
parentheses	adverb
hyphen	article

💡 Effective and non-judgmental student-to-student feedback usually requires a checklist with questions such as: *Is the main idea clear? Does the writer use periods? Etc.*

💡 Invite a local author to talk to the class about his or her writing process.

INTRODUCE THE TOPIC

Write these three sentences on the board, leaving off the punctuation: *Writers write for readers* (.) *Do you like to write* (?) *It's very important to write* (!) See if students can identify what's missing and then discuss the content of the sentences.

TEACH THE NEW WORDS

Ask students a series of *or* questions: *Is the student in A going to write or edit his paper?* (write) *Is the student in D going to rewrite or turn in his paper?* (rewrite) *Is #6 a period or a comma?* (period)

PROVIDE PRACTICE

Chalkboard Activity

△ Have students categorize vocabulary:

In the Sentence	**At the End of a Sentence**
comma	*period*

Conversations

△ Put models on the board and practice. Make appropriate substitutions.

A: Did you turn in the assignment?
B: Not yet. I still have to <u>write a first draft</u>.

   B. edit my paper   C. get feedback
   D. rewrite my paper

A: What's wrong with this sentence?
B: You forgot to put in the <u>period</u>.

   7. question mark 8. exclamation mark
   9. quotation marks 10. comma
   11. apostrophe 12. colon 13. semi-colon

Interview Questions

1. Do you like to write?
2. What kind of writing do you do in your first language?
3. Do you like to edit other people's papers?
4. Do you remember any feedback you got on a paper? What was it?

Listening: Question Dictation

△ Dictate sentences about the topic, speaking naturally and encouraging students to ask for clarification. *(A good what?)* E.g.:

1. *What makes a good writer?*
2. *A good writer writes a first draft.*
3. *A first draft has the writer's ideas.* Etc.

Once the sentences are written, volunteers can write their work on the board for the class to correct and discuss.

EXPAND THE LESSON
Problem Solving

△ Have students brainstorm solutions. *Miguel hates to write. He can never think of anything to write about. When his teacher gives Miguel feedback, she puts red marks all over the paper. What advice do you have for Miguel?*

Workbooks, pp. 114–115
Classic Classroom Activities, Unit 9
Related Dictionary Pages
• The Calendar, pp. 18–19
• North America and Central America, pp. 122–123
• The World, pp. 124–125

TOPIC NOTES

In the U.S., the study of U.S. history encompasses the history of the very first Asian-Pacific peoples, as well as Europeans who settled here, and Africans who were brought as slaves. Also included is the story of democratic values, regional folklore, and cultural contributions.

Included on the time line here are the immigrations of large numbers of particular groups such as Mexicans and Armenians. For many groups, there was more than one wave of immigration, but only the first is noted.

Note: the word *popular* in entries like *TV popular* implies a time when the invention started becoming a household item.

TEACHING TIPS
Related Vocabulary

scientist	inventor
politician	astronaut*
leader	document
democracy	folklore

☼ Bring in a world map so that students can mark with labels the most common years of immigration from that country.

⚠ It is not intended that all the events or dates on these pages be covered in one lesson. Teach one portion of the time line, or only one type of event, or invention, etc., at a time.

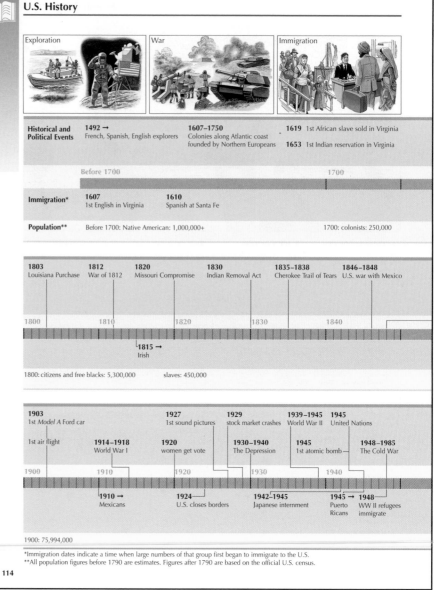

U.S. History

Exploration   War   Immigration

Historical and Political Events	1492 → French, Spanish, English explorers	1607–1750 Colonies along Atlantic coast founded by Northern Europeans	1619 1st African slave sold in Virginia 1653 1st Indian reservation in Virginia

Before 1700   1700

Immigration*	1607 1st English in Virginia	1610 Spanish at Santa Fe

Population**	Before 1700: Native American: 1,000,000+	1700: colonists: 250,000

1803 Louisiana Purchase	1812 War of 1812	1820 Missouri Compromise	1830 Indian Removal Act	1835–1838 Cherokee Trail of Tears	1846–1848 U.S. war with Mexico

1800   1810   1820   1830   1840

1815 → Irish

1800: citizens and free blacks: 5,300,000   slaves: 450,000

1903 1st *Model A* Ford car		1927 1st sound pictures	1929 stock market crashes	1939–1945 World War II	1945 United Nations

1st air flight   1914–1918 World War I   1920 women get vote   1930–1940 The Depression   1945 1st atomic bomb   1948–1985 The Cold War

1900   1910   1920   1930   1940

1910 → Mexicans   1924 U.S. closes borders   1942–1945 Japanese internment   1945 → Puerto Ricans   1948 WW II refugees immigrate

1900: 75,994,000

*Immigration dates indicate a time when large numbers of that group first began to immigrate to the U.S.
**All population figures before 1790 are estimates. Figures after 1790 are based on the official U.S. census.

114

INTRODUCE THE TOPIC

Ask students to look at the dates on pages 114–115 and identify the year they were born. Ask them to identify other years which are important to them and explain why.

Have students look at the immigration component and find when their group first began to come to the United States. Some countries are grouped together under a larger division, such as Southern Europeans.

Bring in pictures of historical events and talk about when they took place. Possibilities include the pilgrims landing at Plymouth Rock, the Civil War, and the first moon landing.

Draw or bring in pictures of three inventions on the time line (e.g., telephone, airplane, TV). Have students guess when they were invented.

TEACH THE NEW WORDS

Ask students to identify the picture based on your description. E.g.: *This shows people coming to live in the United States from another country. Before airplanes, most people came in by boat or ship. Today most people fly here. This movement of people is called "immigration." (#3) This picture shows people choosing a new president or governor by voting. Whoever gets the most votes gets the job. We call this an "election." (#5)* Etc.

Teach the six words at the top of the pictures and use the time line to point out examples of each event. Have students find similar events on the time line. Discuss what the outcome was.

PROVIDE PRACTICE
Chalkboard Activities

△ Have students categorize vocabulary:

Inventions	Wars	Movements
TV	World War I	civil rights

△ Have students find the years for these (or other) events:

Revolutionary War	<u>1775-1783</u>
U. S. war with Mexico	_____
1st light bulb	_____
1st air flight	_____
United Nations chartered	_____

△ Draw a time line from the date of birth of your oldest student. Have volunteers come to the board and write in important events from the time line in the dictionary, from their own country's history, or other world events.

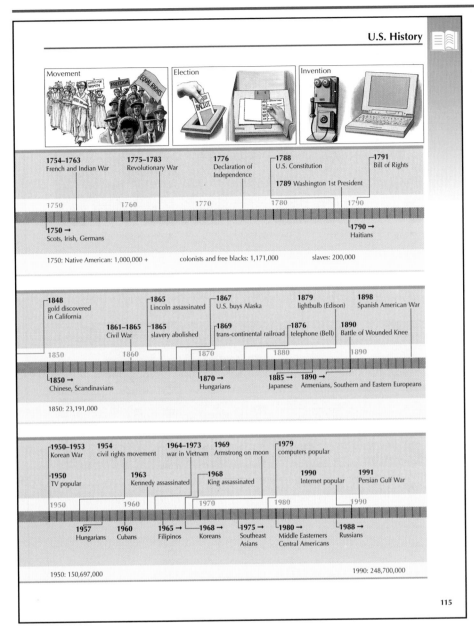

4. *The Irish began to come to the United States in **1840**.*

5. *The U.S. war with Mexico started in **1846**.*

6. *In **1867**, the United States bought Alaska.*

7. *The Japanese began to come to the United States in **1885**.*

8. *In **1903**, the Wright Brothers made the first successful air flight.*

9. *In **1929**, the stock market crashed.*

10. *In **1969**, Neil Armstrong walked on the moon.*

EXPAND THE LESSON
Discussion Questions

1. Many inventions have changed the world. Which invention has most changed the way you live? What invention do you think will be the next important one?

2. What are some of the reasons people from your country came to the United States?

Speeches: A Short History Report

1. Have students look up one event in an encyclopedia or pictorial history book.

2. Write the following words on the board as an example:

   Who: English settlers
   What: sailed across the Atlantic to America and landed
   When: in 1620
   Where: Plymouth Rock, now in Massachusetts.

3. Discuss ways to write the sentences explaining what happened.

Silent Drill: In What Century?

1. Each student needs three sheets of paper. They write the following dates, large and dark, one on each sheet: *1700s, 1800s, 1900s.*

2. Ask students when different events occurred. E.g.: *In what century was Kennedy assassinated?*

3. After students hold up their answers, tell them the correct century.

GAMES
I'm Thinking of....

1. Divide students into teams of 4–6. Each team takes turns guessing which event you are thinking about. Give them clues.

   Teacher: *I'm thinking of something on the time line that happened in the 1920s.*
   Team B: *Is it "women get the vote"?*
   Teacher: *Yes.*

2. For advanced students, have them use the past tense. *(Is it that women got the vote?)*

Conversations

△ Put models on the board and practice. Make appropriate substitutions.

A: When did the _Haitians_ begin to immigrate to the United States?
B: The book says in *[1790].*
  Hungarians, Japanese, Southern Europeans, Irish, etc.

A: Do you know when the _lightbulb_ was invented?
B: Let me check. The book says *[in 1879].*
  telephone, model A Ford car

A: When was _the war in Vietnam_?
B: Let me look. The book says from *[1964 to 1973.]*
  the French and Indian War, the Revolutionary War, the Civil War, World War I, World War II, etc.

Interview Questions

1. What happened around the time you were born?

2. What happened around the time your parents were born?

3. Which events of U.S. history did you hear discussed in your country?

4. Which events on the time line are the most interesting to you?

5. What invention was the most important? Why?

Listening: Listen and Write

△ Have students write the date as you say when the historical event occurred.

1. *The first African slaves arrived in **1619**.*

2. *The Declaration of Independence was signed in **1776**.*

3. *The U.S. Constitution was written in **1788**.*

Unit 9　U.S. Government and Citizenship　page 116

Workbooks, p. 116
Classic Classroom Activities, Unit 9
Related Dictionary Pages
• U.S. History, pp. 114–115
• North America and Central America, pp. 122–123

TOPIC NOTES

In the U.S., there are four levels of government: city, county, state, and federal. All 50 states have three branches of government, but each city and county has its own way of organizing its government. All levels of government levy taxes. Income tax is usually paid to the federal and state governments.

TEACHING TIPS
Related Vocabulary

election*	freedom
vote	mayor
democracy	governor
cabinet	city council
Constitution	city commission
Bill of Rights	public services

🔅 Review events from *U.S. History*, pages 114–115, such as the writing of the Declaration of Independence, the Constitution, and the Bill of Rights, that formed the foundation of U.S. government.

🔅 Bring in federal and state tax forms, voter registration forms, and election ballots so that students can become familiar with them.

🔅 Introduce students to the opportunities U.S. citizens have, such as running for public office and traveling with a U.S. passport.

U.S. Government and Citizenship

BRANCHES OF GOVERNMENT

Legislative

Executive

Judicial

1. The House of Representatives
2. congresswoman / congressman
3. The Senate
4. senator

5. The White House
6. president
7. vice president

8. The Supreme Court
9. chief justice
10. justices

Citizenship application requirements

A. **be** 18 years old

B. **live** in the U.S. for five years

C. **take** a citizenship test

Rights and responsibilities

D. **vote**

E. **pay** taxes

F. **register** with Selective Service*

G. **serve** on a jury

H. **obey** the law

*Note: All males 18 to 26 who live in the U.S. are required to register with Selective Service.

116

INTRODUCE THE TOPIC

Ask students to cover the word list in the top section, look at the pictures, and name the items they already know.

Talk about the last local or federal election. Discuss who ran and who was elected.

Elicit from students what they know about becoming a U.S. citizen. Write their responses on the chalkboard. Compare them to the list on the page.

TEACH THE NEW WORDS

Ask students to identify the number of a particular picture based on your description. *This has 100 elected officials called "Senators," two from each state. It's called "the Senate."* (#3) *We give money to the government every year in April. Your rate for income taxes is based on the money you make.* (E)

PROVIDE PRACTICE
Chalkboard Activity

△ Have students categorize vocabulary:

Branch	Title	Place
executive	*vice president*	*White House*

Conversations

△ Put models on the board and practice. Make appropriate substitutions.

A: Did you hear what *President [Riley]* said?
B: What?
A: *[He]'s* not going to run for office again.
  2. congressman 2. congresswoman
  4. senator

A: Next *[Tuesday]* is a big day for me.
B: Why?
A: I'm going to *vote* for the first time!
  E. pay taxes F. register with Selective Service
  G. serve on a jury

Interview Questions

1. Are the citizenship requirements too difficult? Are they too easy?
2. If you were president, what changes would you try to make in the United States?

Listening: Listen and Write

△ Have students close their books and write vocabulary words #1–10 as you say them in random order.

EXPAND THE LESSON
Discussion Question

The right to vote, to free speech, and to a speedy and public trial for the accused are examples of some rights of U.S. citizenship. Which of these do you think is the most important? Why?

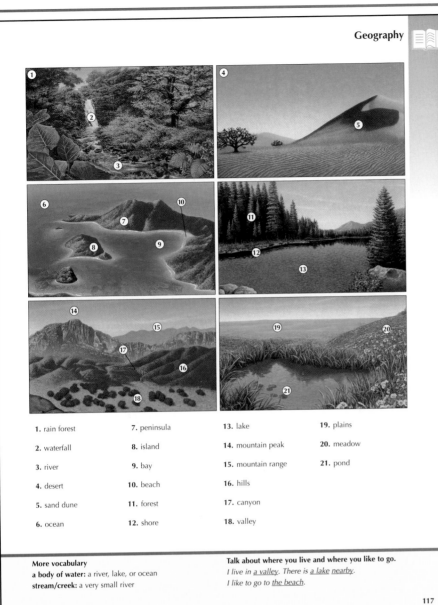

Geography

1. rain forest
2. waterfall
3. river
4. desert
5. sand dune
6. ocean
7. peninsula
8. island
9. bay
10. beach
11. forest
12. shore
13. lake
14. mountain peak
15. mountain range
16. hills
17. canyon
18. valley
19. plains
20. meadow
21. pond

More vocabulary
a body of water: a river, lake, or ocean
stream/creek: a very small river

Talk about where you live and where you like to go.
I live in a valley. There is a lake nearby.
I like to go to the beach.

117

Workbooks, p. 117
Classic Classroom Activities, Unit 9
Related Dictionary Pages
• North America and Central America, pp. 122–123
• The World, pp. 124–125
• Energy and the Environment, p. 126

TOPIC NOTES

In the U.S., it's possible to see all the physical features that are depicted on page 117. U.S. **mountain ranges** include the Rockies in the West and the Appalachians in the East.

More than 50% of the different animals and plants found on earth are in the **rainforests.** These forests also supply the earth with a large percentage of its oxygen, and their deforestation is a world-wide concern. Rainforests exist in Hawaii, Florida, and Oregon.

A **lake** is usually a fresh-water inland body of water. The Great Lakes are the five largest lakes in the United States.

An **island** is a land mass completely surrounded by water. The state of Hawaii consists of nine main islands.

TEACHING TIPS
Related Vocabulary

land	jungle
physical feature	volcano
continent	lagoon
ocean floor	cliff
continental shelf	glacier
plateau	cave

Have students draw travel posters highlighting the geographical features of different countries.

INTRODUCE THE TOPIC

Post four nature scenes (from a calendar or magazine) around the room. Have students "vote with their feet" by standing next to their favorite scene. Count the "votes" and discuss why each group liked its scene.

TEACH THE NEW WORDS

Describe and name the geographical features on the page, while students call out the correct numbers. *This is an ocean, a large body of water, like the Pacific or Atlantic.* (#6)

PROVIDE PRACTICE
Chalkboard Activity

△ Have students categorize vocabulary:

Water
river

Land
rainforest

Conversations

△ Put models on the board and practice. Make appropriate substitutions.

A: Where are you going on your vacation?
B: I'm going to the *desert*.
  10. beach 11. forest 13. lake

A: Is there *a river* near here?
B: Yes, there is, about *[25]* miles away.
  2. a waterfall 4. a desert 5. a sand dune, etc.

Interview Questions

1. Which do you prefer: going to the ocean or to a lake? to the desert or the forest?
2. Would you rather live on an island or on a mountain?

Listening: Listen and Draw

△ Direct students, step by step, to draw a picture using some of the geographical features on page 117. E.g.:
  1. *Draw a mountain on the right side of the page.*
  2. *Draw a lake at the bottom of the mountain.*
  3. *Draw a river coming from the lake and going across the page.*
  4. *Draw a small forest behind the lake.* Etc.

EXPAND THE LESSON
Discussion Question

Rainforests are very important to the earth's ecology, but they are being cut down for their wood and to make room for farms and housing. What can people and governments do about this problem?

Workbooks, p. 118
Classic Classroom Activities, Unit 9
Related Dictionary Pages
• Numbers and Measurements, p. 14–15

TOPIC NOTES
In the U.S., math is taught in every grade, but not all students take the advanced classes of **algebra, geometry,** etc. Most students learn how to use a calculator in their classes as well.

TEACHING TIPS
Related Vocabulary

add*	plus
subtract	minus
multiply	divide
times	goes into
equal(s)	parallelogram
quadrangle	whole number
fraction*	percent*

☼ Review pages 14–15, *Numbers and Measurements*. Give students practice in both listening to and saying numbers up to 100 so that they can talk easily about the numbers on this page as well as about various math problems.

☼ Your students may depict math operations, signs, and symbols differently. Ask students to put problems on the board and show you how they indicate multiplication, division, etc. Student volunteers can solve the problems.

☼ Cut out various 2-D shapes in one color of paper and the various 3-D shapes in another. Use dotted lines to show the solids are three-dimensional. Bring in pictures or actual items representing the shapes and identify them: soda cans as cylinders, road cones as cones, a pair of dice as cubes.

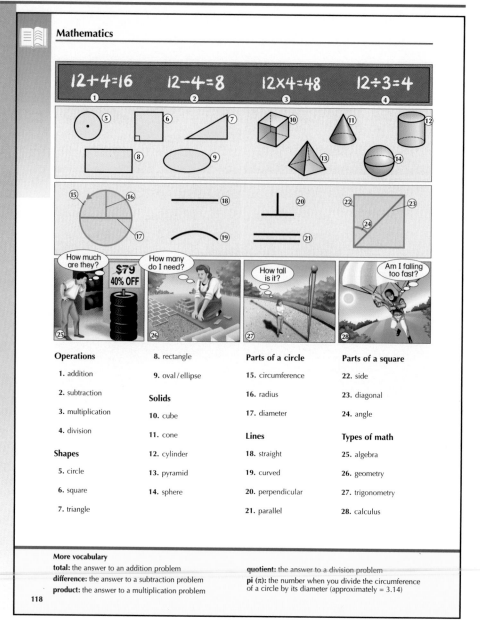

Mathematics

12+4=16   12−4=8   12×4=48   12÷3=4

Operations	8. rectangle	Parts of a circle	Parts of a square
1. addition	9. oval/ellipse	15. circumference	22. side
2. subtraction	**Solids**	16. radius	23. diagonal
3. multiplication	10. cube	17. diameter	24. angle
4. division	11. cone		
	12. cylinder	**Lines**	**Types of math**
Shapes	13. pyramid	18. straight	25. algebra
5. circle	14. sphere	19. curved	26. geometry
6. square		20. perpendicular	27. trigonometry
7. triangle		21. parallel	28. calculus

Speech bubbles: "How much are they?" $79 40% OFF   "How many do I need?"   "How tall is it?"   "Am I falling too fast?"

More vocabulary
total: the answer to an addition problem
difference: the answer to a subtraction problem
product: the answer to a multiplication problem
quotient: the answer to a division problem
pi (π): the number when you divide the circumference of a circle by its diameter (approximately = 3.14)

118

INTRODUCE THE TOPIC
Ask students to cover the word list, look at the pictures, and name the math operations, shapes, etc., they know.

Walk around the room and name some of the shapes and solids you see. For each one, have students name other items with the same shape.

Write on the board a simple word problem. Solve the problem with students, explaining the solution.

TEACH THE NEW WORDS
Ask students a series of *or* questions about the shapes, solids, and lines. *Is #12 a cylinder or a cube?* (cylinder) *Is #7 a circle or a triangle?* (triangle)

Explain the different types of math depicted on the page and have students point to the various problems.

PROVIDE PRACTICE
Chalkboard Activities
△ Have students categorize vocabulary:

Shapes	**Solids**
triangle	*sphere*

△ Put different math problems on the board. Have students call out the operation necessary to solve each. E.g.:

107−27=80   **76+12=88**
subtraction   *addition*

Conversations
△ Put models on the board and practice. Make appropriate substitutions.

A: Can I help you with your *algebra*?
B: Yes, I can't do this problem.
    26. geometry 27. trigonometry 28. calculus

A: How do you get the volume of a *cube*?
B: Sorry, I don't know that yet.
    11. cone 12. cylinder 13. pyramid

Interview Questions
1. Do you like to study math?
2. How do you use math outside of school?

Listening: Listen and Draw
△ Have students draw shapes, solids, and lines as you give commands. E.g.:
1. *Draw a circle.*
2. *Draw a straight line.*
3. *Draw a box.* Etc.

EXPAND THE LESSON
Language Workout
△ Copy this text on the board and discuss its meaning.
Joe loves Mia. Mia loves Bill. This *love triangle* will only cause problems.

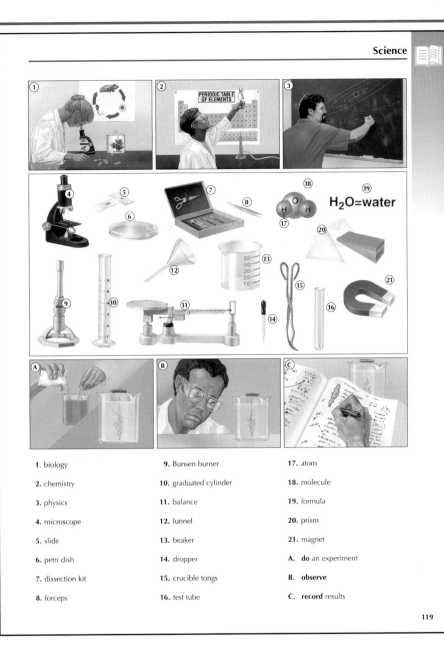

Science

1. biology
2. chemistry
3. physics
4. microscope
5. slide
6. petri dish
7. dissection kit
8. forceps
9. Bunsen burner
10. graduated cylinder
11. balance
12. funnel
13. beaker
14. dropper
15. crucible tongs
16. test tube
17. atom
18. molecule
19. formula
20. prism
21. magnet
A. **do** an experiment
B. **observe**
C. **record** results

119

Workbooks, p. 119
Classic Classroom Activities, Unit 9
Related Dictionary Pages
• Weights and Measures, p. 57
• Geography, p. 117
• The Universe, p. 127

TOPIC NOTES

In the U.S., mandatory general science education begins in kindergarten and continues through middle school. By about the eighth grade students have the opportunity to study specific fields of science such as biology, chemistry, and physics.

TEACHING TIPS
Related Vocabulary

scientist	information science
researcher	health sciences
laboratory (lab)	geology
electron	astronomy
neutron	engineering
periodic table of the elements	

Grammar: The suffix -*logy*
Students may be interested to know that -*logy* means the "study of" or "science of." Mention a number of sciences that have this suffix, e.g., *biology, geology, archeology, psychology.*

☼ Record a science program from a public television station. Preview critical vocabulary and concepts with students, then show a segment or two of the tape. Discuss the segment(s) with the class and encourage students to watch the program at home.

INTRODUCE THE TOPIC

Demonstrate this experiment in air pressure. Take a small glass with a 2 to 2-1/2 inch diameter. Fill the glass to the top with water, wet the rim, and lay a 3"x 5" card on top of the glass. Hypothesize: *I think the water will pour out.* Turn the glass and card over above a bucket or other plastic container. The water should stay in the glass. Record each step and discuss the experiment with the class.

TEACH THE NEW WORDS

Ask students a series of *or* questions. *Is #5 a slide or a dissection kit?* (slide) *Is #20 a prism or a petri dish?* (prism)

PROVIDE PRACTICE
Chalkboard Activity

△ Have students categorize vocabulary:

Biology	**Chemistry**	**Physics**
microscope	*test tube*	*magnet*

Conversations

△ Put models on the board and practice. Make appropriate substitutions.

A: What science class did you get?
B: I'm taking *physics* with [*Ms. Quast*].
  1. biology 2. chemistry

A: Hand me the whatchamacallit, OK?
B: You mean the *dissection kit?*
A: Yeah, that's right.
  5. slide 6. petri dish 8. forceps 9. Bunsen burner 10. graduated cylinder, etc.

A: Wasn't the lecture on *atoms* great?
B: Not to me! I'm totally confused.
  18. molecules 19. formulas 20. prism 21. magnets

Interview Questions

1. Do you like to do experiments?
2. Do you like to read about scientists' work? Which?

Listening: Listen and Write

1. Write the elements *iron, silver, gold, neon, helium,* and *mercury* on the board. Show pictures or examples of each (iron skillet, silver and gold chains, neon light, helium balloon, thermometer).

2. Dictate these symbols for students to write on a separate piece of paper: 1) Ag 2) Ne 3) He 4) Me 5) Fe 6) Au

3. Help students match the symbols to the elements.

EXPAND THE LESSON
Discussion Question

What do you think scientists will discover in the next ten years?

Workbooks, p. 120
Classic Classroom Activities, Unit 9
Related Dictionary Pages
- Electronics and Photography, pp. 164–165
- Entertainment, pp. 166–167

TOPIC NOTES

In the U.S., both instrumental music and vocal music entertain and inspire almost everyone. Music has served as an instrument of political dissent and as a source of ethnic and national pride. Music appreciation provides an understanding of history, culture, and tradition as it connects generations and reflects changing society.

📁 The most frequently sung music in the world is "Happy Birthday to You."

TEACHING TIPS

Related Vocabulary

concert	banjo
composer	harp
rehearsal	cymbals
choir/chorus*	harmonica
marching band	pick/plectrum
speaker	tune (v)
strum	

Grammar: Word endings
Adding the suffix -ist or the word player to the name of an instrument creates the word for the player of that instument, e.g., violinist, saxophone player. One exception is drummer.

💡 Singing together reinforces vocabulary and reduces classroom stress. Use songs in prewriting activities, cloze–style dictations, and focused listening activities.

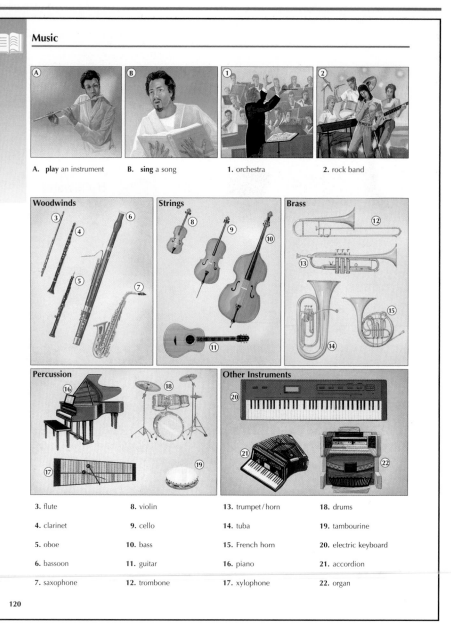

Music

A. **play** an instrument   B. **sing** a song   1. orchestra   2. rock band

Woodwinds   **Strings**   **Brass**

Percussion   **Other Instruments**

3. flute	8. violin	13. trumpet/horn	18. drums
4. clarinet	9. cello	14. tuba	19. tambourine
5. oboe	10. bass	15. French horn	20. electric keyboard
6. bassoon	11. guitar	16. piano	21. accordion
7. saxophone	12. trombone	17. xylophone	22. organ

120

INTRODUCE THE TOPIC

Ask students what instruments they play and how they learned.

Ask students to name instruments they hear as you play a variety of instrumental recordings—classical, jazz, folk, etc.

TEACH THE NEW WORDS

Act out a "class orchestra," assigning students to different sections (e.g., brass, strings). Use TPR commands to guide students through the target vocabulary. *Pick up the violin. Now, pick up the bow. Put the bow over the strings. Ready? Play!*

Chalkboard Activity

△ Have students categorize vocabulary by what is used:

Breath	Bow	Hands Only
flute	violin	piano

Conversations

△ Put models on the board and practice. Make appropriate substitutions.

A: Would you like to learn to play the <u>drums</u>?
B: Maybe. I'd really like to play the [violin].

3. flute 4. clarinet 5. oboe 6. bassoon 7. saxophone 8. violin, etc.

INTERVIEW QUESTIONS

1. Which instruments can you play?
2. Do you like to sing? Do you prefer to sing alone or in a group?
3. Do you prefer rock bands or orchestra music?
4. What's a song you know in your language?
5. Name an instrument that's popular in your country.

Listening 📼 #35, p. 222

"Mr. Porter's Opus" Students listen to Mr. Porter describe the musical instruments. They write the names of the instruments as they are described.

EXPAND THE LESSON

Language Workout

△ Copy this sentence on the board and discuss its meaning:
Lee didn't want to tell his parents about the car accident, but he had to *face the music.*

More School Subjects

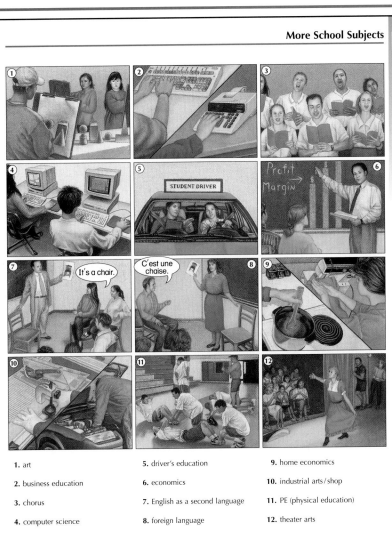

1. art
2. business education
3. chorus
4. computer science
5. driver's education
6. economics
7. English as a second language
8. foreign language
9. home economics
10. industrial arts/shop
11. PE (physical education)
12. theater arts

More vocabulary
core course: a subject students have to take
elective: a subject students choose to take

Share your answers.
1. What are your favorite subjects?
2. In your opinion, what subjects are most important? Why?
3. What foreign languages are taught in your school?

121

Workbooks, p. 121
Classic Classroom Activities, Unit 9
Related Dictionary Pages
• School, p. 5
• Types of Schools, p. 112
• English Composition–Music, pp. 113–120

TOPIC NOTES

In the U.S., students take specific school subjects as their core courses to fulfill academic requirements, and elective subjects to supplement their core coursework.

At one time, **home economics** and **shop** classes were segregated by gender. Now they are coeducational.

Physical education, often called PE, is the general term for all sports and fitness courses. In addition to general PE courses, team sports such as football and individual sports such as track and field are often offered.

TEACHING TIPS
Related Vocabulary

marching band	metal shop
journalism	wood shop
drama	sewing
typing	cooking
auto shop	class schedule

Usage: The words *education, economics, composition,* and *literature* are often shortened when part of a course title. We usually say *driver's ed, home ec, English comp* and *American lit.*

💡 Have students create their ideal class schedules using the target vocabulary and their imaginations. Survey the class about students' favorite subjects. Create a bar graph showing students' preferences.

INTRODUCE THE TOPIC

Take a survey of how many students know how to draw, type, drive, or cook. Then survey students to find out if they learned to do these things at school or from their families.

Talk about your experiences, taking any one of the subjects on the page.

TEACH THE NEW WORDS

Demonstrate the different activities associated with each subject as you name it. Have students point to the appropriate pictures as they say the course names. *In art classes, you paint, draw, and make sculptures.*

PROVIDE PRACTICE
Chalkboard Activity

△ Have students categorize vocabulary:

Academic	Vocational	Fine Arts
economics	*business ed*	*art*

Conversations

△ Put models on the board and practice. Make appropriate substitutions.

A: I love to *[sing]*!
B: Why don't you take *chorus*?
   9. home economics 12. theater arts
A: Oh, no! I'm going to be late for third period.
B: What's so special about third period?
A: It's my *art* class!
   2. business education 3. chorus
   4. computer science 5. driver's education
   6. economics, etc.

Interview Questions

1. Would you prefer to take an economics or a home economics class?
2. Would you prefer to take a theater arts or an industrial arts class?
3. What PE classes do you like?

Listening: Interactive Dictation

△ Have students close their books. Make up and dictate a class schedule, speaking naturally and encouraging students to ask for clarification. (*What time? What class?*) Students should write only the time and the name of the course. E.g.:
   1. *At* **8:00,** *Sally has* **PE.**
   2. *Her second class at* **9:00** *is* **English.** Etc.

EXPAND THE LESSON
Problem Solving

△ Have students brainstorm solutions. *Jung can take one more class. His father wants him to take economics, but Jung wants to take a theater arts class. He likes economics, but he wants to try acting. What can he say to his father?*

Workbooks, pp. 122–123
Classic Classroom Activities, Unit 9
Related Dictionary Pages
• Prepositions, p. 13
• Numbers and Measurements, pp. 14–15
• Geography, p. 117
• The World, pp. 124–125

TOPIC NOTES

In the U.S., borders are shared with only two other nations: Canada and Mexico. Of its 50 states, 49 are on the North American continent; the 50th, Hawaii, is a group of Pacific Ocean islands. Central America lies south of North America and is linked to South America by the Isthmus of Panama.

TEACHING TIPS
Related Vocabulary

country*	border
region	coastal
state*	inland
capital	island*
territory	time zone*
area	surround

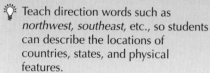 Teach direction words such as *northwest, southeast,* etc., so students can describe the locations of countries, states, and physical features.

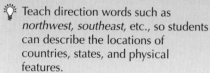 Have student groups choose one region from the word list. On the board, write *geography, climate, food, industry,* and *places to see.* Have each group research these topics for their area at the library or at home. Have groups use magazine pictures or students' own drawings to create a collage about their region. Post the collages around the room.

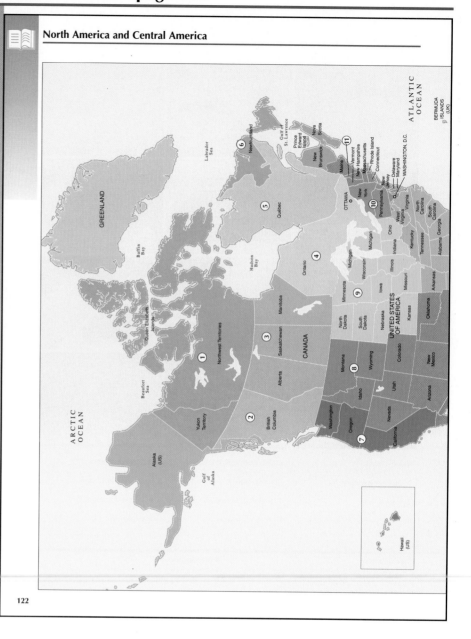

North America and Central America

INTRODUCE THE TOPIC

Tell a story about the travel itinerary of a famous celebrity. Using a map, trace an imaginary North American tour. *Did you hear about Whitney Houston's concert schedule? Her first Canadian concert stop will be Vancouver, British Columbia. That province is west of Alberta. The next concert will be....*

Draw a large sketch of the U.S. and mark an X in the middle to indicate Kansas. Have students brainstorm a list of all other U.S. states they know and tell you where each state is in relation to Kansas. *(Florida is southeast of Kansas.)*

Ask questions about travel from your city to other regions. *Should we fly or take a ship to Panama? Where can we cross the border to Mexico?*

TEACH THE NEW WORDS

Say the words and have students repeat them as they point to the correct regions on the map.

PROVIDE PRACTICE
Chalkboard Activities

△ Have students categorize vocabulary:

1. Coastal	**Inland**
El Salvador	*Nevada, U.S.*

2. Countries	**States/Provinces**
Cuba	*New York*

△ Have students sequence the countries and/or states on a trip north from Panama to Alaska.

_____	**Arizona**	___1___	**Panama**
_____	**Guatemala**	_____	**Alberta**
_____	**Puebla**	_____	**Alaska**
_____	**Oregon**	_____	**Zacatecas**

Conversations

△ Put models on the board and practice. Make appropriate substitutions.

A: Where is *[Florida]* located?
B: It's in the U.S.
A: I still don't see it.
B: It's part of the *[Southeast].*

A: Pack your fishing pole! We're sailing to the *Pacific Northwest.*
B: Great! I've never been there before!

16. Gulf Coastal Plain 17. Southern Uplands 19. Yucatan Peninsula

A: I'd like to visit *[Quebec].*
B: Where's that?
A: It's next to *[Ontario].*

Interview Questions

1. Which cities in North America have you visited?

2. Which countries on these pages have you visited?

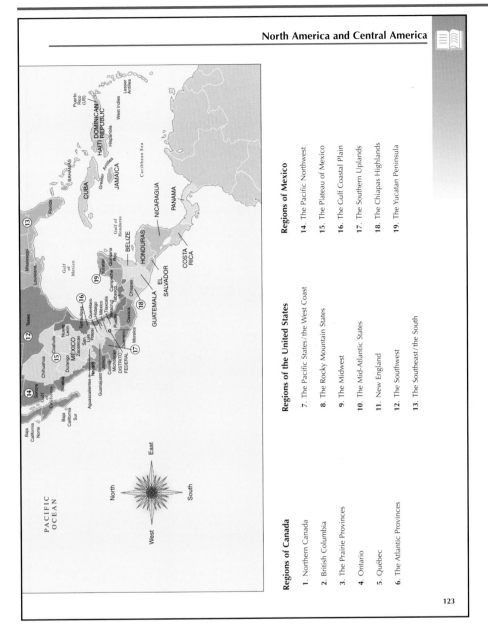

North America and Central America

Regions of Mexico

14. The Pacific Northwest
15. The Plateau of Mexico
16. The Gulf Coastal Plain
17. The Southern Uplands
18. The Chiapas Highlands
19. The Yucatan Peninsula

Regions of the United States

7. The Pacific States/the West Coast
8. The Rocky Mountain States
9. The Midwest
10. The Mid-Atlantic States
11. New England
12. The Southwest
13. The Southeast/the South

Regions of Canada

1. Northern Canada
2. British Columbia
3. The Prairie Provinces
4. Ontario
5. Québec
6. The Atlantic Provinces

123

3. If you could move anywhere tomorrow, where would that be?
4. Where on this map would you dislike living? Why?
5. In your opinion, which place has the best climate? the safest cities?
6. If you wanted to go skiing or ice skating, where would you go?
7. Do you have family or friends in any of these areas? Where?
8. Which regions do you think are popular tourist destinations? Why?
9. When you retire, where would you want to live? Why?
10. In your opinion, where is the best vacation place for swimming and fishing?

Listening: Descriptions

△ Have students look at pages 122–123 and write the name for each location you describe.

1. *This Mid-Atlantic state is north of Pennsylvania and southeast of Ontario.* (New York)
2. *This Southwest state is bordered by California to the west and Sonora to the south.* (Arizona)
3. *This Central American country borders four other countries.* (Guatemala)
4. *This Atlantic province is east of Quebec and is bordered by Maine to the south.* (New Brunswick)
5. *Mexico D.F., Durango, and Zacatecas are states in this region.* (The Plateau of Mexico)
6. *This territory in Northern Canada is east of Alaska.* (Yukon)

EXPAND THE LESSON

Discussion Questions

1. In your opinion, is it better to live in an urban area or a more rural region? Give some reasons.
2. Many regions depend on tourism for their economic success. How can a province or state encourage visits by tourists?
3. Which North American or Central American cities would be best for the Summer Olympic games? the Winter Olympic games?

Speeches

1. Write the following incomplete sentences on the board and brainstorm ways to complete them:

   _____ is the best place to visit!

   The most popular tourist attraction there is _____.

   The best time to visit is in the (spring, summer, fall, winter) because you can _____.

   _____ is famous for its _____.

   When you go, make sure and bring your _____.

   Have a great time in _____!

2. Help students with the pronunciation of these phrases by tapping out the rhythm and/or using your hand to indicate rising and falling intonation.
3. Give each student a 3″ x 5″ card on which to write a short speech, using the phrases from the board and adding their own ideas.
4. Have students practice their speeches with partners or in groups.
5. Students can memorize or use their cards to give the speeches in front of the class.

GAMES

Memory Game

1. Divide the class into two teams.
2. Have students study the maps on pages 122–123.
3. Quiz alternate teams with true/false statements about the map. *Maine is in New England.* (true) *Baja California Norte is in the United States.* (false)
4. Correct answers get one point.
5. The game ends when one team gets ten points.

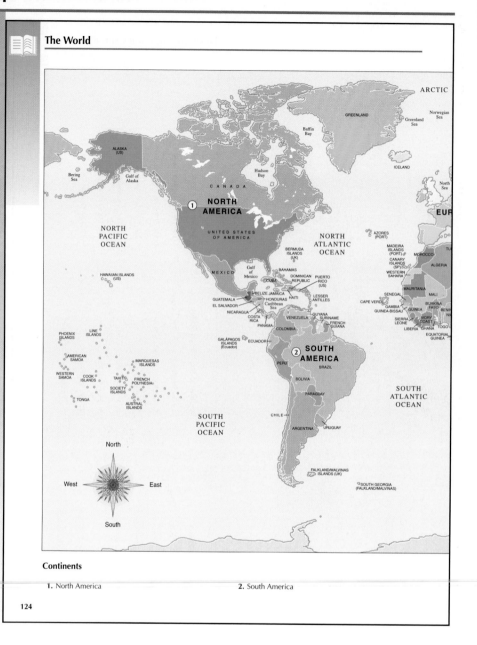

Workbooks, pp. 124–125
Classic Classroom Activities, Unit 9
Related Dictionary Pages
- North America and Central America, pp. 122–123
- The Universe, p. 127

TOPIC NOTES

In the U.S., most people can trace their family heritage back to other countries. U.S. citizens call themselves "Americans" when they are outside U.S. borders, but often refer to their heritage when inside the U.S. *We came here from Japan in the 20s. I may be Italian, but I hate pasta.*

In 1950, there were 82 countries in the world. By 1996, there were 192. The map on these pages reflects national borders as of 1997.

TEACHING TIPS
Related Vocabulary

country*	ocean*
border	sea*
north/south pole	compass rose
Arctic circle	north*/south*
Middle East	east*/west*
body of water	government*
mountain range*	United Nations*

Teach students how to say the nationalities of everyone in the class. Give examples for all the countries represented. *Juan is from Brazil. He's Brazilian.*

Have students group themselves by native countries or by the country they would most like to visit. Take a photo of each group and write the students' names on individual cards. Place the photos and cards around a world map.

The World

Continents
1. North America   2. South America

124

INTRODUCE THE TOPIC

Ask students to name all the countries they know. List these countries on the board and have students tell you whether they are in Africa, Asia, Europe, South America, North America, or Australia.

Draw a rough outline of a world map on the board. Have volunteers use colored chalk to follow your commands and mark various locations. *Make a blue X on an ocean. Make a star on our location on the map. Make a red X on a place with a hot climate.* Etc.

Bring in and post travel posters from different places such as Tahiti, Paris, Tokyo, or Moscow. Ask students which places they've been to, whether they'd like to go there, and why or why not.

TEACH THE NEW WORDS

Ask students a series of *or* questions about the vocabulary. *Is the U.S. in North or South America?* (North America)

PROVIDE PRACTICE
Chalkboard Activities

Have students categorize vocabulary:

North America		**South America**
United States		*Ecuador*

Asia	**Africa**	**Europe**
China	*Kenya*	*France*

Have students sequence the countries they would travel through on a trip from Portugal to Afghanistan.

_____	Greece	_1_	Portugal
_____	Saudi Arabia	_____	Afghanistan
_____	Spain	_____	Turkey
_____	Iran	_____	Italy

Conversations

Put models on the board and practice. Make appropriate substitutions.

A: I'm so excited! Next week we're flying to *Australia!*

B: How long a flight is it?

A: I'm not sure. I think it's about *[16]* hours.

   1. North America 2. South America, etc.

A: If you could live on any continent in the world, where would you live?

B: I would live in *Asia.* How about you?

A: I can't decide.

   3. Europe 5. Africa 6. Australia, etc.

A: Where's *[Albania]?* I can't find it on the map.

B: It's in *Europe.*

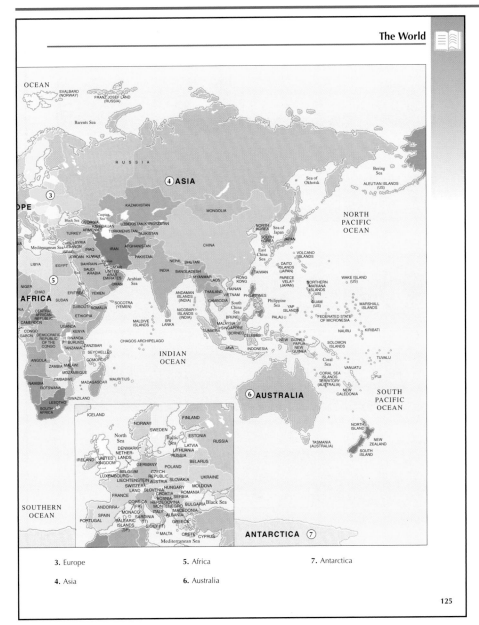

The World

3. Europe   5. Africa   7. Antarctica

4. Asia   6. Australia

125

EXPAND THE LESSON

Problem Solving

△ Have students brainstorm solutions.

1. *Chan is from Vietnam. All his classmates are from El Salvador and Mexico. His classmates do not understand that Chan didn't grow up in China and keep asking questions about China. What can Chan do?*

2. *Anya's country is at war with Masha's country. Their English teacher asks them to pair up to practice a conversation. The women do not want to work together. What do you think they should do?*

Discussion Questions

1. When two countries are fighting, do you think other countries should get involved?

2. Is world peace possible? Why or why not?

3. Many countries want to close their borders. Should countries be allowed to do this? Why or why not?

Drawing Activity

1. Tell students they are going to be making posters to promote world peace. Brainstorm slogans with the class, such as "Give Peace a Chance" and "World Peace Now." List the suggestions on the board.

2. Divide students into groups of four and give each group a piece of posterboard, scratch paper, markers, magazines, scissors, and glue.

3. Tell the groups they must work together to create a design with something from each continent, such as continent outlines, the people, or landmarks.

4. Give students 10–15 minutes to come up with their slogan and plan their design while you monitor and assist as needed.

5. Give students additional time to create their posters.

6. Have a volunteer from each group bring the finished poster to the front and show it to the class.

GAMES

Memory Game

1. Divide the class into two teams.

2. Have students study the countries on pages 124–125.

3. Alternately quiz the teams with true/false statements about the map. *France is in North America.* (false) *Kenya is in Africa.* (true)

4. Correct answers get one point.

5. The game ends after 15 statements.

Interview Questions

1. Name three countries you want to visit.

2. Name three countries you don't want to visit.

3. Have you been to a country with a hot climate? Which one? Did you like it?

4. Have you been to a country with a cold climate? Which one? Did you like it?

5. Which oceans have you seen?

6. In your opinion, which continent is best? Why?

7. In your opinion, which country has the best food?

8. In your opinion, which country has the best climate?

9. Where is your language spoken?

10. Do you speak any other languages? Where is that language spoken?

Listening: Interactive Dictation

△ Have students close their books. Dictate the sentences below, speaking naturally and encouraging students to ask for clarification. *(Where? How do you spell "Mexico"?)*

1. *Mexico is in Central America.*

2. *Peru is in South America.*

3. *Italy is in Europe.*

4. *Ethiopia is in Africa.*

5. *New Zealand is southeast of Australia.*

6. *India is in Asia.*

7. *Kenya is in Africa.*

8. *Chile is in South America.*

9. *Canada is north of the United States.*

10. *Guatemala is south of Mexico.*

Workbooks, p. 126
Classic Classroom Activities, Unit 9
Related Dictionary Pages
- Prepositions, p. 13
- Emergencies and Natural Disasters, pp. 102–103
- Geography, p. 117
- The World, pp. 124–125

TOPIC NOTES

In the U.S., more energy is consumed and more garbage is generated than in any other nation in the world. Today, economics, technology, and a desire to preserve the earth are all fueling the conservation, or "green," movement.

📁 Paper is the most recycled material in the U.S., followed by metals like aluminum and steel.

TEACHING TIPS
Related Vocabulary

gasoline*	solid waste
propane gas	smokestack
uranium	dam
refinery	power lines
mine	ozone layer
geyser	contaminate

Grammar: The suffix *-tion*
Verbs such as *conserve, radiate,* and *pollute* change to nouns with a *-tion* ending; e.g., *conservation, pollution.*

💡 Bring in a ceramic cup, a plastic cup, and a paper cup. Talk about the resources needed to produce them and the pollution they create when discarded. Brainstorm ways to reuse or recycle these materials.

💡 Talk about places which accept recycled materials in your area.

Energy and the Environment

Energy resources

1. solar energy   2. wind   3. natural gas   4. coal

5. hydroelectric power   6. oil/petroleum   7. geothermal energy   8. nuclear energy

Pollution

9. hazardous waste   10. air pollution/smog   11. acid rain   12. water pollution

13. radiation   14. pesticide poisoning   15. oil spill

Conservation

A. recycle   B. save water/conserve water   C. save energy/conserve energy

Share your answers.
1. How do you heat your home?
2. Do you have a gas stove or an electric stove?
3. What are some ways you can save energy when it's cold?
4. Do you recycle? What products do you recycle?
5. Does your market have recycling bins?

126

INTRODUCE THE TOPIC

Ask students to call out types of energy resources and pollution they already know.

Draw a picture of a kite, a TV, a car, and a truck. Talk about the energy needed to power these items and the pollution that can result. *Cars run on gasoline, which is made from crude oil. Car exhaust contains carbon monoxide, which pollutes the air.*

TEACH THE NEW WORDS

Describe and name each picture on the page and have students call out the correct number. *The sun's rays are a source of solar energy. Solar energy is used to heat homes. Some cars even run by solar power!* (#1)

PROVIDE PRACTICE
Chalkboard Activity

Have students categorize vocabulary:

Polluting	Nonpolluting
coal	*solar power*

Conversations

△ Put models on the board and practice. Make appropriate substitutions.

A: What makes that machine work?
B: I think it runs on *natural gas.*
    4. coal 5. hydroelectric power
    8. nuclear energy

A: Please sign my petition.
B: What's it for?
A: We want to stop *hazardous waste* in this state.
    10. air pollution 12. water pollution
    14. pesticide poisoning 15. oil spills

Interview Questions

1. Do you recycle in your home? What do you recycle?
2. What types of pollution worry you?

Listening: Interactive Dictation

△ Have students close their books. Dictate questions about the page. Speak naturally and encourage students to ask for clarification. (*Where are the what?*) Have students check their work and then write the answers working in pairs. E.g.:
1. *Where do the solar panels go?*
2. *What are some hazardous waste products?*
3. *What do you recycle?* Etc.

EXPAND THE LESSON
Discussion Question

What environmental problems exist in your community? How can you help?

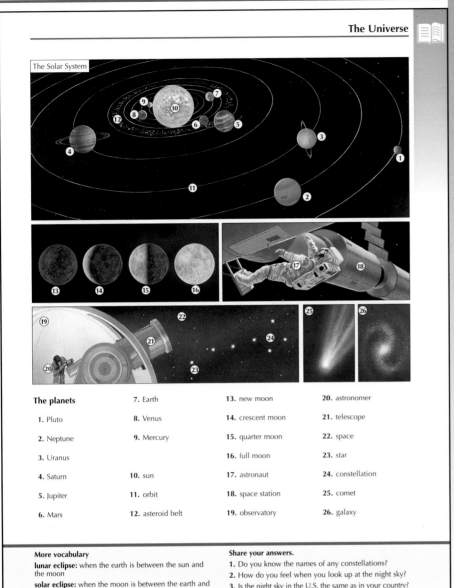

The Universe

The Solar System

The planets

1. Pluto	7. Earth	13. new moon	20. astronomer
2. Neptune	8. Venus	14. crescent moon	21. telescope
3. Uranus	9. Mercury	15. quarter moon	22. space
4. Saturn	10. sun	16. full moon	23. star
5. Jupiter	11. orbit	17. astronaut	24. constellation
6. Mars	12. asteroid belt	18. space station	25. comet
		19. observatory	26. galaxy

More vocabulary
lunar eclipse: when the earth is between the sun and the moon
solar eclipse: when the moon is between the earth and the sun

Share your answers.
1. Do you know the names of any constellations?
2. How do you feel when you look up at the night sky?
3. Is the night sky in the U.S. the same as in your country?

127

Workbooks, p. 127
Classic Classroom Activities, Unit 9
Related Dictionary Pages
• Numbers and Measurements, pp. 14–15
• Prepositions of Motion, p. 105

TOPIC NOTES

In the U.S., NASA (National Aeronautics and Space Administration) oversees space technology and exploration programs.

As far back as 1543, Nicolaus Copernicus produced a **solar system** model with the **sun** at its center. This model provided the basis for modern astronomy.

On July 20th, 1969, at 10:56 EST, Apollo 11 astronaut Neil Armstrong, first person to set foot on the moon, declared, "That's one small step for man; one giant leap for mankind."

TEACHING TIPS
Related Vocabulary

nova	booster rocket
gravity	satellite
space shuttle	black hole
orbit (v)	atmosphere
nebula	UFO
Milky Way	meteor

Usage: *Space* refers to what is outside the earth's air; it also defines something measurable in length, width, and depth. *I'd love to explore outer* space. *Keep some space between you and the next car.*

If your class meets in the evening, observe the sky together.

Plan a trip to a space museum, observatory, or planetarium if there is one in your area.

INTRODUCE THE TOPIC
Draw a picture of the earth, sun, and moon. Draw arrows to talk about the position, rotation, and orbit of each.

Mime looking through a telescope and talk about what you see. *It's a clear night, with lots of stars. There's the constellation Orion. And look! There's the planet Venus.*

TEACH THE NEW WORDS
Ask students a series of *yes/no* questions about the pictures. *Is the asteroid belt near the sun?* (yes) *Does Saturn have rings?* (yes) *Is the astronaut looking through a telescope?* (no)

PROVIDE PRACTICE
Chalkboard Activity
△ Draw the solar system, including the sun and the nine planets. Have students close their books and label each planet they know.

Conversations
△ Put models on the board and practice. Make appropriate substitutions.

A: It's very cloudy tonight.
B: Too bad. I wanted to see that *full moon*.
    14. crescent moon 15. quarter moon
    24. constellation 25. comet

A: NASA is building a new *telescope*.
B: That's great. Do you think we'll learn more about *[Mercury]*?
    18. space station 19. observatory

Interview Questions
1. Do you look at the stars? Where do you go to see them?
2. Would you like to take a space shuttle to the moon? Why or why not?
3. Do you think there is life on other planets? Which ones?

Listening: Checklist
1. Have students make a checklist with these headings: *Planets, Stars,* and *People.*
2. Randomly list vocabulary from the page, while students make a check under the appropriate column.
3. Have students give their tallies. (Planets, 9; Stars, 4; People, 2)
4. Students make a new checklist. Repeat the activity until tallies are accurate.

EXPAND THE LESSON
Discussion Question

Do you think the government should spend money to explore space? Why?

Language workout

△ Copy this sentence on the board: When Lisa talks about her boyfriend she has *stars in her eyes.*

Workbooks, p. 128
Classic Classroom Activities, Unit 10
Related Dictionary Pages
- Geography, p. 117
- Flowers, p. 129
- Construction, p. 149
- Outdoor Recreation, p. 154

TOPIC NOTES

In the U.S., Arbor Day, an annual tree-planting day, is generally observed in public schools in order to stress the importance of forest preservation. Trees and plants are an important part of the ecosystem, providing support to natural resources such as water and air.

In autumn leaves change their color before they are shed by deciduous trees. Evergreen trees stay green year round. Traveling to certain U.S. regions like the New England states to "see the leaves turn" is popular among tourists.

TEACHING TIPS
Related Vocabulary

eucalyptus	bonsai
poplar	forest*
bush*	timber
hedge*	firewood
fern	sap
fir	acorn

Usage: On a person, the torso is called the *trunk*, the arms and legs are *limbs,* and the base of a hair or a tooth is called the *root*.

Spelling: Plurals
Cactus has two plural spellings: *cactuses* or *cacti.*

☼ Take the class on a nature walk to identify different plants and trees.

Trees and Plants

Parts of a tree

1. twig
2. branch
3. limb
4. trunk
5. root
6. leaf

7. redwood	10. pine	13. maple	16. dogwood
8. birch	11. pinecone	14. willow	17. elm
9. magnolia	12. needle	15. palm	18. oak

Plants

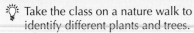

19. holly	21. cactus	23. poison oak	25. poison ivy
20. berries	22. vine	24. poison sumac	

128

INTRODUCE THE TOPIC

Draw a large tree on the board as you talk about each part. *Trees have roots to get water and minerals from the ground. As the tree grows, so do the roots. Do you see this large branch? It's great for hanging a swing!*

Tell a story about a nature walk. *I went walking through some hills where there were lots of plants. One had three shiny leaves and red berries. I picked some. The next day…*

TEACH THE NEW WORDS

Ask students a series of *or* questions about the pictures. *Is #13 a maple or a palm?* (maple) *Does a pine tree have leaves or needles?* (needles) *Do holly plants have berries or pine cones?* (berries)

PROVIDE PRACTICE
Chalkboard Activity

△ Have students categorize vocabulary:

Evergreen Trees	**Trees That Shed Leaves**
holly	*maple*

Conversations

△ Put models on the board and practice. Make appropriate substitutions.

A: Why are you cutting down that *maple tree?*
B: I'm using the wood to make furniture. *[Maple tables]* are beautiful.
  7. redwood 10. pine 14. willow 18. oak

A: Look out! Don't step on that *vine!*
B: Thanks for warning me. I didn't see it.
  19. holly 21. cactus 23. poison oak
  24. poison sumac 25. poison ivy

Interview Questions

1. What's your favorite kind of tree?
2. Do you have any plants in your home? Which ones?

Listening: Descriptions

△ Students write the number of the item as you describe it. E.g.:
1. *This part of the tree grows below the ground.* (#5)
2. *This tree grows in the desert.* (#15)
3. *This plant climbs fences.* (#22) Etc.

EXPAND THE LESSON
Language Workout

△ Copy these sentences on the board and have students guess their meanings.
1. He used to drink too much beer, but this year he's *turning over a new leaf.*
2. If you ask Javier for help, you're *barking up the wrong tree.*

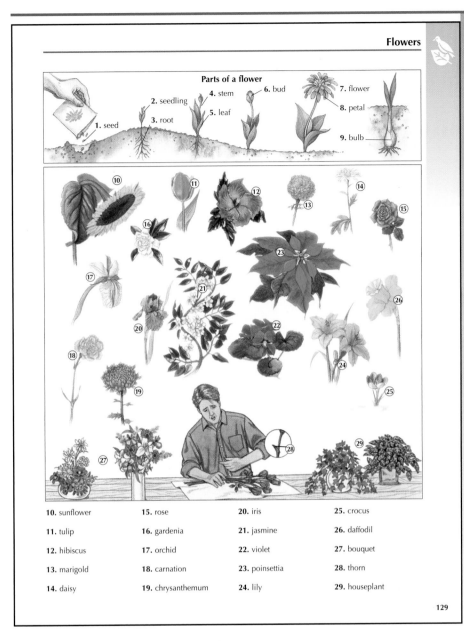

Flowers

Parts of a flower

1. seed
2. seedling
3. root
4. stem
5. leaf
6. bud
7. flower
8. petal
9. bulb

10. sunflower	**15.** rose	**20.** iris	**25.** crocus
11. tulip	**16.** gardenia	**21.** jasmine	**26.** daffodil
12. hibiscus	**17.** orchid	**22.** violet	**27.** bouquet
13. marigold	**18.** carnation	**23.** poinsettia	**28.** thorn
14. daisy	**19.** chrysanthemum	**24.** lily	**29.** houseplant

129

Workbooks, p. 129
Classic Classroom Activities, Unit 10
Related Dictionary Pages
- Colors, p. 12
- Trees and Plants, p. 128
- Places to Go, p. 152

TOPIC NOTES

In the U.S., flower gardening is a popular hobby as well as an important commercial business. Flowers are typically given on anniversaries, birthdays, and on certain holidays. They are given to someone who is ill as a get-well gift and may also be present at funeral services.

A **flower** is the part of the plant that produces seeds. It contains the petals, a pistil, and stamens, which hold pollen.

📁 The Tournament of Roses Parade, held on January 1 in Pasadena, California, is watched worldwide by millions of people. All the parade floats are decorated with 100% natural materials: flowers, seeds, and leaves.

TEACHING TIPS
Related Vocabulary

pansy	greenhouse
petunia	botanical
zinnia	cut* (v)
pollen	arrange* (v)
fragrance	potpourri
annual	blossom
perennial	corsage

Pronunciation: The vowel clusters *ou* in *houseplant* and *ow* in *flower* have the same pronunciation.

🔅 Schedule a field trip to a local nursery or flower shop. Review *Colors,* page 12, to help students identify and describe flowers.

INTRODUCE THE TOPIC

Bring in a potted houseplant in bloom, a small shovel or spoon, and an empty container. Talk about the parts of the plant as you transfer the plant to a larger container. *This African violet has beautiful petals. First, I pick it up by the stem. Next, I…*

Ask students to brainstorm varieties of flowers that they know. Compare their list with the word list on page 129.

TEACH THE NEW WORDS

Describe and name each picture on the page and have students call out the correct number. *Daisies have white petals and a yellow center.* (#14) *Now look at the bouquet. A bouquet is an arrangement of cut flowers. At a wedding, brides often hold a bouquet as they walk down the aisle.* (#27)

PROVIDE PRACTICE
Chalkboard Activity

△ Have students categorize vocabulary:

Pink	**Red**	**Yellow**
carnation	poinsettia	daffodil

Conversations

△ Put models on the board and practice. Make appropriate substitutions.

A: I'm moving this plant. It needs more sun.
B: Good. The *leaves* don't look healthy.
   6. buds 7. flowers 8. petals

A: I want to buy a *carnation* bouquet.
B: What's the occasion?
A: It's *[my mother's birthday]*.
   10. sunflower 11. tulip 14. daisy 15. rose
   19. chrysanthemum 22. violet

Interview Questions

1. What's your favorite flower?
2. Which flowers grow in your country?

Listening: Descriptions

△ Students write the number of the item as you describe it. E.g.:
1. *This part of the stem is sharp.* (#28)
2. *This flower grows on vines.* (#21) Etc.

EXPAND THE LESSON
Discussion Question

Which flowers do you give to express love? sympathy? friendship?

Language Workout

△ Copy this expression on the board and discuss its meaning:
Michelle's garden is beautiful. She has *a green thumb.*

Workbooks, pp. 130–131
Classic Classroom Activities, Unit 10
Related Dictionary Pages
• The World, pp. 124–125

TOPIC NOTES

In the U.S., there are many large aquariums which exhibit and protect marine life and are staffed by marine biologists.

Mammals are warm-blooded animals that breastfeed their young.

Fish are cold-blooded animals that live wholly in water.

Amphibians are animals that are able to live on land and in the water. The word *amphibians* also refers to aircraft and vehicles that can navigate on land and water.

Reptiles are cold-blooded animals with a backbone and short legs or no legs at all.

Worms have a soft rounded body with no backbone or limbs. They live in water, in plants, and underground.

TEACHING TIPS
Related Vocabulary

freshwater	shellfish*
salt water	mollusks
cayman	crustaceans
shell*	school of fish

🔆 Open the dictionary to pages 124–125, *The World,* and have students talk about the kinds of sealife and animal life native to their countries.

🔆 Bring in information and pictures from ecological groups, aquariums, biology textbooks, etc., to enable students to point out the sea and animal life they know about.

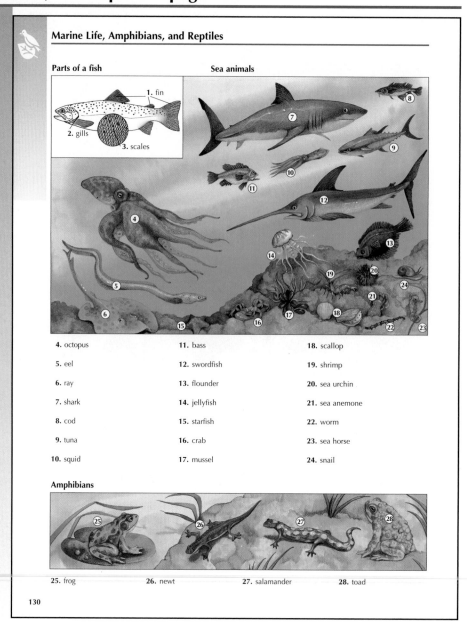

Marine Life, Amphibians, and Reptiles

Parts of a fish
1. fin
2. gills
3. scales

Sea animals

4. octopus	11. bass	18. scallop
5. eel	12. swordfish	19. shrimp
6. ray	13. flounder	20. sea urchin
7. shark	14. jellyfish	21. sea anemone
8. cod	15. starfish	22. worm
9. tuna	16. crab	23. sea horse
10. squid	17. mussel	24. snail

Amphibians

25. frog   26. newt   27. salamander   28. toad

130

INTRODUCE THE TOPIC

Ask students to cover the word list, look at the pictures, and name the marine life, amphibians, and reptiles they know.

Draw a turtle, snake, or whale. Ask students if they know any animal stories about these from their native countries.

Invite students to tell you which animals they have seen in their natural habitat and which they have seen at an aquarium or zoo.

TEACH THE NEW WORDS

Ask students to identify the number of a particular picture based on your description. *This is the largest of all the mammals. It lives in the ocean and comes up for air to breathe. It is a whale.* (#29)

PROVIDE PRACTICE
Chalkboard Activity

△ Have students categorize vocabulary:

Animals We Usually Eat	Animals We Rarely Eat
trout	*seal*

Conversations

△ Put models on the board and practice. Make appropriate substitutions.

A: Look at the *octopus*!
B: Oh, wow! I've never seen one before!
   7. shark 10. squid 14. jellyfish 15. starfish
   20. sea urchin 21. sea anemone
   23. seahorse

A: Any luck fishing?
B: Yes, I caught a *swordfish*.
A: You clean it, and I'll cook it!
   8. cod 9. tuna 11. bass 13. flounder

A: Look at this picture of <u>an alligator</u>!
B: That's really something.
   38. a rattle snake 39. a garter snake
   40. a cobra 41. a lizard 42. a turtle

Interview Questions

1. What fish or animals are native to your country?

2. Do you like to go fishing? What kind of fish do you usually catch?

3. Do you go to aquariums? What fish do you like to watch the most?

4. Are you afraid of any animals on this page? Which ones?

Listening: Listen and Point

△ Have students point to the pictures as you say the vocabulary words. E.g.:

1. *Point to the whale, the largest mammal.* (#29)

2. *Point to the sea lion sitting on a rock.* (#34) Etc.

Marine Life, Amphibians, and Reptiles

Sea mammals

29. whale
30. dolphin
31. porpoise
32. walrus
33. seal
34. sea lion
35. otter

Reptiles

36. alligator
37. crocodile
38. rattlesnake
39. garter snake
40. cobra
41. lizard
42. turtle

131

A–Z Brainstorm

1. Divide students into groups of 3–4.
2. Have students study pages 130–131 for two minutes and close their books.
3. Each group chooses a recorder. The recorder writes the letters A–Z on the left side of his or her paper.
4. As the rest of the group calls out the words, the recorder writes them next to the correct letter.
5. Call time after 5 minutes. The group with the most correct words wins.

Guessing Game

1. Make up index cards with the name of one sea animal, amphibian, or reptile on each.
2. Divide students into groups of 3–4.
3. Give each group 4–5 cards and tell them to place the cards face down in a pile.
4. The first student in each group is "it" and chooses a card without showing it to the group.
5. The others ask *yes/no* questions to find out what card he or she has. *Do you live in water? Do you have fins?* The student with the card answers until someone guesses correctly.
6. The game ends when all students have had a chance to be "it."

Word Links

1. Divide the class into Teams A and B.
2. Write *crocodile* horizontally on the board.
3. Have a volunteer from Team A come up and write a connecting word vertically, using any letter in the word *crocodile*.

```
                          s
c r o c o d i l e
                          a
                          l
```

4. A volunteer from Team B links to either the first or the second word.
5. Play continues until the teams run out of words or board space.

Memory Game

1. Divide the class into two teams.
2. Have students study the creatures on pages 130–131.
3. Alternately quiz the teams with true/false statements. *A crocodile has two legs.* (false)
4. Correct answers get one point.
5. The game ends after 16 statements.

EXPAND THE LESSON

Problem Solving

△ Have students brainstorm solutions.
1. *Laslo loves to go fishing. He always eats the fish he catches. His wife is a vegetarian and will not eat fish. She doesn't like it when Laslo fishes. What can they do?*
2. *Jill's nine-year-old daughter is afraid of snakes and lizards. What can she do so her daughter isn't so afraid?*

Discussion Questions

1. The population of whales has severely decreased because of whale hunting. Do you think this is a problem? Why or why not?
2. Some people in the U.S. have interesting pets. In your opinion, do any of the animals on this page make good pets? Why or why not?

Language Workout

△ Copy these sentences on the board and discuss their meanings.
1. Kenny must be upset about something. He is a *real crab* today.
2. Sometimes Mario is *as slow as a snail.* He never gets the work done!

GAMES

Scrambled Words

1. Have students number their papers 1–10.
2. Spell ten vocabulary words out loud in scrambled order, e.g., c-b-r-a (crab); l-e-w-a-h (whale).
3. Students unscramble the words.
4. The game ends when one student has unscrambled all the words.

Workbooks, p. 132
Classic Classroom Activities, Unit 10
Related Dictionary Pages
- Colors, p. 12
- Household Problems and Repairs, pp. 48–49
- Geography, p. 117
- Flowers, p. 129
- Outdoor Recreation, p. 154

TOPIC NOTES

In the U.S., there are 74 endangered species of birds. Pollution, hunting, and urbanization have destroyed natural habitats. The U.S. National Wildlife Refuge System and conservation groups have helped stop the extinction of many birds. At the same time, many people fear insects and spiders and seek to eliminate them. While some "pests" can spread disease, cause injury, and even death, the majority are harmless and in fact beneficial to nature.

Caterpillars are actually a larval state of moths and butterflies. Caterpillars spin cocoons, change into pupae, and then become winged insects.

TEACHING TIPS
Related Vocabulary

crow	dragonfly
seagull	cricket
swan	firefly
flamingo	prey
ostrich	aviary
stork	sting (v)
parrot	insecticide

☼ Take a nature walk with the class. Have students create a list of the birds, insects, and spiders they find.

Birds, Insects, and Arachnids

Parts of a bird

1. beak/bill
2. wing
3. nest
4. claw
5. feather

6. owl	9. woodpecker	12. penguin	15. peacock
7. blue jay	10. eagle	13. duck	16. pigeon
8. sparrow	11. hummingbird	14. goose	17. robin

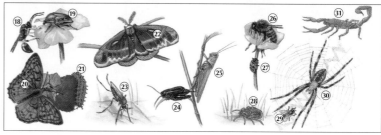

18. wasp	22. moth	26. honeybee	30. spider
19. beetle	23. mosquito	27. ladybug	31. scorpion
20. butterfly	24. cricket	28. tick	
21. caterpillar	25. grasshopper	29. fly	

132

INTRODUCE THE TOPIC

Bring in a picture of a common insect or spider and describe it.

Ask students to name birds they know. Talk about the color, habitat, or unusual traits associated with each one. *Owls are brown birds that live in wooded areas. They are nocturnal—they sleep in the day. Owls make a "hooting" sound.*

TEACH THE NEW WORDS

Ask students a series of *or* questions about the top picture. *Is #12 a penguin or a pigeon?* (penguin) *Does the hummingbird have a long beak or long claw?* (beak)

Name and describe target words in the bottom picture and have students call out the number. *A spider is black or brown. It catches other insects in a web and eats them.* (#30)

PROVIDE PRACTICE
Chalkboard Activity

△ Have students categorize vocabulary:

1. Eats Other Animals   **Eats Plants**
   eagle   *beetle*

2. Scary   **Not Scary**
   spider   *ladybug*

Conversations

△ Put models on the board and practice. Make appropriate substitutions.

A: Look up there! It's _a blue jay_!
B: I can't see it. Can I borrow your binoculars?

   6. an owl 8. a sparrow 9. a woodpecker
   10. an eagle 13. a duck 14. a goose
   16. a pigeon 17. a robin

A: Let's go camping next weekend.
B: Aren't there a lot of _mosquitoes_?
A: Maybe. I'm bringing *[long pants]*.

   18. wasps 28. ticks 31. scorpions

Interview Questions

1. Do any birds live near your home?
2. Do you have a bird feeder?
3. Do you ever go bird hunting? bird watching?
4. Do any insects or spiders bother you? Which ones are you afraid of?

Listening: Descriptions

△ Students write the number of the item as you describe it.

1. *This bird has beautiful multicolored feathers.* (#15)
2. *This insect builds a hive and makes honey.* (#26)

EXPAND THE LESSON
Discussion Question

The bald eagle is the U.S. national bird. Can you name other birds that are symbols for states, countries, or sports teams?

Domestic Animals and Rodents

Farm animals

1. goat	**3.** cow	**5.** hen	**7.** sheep
2. donkey	**4.** horse	**6.** rooster	**8.** pig

Pets

9. cat	**11.** dog	**13.** rabbit	**15.** parakeet
10. kitten	**12.** puppy	**14.** guinea pig	**16.** goldfish

Rodents

17. mouse	**19.** gopher	**21.** squirrel
18. rat	**20.** chipmunk	**22.** prairie dog

More vocabulary
Wild animals live, eat, and raise their young away from people, in the forests, mountains, plains, etc.
Domesticated animals work for people or live with them.

Share your answers.
1. Do you have any pets? any farm animals?
2. Which of these animals are in your neighborhood? Which are not?

133

Workbooks, p. 133
Classic Classroom Activities, Unit 10
Related Dictionary Pages
• Household Problems and Repairs, pp. 48–49
• Mammals, pp. 134–135

TOPIC NOTES

In the U.S., domestic animals such as **cats** and **dogs** are kept as **pets**—animals that provide companionship and/or security for their owners. Birds, fish, **rabbits, horses, rodents,** and reptiles are also kept as common pets.

Dog owners are usually required to have their dogs licensed and given rabies shots. Cat and dog owners are encouraged to spay or neuter their pets.

A rodent that is not in the home by invitation is considered a **pest**. Homeowners use traps or call the exterminator to kill mice, rats, and gophers.

📁 Census projections for the year 2000 say that 50.6% of U.S. households will have one or more pets. This is a drop from the 1993 figure of 52.3%.

TEACHING TIPS
Related Vocabulary

veterinarian	exterminator*
pet food*	pest*
cage	rabies shot
fish bowl	spay

⚠ Different cultures have different attitudes about animals in the home. It may be useful to have a guided class discussion on the benefits and liabilities of having a pet.

Spelling: Irregular plurals
sheep—sheep, mouse—mice.

INTRODUCE THE TOPIC

Survey the class to find out how many students have had a cat, a dog, or other animal as a pet.

Ask students to name all the farm animals they know. Write the list on the board and have students compare it to the word list on page 133.

TEACH THE NEW WORDS

Name and describe each animal and have students call out each number. *This is an orange and white cat. (#9)*

Ask students a series of *yes/no* questions. *Is #9 a cat or a dog?* (cat)

PROVIDE PRACTICE
Chalkboard Activity

△ Have students categorize vocabulary:

Pets	Pests	Both
cat	*gopher*	*mouse*

Conversations

△ Put models on the board and practice. Make appropriate substitutions.

A: Do you have any pets?
B: Yes, I have a <u>cat</u> named *[Leo]*.
   10. kitten 11. dog 12. puppy 13. rabbit 14. guinea pig, etc.

A: I took a trip to a farm.
B: Was it interesting?
A: I thought the <u>cows</u> were *[cool]*.
   1. goats 2. donkeys 4. horses 7. sheep 8. pigs, etc.

A: There's another <u>mouse</u> in the house!
B: I'll call the exterminator.
   18. rat 19. gopher 20. chipmunk 21. squirrel

Interview Questions

1. What's your favorite domestic animal?
2. Which of these animals have you seen? Which have you touched?
3. Are you allergic to any animals?

Listening 📟 #36, p. 222

"Animals! Animals!" Students listen to an animal TV show host and point to each animal he describes.

EXPAND THE LESSON
Problem Solving

△ Have students brainstorm solutions. *Pat and Jo are retired. Their cat, Tiger, is eight years old. Last month their rent went up $50.00. A building nearby has a cheaper apartment, but there are no pets allowed. What should they do?*

GAME
Scrambled Words

1. Scramble ten animal names on the board; e.g., w-o-c (cow), i-p-g (pig).
2. Have two student volunteers race to unscramble the words. (They can ask classmates for help.)

Unit 10 Mammals page 134

Workbooks, pp. 134–135
Classic Classroom Activities, Unit 10
Related Dictionary Pages
- Colors, p. 12
- The World, pp. 124–125
- Domestic Animals and Rodents, p. 133

TOPIC NOTES

In the U.S., the Endangered Species Act of 1973 protects animals that are threatened with extinction. Species of the **bat, deer,** prairie dog, and **wolf** are on the endangered species list.

Asian **elephants**, giant **pandas**, gorillas, **leopards,** and **orangutans** are also threatened. Wildlife reserves, protection of animal habitats, and zoo breeding programs are helping to prevent extinction.

TEACHING TIPS
Related Vocabulary

African	wildlife
Asian	habitat
Australian	endangered species
North American	extinct
South American	nurse (young)

Spelling: Plurals
These words are the same in the singular and plural: *moose, deer, bison*. These words have irregular plurals: *hoof— hooves; wolf—wolves*. The plural of *zebra* is either *zebras* or *zebra*.

- Introduce the top of page 134, then the top of page 135. Teach the parts of the animals after students are familiar with their names.

- Tape a nature show about a mammal and show it to the class, turning off the audio and narrating it at the appropriate level of English.

Mammals

1. moose	5. wolf	9. beaver	13. raccoon
2. mountain lion	6. buffalo / bison	10. porcupine	14. deer
3. coyote	7. bat	11. bear	15. fox
4. opossum	8. armadillo	12. skunk	

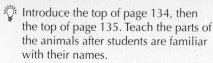

16. antler	18. whiskers	20. paw	22. tail
17. hoof	19. coat / fur	21. horn	23. quill

134

INTRODUCE THE TOPIC

Encourage students to name all the different four-legged animals they know. List them on the board and have students tell you which animals can be found in their countries.

Bring in pictures of animals from four different continents, e.g., a gorilla, a coyote, a koala, and a camel. Have students tell you where they are from and how they are similar.

Talk about a famous mammal such as Koko (the gorilla who understands sign language) or a mammal currently in the news.

Ask students to brainstorm the reasons for the importance of studying and caring for animals. Write their ideas on the board and refer to them throughout the lesson.

TEACH THE NEW WORDS

Name and describe those animals on pages 134–135 that students do not know. For the North American mammals, identify their location within the U.S. *Look, #3 is a coyote. Coyotes are light brown and have yellow eyes. Coyotes live in the southwestern U.S.* For the mammals on page 135, emphasize the countries where they can be found. *#42 is an elephant. This is the largest land mammal. It's gray or brown. Asian elephants are found in India. African elephants are found in Africa.*

Say each word on the bottom of the page and relate it to the appropriate animal(s). *#16 shows an antler. Deer and moose have antlers.* Have students repeat the target words and point to the correct pictures.

PROVIDE PRACTICE
Chalkboard Activity

△ Have students categorize vocabulary:

1. Whiskers	No Whiskers
raccoon	*bat*

2. Long Tail	Short Tail
fox	*deer*

3. In the same family as…

Cats	Dogs	Apes
tiger	*bear*	*gorilla*

Conversations

△ Put models on the board and practice. Make appropriate substitutions.

A: Is that a *moose*?
B: No, I think it's a *deer*.

    5. wolf/3. coyote
    9. beaver/12. skunk
    13. raccoon/10. porcupine, etc .

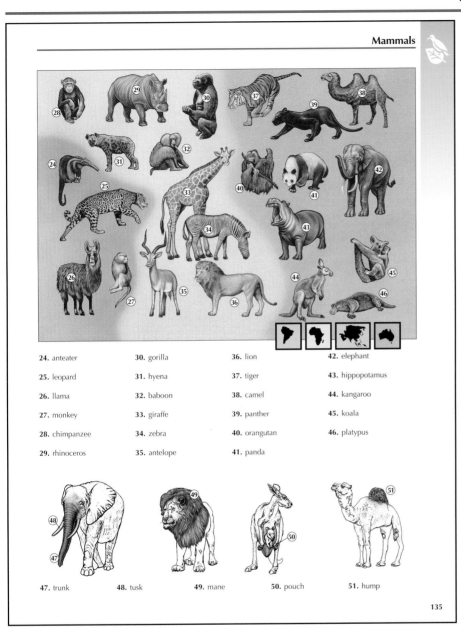

Mammals

24. anteater	30. gorilla	36. lion	42. elephant
25. leopard	31. hyena	37. tiger	43. hippopotamus
26. llama	32. baboon	38. camel	44. kangaroo
27. monkey	33. giraffe	39. panther	45. koala
28. chimpanzee	34. zebra	40. orangutan	46. platypus
29. rhinoceros	35. antelope	41. panda	

47. trunk	48. tusk	49. mane	50. pouch	51. hump

135

A: The _fox_ is a very _[intelligent]_ animal.
B: How do you know?
A: I saw a TV show about them.
  5. wolf 7. bat 30. gorilla 41. panda

A: Now that we're at the zoo, what do you want to see first?
B: Let's go see the _armadillo_ exhibit.
A: Great! I love _[armadillos]_.
  2. mountain lion 24. anteater 26. llama
  27. monkey 37. tiger 38. camel
  40. orangutan 42. elephant

A: Have you ever seen _a panther_?
B: Never in the wild, only at the zoo.
  33. a giraffe 34. a zebra 35. an antelope
  39. a rhinoceros 44. a kangaroo
  45. a koala 46. a platypus

Interview Questions

1. Which animal on these pages do you like best? Which do you like least?
2. Have you ever touched one of these animals? Which one?
3. How many of these animals have you seen?
4. Do you like zoos? Why or why not?

Listening: Listen and Point

Describe mammals by their size, color, features, and habitats. Have students listen and point to the matching picture. Speak naturally and repeat your description (or portions of it) as students request. E.g.:

1. _This large animal has antlers and a dark brown coat. It lives in the northern U.S. and Canada._(#1)
2. _This large brown animal likes to swim in the river. It's sometimes called a hippo._ (#43) Etc.

EXPAND THE LESSON
Problem Solving

△ Have students brainstorm solutions. _Maria's sister-in-law gave her an expensive sweater with a fox collar. Maria does not wear fur because she does not think it is right to kill animals for their coats. What should she say or do about the gift?_

Discussion Questions

1. Some people do not like zoos because the animals are not free. Some animals would be extinct if zoos did not protect and breed them. What is your opinion of zoos?
2. Which is more important to protect: animal habitats or people's jobs?

Language Workout

△ Write these sentences on the board and discuss their meanings.
1. Justin, get _your paws_ off those cookies.
2. Domingo, stop that _monkey business_ and eat your dinner.

GAMES
Word Links

1. Divide the class into Teams A and B.
2. Have students study the words on pages 134–135 for 2 minutes and then close their books.
3. Write the word _rhinoceros_ horizontally on the board.
4. Have a volunteer from Team A come up and write a connecting word vertically, using any letter in the word _rhinoceros._

```
r h i n o c e r o s
      y
      e
      n
      a
```

5. A volunteer from Team B then comes up and links to either the first or the second word on the board.
6. Play continues until the teams run out of words or board space.

What Animal Is It?

1. Write eight different animals' names on slips of paper.
2. Have a volunteer choose a slip and draw the animal on the board.
3. The class has to guess the identity of the animal within 60–90 seconds.
4. The game ends after all the cards have been used, or after 15 minutes, whichever comes first.

Workbooks, pp. 136–137
Classic Classroom Activities, Unit 11
Related Dictionary Pages
• Job Skills, p. 140
• Job Search, p. 141

TOPIC NOTES

In the U.S., people often identify themselves by their occupations or jobs. During introductions, *What's your name?* is frequently followed by the question *What do you do?*

Administrative assistants work with upper management or executives. Assistants help plan and organize the boss's projects and often have their own clerical staffs.

A **caregiver** who takes care of babies and children is also called a **baby-sitter.** A caregiver can also care for disabled adults or the elderly. A caregiver who works in the home of an ill or disabled person and has some basic medical training is called a **home attendant.**

TEACHING TIPS

Related Vocabulary (A–H)

career	designer*
electrician*	hotel worker
astronaut*	factory worker*
childcare worker*	farmer/grower*
construction worker*	

(See pp. 138–139 for more job titles.)

Usage: *What do you do?* is the colloquial question used to inquire about a person's occupation. The questions *What's your job? Where do you work?* or *Who do you work for?* are also used.

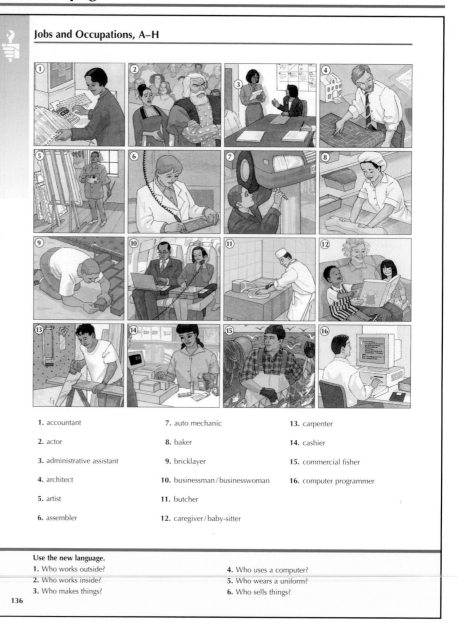

Jobs and Occupations, A–H

1. accountant
2. actor
3. administrative assistant
4. architect
5. artist
6. assembler
7. auto mechanic
8. baker
9. bricklayer
10. businessman / businesswoman
11. butcher
12. caregiver / baby-sitter
13. carpenter
14. cashier
15. commercial fisher
16. computer programmer

Use the new language.
1. Who works outside?
2. Who works inside?
3. Who makes things?
4. Who uses a computer?
5. Who wears a uniform?
6. Who sells things?

136

INTRODUCE THE TOPIC

Ask questions about students' work experience. *Do you work after school? before school? How many different jobs have you had? What's your occupation?*

Ask students to name all the jobs they know that start with the letter *b.* List their ideas on the board and then have them find the words on page 136 or in the index at the back of their picture dictionaries.

Talk about your own job history, describing the jobs you've had, how you trained for them, where you worked, and the tools you used.

Bring in a loaf of bread, a hammer, a computer disk, a frying pan, a flower, and a needle and thread. Have students guess the occupations associated with these items. (baker, carpenter, computer programmer, cook, florist, garment worker)

TEACH THE NEW WORDS

Name and describe 8–10 jobs at a time. Use the picture on the page, gestures, and items in the classroom to create comprehensible information about the tools and location associated with each occupation. *Look at #1. This woman is an accountant. She's working in an office, using an adding machine. An accountant works with numbers. The long papers have information about the company's money.*

PROVIDE PRACTICE

Chalkboard Activity

△ Have students categorize vocabulary:

1.

Outdoor Jobs	Indoor Jobs	Both
bricklayer	accountant	actor

2. Works Mostly With…

Money	People	Things
cashier	caregiver	assembler

Conversations

△ Put models on the board and practice. Make appropriate substitutions.

A: Does *[Felix]* like *[his]* new job?
B: Yes, *[he]* loves being an *accountant!*
  2. actor 3. administrative assistant
  4. architect 5. artist 6. assembler
  7. auto mechanic 23. engineer

A: *[Tasha's]* working as a *caregiver.*
B: I thought *[she]* was *an actor!*
A: Yes, but *[she]* couldn't find work in the field.
  28. gas station attendant/29. a graphic artist
  18. delivery person/17. a cook
  26. gardener/25. a florist, etc.

A: *[Yee]* just finished *[his]* training!
B: That's wonderful. Now *[he's]* a real *doctor!*
  11. butcher 19. dental assistant 20. dentist
  23. engineer 24. firefighter 30. hairdresser, etc.

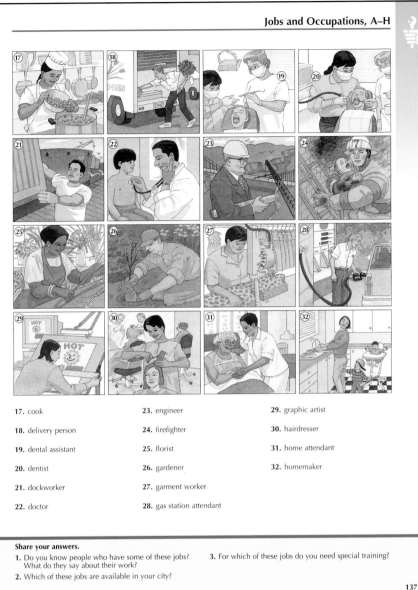

Jobs and Occupations, A–H

17. cook
18. delivery person
19. dental assistant
20. dentist
21. dockworker
22. doctor
23. engineer
24. firefighter
25. florist
26. gardener
27. garment worker
28. gas station attendant
29. graphic artist
30. hairdresser
31. home attendant
32. homemaker

Share your answers.

1. Do you know people who have some of these jobs? What do they say about their work?
2. Which of these jobs are available in your city?
3. For which of these jobs do you need special training?

137

A: Being a *gardener* is hard work.
B: I know. I'm exhausted.

9. brick layer 13. carpenter
15. commercial fisher 21. dockworker
28. gas station attendant 32. homemaker

Interview Questions

1. What's a job you'd like to have? Why?
2. What's the one job on these pages you wouldn't want? Why?
3. If you were an actor, what part would you like to play?
4. If you were a babysitter, what age child would you like to take care of?
5. If you were a cashier, what kind of store would you like to work in?

Listening 🔊 #37, p. 223

"Are They Hiring?" Students take notes on the jobs that the job counselor describes and circle the best job for each person.

EXPAND THE LESSON

Problem Solving

△ Have students brainstorm solutions.

1. *Bernice is a garment worker in a factory with poor lighting, no air-conditioning, and no heat. Bernice doesn't want to lose her job, but she's angry about the conditions. What can she do about her situation?*
2. *Gregor, an actor who also works as a cook, is hoping to get a part in an important movie. This morning he found out that his audition for the movie starts at the same time as his restaurant job. What can he do?*

Discussion Questions

1. Which of these jobs are done by both women and men in your country? Are there any jobs only done by women? by men? Discuss why you think this happens.
2. Which jobs on these pages pay the best salary? Discuss the reasons why.

GAMES

Definition Bingo

1. Have students fold a blank sheet of paper into 16 squares.
2. Dictate 16 occupations and have students write them in random order on their papers.
3. Tell students they will be circling different words on their papers as they hear you define them. Explain that when they get four circled words in a row (horizontally, vertically, or diagonally), they shout "Bingo!"
4. Give a sample definition. *If you have this occupation, you help the dentist work with the patients.* Make sure all students have circled the words *dental assistant* on their papers.
5. Call out definitions until one student gets Bingo.
6. Continue playing until five players have gotten Bingo.

What's My Job?

1. Have a student volunteer secretly choose one of the jobs on pages 136–137 and write it down on a piece of paper.
2. Once the student has decided on his or her job, the other students take turns asking *yes/no* questions to determine which job it is. Questions can focus on the clothing, location, and/or the actions of the worker in the picture. *Do you wear a suit on this job?* (no) *Do you work outside?* (yes) *Do you work with flowers?* (no) *Do you work with bricks?* (yes) *Are you a bricklayer?* (yes)
3. The person who guesses correctly comes up to the front and chooses a job, continuing the game.
4. End the game after 5 rounds or 20 minutes, whichever comes first.

Charades

1. Write jobs #1–32 on slips of paper and put them into a box or hat.
2. Divide the class into two teams.
3. Students take turns picking a slip and acting out the job for their team.
4. Teams get a point for each job they guess.
5. The game ends after 6–8 rounds.

Workbooks, pp. 138–139
Classic Classroom Activities, Unit 11
Related Dictionary Pages
- Jobs and Occupations A–H, pp. 136–137
- Job Skills, p. 140
- Job Search, p. 141

TOPIC NOTES

In the U.S., people in the workforce are protected from discrimination on the basis of gender, age, or race. Jobs, such as firefighter, **police officer,** and fighter pilot, are open to both sexes and eligibility is based on ability, not gender.

A **reporter** may report and write news stories for a TV station, a newspaper, or a magazine. The on-camera personality who reads the news is called an *anchorperson* or *anchor.*

In 1996, 85% of U.S. workers were satisfied with their jobs, 14% were not, and 1% were not sure.

TEACHING TIPS

Related Vocabulary (H–W)

letter carrier*	Realtor*
parking attendant	typist
pilot*	X-ray technician*
plumber*	zookeeper*

(See pp. 136–137 for more job titles.)

Usage: Job titles have changed in order to apply to both men and women: *actor* for *actor/actress, commercial fisher* for *fisherman, delivery person* for *delivery man, firefighter* for *fireman, police officer* for *policeman, postal worker* for *postman, repair person* for *repair man, sanitation worker* for *garbage man,* and *server* for *waiter/waitress.*

Jobs and Occupations, H–W

你好 He says "Hi".

33. housekeeper	39. model	45. postal worker
34. interpreter / translator	40. mover	46. printer
35. janitor / custodian	41. musician	47. receptionist
36. lawyer	42. nurse	48. repair person
37. machine operator	43. painter	
38. messenger / courier	44. police officer	

Talk about each of the jobs or occupations.
She's *a housekeeper. She works in a hotel.*   She's *a nurse. She works with patients.*
He's *an interpreter. He works for the government.*

INTRODUCE THE TOPIC

Act out two or three of the most common jobs from these pages and have students guess the job.

Ask students to name all the jobs they know that start with the letter *m.* List their ideas on the board and then have them see how many of their words are listed in the word list on page 138 or in the index at the back of their picture dictionaries.

Talk about the different "jobs" we do in our daily lives: cook, driver, gardener, messenger, mover, repair person, etc. Determine which job the majority of students do most often, and which jobs they almost never do.

Ask students to brainstorm a list of places where a janitor and a receptionist might work. Have students look at page 138 to see which locations are depicted.

TEACH THE NEW WORDS

Name and describe 8–10 jobs at a time. Use the picture on the page, gestures, and items in the classroom to create comprehensible information about the tools and locations associated with each occupation. *Look at #34. He's an interpreter. This man can speak two or more languages. He helps people who don't speak the same language to communicate.*

Ask students a series of *or* questions about the jobs with which they're familiar. *Look at #42. Is she a nurse or a police officer?* (nurse) *Is #55 a stock clerk or a salesperson?* (stock clerk)

PROVIDE PRACTICE

Chalkboard Activity

△ Have students categorize vocabulary:

College Degree	**Vocational School**
interpreter	*machine operator*

On-the-Job Training	**Other**
housekeeper	*musician*

Conversations

△ Put models on the board and practice. Make appropriate substitutions.

A: I'm looking for work as a *janitor.*
B: You're in luck! We have an opening.
  33. **housekeeper** 37. **machine operator**
  40. **mover** 43. **painter** 53. **server,** etc.

A: Does your *[daughter]* work?
B: No, *[she's]* a full-time student. *[She's]* studying to be *an interpreter.*
  34. a translator 41. a musician 42. a nurse
  44. a police officer 58. a teacher, etc.

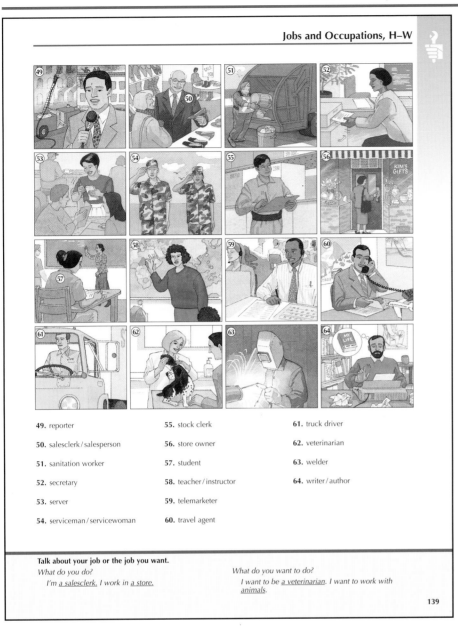

Jobs and Occupations, H–W

49. reporter
50. salesclerk / salesperson
51. sanitation worker
52. secretary
53. server
54. serviceman / servicewoman

55. stock clerk
56. store owner
57. student
58. teacher / instructor
59. telemarketer
60. travel agent

61. truck driver
62. veterinarian
63. welder
64. writer / author

Talk about your job or the job you want.
What do you do?
   I'm a salesclerk. I work in a store.

What do you want to do?
I want to be a veterinarian. I want to work with animals.

139

A: I wish I were a *reporter*!
B: That would be *[an exciting]* job.
   36. lawyer **39.** model **60.** travel agent
   64. writer

A: What's *[Vince]* doing these days?
B: *[He's]* a *lawyer* at *[ABC company]*.
A: Wow! Do you think he could help me get a job there?
B: I don't know. I'll ask.
   38. messenger **47.** receptionist
   50. salesclerk **52.** secretary, etc.

Interview Questions

1. Which of these jobs would you like to have? Why?
2. Which of these jobs would you hate? Why?
3. If you were a store owner, what kind of store would you like to own?
4. If you were a salesclerk, what would you like to sell?

5. Which job do you think is more dangerous: police officer, reporter, or serviceman/service woman? Why?

Listening 🔊 #37, p. 223

"Are They Hiring?" People at a job agency talk about the work they want. Students listen and point to the picture they hear described.

EXPAND THE LESSON
Problem Solving

△ Have students brainstorm solutions.
1. *Carl is a custodian. His supervisor asked him out, but he turned her down. After that she started to complain about his work. What advice would you give Carlos? What advice would you give if this happened to a woman whose supervisor was a man?*

2. *It's 4:00 P.M., and Will's boss says that he needs him to work late. Will's wife leaves for her job at 4:15. Their son has to be picked up from daycare by 6:00 P.M. What are Will's options?*

Discussion Questions

1. Some people think high school students should not have to work; other people think work experience should be a part of education. What do you think?
2. In 1960, 29% of U.S. women with children under six years of age worked. By 1995, the percentage had jumped to 60%. How does this change family life?

GAMES
Class Go-Around: Job Search

1. Begin by saying *I'm looking for a job as a painter*.
2. The first student volunteer repeats the sentence and adds another job. *I'm looking for a job as a painter or a nurse*.
3. The next student volunteer continues the chain, adding another job.
4. Stop after the tenth student and begin the game again.

Spell Check

1. Divide the class into two teams.
2. Give teams 10 minutes to study the spelling of the words on pages 138–139.
3. Have teams line up on either side of the room.
4. Tell the first student on each team a word from the pages and have him or her write it on the board.
5. Team members who spell the word correctly sit down and earn a point for their team.
6. Team members who make a mistake go to the end of the line, so that they can have another chance.
7. The game ends when all the team members of one team are seated.

A–Z Brainstorm

1. Divide students into groups of 3–4.
2. Have students study pages 138–139 for 2 minutes and close their books.
3. Each group chooses a recorder, who writes the letters *A–Z* on the left side of his or her paper.
4. As the group calls out the words, the recorder writes them down next to the letter the word begins with.
5. Call time after 5 minutes. The group with the most correct words wins.

Workbooks, p. 140
Classic Classroom Activities, Unit 11
Related Dictionary Pages
• Jobs and Occupations, pp. 136–139
• Job Search, p. 141

TOPIC NOTES

In the U.S., one can acquire job skills on-the-job, as an apprentice, in high schools and vocational education centers, and in colleges and universities. Most resumes list responsibilities and job skills as well as jobs held.

Work on a computer is a very broad skill category. Most job applications ask which software programs the applicant can use. Many applications ask if one can **type**, but this can refer to typing on a computer keyboard also.

Do manual labor means to do physical work that does not require lengthy training.

TEACHING TIPS
Related Vocabulary

bake*	learn*
clean*	lift
deliver*	paint*
design*	sing*
draw*	write*

Grammar: The modal *can*
Introduce or review the modal forms *can* and *can't* so that students are able to talk about their abilities.

- Teach the past tense of the verbs on the page so that students can talk about what jobs they have performed.

- Bring in want ads and talk about what specific job skills are required for various jobs.

Job Skills

A. **assemble** components	G. **repair** appliances	M. **type**
B. **assist** medical patients	H. **sell** cars	N. **use** a cash register
C. **cook**	I. **sew** clothes	O. **wait on** customers
D. **do** manual labor	J. **speak** another language	P. **work** on a computer
E. **drive** a truck	K. **supervise** people	
F. **operate** heavy machinery	L. **take care** of children	

More vocabulary
act: to perform in a play, movie, or TV show
fly: to pilot an airplane
teach: to instruct, to show how to do something

Share your answers.
1. What job skills do you have? Where did you learn them?
2. What job skills do you want to learn?

140

INTRODUCE THE TOPIC

Describe some of the jobs you have had and act out the various job skills as you talk. *In 1988 I worked in a market, so I know how to use a cash register. I was a waitress in the summers, so I can wait on tables.*

Survey students on their job skills. Ask questions such as *How many of you can type? How many can drive a truck? Sew clothes?* Write or graph their responses on the board.

TEACH THE NEW WORDS

Ask students to identify the letter of a particular picture based on your description. *This woman is making clothes. She knows how to sew clothes.* (I) *This man works for a furniture company. He can drive a truck.* (E) Etc.

PROVIDE PRACTICE
Chalkboard Activity

△ Write these jobs on the board and have students brainstorm various job skills needed for each:

Pizza Restaurant Manager	Car Lot Office Manager
cook	*sell cars*
wait on customers	*work on a computer*

Conversations

△ Put models on the board and practice. Make appropriate substitutions.

A: We need someone who can *type*.
B: No problem. I can *[type]* really well.
 A. assemble components
 B. assist medical patients C. cook, etc.

A: What do you do now?
B: I *do manual labor*.
 F. operate heavy machinery G. repair appliances H. sell cars, etc.

Interview Questions

1. Which job skills do you have?
2. Which ones would you like to learn?
3. Which ones do not interest you?
4. Do you prefer to learn on-the-job or in classes? Why?

Listening: Listen and Point

△ Have students point to the pictures as you say the vocabulary words.
1. This woman sells cars. (H)
2. This man sews clothes. He's making a dress. (I)

EXPAND THE LESSON
Problem Solving

△ Have students brainstorm solutions. *Max makes money for his family. He's 25 years old and works full-time. He wants to learn new job skills but doesn't have time. What advice can you give him?*

Job Search

A. **talk** to friends

B. **look** at a job board

C. **look** for a help wanted sign

D. **look** in the classifieds

E. **call** for information

F. **ask** about the hours

G. **fill out** an application

H. **go** on an interview

I. **talk** about your experience

J. **ask** about benefits

K. **inquire** about the salary

L. **get hired**

141

Workbooks, p. 141
Classic Classroom Activities, Unit 11
Related Dictionary Pages
• Jobs and Occupations, pp. 136–139
• Job Skills, p. 140

TOPIC NOTES

In the U.S., the term *labor force* refers to all people over 16 who are employed or seeking work. In the 1970s, an average worker changed jobs only once during the decade; 21st century predictions indicate fewer than 1/3 of the workforce will enjoy this job stability.

📁 Urban areas projected to gain the most new jobs between 1993 and 2015 are Atlanta, Georgia; Washington, D.C.; and Los Angeles–Long Beach, California.

TEACHING TIPS
Related Vocabulary

talk to a job counselor	raise
call an employment agency	pension
provide a reference	paycheck
write a resume	get fired
wage	get laid off

🔅 Review page 4, *Personal Information,* to assist students in filling out job applications. Stress accuracy as well as legibility.

🔅 Bring in application forms and sample resumes to assist students in looking for a job.

🔅 Help students gain confidence during job interviews by discussing appropriate dress and hygiene, legal and illegal hiring practices and interview strategies.

INTRODUCE THE TOPIC

Survey the class to find out how students find work. Ask questions such as *How many of you found a job in the newspaper? How many looked in a store window? Have friends or family helped?*

Bring in sample job ads from the classifieds. Read the ads together; then ask students comprehension questions about the ads. *Do you need experience? What's the salary?*

TEACH THE NEW WORDS

Ask students to identify the letters of particular pictures (first in order and then randomly) based on your descriptions. *Dan talks to his friends. Maybe his friends know about a job opening.* (A) *Dan checks the listings at the career center. He looks at a job board.* (B)

PROVIDE PRACTICE
Chalkboard Activity

△ Put job-interview questions on the board.
   Do you have any experience?
   How much is the starting salary? Etc.
   Have students identify the speaker as the interviewer or the applicant.

Conversations

△ Put models on the board and practice. Make appropriate substitutions.

A: How did you get your job at *[Pizza Palace]?*
B: I *talked to friends.*
   B. looked at a job board
   C. looked for a help wanted sign
   D. looked in the classifieds

A: How did your interview go?
B: OK, but I wasn't sure how to *talk about my experience.*
   F. ask about the hours J. ask about benefits
   K. inquire about the salary

Interview Questions

1. Are you working? Looking for a job?
2. What's one question you would ask at an interview?

Listening: Listen and Point

△ Say sentences using job-search verbs A–L and have students point to the correct picture. E.g.:
1. *Can I work overtime?* (F)
2. *I worked in a market in China.* (I) Etc.

EXPAND THE LESSON
Discussion Questions

1. Some interviewers may ask illegal questions about marital status, race, or religion. How should you answer these types of questions?
2. Some employers pay workers in cash with no receipt. Do you think payment "under the table" is a good idea?

141

Workbooks, pp. 142–143
Classic Classroom Activities, Unit 11
Related Dictionary Pages
• A Classroom, pp. 2–3
• The Telephone, p. 9
• Job Search, p. 141
• Computers, p. 144

TOPIC NOTES

In the U.S., almost all office workers have at least a high school education. Their work involves recording, storing, and distributing information so that the managers can use this information to operate the business and to make administrative decisions.

A **microcassette transcriber** is a tape recorder which can play back recorded information at different speeds.

TEACHING TIPS
Related Vocabulary

employee lounge	mailroom
reception area	conference room
water cooler	bulletin board*
coat closet	storage room
e-mail	in/out box
documents	coffee break

Usage: The polite way to ask someone to do a task such as take a message is to use *Could you please…?*

- Have a school office worker come to speak to your class about their job responsibilities, office etiquette, and what it is like to work in an office.

- Make a copy of an ad from an office supply store so students can see how much these items cost.

⚠ Students may be unfamiliar with some of the machines on this page, such as a postal scale or paper shredder.

An Office

1. desk	**6.** desk calendar	**11.** file folder
2. typewriter	**7.** desk pad	**12.** file clerk
3. secretary	**8.** calculator	**13.** supply cabinet
4. microcassette transcriber	**9.** electric pencil sharpener	**14.** photocopier
5. stacking tray	**10.** file cabinet	

A. **take** a message	**D.** **type** a letter	**G.** **staple**
B. **fax** a letter	**E.** **make** copies	**H.** **file** papers
C. **transcribe** notes	**F.** **collate** papers	

Practice taking messages.
Hello. My name is Sara Scott. Is Mr. Lee in?
*   Not yet. Would you like to leave a message?*
Yes. Please ask him to call me at 555-4859.

Share your answers.
1. Which office equipment do you know how to use?
2. Which jobs does a file clerk do?
3. Which jobs does a secretary do?

142

INTRODUCE THE TOPIC

Bring in office supplies not found in the classroom and pass them around. Talk about what they are used for.

Ask students to tell you all the items they would expect to find on the desk of the school secretary. Write their words on the board and have students compare their list with the words on pages 142–143.

Talk about a typical day in the life of an office worker. Act out the actions as you say them. *I take a lot of messages. I also make a lot of copies.*

TEACH THE NEW WORDS

Ask students a series of *or* questions about the pictures. *Is #1 a desk or a file folder?* (desk) *Is #16 a postal scale or an electric pencil sharpener?* (electric pencil sharpener)

Act out verbs A–H, talking about what you are doing. Have students point to the pictures. *I am transcribing notes my boss made last night. He speaks fast, but I can slow him down on the machine.* (C)

PROVIDE PRACTICE
Chalkboard Activities

△ Have students categorize vocabulary:

Write on These
organizer

Keep Papers Together with These
rubberbands

△ Generate a list of office machines and supplies and have students determine which office it would be in.

	1960 Office	2000 Office
typewriter	✓	
fax machine		
postal scale		
Etc.		

Conversations

△ Put models on the board and practice. Make appropriate substitutions.

A: Ron, where is my *desk calendar*?
B: I think it's next to the *[paper shredder]*.
A: Things are always moving around in this office!

   8. calculator **9.** electric pencil sharpener
   17. rotary card file **18.** legal pad
   26. clipboard **28.** stapler
   34. Post-it notes, etc.

A: Katie, could you *fax a letter*?
B: Sure, when I've finished this.

   C. transcribe these notes **D.** type a letter
   E. make copies **F.** collate these papers
   H. file these papers

A: This office could use a *fax machine*!
B: I know. We're the only *[doctor's]* office that doesn't have one.
A: Maybe you could talk to the boss about it.

   8. calculator **14.** photocopier
   16. postal scale **24.** paper shredder

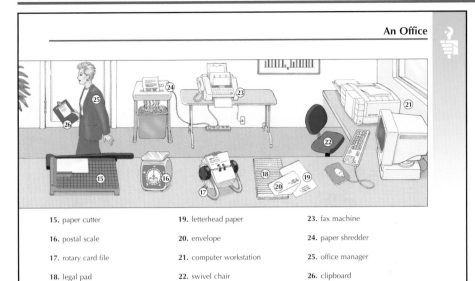

An Office

15. paper cutter
16. postal scale
17. rotary card file
18. legal pad
19. letterhead paper
20. envelope
21. computer workstation
22. swivel chair
23. fax machine
24. paper shredder
25. office manager
26. clipboard

27. appointment book
28. stapler
29. staple
30. organizer
31. typewriter cartridge
32. mailer
33. correction fluid
34. Post-it notes
35. label
36. notepad
37. glue
38. rubber cement
39. clear tape
40. rubber stamp
41. ink pad
42. packing tape
43. pushpin
44. paper clip
45. rubber band

Use the new language.
1. Which items keep things together?
2. Which items are used to mail packages?
3. Which items are made of paper?

Share your answers.
1. Which office supplies do students use?
2. Where can you buy them?

143

Interview Questions

1. Do you know anyone who works in an office? Do they like their work?
2. What office machines do you think are essential? Which are not important?
3. What office equipment and supplies do you have in your home?
4. Which jobs in an office do you think you would like the most? The least?
5. If you were a secretary, what kind of office would you like to work in?
6. If you didn't know how to work a fax machine, how would you find out?

Listening: Interactive Dictation

△ Dictate this purchase order for office supplies. Speak naturally and encourage students to ask for clarification. (*How many envelopes?*)
1. *5 boxes of envelopes*
2. *10 appointment books*
3. *15 boxes of paper clips*
4. *50 mailers*
5. *2 boxes of letterhead paper*
6. *25 file folders*
7. *30 note pads*
8. *4 boxes of push pins*

EXPAND THE LESSON
Problem Solving

△ Have students brainstorm solutions.
1. *Rosa is a file clerk and wants to be a secretary. She speaks English well and can use the computer, but she hasn't been promoted to secretary. She doesn't understand why. What can she do?*
2. *Larry's boss is always giving him more work than he can do. No matter how hard he works, his in-box is full. Talking to the boss doesn't seem to help. What can he do?*

Discussion Questions

1. There are millions of office workers in the United States. What kind of people do you think would like this job? What skills do you need to be a good office worker?
2. Office work used to mean that you had a boss and worked in an office. Nowadays, you may do office work in your own home and may be self-employed. What are the advantages and disadvantages of working at home?

Language Workout

△ Copy these sentences on the board and discuss their meanings.
1. Barbara is a single mom and works hard. She's the *glue that keeps that family together.*
2. Mr. Elwing never looks at any of the work that passes his desk. He just *rubber stamps* everything his secretary sends him.

What Do I Need?

1. Tell students different tasks you need to accomplish or different problems you have, such as *I've made a few mistakes on these papers.*
2. Students tell you what equipment or supplies you need. (*You need correction fluid.*)

GAMES
Guess What!

1. Bring in 10–20 small paper bags, each containing a different office supply. Number each bag.
2. Have students work in pairs. Distribute the bags and have students guess what the object is by feeling the object inside the bag. (Do not bring in push pins or staples.)
3. Have students keep a list of their guesses on a separate piece of paper.
4. The activity ends when all students have had a chance to guess what is in all the bags. Then check the contents.

Backwards Dictionary

1. Divide students into two teams.
2. Give definitions or descriptions of each vocabulary word to one team at a time and have each team guess what the word is. *You type letters on it. It's been around for over 100 years. What is it?* (typewriter) *You put a pencil into it and it comes out sharp. You plug it into the wall. What is it?* (electric pencil sharpener)
3. The team with the most correct answers wins.

Workbooks, p. 144
Classic Classroom Activities, Unit 11
Related Dictionary Page
• An Office, pp. 142–143

TOPIC NOTES

In the U.S., personal computers have changed the way almost all businesses conduct their affairs. They are in more and more classrooms and are the number one leisure time activity. Every year new models and software increase the tasks computers are able to accomplish.

Hardware refers to any part of the machine and its components. **Software** is the program that is entered into the computer by **disks** (diskettes) and CDs (compact discs). A **laptop** is a small, portable computer.

The **mouse** was so named because it was the same size as the animal.

TEACHING TIPS
Related Vocabulary

input	fax*
output	multimedia
tower	e-mail
ROM (read-only memory)	
RAM (random-access memory)	

Pronunciation: *CPU* is pronounced letter by letter: /C-P-U/. With *ROM* and *RAM*, however, the letters are pronounced as a word: /rom/ and /ram/.

⚠ Some people have not had the opportunity to use computers. Words such as *memory* or *mouse* will require simple explanations. If your classroom does not have a computer, bring in disks, a mouse, etc., so that students can become familiar with them.

Computers

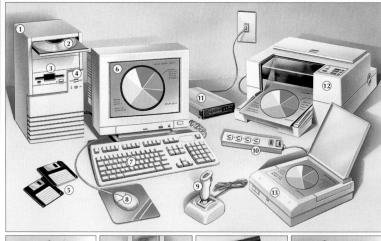

Hardware

1. CPU (central processing unit)
2. CD-ROM disc
3. disk drive
4. power switch
5. disk/floppy
6. monitor/screen
7. keyboard
8. mouse
9. joystick
10. surge protector
11. modem
12. printer
13. scanner
14. laptop
15. trackball
16. cable
17. port
18. motherboard
19. slot
20. hard disk drive

Software

21. program/application
22. user's manual

More vocabulary
data: information that a computer can read
memory: how much data a computer can hold
speed: how fast a computer can work with data

Share your answers.
1. Can you use a computer?
2. How did you learn? in school? from a book? by yourself?

144

INTRODUCE THE TOPIC

Tell students how you learned to use a computer, what you use it for, and how it has changed the way you do things.

Talk about different businesses that use computers.

Ask students to tell you the parts of a computer. Write their words on the board and have students compare their list with the words on page 144.

TEACH THE NEW WORDS

Ask students to identify the number of a particular picture based on your description. *This is the part of the computer where you type the words. It's called the "keyboard." (#7) This is where you put in the disks. It's called the "disk drive." (#3) This moves the arrow around on the screen. It's called the "mouse." (#8)*

PROVIDE PRACTICE
Chalkboard Activity

△ Have students categorize vocabulary:

Input Device	Output Device
mouse	*printer*

Conversations

△ Put models on the board and practice. Make appropriate substitutions.

A: My computer is not working.
B: What do you think is the problem?
A: I think I have to replace the _disk drive_.

> 6. monitor 7. keyboard 8. mouse
> 9. joystick 16. cable 18. motherboard
> 20. hard disk drive

A: I bought a new _CPU_ today.
B: Did you need one?
A: No, but the old one was too slow.

> 11. modem 12. printer 13. scanner
> 14. laptop

Interview Questions

1. Have you used a computer? What for?
2. Where do you see computers used?

Listening: Interactive Dictation

△ Dictate these rules for using the computer. Speak naturally and encourage students to ask for clarification. (*Too close to what?*)

1. *Don't sit too close to the monitor.*
2. *Don't leave disks in the disk drive.*
3. *Don't put drinks near the keyboard.*
4. *Don't put magnetic objects on the disks.*
5. *Don't turn off the power switch.*

EXPAND THE LESSON
Discussion Question

How have computers changed the way you do things? How do they benefit society? What problems do they cause?

A Hotel

1. valet parking	8. front desk	15. housekeeper
2. doorman	9. desk clerk	16. pool
3. lobby	10. guest room	17. pool service
4. bell captain	11. guest	18. ice machine
5. bellhop	12. room service	19. meeting room
6. luggage cart	13. hall	20. ballroom
7. gift shop	14. housekeeping cart	

More vocabulary
concierge: the hotel worker who helps guests find restaurants and interesting places to go
service elevator: an elevator for hotel workers

Share your answers.
1. Does this look like a hotel in your city? Which one?
2. Which hotel job is the most difficult?
3. How much does it cost to stay in a hotel in your city?

145

Workbooks, p. 145
Classic Classroom Activities, Unit 11
Related Dictionary Pages
• Apartments, pp. 36–37
• A Restaurant, pp. 62–63
• Places to Go, p. 152

TOPIC NOTES

In the U.S., hotels and motels provide the dining facilities, meeting rooms, and guest rooms for more than 10 million people who attend conventions each year.

The **hotel** on this page would be found within a city or at a resort. A motor hotel, or motel, is usually found along major highways. Both kinds of hotels cater to business people and vacationers, although their rates vary based on their location, facilities, and amenities.

There is usually an additional charge for **room service** (food delivered to guest rooms).

TEACHING TIPS
Related Vocabulary

motel*	business trip
resort	vacation*
reservation	queen-size bed, etc.
amenity	nonsmoking room
gratuity	hotel chain

Usage: The term *housekeeper* is preferred over *maid*.

Make a reservation at a hotel over the phone. Record the conversation and play it in class. Have students listen for the clerk's questions.

INTRODUCE THE TOPIC

Ask students to name the hotels or motels in your city or area. Take an informal survey to find out where students have stayed.

Bring in a class set of brochures from hotels or motels in nearby vacation spots. Have students vote on where they'd like to stay.

TEACH THE NEW WORDS

Ask students a series of *or* questions about the pictures. *Is the doorman near the lobby or the guest room?* (lobby) *Is the guest in the hall or in the guest room?* (guest room)

PROVIDE PRACTICE
Chalkboard Activity

△ Have students categorize vocabulary:

Workers	Locations	Other
bell captain	*lobby*	*luggage cart*

Conversations

△ Put models on the board and practice. Make appropriate substitutions.

A: I heard *[Sam]* got a new job.
B: Yep! *[He]*'s a *doorman* at the *[Jilton]*!
   4. bell captain 5. bell hop 9. desk clerk
   15. housekeeper

A: Where do you want to meet?
B: Let's meet *in the lobby*.
   7. in the gift shop 8. by the front desk
   13. in the hall 16. by the pool 18. by the
   ice machine 19. in the meeting room
   20. in the ballroom

Interview Questions

1. Is there a hotel or motel near your home? What's its name?
2. Do you know anyone who works in a hotel? What does he or she do?
3. Have you ever stayed in a hotel? Where? When? Was it a good experience?

Listening: Interactive Dictation

△ Have students make three columns headed *job, hours,* and *wages* on a piece of paper. Make statements about 4 or 5 hotel job openings, being sure to give the title, hours, and pay rate. Speak naturally and repeat information upon request.

GAME
Memory Game

1. Divide the class into two teams.
2. Have students study the scene on page 145.
3. Quiz alternate teams with true/false statements about the scene. *The bell captain is opening the door.* (false) *The doorman is in the lobby.* (false)
4. Correct answers get one point.
5. The game ends after 15 statements.

145

Unit 11   A Factory   page 146

Workbooks, p. 146
Classic Classroom Activities, Unit 11
Related Dictionary Pages
- Jobs and Occupations, pp. 136–139
- Job Skills, p. 140
- Job Safety, p. 147
- Tools, pp. 150–151

TOPIC NOTES

In the U.S., factories mass-produce and distribute a wide variety of products. The fastest growing manufacturing companies produce machine tools, electronic components, and surgical instruments. Government regulation and competition from imported products have changed U.S. industry policies. Factory management has been forced to *downsize,* which has resulted in layoffs and changes in factory operations.

📁 On March 25, 1911, 145 immigrant women died in a factory sweatshop in New York City. The Triangle Shirtwaist fire is remembered as the start of better factory conditions in the U.S.

TEACHING TIPS
Related Vocabulary

shift	sweatshop
freight	lay off (v)
work station	supervise*
badge/ID card	promote
union	punch in/out
strike	swipe in/out

Grammar: Active and passive voice Practice both forms with target verbs A–C: *General Motors manufactures cars. Cars are manufactured by General Motors.*

💡 A good follow-up lesson is page 147, *Job Safety.*

A Factory

1. front office
2. factory owner
3. designer
4. time clock
5. line supervisor
6. factory worker
7. parts
8. assembly line
9. warehouse
10. order puller
11. hand truck
12. conveyor belt
13. packer
14. forklift
15. shipping clerk
16. loading dock

A. design
B. manufacture
C. ship

146

INTRODUCE THE TOPIC

Describe the factory production of a consumer product. Bring in realia such as a small lamp or toy to assist in describing the product from start to finish. *First, the designer draws a picture showing what the new lamp will look like. This lamp has three parts…*

Talk about a typical day in the life of a factory worker. Act out various tasks in the factory. *First, I punch in at the time clock, 7:00 A.M. sharp. Next, I take my seat on the assembly line…*

TEACH THE NEW WORDS

Ask students to identify the letter of a particular picture based on your description. *He's counting the boxes on the dock. He's a shipping clerk. (#15)*

PROVIDE PRACTICE
Chalkboard Activity

△ Have students categorize vocabulary:

People	Places	Machines
packer	loading dock	hand truck

Conversations

△ Put models on the board and practice. Make appropriate substitutions.

A: Are those *[lamp]* parts ready?
B: Yup. Put them on the *assembly line*.
   11. hand truck 12. conveyor belt
   14. forklift 16. loading dock

A: The *factory workers* are on strike.
B: What are they striking for?
A: They want *[health benefits]*.
   10. order pullers 13. packers
   15. shipping clerks

Interview Questions

1. Do you know anyone who works in a factory? What does he or she do?
2. Would you rather design something, manufacture it, or sell it?

Listening: 📼 #38, p. 224

"Castillo's Lamp Factory" Students point to the people or things they hear.

EXPAND THE LESSON
Problem Solving

△ Have students brainstorm solutions. *Marta wants a promotion to line supervisor. The owner says that she is qualified, but that he prefers men for that job. What should she do?*

146

Job Safety

1. electrical hazard
2. flammable
3. poison
4. corrosive
5. biohazard
6. radioactive
7. hazardous materials
8. dangerous situation

9. safety goggles
10. safety glasses
11. safety visor
12. respirator
13. earplugs
14. safety earmuffs
15. safety vest
16. back support
17. latex gloves
18. hair net
19. hard hat
20. safety boot
21. toe guard
22. fire extinguisher
23. careless
24. careful

147

Workbooks, p. 147
Classic Classroom Activities, Unit 11
Related Dictionary Pages
• Jobs and Occupations, pp. 136–139
• A Factory, p. 146
• Construction, p. 149

TOPIC NOTES

In the U.S., the total number of injuries and deaths due to workplace accidents becomes smaller every year. Safety regulations, government standards, and workplace education have all contributed to the decline of dangerous working conditions.

Construction workers ranked third in a recent survey of most dangerous jobs (32 deaths per 100,000 workers). Only taxi drivers and loggers had more fatalities.

TEACHING TIPS
Related Vocabulary

electrocute   chemical
ignite   fire-retardant
contaminate   harness
toxic waste   face mask
clean up*   workmen's compensation

Grammar: Modal verbs *should* and *must* Have students practice giving strong advice about safety equipment on the page. *You should put on safety glasses. You must wear a hard hat.*

Using pages 136–139, *Jobs and Occupations,* have students brainstorm dangerous situations and safety equipment they might use.

For students with little workplace experience, the topic of job safety can be extended to the home.

INTRODUCE THE TOPIC

Talk about job safety. Discuss the safety equipment on the page and help students identify which parts of the body each safety item protects.

Take a survey to find out how many students wear safety equipment at work.

Draw a skull and crossbones on the board. Ask students where they would see this sign and to brainstorm a list of potentially dangerous materials.

TEACH THE NEW WORDS

Ask students to call out the number of each picture you describe. *Flammable things can catch fire or explode. You mustn't smoke near flammable items like gasoline. (#2) A safety vest protects your chest and back. They're usually orange. (#15)*

PROVIDE PRACTICE
Chalkboard Activity

△ Have students categorize vocabulary:

Head	Face	Body
hair net	safety goggles	back support

Conversations

△ Put models on the board and practice. Make appropriate substitutions.

A: Watch out! That's *flammable*.
B: Thanks. I didn't see the sign.
   3. poison 4. corrosive 5. a biohazard
   6. radioactive

A: This area is restricted.
B: It's OK. I'm wearing my *safety goggles*.
   10. safety glasses 13. ear plugs 15. safety vest 19. hard hat 20. safety boots

Interview Questions

1. Are there any hazardous materials in your home? at your work? What kind?
2. Did you ever have a dangerous job?
3. Do you have a fire extinguisher in your home?

Listening: #38, p. 224

"Castillo's Lamp Factory" Students write an "H" when they hear a safety hazard and an "E" when they hear a piece of safety equipment.

EXPAND THE LESSON
Problem Solving

△ Have students brainstorm solutions. *Hugo has a job in a welding factory. He is a good welder, but he doesn't speak much English. How can Hugo be sure he understands the safety rules and regulations?*

Workbooks, p. 148
Classic Classroom Activities, Unit 11
Related Dictionary Pages
- Fruit, p. 50
- Vegetables, p. 51
- Meat and Poultry, p. 52
- Domestic Animals and Rodents, p. 133

TOPIC NOTES

In the U.S., farmers produce crops for domestic consumption and foreign export. The U.S. has the world's most efficient farms, thanks to climate, irrigation, automation, and genetic engineering. The largest farms are highly specialized and produce the most; small family farms have declined.

Farms and ranches are the main employers of migrant laborers, men and women who travel for seasonal work.

Livestock refers to farm animals such as **cattle,** hogs, chickens, and turkeys. About 50% of U.S. farm income is from livestock and dairy products.

In 1880, almost 44% of U.S. residents lived on farms. By 1992, only about 2% did.

TEACHING TIPS
Related Vocabulary

pasture	combine (n)
grove	silo
plantation	pitchfork
chicken coop	till
pen	graze
plow	raise

Using the maps on pages 122–123, have students discuss crops and animals that are found in various regions.

Bring in pictures of farmhouses, barns, and silos to discuss the daily workings of farms and ranches.

Farming and Ranching

1. rice	**8.** farmworker	**15.** farmer/grower	**22.** rancher
2. wheat	**9.** tractor	**16.** orchard	**A.** **plant**
3. soybeans	**10.** farm equipment	**17.** corral	**B.** **harvest**
4. corn	**11.** barn	**18.** hay	**C.** **milk**
5. alfalfa	**12.** vegetable garden	**19.** fence	**D.** **feed**
6. cotton	**13.** livestock	**20.** hired hand	
7. field	**14.** vineyard	**21.** steers/cattle	

148

INTRODUCE THE TOPIC

Survey the class, asking students if they ever lived on a working farm or ranch.

Ask students to brainstorm a list of animals they might find on a farm.

Talk about farming in the 1800's and now. Contrast equipment and methods used, as well as the labor required.

TEACH THE NEW WORDS

Ask students a series of *or* questions about the pictures. *Is #3 soybeans or rice?* (soybeans) *Is the rancher on a tractor or a horse?* (horse)

PROVIDE PRACTICE
Chalkboard Activity

△ Have students brainstorm what each of these areas contains: **field, barn, orchard, vineyard, vegetable garden, corral.**

Conversations

△ Put models on the board and practice. Make appropriate substitutions.

A: Is it time to harvest the *rice?*
B: Almost. The farmers say it's going to be a *[great]* crop.
  2. wheat 3. soybeans 4. corn 5. alfalfa
  6. cotton

A: There's a pig in the *orchard!*
B: Oh, no! It's eating the *[apples]!*
  7. field 12. vegetable garden 14. vineyard

Interview Questions

1. Would you like to work on a farm or ranch? Why?
2. Have you ever milked cows? Fed pigs?

Listening: Listen and Point

△ Have students point to the pictures as you describe them. E.g.:
1. *Animals sleep in this building. Farmers keep tools in here, too.* (#11)
2. *This machine pulls farm machinery. Farmers sit on it.* (#9) Etc.

EXPAND THE LESSON
Language Workout

△ Copy these sentences on the board and discuss their meanings.
1. It's midnight, and I'm really tired. Time to *hit the hay.*
2. Will Sylvia vote Democrat or Republican? Who knows? She's *sitting on the fence.*

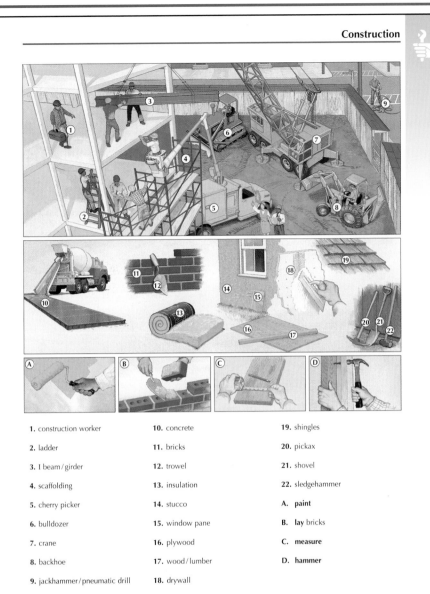

Construction

1. construction worker
2. ladder
3. I beam / girder
4. scaffolding
5. cherry picker
6. bulldozer
7. crane
8. backhoe
9. jackhammer / pneumatic drill

10. concrete
11. bricks
12. trowel
13. insulation
14. stucco
15. window pane
16. plywood
17. wood / lumber
18. drywall

19. shingles
20. pickax
21. shovel
22. sledgehammer

A. paint
B. lay bricks
C. measure
D. hammer

149

Workbooks, p. 149
Classic Classroom Activities, Unit 11
Related Dictionary Pages
- Prepositions of Motion, p. 105
- Jobs and Occupations, pp. 136–139
- Job Skills, p. 140
- Job Safety, p. 147
- Tools, pp. 150–151

TOPIC NOTES

In the U.S., residential and commercial construction work is booming in many suburban areas, while work in other areas may be primarily road maintenance or repair of existing structures. Construction work is sometimes seasonal. As the demand for workers increases, day laborers may appear, often accepting lower wages than licensed tradespeople.

Construction workers can work independently or as part of a work crew. Contractors or builders hire tradespeople such as masons, painters, carpenters, and roofers.

TEACHING TIPS
Related Vocabulary

blueprints	studs
level*	orange cone
wheelbarrow*	detour
cement	restricted area
cement mixer	demolition
fiberglass	remodel

Teach occupations on pages 136–139 that use the machines and materials depicted here.

Review page 147, *Job Safety,* in order to describe what safety precautions the construction workers have to take. *The construction worker is wearing a hard hat.*

INTRODUCE THE TOPIC

Ask students to cover the words at the bottom of the page and name the items they already know.

Bring in copies of a flyer from a home improvement center. Tell the class you are building a new patio. Have students help you pick out some supplies and equipment.

TEACH THE NEW WORDS

Describe the scenes, emphasizing the vocabulary. *Look at #3. The construction worker is holding an I beam.* Have students repeat the target words.

PROVIDE PRACTICE
Chalkboard Activity

△ Have students categorize vocabulary:

Machines
crane

Materials
bricks

Conversations

△ Put models on the board and practice. Make appropriate substitutions.

A: Can you operate a *crane*?
B: No, but I'd like to learn how.
    **5. cherry picker 6. bulldozer 8. backhoe
    9. jack hammer 22. sledgehammer**

A: Did you order the extra *cement*?
B: Yes, it arrived yesterday.
A: That's good. This condo is going to look [great].
    **11. bricks 13. insulation 14. stucco
    16. plywood 17. lumber
    18. drywall 19. shingles**

Interview Questions

1. Have you ever painted your home?
2. What machines or tools on this page can you use?

Listening: Checklist

1. Have students make checklists with these three headings: *Machines, Hand Tools, Building Materials.*
2. Randomly list words from the page, while students make a check under the appropriate column.
3. Have students tell you their tallies. (Correct tallies are: Machines, 5; Tools, 4; and Materials, 10)
4. Repeat the activity until all tallies are accurate.

EXPAND THE LESSON
Discussion Questions

1. What are the advantages and disadvantages of wood, brick, and stucco in house construction?
2. Why are construction jobs so dangerous? What safety tips do you know to reduce injuries?

Workbooks, pp. 150–151
Classic Classroom Activities, Unit 11
Related Dictionary Pages
- Household Problems and Repairs, pp. 48–49
- Parts of a Car and Car Maintenance, pp. 108–109
- Job Safety, p. 147
- Construction, p. 149

TOPIC NOTES

In the U.S., many people own basic tools for small repairs. There are many classes, computer programs, books, and magazines on basic home carpentry, wiring, plumbing, and painting.

Many hand tools that are not electric, such as the **screwdriver,** have electric or battery-operated counterparts.

TEACHING TIPS
Related Vocabulary

measure*	cut*
paint (v)*	saw (v)
chain saw	soldering iron
welding torch	work bench
tool box	ladder*
carpenter*	painter*
do-it-yourselfer	

Grammar: *Paint, hammer, saw, nail, bolt, wire, chisel,* and *plane* are also verbs.

Usage: Electrical tools are often called *power tools.* For example, a *power sander* is run on electricity.

- Review page 149, *Construction,* and pages 48–49, *Household Problems and Repairs.* Talk about the tools that are illustrated.

- Bring in newspaper flyers of tool sales and talk about the quality and prices of the tools shown in the ads.

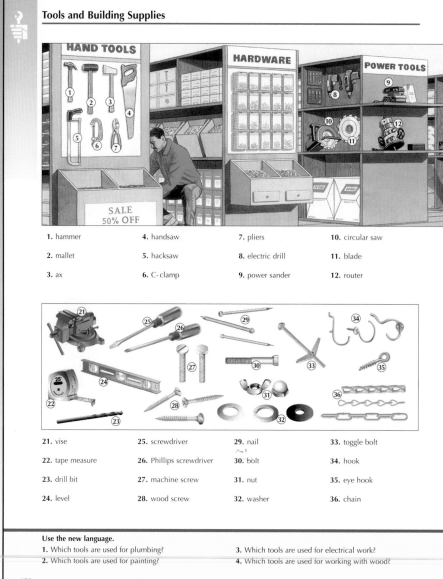

Tools and Building Supplies

HAND TOOLS / HARDWARE / POWER TOOLS

SALE 50% OFF

1. hammer	4. handsaw	7. pliers	10. circular saw
2. mallet	5. hacksaw	8. electric drill	11. blade
3. ax	6. C-clamp	9. power sander	12. router

21. vise	25. screwdriver	29. nail	33. toggle bolt
22. tape measure	26. Phillips screwdriver	30. bolt	34. hook
23. drill bit	27. machine screw	31. nut	35. eye hook
24. level	28. wood screw	32. washer	36. chain

Use the new language.
1. Which tools are used for plumbing?
2. Which tools are used for painting?
3. Which tools are used for electrical work?
4. Which tools are used for working with wood?

150

INTRODUCE THE TOPIC

Tell students about a recent repair or a project you accomplished using some of the tools on the page. Talk about what you did and how long it took.

Walk around the classroom, pointing out small problems that could be repaired such as a crack in the ceiling. Ask students what you would need to fix the problem.

Bring in hand tools and some of the simple hardware on this page. Take an informal class survey asking students which of the items they have in their homes.

TEACH THE NEW WORDS

Ask students to identify the number of a particular picture based on your description. *You use this to cut wood. It's a handsaw.* (#4)

Ask students a series of *yes/no* questions about the pictures. *Is #6 a C-clamp?* (yes) *Is #45 a paint roller?* (no) *Do you use nails with a hammer?* (yes) *Does a mallet hold things together?* (no)

PROVIDE PRACTICE
Chalkboard Activity

△ Have students categorize vocabulary. Some words may fit in two categories:

1. Paint
sandpaper

Electrical
wire

Plumbing
wrench

Carpentry
hammer

2. Make a Bookcase
saw

Fix a Leak
wrench

Conversations

△ Put models on the board and practice. Make appropriate substitutions.

A: Hey, Joe. Could you get me the *hammer?*
B: Here you go.
A: Thanks. I'll give it right back.
    2. mallet 3. ax 4. handsaw 6. C-clamp 8. electric drill 12. router, etc.

A: Please tell me where I can find *nails.*
B: They're on aisle 8 in the *[hardware]* section. I think they're on sale today!
A: Thanks.
    19. spray guns 28. wood screws 30. bolts 31. nuts 32. washers 33. toggle bolts 34. hooks, etc.

A: Do I need special instruction to run the *power sander?*
B: Yes. Wait, I'll show you.
    8. electric drill 10. circular saw 12. router

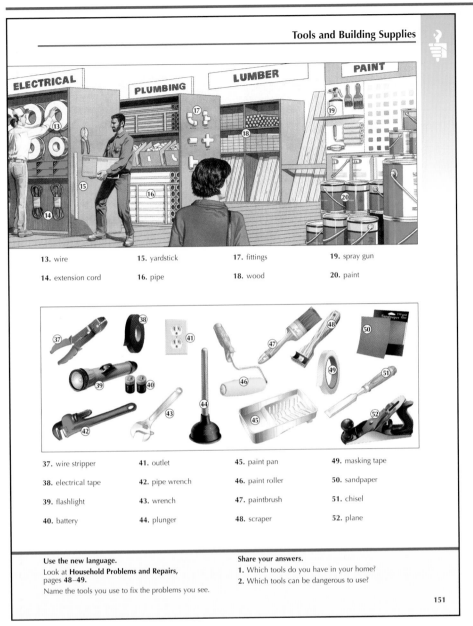

Tools and Building Supplies

13. wire	15. yardstick	17. fittings	19. spray gun
14. extension cord	16. pipe	18. wood	20. paint

37. wire stripper	41. outlet	45. paint pan	49. masking tape
38. electrical tape	42. pipe wrench	46. paint roller	50. sandpaper
39. flashlight	43. wrench	47. paintbrush	51. chisel
40. battery	44. plunger	48. scraper	52. plane

Use the new language.
Look at **Household Problems and Repairs,**
pages **48–49.**
Name the tools you use to fix the problems you see.

Share your answers.
1. Which tools do you have in your home?
2. Which tools can be dangerous to use?

151

EXPAND THE LESSON

Problem Solving

△ Have students brainstorm solutions.
Poy let his brother borrow tools to fix a broken window. His brother has not returned them for over two months. What can Poy do?

Discussion Questions

1. Many people have different ways of doing the same thing. They do things in different order or use different tools to accomplish the same thing. What is one way to paint a room? Fix a pipe? Make a bookcase?

2. In some places, tools are difficult to find or buy. Has there been a time when you didn't have the right tool for a job but you completed the job anyway? What did you do?

3. Some people are lucky enough to learn about using tools from relatives or friends. Where can you go in the community to learn about using the tools on this page?

Language Workout

△ Copy these sentences on the board and discuss their meanings.
1. My friend wants to give up his job even though work is hard to find. He must have a *screw loose.*
2. Every day my mother tells me to study. She is *hammering it into me* to be a good student.

Tool Brainstorm

1. Have students look at pages 48–49, *Household Problems and Repairs.*
2. Have each student choose one household repair problem such as a cracked wall or a dripping faucet.
3. For each problem, students write a list of tools needed to fix the problem.
4. Discuss the final lists with the whole class and talk about any differences of opinion.

GAME

Charades

1. Write the names of tools on slips of paper and put them into a box or hat.
2. Divide students into two teams.
3. Team members take turns picking a word and pantomime using it for their team.
4. Teams get a point for each word they guess.
5. The game ends when all the slips are gone.

Interview Questions

1. Which tools on the pages do you think are the most useful?
2. Which tools do you know how to use?
3. Do you have nails, screws, and hooks in your home?
4. Where do you keep tools you would need in an emergency?

Listening: Listen and Write

△ Have students write the tools and hardware items you name in these sentences. Students can also listen again and identify the places that are mentioned.
1. *Could you please take these **bolts** over to Sam? He's on the roof.*
2. *I need a new **drill bit**. This one is old and dull. There's one in the toolbox.*
3. *Gina, is the **handsaw** in the toolshed? I've got to cut this board.*
4. *We can measure the step with a **yardstick**. Maybe it's in the garage.*
5. *To run this pump I need an **extension cord**. Check the cabinet in the kitchen.*
6. *These **paintbrushes** need to be cleaned. Put them in the sink.*
7. *Here is a new **flashlight**. Put it in a drawer next to the bed.*
8. *Shoot! The plumber left his **wrench** here. Leave it by the door and he can pick it up.*
9. *I've got enough **wood** for the bookcase. It's in the back of my truck.*
10. *Let's use heavy **wire** to hold the fence together. I think the wire is in the storage cabinet.*

Workbooks, p. 152
Classic Classroom Activities, Unit 12
Related Dictionary Pages
• The Park and Playground, p. 153
• The Beach, p. 155
• Entertainment, pp. 166-167

TOPIC NOTES

In the U.S., people often "go out for the day" on Saturday or Sunday.

Amusement parks, theaters, **museums, zoos, botanical gardens,** and **stadiums** are permanent structures with varying exhibits and/or rides.

Carnivals and **fairs** usually come into town for a limited period of time.

Swap meets often occur in structures that were built for other purposes, such as stadiums or drive-in theaters.

📁 Attendance at North American theme parks reached 255 million in 1994.

TEACHING TIPS
Related Vocabulary

park*	parade*
beach*	football*
theme park	national park
theater*	ticket*
air show	admission

Grammar: Articles *a* vs. *the*
Show students the difference between saying *Let's go to the zoo* and *Let's go to a zoo.* In one, the *zoo is* known to the speaker and listener; in the other, the zoo is one of many zoos in the area.

Usage: We use the plural when we talk about liking or disliking something: *I like zoos. I don't like puppet shows.*

💡 Every Monday, have students talk about their weekend activities. *Where did you go? I went…*

Places to Go

1. zoo	**10.** the movies	**19.** county fair
2. animals	**11.** seat	**20.** first place/first prize
3. zookeeper	**12.** screen	**21.** exhibition
4. botanical gardens	**13.** amusement park	**22.** swap meet/flea market
5. greenhouse	**14.** puppet show	**23.** booth
6. gardener	**15.** roller coaster	**24.** merchandise
7. art museum	**16.** carnival	**25.** baseball game
8. painting	**17.** rides	**26.** stadium
9. sculpture	**18.** game	**27.** announcer

Talk about the places you like to go.
I like <u>animals</u>, so I go to <u>the zoo</u>.
I like <u>rides</u>, so I go to <u>carnivals</u>.

Share your answers.
1. Which of these places is interesting to you?
2. Which rides do you like at an amusement park?
3. What are some famous places to go to in your country?

152

INTRODUCE THE TOPIC

Ask students to name local places where they go to to have fun. Write their ideas on the board, as well as locations and admission rates. Have students compare their list to the word list on page 152.

TEACH THE NEW WORDS

Describe and name each picture on the page and have students call out the correct number. *This is a zoo.* (#1) *You can see different animals.* (#2)
Ask students comprehension questions such as *How many animals do you see? What kinds of animals?*

PROVIDE PRACTICE
Chalkboard Activity

△ Have students categorize vocabulary:

Under $10 a Person	Over $10 a Person
zoo	*amusement park*

Conversations

△ Put models on the board and practice. Make appropriate substitutions.

A: Did you have a good weekend?
B: Yes, I did. I went to the <u>zoo</u> on Saturday and <u>the movies</u> on Sunday.

4. botanical gardens/16. a carnival
7. art museum/25. a baseball game
19. county fair/22. a swap meet

A: C'mon!! I want to see the <u>animals</u>!
B: Hold on! I'm buying the tickets.

5. greenhouse 8. painting 9. sculpture
14. puppet show 21. exhibition
25. baseball game

Interview Questions

1. Do you ever go to art museums?
2. Do you ever go to baseball games?
3. Do you ever go to swap meets?
4. Do you like to go on rides? How about rollercoasters?

Listening: 📼 #39, p. 224

"Where Do You Wanna go?" Have students listen as a family discusses where they should spend their weekend. Students point to the place they hear being discussed.

EXPAND THE LESSON
Writing/Drama Activity

1. Divide the class into groups of 4–5 students and tell them they will be making commercials for the places on page 152.

2. Each group chooses a different place from the page and a recorder.

3. Demonstrate a sample commercial for an airshow or a beach resort. *Come to the LA Airshow. You'll see planes, pilots and more! You'll hear…*

4. Each group writes its commercial and performs it for the class.

The Park and Playground

Workbooks, p. 153
Classic Classroom Activities, Unit 12
Related Dictionary Pages
• Trees and Plants, p. 128
• Birds, Insects, and Arachnids, p. 132
• Outdoor Recreation, p. 154
• Sports Verbs, pp. 156–157
• Sports Equipment, p. 161

TOPIC NOTES

In the U.S., neighborhood **parks** are an integral part of urban and suburban communities. They vary from small concrete **playgrounds** surrounded by chain-link fences to large grassy parks with numerous recreational programs. Many parks feature baseball and soccer fields, basketball courts and gymnasiums.
See-saws are also called *teeter-totters.*

TEACHING TIPS
Related Vocabulary

sandtoys	tetherball
handball court	grill
asphalt	Dogs on Leash
(soda) vendor	No Littering
jungle gym	

Grammar: Verb and noun forms
Words such as *bicycle, slide,* and *swing* can be used as either nouns or action verbs: *He's bringing his new bicycle to the park. He bicycled around the lake. Watch me go down the slide. I slide down very fast.*

Arrange a field trip to a local park. A class picnic is a wonderful culminating activity for the class.

1. ball field	8. picnic table	15. sandbox
2. bike path	9. tricycle	16. seesaw
3. cyclist	10. bench	A. **pull** the wagon
4. bicycle/bike	11. water fountain	B. **push** the swing
5. jump rope	12. swings	C. **climb** on the bars
6. duck pond	13. slide	D. **picnic/have** a picnic
7. tennis court	14. climbing apparatus	

153

INTRODUCE THE TOPIC

Ask questions about a neighborhood park or playground. *Is the park large or small? Are there a lot of trees? Is there a special area for children? What kinds of sports can you play? Are you allowed to cook food?*

Have students brainstorm a list of parks they like or things they enjoy doing at the park.

TEACH THE NEW WORDS

Describe a perfect park day. Ask students to identify the number of particular pictures based on your description. *I'll sit on the bench and read the newspaper. (#10) My daughter will play in the sandbox. (#15)*

PROVIDE PRACTICE
Chalkboard Activity

△ Have students categorize vocabulary:

Play Equipment	**Places in the Park**
swing	ballfield

Conversations

△ Put models on the board and practice. Make appropriate substitutions.

A: It's a nice day. Let's go over to the *ballfield*.
B: Great. I'll bring *[my glove]*.
A: That's a good idea.

    6. duck pond 7. tennis court 15. sandbox

A: Look at my son! He can *pull the wagon* all by himself!
B: You must be very proud.
A: I am. He's only *[three]* years old.

    B. push the swing C. climb on the bars

Interview Questions

1. Do your friends or family have get-togethers at the local park? For what occasion?
2. What do you like to do at the park?

Listening: Interactive Dictation

△ Have students close their books as you dictate questions about page 153. Have them check their work and then work in pairs to write the answers.

1. *Where are the picnic tables?*
2. *How many people are riding bicycles?*
3. *Who is feeding the ducks?*
4. *What sports are people playing?*

EXPAND THE LESSON
Discussion Question

Some parks are not safe. How can the government and community improve them?

Unit 12 Outdoor Recreation page 154

Workbooks, p. 154
Classic Classroom Activities, Unit 12
Related Dictionary Pages
• Places to Go, p. 152
• Sports Verbs, pp. 156–157
• Team and Individual Sports, pp. 158–159
• Winter Sports and Water Sports, p. 160
• Sports Equipment, p. 161

TOPIC NOTES

In the U.S., 19.5% of the population camps regularly. There are over 7 million acres of National Park land, and numerous acres of county and state parks as well. People go **backpacking,** carrying all their supplies into the wilderness, or drive into campgrounds and camp in **tents,** campers, or RV's (recreational vehicles).

U.S. Census figures show that 67% of all bikes sold in 1993 were mountain bikes: bikes that can handle unpaved roads.

TEACHING TIPS
Related Vocabulary

fish hook	lake*
tackle box	river*
gear	hill*
hunting	mountain climbing
rifle	trail

Grammar: Gerunds
The *-ing* form of a verb is called a gerund when it's used as a noun: ***Hiking** helps you stay healthy.* Name the verbs within gerunds on the page: *hiking—hike, camping—camp, etc.*

🔅 Many yellow pages list local recreation areas, including user fees, types of facilities, and the availability of food and rentals.

🔅 Have students plan a hike in a local state park. Have groups make a list of all necessary supplies.

Outdoor Recreation

1. camping	4. rafting	7. backpacking
2. boating	5. fishing	8. mountain biking
3. canoeing	6. hiking	9. horseback riding

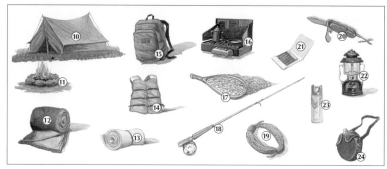

10. tent	15. backpack	20. multi-use knife
11. campfire	16. camping stove	21. matches
12. sleeping bag	17. fishing net	22. lantern
13. foam pad	18. fishing pole	23. insect repellent
14. life vest	19. rope	24. canteen

154

INTRODUCE THE TOPIC

Talk about outdoor activities that are popular in your area. Survey the class to find out how many students have participated in these activities.

TEACH THE NEW WORDS

Demonstrate the activities, #1–9, naming them as you do them.
Bring in realia that matches #10-–24 and see which items students can name. Identify items students can't name.

PROVIDE PRACTICE
Chalkboard Activities

△ Have students categorize vocabulary:

Water	**Land**
rafting	*backpacking*

△ Have students create two matching lists:

Sport	**Equipment**
hiking	*backpack*

Conversations

△ Put models on the board and practice. Make appropriate substitutions.

A: Ah! I love being outdoors!
B: I know! Isn't <u>*hiking*</u> great?

> 1. camping 2. boating 3. canoeing
> 4. rafting 5. fishing 7. backpacking
> 8. mountain biking 9. horseback riding

A: You forgot to bring the <u>*matches*</u>!!
B: No, I didn't. Look in the tent.

> 12. sleeping bag 13. foam pad 16. camping stove 19. rope 20. multi-use knife 22. lantern 23. insect repellent 24. canteen

Interview Questions

1. Do you go camping? Where?
2. Do you go fishing? Where?
3. Name an activity you don't like.
4. Do you like hiking or horseback riding?
5. Would you rather go rafting or canoeing?

Listening: Interactive Dictation

△ Have students close their books as you dictate these five safety rules. Speak naturally and encourage students to ask for clarification. (*Never what?*)

1. *Never go hiking without a canteen.*
2. *Always put out your campfires.*
3. *Wear insect repellent on clothing.*
4. *Always wear a life vest when boating.*
5. *Never go rock climbing alone.*

EXPAND THE LESSON
Discussion Questions

1. In your opinion, what are the most important items to bring with you when you are camping?
2. Which of these outdoor activities are dangerous? Why do people do them? What safety equipment should be used?

154

The Beach

1. ocean/water	**10.** sand castle	**19.** lifesaving device
2. fins	**11.** cooler	**20.** lifeguard station
3. diving mask	**12.** shade	**21.** seashell
4. sailboat	**13.** sunscreen/sunblock	**22.** pail/bucket
5. surfboard	**14.** beach chair	**23.** sand
6. wave	**15.** beach towel	**24.** rock
7. wet suit	**16.** pier	
8. scuba tank	**17.** sunbather	
9. beach umbrella	**18.** lifeguard	

More vocabulary
seaweed: a plant that grows in the ocean
tide: the level of the ocean. The tide goes in and out every twelve hours.

Share your answers.
1. Are there any beaches near your home?
2. Do you prefer to spend more time on the sand or in the water?
3. Where are some of the world's best beaches?

155

Workbooks, p. 155
Classic Classroom Activities, Unit 12
Related Dictionary Pages
• Clothing II, p. 66
• Marine Life, Amphibians, and Reptiles, pp. 130–131
• Sports Verbs, pp. 156–157
• Winter Sports and Water Sports, p. 160

TOPIC NOTES

In the U.S., there are **beaches** on the Pacific and Atlantic Oceans, the Gulf of Mexico, the Great Lakes, and numerous other natural and man-made sounds and lakes. Beaches provide excellent places for recreation, and their surrounding waters support numerous ecosystems. However, beaches near urban areas are threatened by erosion, pollution, and recreational overuse.

Piers are wood plank structures that extend out into the lake or ocean, providing docking and fishing areas. Food stands, souvenir shops, arcade games, and rides can also be found on some piers.

TEACHING TIPS
Related Vocabulary

sand chair	bodysurfing
sand dune*	jetski
rescue	windsurfing
dune buggy	riptide
boardwalk	kickboard

☀ Bring in pictures from magazines and travel brochures to give students added practice describing beach areas.

INTRODUCE THE TOPIC

Draw a picture of a large beach bag. Announce, "It's a beautiful day—let's go to the beach!" Have students brainstorm items to put in the bag.

Act out a beach scene, using comedy as you tell a "shark tale." *It was Sunday morning at Baywatcher Beach. Lifeguard Dan looked through his binoculars and saw fins. Was it a swimmer or…a shark?!*

TEACH THE NEW WORDS

Ask students to identify the number of a particular picture based on your description. *You stand on it to ride the waves. It's a surfboard.* (#5)

PROVIDE PRACTICE
Chalkboard Activity

△ Have students categorize vocabulary:

In Water	On Land	Both
wave	*cooler*	*lifeguard*

Conversations

△ Put models on the board and practice. Make appropriate substitutions.

A: Can I borrow your <u>sunscreen</u>?
B: Sure. But please give it back when you're done.
   2. fins 3. diving mask 5. surfboard
   8. scuba tank 13. sunblock
   15. beach towel 22. pail

A: Do you see the kids anywhere?
B: Yes, there over near the <u>cooler</u>.
A: Oh, I see them. This beach is so crowded!
   4. sailboat 9. beach umbrella
   10. sand castle 20. lifeguard station

Interview Questions

1. Do you like to go to the beach? Where do you go?
2. Do you wear sunscreen or sunblock? Why or why not?

Listening: 📼 #40, p. 224
"Take Me Out To The Beach Please"
Students point to the items at the beach they hear mentioned in the song.

EXPAND THE LESSON
Discussion Question

Many beach areas are destroyed because of overuse and pollution. What would you recommend to save the beaches?

Language Workout

△ Copy these sentences on the board and discuss their meanings.
1. Be quiet—*don't make waves.*
2. Her $25 raise is just *a drop in the bucket.*

Unit 12   Sports Verbs   page 156

Workbooks, pp. 156–157
Classic Classroom Activities, Unit 12
Related Dictionary Pages
• Team Sports, p. 158
• Individual Sports, p. 159
• Winter Sports and Water Sports, p. 160
• Sports Equipment, p. 161

TOPIC NOTES

In the U.S., sports are an important part of people's leisure time. Children sometimes start practicing throwing and catching a ball before they are three years old. Swimming lessons for infants are also becoming popular.

Ride has two meanings: 1) In sports, ride means to have control of an animal or machine, such as a bicycle, horse, or surfboard. *She rides well.* 2) Ride also means to be conveyed by a vehicle, such as a bus or car. *He rides the bus to school.* **Work out** means to exercise or lift weights.

TEACHING TIPS
Related Vocabulary

lift	fall*
bowl	skip
push*	pull*
strike out	slide*
climb*	

Grammar: Transitive Verbs
In sports, *throw, catch, pitch, hit, pass, shoot, kick, serve,* and *swing* are often used as transitive verbs. *He throws the ball well. She swings the racket easily.*
Note: Some of the above verbs can also be intransitive. E.g.:
He likes to swing *on the swings.*

Sports Verbs

A. walk	E. catch	I. shoot	M. tackle
B. jog	F. pitch	J. jump	
C. run	G. hit	K. dribble / bounce	
D. throw	H. pass	L. kick	

Practice talking about what you can do.
I can swim, but I can't dive.
I can pass the ball well, but I can't shoot too well.

Use the new language.
Look at **Individual Sports, page 159.**
Name the actions you see people doing.
The man in number 18 is riding a horse.

156

INTRODUCE THE TOPIC

Act out various actions: running, walking, throwing a ball, etc. Describe what you are doing. *I run every morning until I get tired. Then I walk. I like to play baseball, too. I swing the bat hard before my turn at the plate. When I hit the ball far, I'm really happy.*

Write on the board two sports depicted on the page. Ask students to brainstorm the verbs used in each sport. Compare their lists with the word list on pages 156–157.

Bring in various sports equipment: a baseball, baseball bat, skates, etc. Talk about how they are used. *In baseball you can throw the ball, hit it, or catch it. You hit the ball with a baseball bat. When I skate, I like to use these new inline skates.*

TEACH THE NEW WORDS

Ask students to identify the letter of a particular picture based on your description. *Julio swims everyday in the pool.*(T) *Mark and Roger play baseball. Mark can throw really well.* (D)

PROVIDE PRACTICE
Chalkboard Activity

△ Have students categorize vocabulary:

1. Arms	Legs	Both
throw	kick	tackle

2. With Someone	By Yourself
catch	walk

Conversations

△ Put models on the board and practice. Make appropriate substitutions.

A: You really *throw* the ball well!
B: Thanks, Coach!

E. catch F. pitch G. hit H. pass I. shoot
K. dribble N. serve

A: How often do you *jog?*
B: I try to do it *[three times a week],* but sometimes I don't.
A: I don't ever *[jog],* but I'd like to try it sometime.

A. walk C. run P. exercise
S. dive T. swim V. skate W. ride

A: Look at *[Katie]!!* Look how well *[she] throws!*
B: Yeah, too bad *[she's]* not on our team!

C. runs E. catches F. pitches G. hits
H. passes I. shoots J. jumps K. dribbles
L. kicks M. tackles N. serves S. dives

Interview Questions

1. Do you like to do physical activity? What things do you do?
2. Do you exercise? What kind of exercise do you do?

Sports Verbs

N.	serve	R.	bend	V.	skate	Z.	finish
O.	swing	S.	dive	W.	ride		
P.	exercise / work out	T.	swim	X.	start		
Q.	stretch	U.	ski	Y.	race		

Share your answers.
1. What do you like to do?
2. What do you have difficulty doing?
3. How often do you exercise? Once a week? Two or three times a week? More? Never?
4. Which is more difficult, throwing a ball or catching it?

157

3. Does your family play sports together?
4. Which of these activities are most popular in your country?

Listening: 🔊 #41, p. 225
"The Oakwood News" Students point to different sports as they hear Karl and Gina picking photographs for the newspaper.

EXPAND THE LESSON
Problem Solving
△ Have students brainstorm solutions.
1. *Hilo's doctor says he has to exercise more, but Hilo says it's too boring. His wife is worried. What can she do about it?*
2. *Brad's eight-year-old daughter is upset because she is not as good as the other children in sports. What can Brad do?*

Discussion Questions
1. Walking, jogging, and running are very popular in the U.S. Are they popular in your country?
2. Some athletes leave their families to train for hundreds of hours to be able to go to the Olympics. If you were given the chance to train for the Olympics, would you do it? Why or why not?

Language Workout
△ Copy these sentences on the board and discuss their meanings.
1. Charlie has a lot of money in the stock market. He felt terrible last summer when it *took a dive.*
2. Teri lives in a small apartment with her three young children. She cleans her place every day but she always feels like she's *swimming upstream.*

3. Wally is a good worker. Whenever there is a problem he *tackles it head-on.*
4. When Sal's friend asked him to work in his factory, *he jumped at the chance.*
5. At 5:00 on Fridays everyone in Nick's office *races* for the bus.

One-Two-Three
1. Have students close their books.
2. Give three commands in a row. *Show me, "walk," "kick," and "dive."*
3. A student volunteer comes to the front of the room and does the three commands in order.
4. Continue with more three-in-a-row commands.

Variation: Have one of your more able students give the commands.

Scrambled Words
1. Have students number their papers 1–10.
2. Spell out loud ten vocabulary words in scrambled order, e.g., *w-t-r-h-o* (throw); *k-k-c-i* (kick).
3. Give students 5 minutes to unscramble the words.
4. Have student volunteers come to the board to write the correct spelling.

GAMES
Charades
1. Write the verbs A–W on slips of paper and put them into a box or hat.
2. Divide the class into two teams.
3. Team members take turns picking a word and acting it out for their team.
4. Teams get a point for each word they guess.
5. The game ends when all the slips are gone.

Class Go-Around: I Am the Most Athletic!
Note: Talk about boasting. Tell students that athletes in the U.S. are known to boast after games.
1. Begin by saying *I am the most athletic. I pitch really well.*
2. The first student volunteer repeats the sentence and adds another item. *I am the most athletic. I pitch and hit really well.*
3. The next student volunteer continues the chain, adding another item.
4. Stop after the tenth student and begin the game again.

Workbooks, p. 158
Classic Classroom Activities, Unit 12
Related Dictionary Pages
- Sports Verbs, pp. 156–157
- Individual Sports, p. 159
- Winter Sports and Water Sports, p. 160
- Sports Equipment, p. 161

TOPIC NOTES

In the U.S., people are participating in and watching team sports more than ever before. In high school, boys favor **football** while girls favor **basketball**. **Soccer** has been gaining in popularity everywhere. However, among these spectator sports, **baseball**, with 28 professional teams, is still number one.

Baseball and softball are similar games, but the equipment and pitching styles are different. Baseball uses a hardball that is smaller than a softball. In baseball pitching is overhand, whereas softball uses an underhand pitching style.

TEACHING TIPS
Related Vocabulary

field	run (n)
rink	forward (n)
tie	guard
point	pitcher
touchdown	catcher
field goal	halfback
spectator	fullback

- Review pages 156–157, *Sports Verbs*, so that students can talk about the various actions associated with each team sport.
- Bring in the sports section of your local or high school newspaper and talk about the names of various teams and what their current record is.

Team Sports

1. score	3. team	5. player	7. basketball court
2. coach	4. fan	6. official / referee	

8. basketball	11. football	14. volleyball
9. baseball	12. soccer	15. water polo
10. softball	13. ice hockey	

More vocabulary
captain: the team leader
umpire: in baseball, the name for the referee
Little League: a baseball league for children

win: to have the best score
lose: the opposite of win
tie: to have the same score as the other team

158

INTRODUCE THE TOPIC

Ask students what sports they play and which ones they watch on TV. Talk about the most popular sports in different countries.

Discuss the top picture, asking questions such as *How many people do you see playing? What's the score? What's the name of one team?*

TEACH THE NEW WORDS

Ask students to identify the number of a particular picture based on your description. *Look at the man in the striped shirt. He keeps the rules. He is the referee.* (#6) *These boys are trying to make a touchdown. The ball is not round. They can kick it or throw it. They are playing football.* (#11)

PROVIDE PRACTICE
Chalkboard Activity

△ Have students categorize vocabulary. They may use each sport more than once:

Hit	Throw	Run	Kick
baseball	*baseball*	*softball*	*football*

Conversations

△ Put models on the board and practice. Make appropriate substitutions.

A: Look at that <u>coach</u>. She's really mad!
B: Well, her team just lost the game!
　　4. fan 5. player

A: We're having a game of <u>basketball</u> at the park. Come play with us!
B: OK, but I'm new at it.
A: Don't worry! It's a friendly game.
　　9. baseball 10. softball 11. football
　　12. soccer 14. volleyball

Interview Questions

1. What is your favorite sport to watch?
2. What is your favorite sport to play?

Listening: 📼 #42, p. 225

"Coach Wilder, Lakewood High" Students point to the sports they hear the coach talking about.

EXPAND THE LESSON
Discussion Questions

1. Fewer girls than boys take part in sports although that is changing. Do you think sports are as important for girls as for boys? Why or why not?
2. Football is considered a dangerous sport by some people. Do you think high school students should continue to play football? Why or why not?

Individual Sports

1. archery
2. billiards/pool
3. bowling
4. cycling/biking
5. fencing
6. flying disc*
7. golf
8. gymnastics
9. inline skating
10. martial arts
11. racquetball
12. skateboarding
13. table tennis/ Ping-Pong™
14. tennis
15. weightlifting
16. wrestling
17. track and field
18. horse racing

*Note: one brand is Frisbee® (Mattel, Inc.)

Talk about sports.
Which sports do you like?
I like tennis but I don't like golf.

Share your answers.
1. Which sports are good for children to learn? Why?
2. Which sport is the most difficult to learn? Why?
3. Which sport is the most dangerous? Why?

159

Workbooks, p. 159
Classic Classroom Activities, Unit 12
Related Dictionary Pages
- Sports Verbs, pp. 156–157
- Team Sports, p. 158
- Winter Sports and Water Sports, p. 160
- Sports Equipment, p. 161

TOPIC NOTES

In the U.S., people have always participated in individual sports. **Inline skating, skateboarding,** and mountain **biking** are gaining in popularity.

Horse racing is a spectator sport that often involves gambling.

TEACHING TIPS
Related Vocabulary

win*	lose*
score*	practice
play*	compete
squash	handball
skydiving	darts
karate	equestrian
boxing	aerobics

Usage: Explain to students the verbs that are used with the different types of sports:
do: archery, gymnastics, martial arts, track and field
play: billiards, golf, Frisbee, racquetball, table tennis, tennis
go: bowling, cycling, inline skating, skateboarding
Fence, lift weights, race horses, and *wrestle* do not take another verb.

☼ Review *Sports Verbs,* pages 156–157, for the various actions associated with each sport.

☼ Bring in the yellow pages from the telephone book and talk about various places to go bowling, do gymnastics, etc.

INTRODUCE THE TOPIC

Act out one or two of the sports on the page. If you need special equipment or clothing, such as bowling shoes, mime putting those on. Ask students what sport you are showing.

Talk about one or two of the sports that you know. Ask students to identify any of the sports they have participated in recently.

TEACH THE NEW WORDS

Name and describe each sport. Act them out as you talk about each one. Ask students to identify the number of a particular picture based on your description. *I'm using a bow and arrow. I hope I can hit the target. This is called "archery." (#1) I need lots of muscles to do this. Here I go. I hope I can lift these barbells. This is called "weightlifting." (#15)*

PROVIDE PRACTICE
Chalkboard Activity

△ Have students categorize vocabulary. Sports can be used more than once:

Alone	Two People	More Than Two
archery	tennis	tennis

Conversations

△ Put models on the board and practice. Make appropriate substitutions.

A: Do you want to go *bowling*?
B: Thanks, not today. I've already played *racquetball*.
    4. cycling/2. billiards
    9. inline skating/7. golf
    12. skateboarding/14. tennis

A: My son really loves *archery*.
B: That's great. I like to watch, but I don't do it myself.
    3. bowling 4. cycling 5. fencing
    7. golf 8. gymnastics 10. martial arts
    11. racquetball 12. skateboarding

Interview Questions

1. What sports have you tried?
2. Did you play for a long time? Why or why not?

Listening: Interactive Dictation

△ Have students close their books. Dictate sentences including the verbs, *go, play,* and *do.* Speak naturally and encourage students to ask for clarification. *(What's his name? When?)* E.g.:
1. *Mike plays frisbee every Monday.*
2. *Maria does gymnastics every day.*
3. *Cindy goes bowling Friday nights.*
4. *Leo plays golf on Sundays.* Etc.

EXPAND THE LESSON
Discussion Question

Everyone can do some sport. If someone doesn't feel athletic, which sport would you recommend they try? Why?

Unit 12   Winter Sports and Water Sports   page 160

Workbooks, p. 160
Classic Classroom Activities, Unit 12
Related Dictionary Pages
• Sports Verbs, pp. 156–157
• Team Sports, p. 158
• Individual Sports, p. 159
• Sports Equipment, p. 161

TOPIC NOTES

In the U.S., sports lose and gain in popularity as people's tastes change. Young people are taking up **snowboarding** instead of **downhill skiing. Surfing** is still very popular, but the style of surfboards has changed to much smaller boards since the 70s.

While any sport can be dangerous, some, like **scuba diving,** require special training and certification.

TEACHING TIPS
Related Vocabulary

bobsledding	ice hockey*
snowmobiling	tobogganing
body surfing	canoeing*
kayaking	rowing
swimming	diving

Pronunciation: Some languages, such as Spanish, Chinese, Persian, Russian, and Polish, do not have the sound represented by -ing. Practice having students distinguish between *dim/ding, rim/ring, thin/thing,* and *win/wing* before beginning this page.

Grammar: The gerunds (-ing nouns) on this page become verbs by deleting -ing. Add -e in some cases: *ice skating—ice skate, surfing—surf.*

☀ Talk about the special sports equipment on page 161 needed for each sport on this page.

Winter Sports and Water Sports

1. downhill skiing	**3.** cross-country skiing	**5.** figure skating
2. snowboarding	**4.** ice skating	**6.** sledding

7. waterskiing	**9.** surfing	**11.** snorkeling
8. sailing	**10.** sailboarding	**12.** scuba diving

Use the new language.
Look at **The Beach,** page 155.
Name the sports you see.

Share your answers.
1. Which sports are in the Winter Olympics?
2. Which sports do you think are the most exciting to watch?

160

INTRODUCE THE TOPIC

Act out one or two of the sports on this page. If you need special equipment or clothing, such as ice skates, mime putting those on. Ask students to tell what sport you are doing.

Bring in a picture from a magazine of someone doing one of these sports. Talk about where the person is, the clothes they are wearing, and the skills they need.

TEACH THE NEW WORDS

Name and describe each sport. Act them out as you talk about each one. Ask students to identify the number of a particular picture based on your description. *I'm learning how to spin and jump on the ice. This is called "figure skating." (#5) I like being pulled by a boat on water skis. This is called "waterskiing." (#7)*

PROVIDE PRACTICE
Chalkboard Activity

△ Have students categorize vocabulary:

Lessons	**No Lessons**
figure skating	*sledding*

Conversations

△ Put models on the board and practice. Make appropriate substitutions.

A: Why don't you come *waterskiing* with us?
B: Thanks, I d love to!
  8. sailing 9. surfing 10. sailboarding 11. snorkeling, etc.

A: I want to take up *snowboarding*.
B: Me too, but I heard *[snowboarding]* is hard to learn.
A: Not at all. My *[brother]* can teach us!
  1. downhill skiing 3. cross-country skiing 4. ice skating 5. figure skating 6. sledding 7. waterskiing 8. sailing, etc.

Interview Questions

1. Which winter sports do you like?
2. Which water sports are popular in your country?

Listening: Listen and Write

△ Have students write the sports as you say them in random order.

EXPAND THE LESSON
Discussion Questions

1. Sports such as downhill skiing and scuba diving can be dangerous. How can one prevent accidents when doing these sports?
2. Have you ever tried to teach someone a sport? What are some qualities of a good teacher or coach? What are some ways to encourage people to work at a sport?

Sports Equipment

1. golf club	8. target	15. catcher's mask	22. football
2. tennis racket	9. ice skates	16. uniform	23. snowboard
3. volleyball	10. inline skates	17. glove	24. skis
4. basketball	11. hockey stick	18. baseball	25. ski poles
5. bowling ball	12. soccer ball	19. weights	26. ski boots
6. bow	13. shin guards	20. football helmet	27. flying disc*
7. arrow	14. baseball bat	21. shoulder pads	*Note: one brand is Frisbee® (Mattel, Inc.)

Share your answers.
1. Which sports equipment is used for safety reasons?
2. Which sports equipment is heavy?
3. What sports equipment do you have at home?

Use the new language.
Look at **Individual Sports,** page 159.
Name the sports equipment you see.

161

Workbooks, p. 161
Classic Classroom Activities, Unit 12
Related Dictionary Pages
• Sports Verbs, pp. 156–157
• Team Sports, p. 158
• Individual Sports, p. 159
• Winter Sports and Water Sports, p. 160

TOPIC NOTES

In the U.S., sports equipment is sold in sporting goods stores, department stores, and discount stores. One can find good buys for used equipment in the classified ads and at garage sales.

TEACHING TIPS
Related Vocabulary

sporting goods	goggles
snorkel	wet suit
surfboard	life jacket
bindings	athletic shoes
chest protector	batting helmet
weightbelt	elbow pads
pool stick	

Usage: Talk about sports equipment that incorporates the name of the sport, e.g., *baseball bat, football helmet,* etc.

- ☼ Talk about sports equipment in students' countries. Discuss which equipment is the same as that depicted and which is different.
- ☼ Talk about how sports equipment has changed: bats are now also aluminum, skates have in-line wheels, skis are shorter, etc.
- ☼ Have a "garage sale" in your class. Have students bring in used equipment and price it. Invite other classes to join in.

INTRODUCE THE TOPIC

Ask students to look at the dictionary page and name all the items they already know.

Bring in a favorite piece of sport equipment. Talk about when you got it and why it is special.

TEACH THE NEW WORDS

Ask students a series of *or* questions about the pictures. *Is #9 a soccer ball or ice skates?* (ice skates) *Is #20 a football helmet or a catcher's mask?* (football helmet)

Act out using each piece of equipment as you describe it. *I like putting on this baseball glove. I play first base, and this is my lucky glove.*

PROVIDE PRACTICE
Chalkboard Activity

△ Have students categorize vocabulary:

| **For the Sport** | **As Protection** |
| *target* | *shin guards* |

Conversations

△ Put models on the board and practice. Make appropriate substitutions.

A: Oh, no! I can t find my <u>football</u>!
B: Look in your closet. I'm sure it's in there.
    6. bow 7. arrow 11. hockey stick
    14. baseball bat 15. catcher's mask
    16. uniform 17. glove 18. baseball
    20. football helmet, etc.

A: John, can I borrow your <u>weights</u>?
B: OK, but I need them back tomorrow. I'm going to be using them.
    9. ice skates 10. inline skates 13. shin guards
    21. shoulder pads 24. skis 25. ski poles
    26. ski boots

Interview Questions

1. Which sports equipment on this page have you used before?
2. What sports equipment would you give to a ten-year-old child? To an adult?

Listening: ▭ **#42, p. 225**
"Coach Wilder, Lakewood High" Students point to the sports equipment they hear.

EXPAND THE LESSON
Problem Solving

Ned lent Alan his skis. Now Alan says he never borrowed them. What can Ned do?

Language Workout

△ Copy this sentence on the board and discuss its meaning.
Raul was *right on target* when he guessed that Julia didn't like her new boss.

161

Workbooks, pp. 162–163
Classic Classroom Activities, Unit 12
Related Dictionary Pages
- A Yard, p. 39
- Sewing and Alterations, p. 73
- Computers, p. 144

TOPIC NOTES

In the U.S., many people watch television during evening hours that used to be devoted to games and hobbies. Crafting is on the rise, however, as more and more people take pleasure in working with their hands to create things.

A **hobby** is a leisure-time activity that usually involves collecting or creating something for personal satisfaction.

Games come in a variety of media. When people play a game regularly, they can refer to the game as their hobby.

TEACHING TIPS
Related Vocabulary

needlepoint	imagine
basketry	act out
weaving	opponent
jewelry making	winner
pottery	team*
craftsperson	computer game

Grammar: Adverbs of frequency
Review the adverbs *usually, sometimes,* and *never* to help students talk about their leisure-time preferences. *I like to paint. I usually work with oil. Sometimes I work with watercolor. I never work with acrylic paint.*

⚠ Emphasize the artistry of crafts from different cultures. A craft one person views as a hobby may be another person's economic support.

Hobbies and Games

A. **collect** things   B. **play** games   C. **build** models   D. **do** crafts

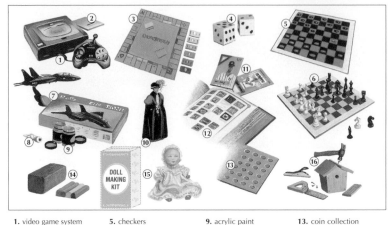

1. video game system	5. checkers	9. acrylic paint	13. coin collection
2. cartridge	6. chess	10. figurine	14. clay
3. board game	7. model kit	11. baseball card	15. doll making kit
4. dice	8. glue	12. stamp collection	16. woodworking kit

Talk about how much time you spend on your hobbies.
I do crafts all the time.
I play chess sometimes.
I never build models.

Share your answers.
1. How often do you play video games? Often? Sometimes? Never?
2. What board games do you know?
3. Do you collect anything? What?

162

INTRODUCE THE TOPIC

Act out one of the activities from pages 162–163, such as knitting or painting, and have students guess what you are doing.

Bring in something from one of your collections or something to do with one of your hobbies. Talk about how you got started.

Ask students to name all the games they know. Write their ideas on the board and then have them compare their list with the games on page 162.

Show an unusual piece of pottery or other handcrafted item and see if anyone can describe how it was made.

Play a game of tic-tac-toe on the board. Divide the class into two teams, play the game, and then elicit the rules of the game from students.

TEACH THE NEW WORDS

Describe and name what each person is doing in the scenes, one scene at a time. Have students call out the correct letter. *The first picture shows people in a living room. A father and older daughter are playing a board game. This family likes to play games. The younger brother is playing a video game.*

Ask students a series of *yes/no* questions about #1–32. *Do you play a video game with dice?* (no) *Do you need glue for a model kit?* (yes)

Give students an opportunity to practice any words they have trouble pronouncing. Elicit those words they feel unsure of and then model those words for them. *What word do you want to practice? "Woodworking kit"? OK, listen. "Kit." "Woodworking kit."*

PROVIDE PRACTICE
Chalkboard Activity

Have students categorize vocabulary:

Collect	**Build**
coins	models

Play	**Pretend with**
chess	paper dolls

Conversations

△ Put models on the board and practice. Make appropriate substitutions.

A: Would you like to see my *stamp collection?*
B: I'd love to.
> 10. figurines 11. baseball cards
> 13. coin collection 30. paper dolls
> 31. action figures 32. model trains

A: I need to buy some *yarn.* Any ideas?
B: *[Yarn's]* on sale at Tom's Craft Shop.
> 8. glue 9. acrylic paint 14. clay

162

Hobbies and Games

E. paint   F. knit   G. pretend   H. play cards

17. yarn

18. knitting needles

19. embroidery

20. crochet

21. easel

22. canvas

23. paintbrush

24. oil paint

25. watercolor

26. clubs

27. diamonds

28. spades

29. hearts

30. paper doll

31. action figure

32. model trains

Share your answers.
1. Do you like to play cards? Which games?
2. Did you pretend a lot when you were a child? What did you pretend to be?
3. Is it important to have hobbies? Why or why not?
4. What's your favorite game?
5. What's your hobby?

163

A: I don't know what to get for *[Rose's 10th birthday]*.
B: Well, she loves to *do crafts*. Why don't you get *a dollmaking kit*?
A: That's a great idea!

    A. collect things/10. a figurine
    B. play games/1. a video game
    C. build models/7. a model kit
    E. paint/22. a canvas
    F. knit/18. knitting needles

A: I win!! I win the game!
B: Relax, it's only *checkers*!
A: I know, but I love to win!

    3. a board game 6. chess

Interview Questions

1. Do you do crafts? Which ones?
2. Do you collect things? What?
3. Do you have any models at home? Which ones?
4. Which do you like better— boardgames or card games?

5. Do you have a favorite artist? Who?
6. Do you like to paint?
7. Do you know how to knit, crochet, or embroider?
8. Pretend you just won the lottery. What will you do in your free time?

Listening 🔊 #43, p. 225

"Who's Doing What?" As the people talk about their crafts and hobbies, students point to the person who is speaking.

EXPAND THE LESSON
Problem Solving

△ Have students brainstorm solutions. *Susie's husband, Mike, goes out on Saturday night and plays cards with his friends. Susie has to take care of the kids and never goes out. Susie feels angry about this. What should she do?*

Discussion Questions

1. Some people think family life was better when people played games, read, or did crafts instead of watching TV. What's your opinion?
2. Do you think video games are good for children? Why or why not?
3. What are the benefits of having a collection? Are there any problems with collecting things?

Language Workout

△ Write these sentences on the board and discuss their meanings.

1. The Browns always stay home together in the evenings. They're a *close-knit* family.
2. George never says what he means. He's always *playing games.*

Drawing/Writing Activity

1. Bring in or show pictures of pottery from different cultures.
2. Have student volunteers come up and draw the pottery shapes on the board.
3. Distribute blank paper and colored markers to the class and have students design a piece of pottery.
4. When finished, students can share their work with a partner.
5. Have students write about their creations, using these prompts:
   What shape did you choose? Why? What colors did you choose? Why? What would you put in your pottery piece?

GAMES
Class Go-Around: Free Time

1. Begin by saying *In my free time, I like to play checkers*.
2. The first student volunteer repeats the sentence and adds another game or a hobby. *In my free time, I like to play checkers and build models*.
3. The next student volunteer continues the chain, adding another game or hobby.
4. Stop after the tenth student and begin the game again.

Questions Only!

1. Divide students into groups of 4–8 and have each group choose a recorder.
2. Have students look at page 162 and come up with as many questions as they can about the scene. *Who is playing cards?* Etc.
3. Recorders write their groups' questions on the board.
4. The group with the most correct questions wins.

Workbooks, pp. 164–165
Classic Classroom Activities, Unit 12
Related Dictionary Pages
• The Telephone, p. 9
• Computers, p. 144
• Entertainment, pp. 166–167

TOPIC NOTES

In the U.S., advances in electronic technology have transformed homes and businesses. It took 70 years after the telephone was invented for it to be installed in 50% of all U.S. homes, while it took television only 8 years.

Competition from imported products has resulted in lower prices and more variety in state-of-the-art electronic components and accessories.

Cameras and video camera equipment are widely marketed for professionals and hobbyists alike.

TEACHING TIPS
Related Vocabulary

flash attachment	negatives
darkroom	reprints
satellite dish	copy a tape
laser disc player	recharge a battery
audiocassette	program a VCR
boombox	cable box
CB/ham radio	

Pronunciation: Word stress
The noun *record* has the stress on the first syllable: *I have a new **re**cord.* The verb *record* has the stress on the second syllable: *I want to re**cord** that new song.*

 Take pictures of students and make up a class photo album, or put them on a bulletin board.

Electronics and Photography

1. clock radio	**8.** VCR (videocassette recorder)	**15.** personal radio-cassette player
2. portable radio-cassette player	**9.** remote control	**16.** headphones
3. cassette recorder	**10.** videocassette	**17.** adapter
4. microphone	**11.** speakers	**18.** plug
5. shortwave radio	**12.** turntable	
6. TV (television)	**13.** tuner	
7. portable TV	**14.** CD player	

164

INTRODUCE THE TOPIC

Take an informal survey to see how many students like to watch television. Ask students to tell you the different television (or VCR or 35 mm camera) brand names and models that they know of and which ones they would recommend.

Bring in a slide projector or a camera and demonstrate its features. Show some overexposed, underexposed, and out-of-focus photos as you discuss your photographic "skills." *I have a great camera, but these pictures are terrible. Does this one look blurry? It's out of focus.*

Ask questions about various electronic equipment and accessories. *Do you like to listen to music on a CD player or a cassette player? Where do you take it? What kind of radio do you listen to? Do you plug it in or use batteries?*

TEACH THE NEW WORDS

Say the words and have students repeat them as they point to the correct pictures.
Bring in a portable radio/cassette player and act out the role of audio salesperson. Demonstrate the features, using TPR commands to guide students through the target vocabulary. *Try this new model. First, plug it in. Now, press the eject button. Put in the cassette. Press the play button. Rewind the tape when the song is over.*

PROVIDE PRACTICE
Chalkboard Activity

△ Have students categorize vocabulary:

Audio	Visual	Both
portable radio	slides	television

Conversations

△ Put models on the board and practice. Make appropriate substitutions.

A: Where can I buy a good *clock radio*?
B: Try *[Electronic World]*. They carry all the name brands.
   2. portable radio-cassette player 8. VCR
   15. personal radio 29. slide projector

A: I'd like to return this video camera system.
B: What seems to be the problem?
A: The *tripod* is broken.
   21. camcorder 22. battery pack 23. battery charger 25. zoom lens 27. camera case

A: Does this stereo system come with *a microphone*?
B: No, that costs extra.
   9. a remote control 11. speakers
   12. a turntable 13. a tuner 14. a CD player
   16. headphones

164

Electronics and Photography

19. video camera	27. camera case	35. underexposed
20. tripod	28. screen	A. **record**
21. camcorder	29. carousel slide projector	B. **play**
22. battery pack	30. slide tray	C. **fast forward**
23. battery charger	31. slides	D. **rewind**
24. 35 mm camera	32. photo album	E. **pause**
25. zoom lens	33. out of focus	F. **stop** and **eject**
26. film	34. overexposed	

165

Interview Questions

1. Do you have a camera? What kind of pictures do you like to take?
2. Do you have a family photo album? What's your favorite picture?
3. Do you know how to use a slide projector?
4. What kind of radio do you like? Do you use an alarm or music to wake up?
5. In your opinion, what companies manufacture good quality televisions? Cameras?
6. How do you listen to music: on records, cassettes, or CDs?
7. Do you tape music or television programs? What kind?
8. Do you ever rent videos? Where do you rent them?
9. Where can you get the best deals on photographic or electronic items?

Listening: Definitions

△ Read the following sentences and have students write the number of the item on a separate piece of paper.

1. *You can set the alarm to ring or play music on this.* (#1)
2. *You can listen to music with this and except you nobody can hear it.* (#16)
3. *Put all your pictures in this and save your memories.* (#32)
4. *This is the part of a stereo system that plays records.* (#12)
5. *This part of a still or video camera lets you see things both close-up and from a distance.* (#25)
6. *You can play videos or record your favorite programs onto a blank tape with this.* (#8)
7. *This is the part of a radio that receives AM or FM signals.* (#13)

8. *This small item connects electrical equipment to the power source.* (#18)
9. *Adjust the three legs on this support and put a camera on it.* (#20)
10. *This camera records moving pictures and sounds on a videotape.* (#21)

EXPAND THE LESSON

Problem Solving

△ Have students brainstorm solutions.

1. *Sam just bought a 35 mm. camera at a swapmeet. The camera is broken. The seller refuses to take back the camera because it is used. What should Sam do?*
2. *Patricia got a camera for her birthday, but she doesn't know how to take good pictures. What advice could you give Patricia?*

Discussion Questions

1. In your opinion, what is the best way to record and preserve memories: photographs, videotapes, or slides? What are some advantages of each one?
2. Most people listen to music on CD or cassette players. Do you think records will soon disappear completely?
3. Some people buy and sell illegal, or "bootleg," copies of audio or video cassettes. Do you think this is a serious problem?

Language Workout

△ Copy this sentence on the board and discuss its meaning.
The mayor *pulled the plug* on the project because of money problems.

GAME

Word Links

1. Divide the class into Teams A and B.
2. Have students study the words on pages 164 and 165 for 2 minutes and then close their books.
3. Write the word *television* horizontally on the board.
4. Have a volunteer from Team A come up and write a connecting word vertically, using any letter in the word television.

t e l e v i s i o n
u
n
e
r

5. A volunteer from Team B then comes up and links to either the first or the second word on the board.
6. Play continues until the students run out of words or board space.

Unit 12 Entertainment page 166

Workbooks, pp. 166–167
Classic Classroom Activities, Unit 12
Related Dictionary Pages
- Feelings, pp. 30–31
- Music, p. 120
- Electronics and Photography, pp. 164–165

TOPIC NOTES

In the U.S., television viewing remains the number one form of entertainment. Every day more than 75 million Americans tune in to network or cable programs.

People of all ages enjoy live **concerts** and **plays,** with performances by both amateur and professional casts. Venues range from large concert halls to school auditoriums and public recreation centers.

A **soap opera** is neither soap nor an opera; it is a daytime serial TV program. These programs, originally aired on the radio, were first sponsored by soap companies.

TEACHING TIPS
Related Vocabulary

cable service	reserved seating
pay per view	box office
musical	soprano
circus	tenor
cast	paperback
rehearse	novel

Usage: We *watch television*, but can *watch* or *see a movie.*

⚠ Students often confuse *bored* with *boring* and *interested* with *interesting.* Give a number of examples of how these words are used. *That movie was boring. I was really bored when I saw it.*

Entertainment

Types of entertainment

1. film/movie

2. play

3. television program

4. radio program

5. stand-up comedy

6. concert

7. ballet

8. opera

Types of stories

9. western

10. comedy

11. tragedy

12. science fiction story

13. action story/ adventure story

14. horror story

15. mystery

16. romance

166

INTRODUCE THE TOPIC

Bring in the entertainment section of the local newspaper and talk about several upcoming local events. *There's a folkloric and classical dance festival on Saturday. Julio Iglesias is in concert, singing popular music selections.* Ask for a show of hands for events students would like to attend.

Ask students to name their favorite television programs. Talk about why these shows are entertaining. Make a checklist on the board as you survey students. Do they like these programs because they are exciting, funny, informative, or have a famous celebrity?

Mime reading funny, sad, boring, and interesting books. See if students can tell how you feel about each book.

TEACH THE NEW WORDS

Ask students to call out the number of each picture you describe. *I enjoy this nature program —those gorillas are amazing. (#22) News with Tom Smith tells me what's happening in the world. (#17)*

PROVIDE PRACTICE
Chalkboard Activity

△ Have students categorize vocabulary. They may use programs more than once:

Entertain	Educate
situation comedy	*news*

Conversations

△ Put models on the board and practice. Make appropriate substitutions.

A: What do you want to do tonight?
B: I hear there's a new *movie* downtown. How does that sound?

2. play 6. concert 7. ballet 8. opera

A: Let's rent *a western* at Videostore.
B: I'd prefer something else. Those films are too *[violent].*

10. a comedy 12. a science fiction story
13. an action story 14. a horror story
15. a mystery 16. a romance

A: Don't change the channel! My favorite *sitcom* is coming on.
B: What program is that?
A: *[I Love Lucy].* I really like it.

19. cartoon 20. talk show 21. soap opera
22. nature program 23. game show
24. children's program 25. shopping program

Interview Questions

1. What types of entertainment are popular in your native country?

2. Is there entertainment in your country that you can't enjoy here? What is it?

Entertainment

Types of TV programs

17. news

18. sitcom (situation comedy)

19. cartoon

20. talk show

21. soap opera

22. nature program

23. game show / quiz show

24. children's program

25. shopping program

26. **serious** book

27. **funny** book

28. **sad** book

29. **boring** book

30. **interesting** book

167

---

3. Have you ever been to a ballet or an opera? Did you enjoy it?

4. Did you ever act in a play? What role did you play?

5. What do you think is the best entertainment for a family to enjoy together?

6. What was your favorite entertainment when you were ten years old? Do ten-year-olds like it today?

7. Which types of television programs do you watch most often? Most infrequently?

8. How do you find out the news—from TV, radio, or newspaper?

Listening: 🔊 Tapescript #44, p. 226

"Channel Changers" Students listen to a family talking about TV shows and point to the pictures as they are described.

EXPAND THE LESSON

Problem Solving

△ Have students brainstorm solutions.

1. *Rosie is with a friend at a rock concert. She can't stand the loud music. Her friend spent a lot of money for the tickets. What can Rosie do?*

2. *Alberto loves to read. He is on a tight budget. How can he get books and magazines without spending a lot of money?*

3. *What do you think about laws that ban loud music in public places?*

Discussion Questions

1. Many people say that news programs show too many crimes and disasters. What do you think?

2. What kinds of television programs can you learn the most from? What channels are these programs on?

---

3. In your opinion, can watching television help improve your English?

4. Do you have a favorite radio station? What do you listen to most often: news, weather, sports, or music?

5. Many stories have heroes and villains. Can you name some from movies or books?

6. Name a popular game show. Describe how contestants win money or prizes.

7. How do television and radio programs sell things?

8. Film ratings (G, PG, PG-13, R) give information about a movie's language, violence, and sexual content. What do you think about ratings for television and music?

Language Workout

△ Copy these sentences on the board and discuss their meanings.

1. Juan hasn't heard about the job yet, but that's OK. *No news is good news.*

2. Ella has a new boyfriend every week. Her life is a real *soap opera!*

Speeches: "Movie Critic"

1. Write the following incomplete sentences on the board and have students brainstorm ways to complete them:

> **One of my favorite movies is…**
> **This movie is…(western, comedy, mystery, etc.) starring…**
> **The story takes place in…**
> **I liked the part when…**
> **The ending is great because…**

2. Help students with the pronunciation of these phrases by tapping out the rhythm and/or using your hand to indicate rising and falling intonation.

3. Give each student a 3″ x 5″ card on which to write a short movie review, using the phrases from the board and adding his or her own ideas.

4. Have students practice their movie reviews with partners or in groups.

5. Students can memorize or use their cards to give the reviews in front of the class.

GAME

Backwards Dictionary

1. Divide students into two teams.

2. Give definitions or descriptions of the vocabulary words to one team at a time and have them guess what the word is. *This program gives information about what's happening in the world.* (news) *This type of story usually has cowboys and horses.* (western)

3. The team with the most correct answers wins.

Workbooks, p. 168
Classic Classroom Activities, Unit 12
Related Dictionary Pages
- The Calendar, pp. 18–19
- North America and Central America, pp. 122–123
- The World, pp. 124–125
- Entertainment, pp. 166–167

TOPIC NOTES

In the U.S., a mix of cultures ensures that there are celebrations every month of the year. Traditional festivals and religious holidays are often observed cross-culturally within different communities. (**Christmas** is an example of such a holiday.)

On legal holidays (which are created by the government), government offices, banks, schools, and some businesses are closed. The government, however, does not have the power to declare a national holiday when all businesses and government offices must be closed.

TEACHING TIPS
Related Vocabulary

New Year's Eve	Memorial Day
Lunar New Year	Flag Day
President's Day	Father's Day
Saint Patrick's Day	Labor Day
April Fool's Day	Hanukkah/Chanukah
Easter	observe
Mother's Day	honor

Usage: We sometimes refer to the *eve* of a holiday, meaning the evening before the holiday begins. Some holidays are celebrated on both the eve and day of the holiday: e.g., *New Year's Eve* and *New Year's Day*.

☀ Have the class make cards for an upcoming holiday and "send" them to students in another classroom.

Holidays

1. New Year's Day	8. fireworks	15. Thanksgiving
2. parade	9. flag	16. feast
3. confetti	10. Halloween	17. turkey
4. Valentine's Day	11. jack-o'-lantern	18. Christmas
5. card	12. mask	19. ornament
6. heart	13. costume	20. Christmas tree
7. Independence Day / 4th of July	14. candy	

168

INTRODUCE THE TOPIC

Show students a calendar page for the current month and ask them to identify any holidays they know of.

Ask students to name different ways they celebrate the New Year, being sure to point out that the New Year comes at different times for different people. Ask students questions such as *What do you eat? What do you wear? Where do you go? What do you do?*

TEACH THE NEW WORDS

Describe and name each holiday, focusing on the dates, the identifying elements, and the associated colors.

Ask students a series of yes/no questions about the holidays. *Is Halloween in May?* (no) *Is Independence day on June 4th?* (no)

PROVIDE PRACTICE
Chalkboard Activity

△ Have students categorize the vocabulary and add other holidays:

Winter	**Spring**
Christmas	*Easter*

Summer	**Fall**
July 4th	*Halloween*

Conversations

△ Put models on the board and practice. Make appropriate substitutions.

A: Wasn't George's *costume* great?
B: Yes, he's so [*creative*]!

> 5. card 9. flag 11. jack o'lantern 12. mask 19. ornament 20. Christmas tree

Interview Questions

1. What holiday do you celebrate that is not on page 168?
2. Is there an Independence Day in your native country? When is it?

Listening 🔊 #45, p. 226

"Where's the Party?" Students hear people inviting each other to holiday parties and point to the holidays they hear.

EXPAND THE LESSON
Problem Solving

△ Have students brainstorm solutions. *During the month of Ramadan, Ali, a Moslem, cannot eat or drink during the day. His teacher brought in a cake for a classmate, and Ali doesn't want to upset the teacher. What should he say when the teacher offers him cake?*

A Party

A. plan a party

B. invite the guests

C. decorate the house

D. wrap a gift

E. hide

F. answer the door

G. shout "surprise!"

H. light the candles

I. sing "Happy Birthday"

J. make a wish

K. blow out the candles

L. open the presents

Practice inviting friends to a party.
I'd love for you to come to my party next week.
Could you and your friend come to my party?
Would your friend like to come to a party I'm giving?

Share your answers.
1. Do you celebrate birthdays? What do you do?
2. Are there birthdays you celebrate in a special way?
3. Is there a special birthday song in your country?

169

Workbooks, p. 169
Classic Classroom Activities, Unit 12
Related Dictionary Pages
• The Calendar, pp. 18–19
• A Graduation, pp. 32–33
• Food Preparation, p. 58
• Entertainment, pp. 166–167

TOPIC NOTES

In the U.S., parties are thrown to celebrate numerous events. The most common of these are birthdays, anniversaries, graduations, new jobs, new homes, upcoming weddings or babies, or retirements.

Children's birthday parties usually include games, a cake, and presents. Adult birthday parties may include all of the above but may also center around a meal and have music.

It is traditional to match the number of candles on the birthday cake with the birthday person's age plus one for good luck. The birthday person usually **makes a wish** and **blows out** all **the candles**.

TEACHING TIPS
Related Vocabulary

anniversary*	decorations
retirement	banner*
bon voyage	balloon
wedding shower	gift wrap
baby shower	caterer*
housewarming	dance floor*

Review these words in the phrases on page 169: *party, guest, house, gift/present, door, candles, wish.*

Students can plan a surprise "thank you" party for someone on the school staff, creating invitations, decorations, and a commemorative plaque for the guest of honor.

INTRODUCE THE TOPIC

Bring in party decorations and a box of cookies and have students guess the topic.

Talk about a recent birthday party you have attended. Tell students the age of the guest of honor, the kind of food that was served, the activities at the party, and the kinds of gifts that were given.

TEACH THE NEW WORDS

Act out the sequence (A–L). Have students follow along in their books and tell you what you are doing. *Susan is having a birthday. Hmmm. It would be nice to have a party for her, but where? Who's going to come? What will we eat? What do I have to do?* (plan a party)

PROVIDE PRACTICE
Chalkboard Activity

△ Have students categorize vocabulary:

Host	Guests	Guest of Honor
decorate	*wrap a gift*	*make a wish*

Conversations

△ Put models on the board and practice. Make appropriate substitutions.

A: Isn't it fun to have surprise parties?
B: It sure is. Especially the part when we *shout "surprise."*

C. decorate the house E. hide I. sing "Happy Birthday" L. open the presents

Interview Questions

1. Do you like birthday parties?
2. Do you ever decorate your home for special occasions? What do you use?
3. Is there a special birthday song in your language? What is it?

Listening 🔊 #45, p. 226

"Where's the Party?" Students hear people inviting each other to parties, and write down the dates and times.

EXPAND THE LESSON
Hope Gifts

1. Pair students and have them interview their partners about their hopes and wishes for the future.
2. Give each student a piece of colorful construction paper and tell them to write what they wish for their partners on the paper.
3. Have students fold up their papers and exchange their "gifts."

Verb Guide

Verbs in English are either regular or irregular in the past tense and past participle forms.

Regular Verbs

The regular verbs below are marked 1, 2, 3, or 4 according to four different spelling patterns. (See page 172 for the **irregular verbs** which do not follow any of these patterns.)

Spelling Patterns for the Past and the Past Participle	*Example*		
1. Add **-ed** to the end of the verb.	**ASK**	→	**ASKED**
2. Add **-d** to the end of the verb.	**LIVE**	→	**LIVED**
3. Double the final consonant and add **-ed** to the end of the verb.	**DROP**	→	**DROPPED**
4. Drop the final y and add **-ied** to the end of the verb.	**CRY**	→	**CRIED**

The Oxford Picture Dictionary List of Regular Verbs

act (1)
add (1)
address (1)
answer (1)
apologize (2)
appear (1)
applaud (1)
arrange (2)
arrest (1)
arrive (2)
ask (1)
assemble (2)
assist (1)
bake (2)
barbecue (2)
bathe (2)
board (1)
boil (1)
borrow (1)
bounce (2)
brainstorm (1)
breathe (2)
broil (1)
brush (1)
burn (1)
call (1)
carry (4)
change (2)
check (1)
choke (2)
chop (3)
circle (2)
claim (1)
clap (3)
clean (1)
clear (1)
climb (1)
close (2)
collate (2)

collect (1)
color (1)
comb (1)
commit (3)
compliment (1)
conserve (2)
convert (1)
cook (1)
copy (4)
correct (1)
cough (1)
count (1)
cross (1)
cry (4)
dance (2)
design (1)
deposit (1)
deliver (1)
dial (1)
dictate (2)
die (2)
discuss (1)
dive (2)
dress (1)
dribble (2)
drill (1)
drop (3)
drown (1)
dry (4)
dust (1)
dye (2)
edit (1)
eject (1)
empty (4)
end (1)
enter (1)
erase (2)
examine (2)
exchange (2)

exercise (2)
experience (2)
exterminate (2)
fasten (1)
fax (1)
file (2)
fill (1)
finish (1)
fix (1)
floss (1)
fold (1)
fry (4)
gargle (2)
graduate (2)
grate (2)
grease (2)
greet (1)
grill (1)
hail (1)
hammer (1)
harvest (1)
help (1)
hire (2)
hug (3)
immigrate (2)
inquire (2)
insert (1)
introduce (2)
invite (2)
iron (1)
jog (3)
join (1)
jump (1)
kick (1)
kiss (1)
knit (3)
land (1)
laugh (1)
learn (1)

lengthen (1)	pull (1)	start (1)
listen (1)	push (1)	stay (1)
live (2)	race (2)	steam (1)
load (1)	raise (2)	stir (3)
lock (1)	rake (2)	stir-fry (4)
look (1)	receive (2)	stop (3)
mail (1)	record (1)	stow (1)
manufacture (2)	recycle (2)	stretch (1)
mark (1)	register (1)	supervise (2)
match (1)	relax (1)	swallow (1)
measure (2)	remove (2)	tackle (2)
milk (1)	rent (1)	talk (1)
miss (1)	repair (1)	taste (2)
mix (1)	repeat (1)	thank (1)
mop (3)	report (1)	tie (2)
move (2)	request (1)	touch (1)
mow (1)	return (1)	transcribe (2)
need (1)	rinse (2)	transfer (3)
nurse (2)	roast (1)	travel (1)
obey (1)	rock (1)	trim (3)
observe (2)	sauté (2)	turn (1)
open (1)	save (2)	type (2)
operate (2)	scrub (3)	underline (2)
order (1)	seat (1)	unload (1)
overdose (2)	sentence (2)	unpack (1)
paint (1)	serve (2)	use (2)
park (1)	share (2)	vacuum (1)
pass (1)	shave (2)	vomit (1)
pause (2)	ship (3)	vote (2)
peel (1)	shop (3)	wait (1)
perm (1)	shorten (1)	walk (1)
pick (1)	shout (1)	wash (1)
pitch (1)	sign (1)	watch (1)
plan (3)	simmer (1)	water (1)
plant (1)	skate (2)	weed (1)
play (1)	ski (1)	weigh (1)
point (1)	slice (2)	wipe (2)
polish (1)	smell (1)	work (1)
pour (1)	sneeze (2)	wrap (3)
pretend (1)	sort (1)	yield (1)
print (1)	spell (1)	
protect (1)	staple (2)	

Verb Guide

Irregular Verbs

These verbs have irregular endings in the past and/or the past participle.

The Oxford Picture Dictionary List of Irregular Verbs

simple	past	past participle	simple	past	past participle
be	was	been	leave	left	left
beat	beat	beaten	lend	lent	lent
become	became	become	let	let	let
begin	began	begun	light	lit	lit
bend	bent	bent	make	made	made
bleed	bled	bled	pay	paid	paid
blow	blew	blown	picnic	picnicked	picnicked
break	broke	broken	put	put	put
build	built	built	read	read	read
buy	bought	bought	rewind	rewound	rewound
catch	caught	caught	rewrite	rewrote	rewritten
come	came	come	ride	rode	ridden
cut	cut	cut	run	ran	run
do	did	done	say	said	said
draw	drew	drawn	see	saw	seen
drink	drank	drunk	sell	sold	sold
drive	drove	driven	send	sent	sent
eat	ate	eaten	set	set	set
fall	fell	fallen	sew	sewed	sewn
feed	fed	fed	shoot	shot	shot
feel	felt	felt	sing	sang	sung
find	found	found	sit	sat	sat
fly	flew	flown	speak	spoke	spoken
get	got	gotten	stand	stood	stood
give	gave	given	sweep	swept	swept
go	went	gone	swim	swam	swum
hang	hung	hung	swing	swung	swung
have	had	had	take	took	taken
hear	heard	heard	teach	taught	taught
hide	hid	hidden	throw	threw	thrown
hit	hit	hit	wake	woke	woken
hold	held	held	wear	wore	worn
keep	kept	kept	withdraw	withdrew	withdrawn
lay	laid	laid	write	wrote	written

Index

Two numbers are shown after words in the index: the first refers to the page where the word is illustrated and the second refers to the item number of the word on that page. For example, cool [ko͞ol] **10**-3 means that the word *cool* is item number 3 on page 10. If only the bold page number appears, then that word is part of the unit title or subtitle, or is found somewhere else on the page. A bold number followed by ♦ means the word can be found in the exercise space at the bottom of that page.

Words or combinations of words that appear in **bold** type are used as verbs or verb phrases. Words used as other parts of speech are shown in ordinary type. So, for example, **file** (in bold type) is the verb *file*, while file (in ordinary type) is the noun *file*. Words or phrases in small capital letters (for example, HOLIDAYS) form unit titles.

Phrases and other words that form combinations with an individual word entry are often listed underneath it. Rather than repeating the word each time it occurs in combination with what is listed under it, the word is replaced by three dots (...), called an ellipsis. For example, under the word *bus*, you will find ...driver and ...stop meaning *bus driver* and *bus stop*. Under the word *store* you will find shoe... and toy..., meaning *shoe store* and *toy store*.

Pronunciation Guide

The index includes a pronunciation guide for all the words and phrases illustrated in the book. This guide uses symbols commonly found in dictionaries for native speakers. These symbols, unlike those used in pronunciation systems such as the International Phonetic Alphabet, tend to use English spelling patterns and so should help you to become more aware of the connections between written English and spoken English.

Consonants

[b] as in back [băk]
[ch] as in cheek [chēk]
[d] as in date [dāt]
[dh] as in this [dhĭs]
[f] as in face [fās]
[g] as in gas [găs]
[h] as in half [hăf]
[j] as in jam [jăm]

[k] as in key [kē]
[l] as in leaf [lēf]
[m] as in match [măch]
[n] as in neck [nĕk]
[ng] as in ring [rĭng]
[p] as in park [pärk]
[r] as in rice [rīs]
[s] as in sand [sănd]

[sh] as in shoe [sho͞o]
[t] as in tape [tāp]
[th] as in three [thrē]
[v] as in vine [vīn]
[w] as in wait [wāt]
[y] as in yams [yămz]
[z] as in zoo [zo͞o]
[zh] as in measure [mĕzhʹər]

Vowels

[ā] as in bake [bāk]
[ă] as in back [băk]
[ä] as in car [kär] or box [bäks]
[ē] as in beat [bēt]
[ĕ] as in bed [bĕd]
[ë] as in bear [bër]
[ī] as in line [līn]

[ĭ] as in lip [lĭp]
[ï] as in near [nïr]
[ō] as in cold [kōld]
[ö] as in short [shört]
    or claw [klö]
[o͞o] as in cool [ko͞ol]
[o͝o] as in cook [ko͝ok]

[ow] as in cow [kow]
[oy] as in boy [boy]
[ŭ] as in cut [kŭt]
[ü] as in curb [kürb]
[ə] as in above [ə bŭvʹ]

All the pronunciation symbols used are alphabetical except for the schwa [ə]. The schwa is the most frequent vowel sound in English. If you use the schwa appropriately in unstressed syllables, your pronunciation will sound more natural.

Vowels before [r] are shown with the symbol [¨] to call attention to the special quality that vowels have before [r]. (Note that the symbols [ä] and [ö] are also used for vowels not followed by [r], as in *box* or *claw*.) You should listen carefully to native speakers to discover how these vowels actually sound.

Stress

This index follows the system for marking stress used in many dictionaries for native speakers.

1. Stress is not marked if a word consisting of a single syllable occurs by itself.

2. Where stress is marked, two levels are distinguished:

a bold accent [ʹ] is placed after each syllable with primary (or strong) stress, a light accent [ʹ] is placed after each syllable with secondary (or weaker) stress.

In phrases and other combinations of words, stress is indicated for each word as it would be pronounced within the whole phrase or other unit. If a word consisting of a single syllable is stressed in the combinations listed below it, the accent mark indicating the degree of stress it has in the phrases (primary or secondary) is shown in parentheses. A hyphen replaces any part of a word or phrase that is omitted. For example, bus [bŭs(ʹ–)] shows that the word *bus* is said with primary stress in the combinations shown below it. The word ...driver [–drīʹvər], listed under *bus*, shows that *driver* has secondary stress in the combination *bus driver*: [bŭsʹ drīʹvər].

Syllable Boundaries

Syllable boundaries are indicated by a single space or by a stress mark.

Note: The pronunciations shown in this index are based on patterns of American English. There has been no attempt to represent all of the varieties of American English. Students should listen to native speakers to hear how the language actually sounds in a particular region.

Index

Index

Index

Index

Index

Index

Index

Index

...bite [–bīt/] **78**–11
...repellent [–rĭ pĕl/ənt] **154**–23
INSECTS [ĭn/sĕkts] **132**
insert [ĭn sürt/] **97**–A
Inside the body [ĭn/sīd/ dhə bäd/ē] **75**
instant coffee [ĭn/stənt kö/fē] **55**–51
instructor [ĭn strŭk/tər] **5** ✦, **139**–58
instrument [ĭn/strə mənt] **120**–A
insulation [ĭn/sə lā/shən] **149**–13
insurance [ĭn shŏŏr/əns]
...card [–kärd/] **84**–4
...form [–förm/] **84**–5
intercom [ĭn/tər käm/] **36**–8
interesting [ĭn/trə stĭng, ĭn/tə rĕs/tĭng] **167**–30
international call [ĭn/tər näsh/ə nəl köl/] **9**–6
internist [ĭn/tür/nĭst] **86**–2
interpreter [ĭn tür/prə tər] **138**–34
INTERSECTION [ĭn/tər sĕk/shən] **90**–**91**
interview [ĭn/tər vyōō/] **141**–H
intestinal parasites [ĭn tĕs/tə nəl păr/ə sīts/] **79**–16
intestines [ĭn tĕs/tənz] **75**–42
into [ĭn/tōō, –tə] **105**–4
introduce [ĭn/trə dōōs/] **8**–D, F
Invention [ĭn vĕn/shən] **115**
invite [ĭn vīt/] **169**–B
iris [ī/rəs] **129**–20
iron [ī/ərn] **72**–G
iron [ī/ərn] **72**–13
ironed shirt [ī/ərnd shürt/] **72**–20
ironing board [ī/ər nĭng börd/] **72**–14
island [ī/lənd] **117**–8
IV (intravenous drip) [ī/vē/] / [ĭn/trə vē/nəs drĭp/] **87**–27
jack [jăk] **109**–53
jack cheese [jăk/ chēz/] **53**–12
jacket [jăk/ət] **66**–7
jack hammer [jăk/ hăm/ər] **149**–9
jack-o'-lantern [jăk/ə lăn/tərn] **168**–11
jam [jăm] **56**–14
janitor [jăn/ə tər] **138**–3
January [jăn/yōō ĕr/ē] **19**–25
jar [jär(/–)] **56**–2
...of jam [–əv jăm/] **56**–14
jasmine [jăz/mən] **129**–21
jaw [jö] **74**–23
jeans [jēnz] **64**–5
jellyfish [jĕl/ē fĭsh/] **130**–14
jewelry [jōō/əl rē] **69**–8
...store [–stör/] **92**–2
job [jäb(/–)] / [–jäb/]
...board [–börd/] **141**–B
get a... [gĕt/ ə–] **28**–G
JOB SAFETY [jäb/ sāf/tē] **147**
JOB SEARCH [jäb/ sürch/] **141**
JOB SKILLS [jäb/ skĭlz/] **140**
JOBS AND OCCUPATIONS A-H [jäbz/ ən äk/yə pā/shənz] **136**–**137**
JOBS AND OCCUPATIONS H-W [jäbz/ ən äk/yə pā/shənz] **138**–**139**
jockstrap [jäk/străp/] **67**–14
jog [jäg] **156**–B
join the army [joyn/ dhē är/mē] **28**–F
joystick [joy/stĭk/] **144**–9
judge [jŭj] **99**–6
Judicial [jōō dĭsh/əl] **116**
July [jōō lī/] **19**–31, **168**–7
jump [jŭmp] **156**–J

jumper [jŭm/pər] **65**–18
jumper cables [jŭm/pər kā/bəlz] **109**–52
jump rope [jŭmp/ rōp/] **153**–5
jumpsuit [jŭmp/sōōt/] **65**–16
June [jōōn] **19**–30
junior high school [jōōn/yər hī/ skōōl] **112**–6
Jupiter [jōō/pə tər] **127**–5
jury [jŏŏr/ē] **99**–8, **116**
Justices [jŭs/tə səz] **116**–10
kangaroo [kăng/gə rōō/] **135**–44
keep [kēp] **21**–E
ketchup [kĕch/əp, kăch/–] **60**–23
key [kē(/–)] **37**–31
...chain [–chān/] **69**–43
keyboard [kē/börd/] **120**–20, **144**–7
kick [kĭk] **156**–L
kidney [kĭd/nē] **75**–45
kilometers [kĭ läm/ə tərz, kĭl/ə mē/tərz] **15** ✦
kiss [kĭs] **33**–F
KITCHEN [kĭch/ən] **40**
kitchen [kĭch/ən] **63**–10
...timer [–tī/mər] **59**–18
KITCHEN UTENSILS [kĭch/ən yōō tĕn/səlz] **59**
kitten [kĭt/n] **133**–10
knee [nē(/–)] **74**–17
...socks [–säks/] **67**–25
knee-highs [nē/hīz/] **67**–24
knife [(–)nīf(/)] **41**–22, **63**–27
carving... [kär/vĭng–] **59**–12
multi-use... [mŭl/tē yōōs/–, mŭl/tī–] **154**–20
paring... [për/ĭng–] **59**–16
knit [nĭt] **163**–F
knit shirt [nĭt/ shürt/] **65**–20
knitting needles [nĭt/ĭng nēd/lz] **163**–18
koala [kō ä/lə] **135**–45
label [lā/bəl] / [–lā/bəl] **143**–35
prescription... [prĭ skrĭp/shən–] **80**–14
lab technician [lăb/ tĕk nĭsh/ən] **86**–16
ladder [lăd/ər] **149**–2
ladle [lād/l] **59**–7
ladybug [lā/dē bŭg/] **132**–27
lake [lāk] **117**–13
lamb [lăm(/–)] **52**–13, 14, 15
...chops [–chäps/] **52**–15
...shanks [–shăngks/] **52**–13
lamp [lămp] **42**–15, **44**–17
lampshade [lămp/shād/] **44**–18
land [lănd] **111**–O
landlord [lănd/lörd/] **37**–32
language [lăng/gwĭj]
English as a second... [ĭng/glĭsh əz ə sĕk/ənd–] **141**–7
foreign... [för/ən–, fär/–] **141**–8
speak another... [spēk/ ə nä/thər] **140**–J
use the new... [yōōz/ thə nū/–] **143** ✦
lantern [lăn/tərn] **154**–22
laptop [lăp/täp/] **144**–14
large [lärj] **70**–4
last [lăst(/–)]
...name [–nām/] **4**–4
...week [–wēk/] **18**–18
late [lāt] **17**–23
latex gloves [lā/tĕks glŭvz/] **87**–33, **147**–17
laugh [lăf] **33**–H
Laundromat [lön/drə măt/] **90**–1
laundry [lön/drē] **72**–1

Index

Index

Index

Index

Geographical Index

Continents

Africa [ăf/rĭ kə] **125**–5
Antarctica [ănt ärk/tĭ kə, –är/tĭ–] **125**–7
Asia [ā/zhə] **125**–4
Australia [ö sträl/yə] **125**–6
Europe [yŏor/əp] **125**–3
North America [nörth/ ə mĕr/ə kə] **124**–1
South America [sowth/ ə mĕr/ə kə] **124**–2

Countries and other locations

Afghanistan [ăf găn/ə stăn/] **124–125**
Albania [ăl bā/nē ə] **124–125**
Algeria [ăl jïr/ē ə] **124–125125**
American Samoa [ə mĕr/ə kən sə mō/ə] **124–125**
Andorra [ăn dör/ə] **124–125**
Angola [ăng gō/lə] **124–125**
Argentina [är/jən tē/nə] **124–125**
Armenia [är mē/nē ə] **124–125**
Australia [ö sträl/yə] **124–125**
Austria [ö/strē ə] **124–125**
Azerbaijan [ăz/ər bī jän/] **124–125**
Bahamas [bə hä/məz] **122–125**
Bahrain [bä rān/] **124–125**
Bangladesh [băng/glə dĕsh/, băng/–] **124–125**
Barbados [bär bā/dōs] **124–125**
Belarus [bē/lə rōōs/, byĕl/ə–] **124–125**
Belgium [bĕl/jəm] **124–125**
Belize [bə lēz/] **124–125**
Benin [bə nĭn/, –nēn/] **124–125**
Bermuda [bər myōō/də] **122–125**
Bhutan [bōō tän/] **124–125**
Bolivia [bə lĭv/ē ə] **124–125**
Borneo [bör/nē ō] **124–125**
Bosnia-Herzegovina [băz/nē ə hĕr/tsə gō vē/nə] **124–125**
Botswana [bät swä/nə] **124–125**
Brazil [brə zĭl/] **124–125**
Brunei [brōō nī/] **124–125**
Bulgaria [bŭl gĕr/ē ə] **124–125**
Burkina Faso [bər kē/nə fä/sō] **124–125**
Burundi [bōō rōōn/dē] **124–125**
Cambodia [kăm bō/dē ə] **124–125**
Cameroon [kăm/ə rōōn/] **124–125**
Canada [kăn/ə də] **122–125**
Cape Verde [kāp/ vürd/] **124–125**
Central African Republic [sĕn/trəl ăf/rĭ kən rĭ pŭb/lĭk] **124–125**
Chad [chăd] **124–125**
Chile [chĭl/ē] **124–125**
China [chī/nə] **124–125**
Colombia [kə lŭm/bē ə] **124–125**
Comoros [kăm/ə rōz] **124–125**
Congo [käng/gō] **124–125**
Costa Rica [kōs/tə rē/kə, käs/–] **122–125**
Croatia [krō ā/shə] **124–125**
Cuba [kyōō/bə] **122–125**
Cyprus [sī/prəs] **124–125**
Czech Republic [chĕk/ rĭ pŭb/lĭk] **124–125**
Democratic Republic of the Congo [dĕm/ə krăt/ĭk rĭ pŭb/lĭk əv dhə käng/gō] **124–125**
Denmark [dĕn/märk] **124–125**
Djibouti [jĭ bōō/tē] **124–125**
Dominica [dăm/ə nē/kə] **124–125**
Dominican Republic [də mĭn/ĭ kən rĭ pŭb/lĭk] **122–125**
 ̄ador [ĕk/wə dör/] **124–125**
 ̄ē/jĭpt] **124–125**
 ̄r [ĕl săl/və dör/] **122–125**

Equatorial Guinea [ē/kwə tör/ē əl gĭn/ē, ĕk/wə–] **124–125**
Eritrea [ĕr/ə trē/ə] **124–125**
Estonia [ĕ stō/nē ə] **124–125**
Ethiopia [ē/thē ō/pē ə] **124–125**
Fiji [fē/jē] **124–125**
Finland [fĭn/lənd] **124–125**
France [frăns] **124–125**
French Guiana [frĕnch/ gē ăn/ə, –ä/nə] **124–125**
French Polynesia [frĕnch/ păl/ə nē/zhə] **124–125**
Gabon [gă bōn/] **124–125**
Georgia [jör/jə] **124–125**
Germany [jür/mə nē] **124–125**
Ghana [gä/nə] **124–125**
Greece [grēs] **124–125**
Greenland [grēn/lənd, –lănd/] **122–125**
Grenada [grə nā/də] **124–125**
Guatemala [gwä/tə mä/lə] **122–125**
Guinea [gĭn/ē] **124–125**
Guinea-Bissau [gĭn/ē bĭ sow/] **124–125**
Guyana [gī ăn/ə] **124–125**
Haiti [hā/tē] **122–125**
Honduras [hän dŏŏr/əs] **122–125**
Hong Kong [häng/ käng/] **124–125**
Hungary [hŭng/gə rē] **124–125**
Iceland [īs/lənd] **124–125**
India [ĭn/dē ə] **124–125**
Indonesia [ĭn/də nē/zhə] **124–125**
Iran [ĭ rän/, ĭ răn/] **124–125**
Iraq [ĭ räk/, ĭ răk/] **124–125**
Ireland [īr/lənd] **124–125**
Israel [ĭz/rē əl, –rā–] **124–125**
Italy [ĭt/l ē] **124–125**
Ivory Coast [īv/rē kōst/] **124–125**
Jamaica [jə mā/kə] **122–125**
Japan [jə păn/] **124–125**
Java [jä/və] **124–125**
Jordan [jör/dn] **124–125**
Kazakhstan [kä/zăk stän/] **124–125**
Kenya [kĕn/yə, kēn/–] **124–125**
Kiribati [kïr/ə băs/] **124–125**
Kuwait [kōō wāt/] **124–125**
Kyrgyzstan [kïr/gĭ stän/, –stän/] **124–125**
Laos [lows, lä/ōs] **124–125**
Latvia [lăt/vē ə] **124–125**
Lebanon [lĕb/ə nən, –năn/] **124–125**
Lesotho [lə sō/tō, –sōō/tōō] **124–125**
Liberia [lī bïr/ē ə] **124–125**
Libya [lĭb/ē ə] **124–125**
Liechtenstein [lĭk/tən stīn/] **124–125**
Lithuania [lĭth/ōō ā/nē ə] **124–125**
Luxembourg [lŭk/səm bürg/] **124–125**
Macedonia [măs/ə dō/nē ə] **124–125**
Madagascar [măd/ə găs/kər] **124–125**
Malawi [mə lä/wē] **124–125**
Malaysia [mə lā/zhə] **124–125**
Maldives [möl/dēvz, –dīvz] **124–125**
Mali [mä/lē] **124–125**
Malta [möl/tə] **124–125**
Marshall Islands [mär/shəl ī/ləndz] **124–125**
Mauritania [mör/ə tā/nē ə] **124–125**
Mauritius [mö rĭsh/əs] **124–125**
Mexico [mĕk/sĭ kō/] **122–125**
Micronesia [mī/krə nē/zhə] **124–125**
Moldova [mäl dō/və, möl–] **124–125**
Monaco [män/ə kō/] **124–125**

The United States of America
Capital: Washington, D.C. (District Of Columbia)
[wä/shĭng tən dē/sē/, wö/–]

Regions of the United States

Geographical Index

Unit 1 Everyday Language

Tapescript #1 1: side 1
"Whaddya Need?"
Pages 2 and 3, *A Classroom*

Students and teachers are talking about different classroom items. Point to these items in the picture of the classroom on pages two and three.

1. Excuse me, could you move to the right? I can't see the board. I want to copy what Mrs. Simms wrote on the **chalkboard**.
2. Aw, no! Could you help me with this? It keeps rewinding. I'm not good with machines.
3. All right everybody take your seats. Paulo, you sit in that **chair** near Feng Li. Come on, sit down. Yes, that **seat** over there.
4. Now, please! Don't use the **pencil sharpener** in the middle of class. Sharpen your pencils before the bell rings.
5. Mr. Ramirez, I can't find my country on the **map**. It's very small, but it is there. Ah, here it is.
6. Do you know what time it is? I think the **clock** on the wall is wrong. My watch says 2:30.
7. Close your books. I'm going to put a picture on the **overhead projector**. When we work with the overhead, you can close your books.
8. Marty, will you help me get these books out of the **bookcase**? This **bookcase**, over here. I think we're using the books on the bottom shelf.
9. Who can tell me what colors you see on the **screen**? There are many colors up here. Maria, what's one color on the screen?
10. I can't wait to take my turn at the **computer**. There's a computer grammar game I want to try. I wish we had more than one computer in this class!

Tapescript #2
"What Do I Do?"
Pages 6 and 7, *Studying*

Two teachers are giving directions. You will need a piece of paper. Close your book and follow their directions.

Exercise 1.
You need just one sheet of paper. Pick up a pencil with an eraser. Do not use your pen.
1. **Write** the word *talk*, t-a-l-k, on the piece of paper.
2. **Underline** the word.
3. **Circle** the vowel.
4. Erase the *t* and write *w*. Now you have a new word, *walk*, w-a-l-k.
5. **Copy** this word three times.

Exercise 2.
Turn the paper over. Write on the back of the paper. Use a pen. Do not use a pencil. Do not erase your mistakes. I will **dictate a sentence**. I will say the sentence three times.
Listen: *Good students ask questions.*
Write what I say: *Good students ask questions.*
Now check your sentence: *Good students ask questions.*
Check the words while I **spell** them. **Cross out** the mistakes: G-O-O-D Good, S-T-U-D-E-N-T-S students, A-S-K ask, Q-U-E-S-T-I-O-N-S questions.
Write the sentence one more time.
Draw a picture of a good student on the paper.
When you are finished, **pass your paper** up to the front.

Tapescript #3
"What Color Goes Where?"
Page 12, *Colors,* and Page 13, *Prepositions*

Alan Lennard is a supervisor in a warehouse. He is telling his workers where to put the boxes. Close your book. You will need a piece of paper. For page 12, write the colors you hear. For page 13, write the prepositions you hear.

1. Listen up everybody, we've got a big shipment and we need to organize them. Paul, put the **gray** boxes…yeah—those gray boxes—**next to** the door. Next to the door **on the right,** OK?
2. All right, Irene, get those **orange** boxes and put them **between** the windows on the back wall. That's right, set them right between the windows. Boy, the light makes that orange bright!
3. Paul, you ready for those heavy **purple** boxes now? They need to go on the shelf. Put them on the shelf right there. I don't know why they make the purple boxes so heavy.
4. Irene, I think those light **green** boxes can go **in front of** the others. The light **green** boxes always go in front.
5. Let's move those tall **yellow** boxes **next to** the door, **on the left.** Remember, yellow—on the left. There are already boxes on the other side.
6. We've only got a few more sets to move. Let's put the **red** boxes **above** the ones on the shelves. Right up there, above those boxes. Yep, the red ones belong there.
7. I can't see the **black** boxes anywhere…I hope they came in. They're kind of small boxes… There they are, **behind** the dolly. Let's leave them behind the dolly for now.
8. Do you see the **blue** boxes anywhere? You do? Ah, they're **in** those large boxes over there. Don't get 'em. We can leave them in there

for now. We'll get them later.
9. Paul, take this box from me and put it **under** the table. Yeah, this **pink** box. It's not that it's heavy. I just can't stand looking at pink…it's so cheerful.
10. I'm ready to quit…oh wait, one more set of boxes. Geez, I thought we were done. OK, Irene take those **brown** boxes **below** the **turquoise** boxes to the dumpster. Just the boxes below the turquoise ones go out. The other brown boxes can stay here.

Tapescript #4
"Who's Saying What?"
Page 21, *Shopping*

Different people are talking about sweaters. Point to the person you hear speaking.

1. Can I help you? We've got some wonderful clothes on sale today. What are you looking for? [saleswoman in **A**]
2. I'm shopping for my daughters. They're so difficult to shop for, but these sweaters look perfect. How much are they? [older woman in **A**].
3. I'll **pay** cash **for** these sweaters. I don't like to use credit cards. Here you are, $32.44. I always carry pennies. [older woman in **B**]
4. I hope you three don't mind that your mother still buys you clothes. You know I just love to **give** you things. But don't worry, they were on sale. [older woman in **C**]
5. Mom, these sweaters are great! Where did you **buy** them? This red is perfect. [young woman with black hair in **C**]
6. Oh, I'm going to **keep** this red sweater right here, next to my dark gray jacket. They'll go together perfectly. Yes, I'm definitely going to keep this in the front of the closet. I can wear it everywhere! [woman in **D**]
7. Thank you for letting me **return** this sweater. Usually I hate to take things back and it's a pretty yellow, but I just hate for Mom to spend money on me. I'll take this $10.81 and buy her some flowers. [woman in **E**]
8. I want to **exchange** this sweater for that one. My mom forgot that I prefer blue. It's no problem to exchange it, right? I mean, your ads say, "Exchanges are no problem." So, can I get the blue sweater? [woman in **F**]

Unit 2 People

Tapescript #5
"Hollywood Starrs"
Page 22, *Age and Physical Description*

Hollywood agent Sam Starr is discussing photographs with famous talent director Harry Howard. Point to the people they're describing.

Tapescripts

Sam: Hey, Harry! So, you need some fresh faces for that new TV series? I got some clients that are perfect.

Harry: OK Sam, have a seat. Hey, close the door, would ya? Now, let's take a look at these photos.

Sam: Sure, sure thing. Here ya go. Danny Smith. He's 5, no—6 years old. **Cute** boy, ya know? Need a **6-year-old boy**?

Harry: No, we need older kids. Do you have any **teenagers**?

Sam: OK, OK, I got a **19-year-old girl**—Jennifer Andrews. Real popular with the teens. Take a look. Long blond hair, long legs. She's a rising star, know what I mean?

Harry: A 19-year-old girl? She's over the hill, Sam. Uh, we need people who can change their look. Show me those smaller photos.

Sam: OK, OK, here ya go. I got some fabulous people for commercials. Hold on, just a minute. Ah, here we go. Lucy Rivera. Look at this picture—she's **young**, about 20, nice friendly smile, yeah? And she can go a lot older with makeup and hair. Yeah, in this same picture, she looks **elderly**, right? Gray hair, but that same smile, right? What da ya think?

Harry: Sorry, Sam, we don't need women. But thanks for…

Sam: Hold on. Hold on. I got Tony Marco. See 'im? He's no Tom Cruise. **Heavyset** guy, I think he lifts weights. Real pro, that Tony.

Harry: Tony Marco? C'mon, Sam, this commercial is for a health club! Don't you have any **thin** men? Who's this guy near Tony? I could use him. He's really **slim**.

Sam: Uh…yeah, that's Tony's brother, Dean Marco. Yeah, he's thin, all right. He dropped me to start…a movie career. OK, wait a minute. I got another photo. Yeah, yeah, hey, I just signed Burt Conners. You know, he coaches the Special Olympics.

Harry: Hmm, he's that **physically challenged** athlete, right? I saw his sports ad… Well, I'll call him in for an interview. OK, Sam?

Sam: Super, Harry. Now we're doing some business together, heh? Hey, while we're looking at these pictures, how about a **baby** for that diaper commercial? I got a great 10-month-old, not much experience, but…

Harry: No, Sam.

Sam: OK, OK. How about a **senior citizen**? I got George Edwards, gray hair, mature, good-looking guy. Hey, do ya need a senior citizen for that health club ad?

Harry: Sam, don't push your luck. I have a meeting. Good-bye.

Harry? Hey, Harry, wait just a ⁺e. I got more pictures to show you, here's one…

Harry: Sam, good-bye.

Tapescript #6
"Trends Hair Salon"
Page 23, *Describing Hair*

Vincente is a world famous hair stylist. He is describing popular hair styles. Close your book. You will need a piece of paper. Fold the paper into three sections. Label the first section *color*. Label the second section *length*. Label the third section *style*. Make a check in the first section when you hear a different hair color. Make a check in the second section when you hear a different length. Make a check in the third section when you hear a different style.

Voice: Vincente, we're ready. Lights! Camera! anddddd Action!

Vincente: Hello, I'm Vincente. This is a very exciting time for me and my new salon, Trends Hair Salon. Let me share some of our newest hair creations for men and women. At Trends, we are always on the cutting edge.

Well, you know that many of our clients have **brown hair**. Brown may be a common hair color, but it is certainly not a boring one! No, no, we have new techniques for weaving beautiful highlights into this dark colored hair. Of course, we do charge extra for **long hair**. At Trends, our stylists all do the finest work, and well, long hair does take more time.

Many customers ask me, "Vincente, my hair is so **straight**. I'm so tired of curling and setting my hair. What should I do?" Well, I say to them, "Throw away those rollers and curlers!" Straight hair can look fabulous with the right cut. And I do mean cut, cut, cut. **Short hair** is very fashionable right now. Ladies, don't be afraid to show your face. Short hair is fresh, it's sassy—and it's easy to take care of. Wash, towel dry, and *voila!* Perfect every time.

Now, let's talk about **black hair**. Aha, you want to know if my black hair is natural? Yes… Actually I have **gray hair**. But you know, at Trends, every hair color is a beautiful one! Gray makes one look, well…mature.

So, let me tell you about our newest look for spring. **Curly hair** is in—it's fresh, it's bouncy, and it's…well, what can I say? With curly hair, you feel light and so free. We can perm your hair using only the safest chemical process. And, no, no, no-never do this at home.

Well, now let me see…we all know **blond hair** is lovely, but you need to use my Trends conditioner with sunscreen to keep your hair healthy. Hmmm, maybe you want to cut your **shoulder-length** hair? Let me show you some pictures of our Trends models in their fabulous, shoulder-length styles. Just lovely, aren't they?

You know, at Trends Hair Salon, we always listen to our customers, but sometimes the customer is wrong. Let me tell you, I have this customer with bright **red, wavy hair** and she wants to perm and color her hair. I tell her no-your hair is already wavy, already a beautiful red-please don't ask for this. Does she listen to Vincente? No! What a disaster!

Voice: Cut! Vincente are you OK?

Vincente: Excuse me, but you know, for a professional this is very upsetting. Can we start from the beginning please?

Tapescript #7
"Family Is Family!"
Pages 24 and 25, *Family*

Tom Lee, Ana Garcia and Lisa Smith are talking about their families. Point to the people they are talking about.

1. Tom Lee: Let me tell you about my family. We are Chinese and I was the first one in my family to be born in the United States. My name is Tom Lee. My **grandfather** is the oldest in our family, of course. He came here from Vietnam in 1974. His friends call him Lu. My **grandmother** came with him and she was really scared. My **father** came too. He was my age. His name is Chang. Of course, I never call him that—too disrespectful. He met my **mother** at Los Angeles High School. They knew each other for four years before they got married. My mother's name is Rose.

I have a younger **brother** named Alex. He just started first grade. Sometimes we go to my **Aunt** Helen's house. She's my father's younger sister and was born in Los Angeles. My **Uncle** Daniel is her husband. Uncle Daniel only talks about baseball and his restaurant business. My **cousin** Emily is OK. She loves to sing, but I don't. Well, that's it. Did I forget someone? Oh, just my **sister**. Her name is Lily, she's older than me, she takes dance lessons, but I don't do that either.

2. Ana Garcia: Hello. My name is Ana Garcia de Sanchez. I am a computer programmer and so is my **husband** Tito—that's how we met. His mother, my **mother-in-law** Berta, doesn't understand why I still work—she's from the old country. My **father-in-law** Mario understands. He says times are changing. He's right about that! My **sister-in-law** Marta works too, but she works at home as a writer for the Spanish newspaper. My **brother-in-law** Carlos thinks his wife has a great job. Lucky for me that sometimes my **niece** Alice baby-sits for me. She says she likes to watch Felix, my **son**. My son loves her too. Well, gotta go! I'm off to the market with my **daughter** Sara. Everyone helps around here. I'm happy about that!

3. Lisa Smith: Hi, guys! I'm Lisa Smith. I'm ten years old and I guess you could say I have a large family! But they are in two different houses. It took me a while to get used to it. During the week, I live with my mother. Her name is Carol. She married Rick who is my **stepfather**. He's OK—nice, but quiet. After my mom and Rick got married, they had two kids. David is my **half brother**. He has his own room. Mary is my **half sister**. She and I sleep in the same room. I don't mind. She's really cute. In this house, I'm the oldest and I get to do things Mary and David can't do—like go to bed late. On the weekends, I'm with my dad. His name is Dan. At my Dad's house, I'm the youngest. He married my **stepmother**. I think my stepmom likes having me around. I call her Sue, not Mom. Sue has a daughter who became my **stepsister**. Her name is Kim and she goes to college. My **stepbrother** Bill stays in his room studying all the time. When people ask me if I'm the youngest or the oldest in my family, I always say it depends on which day of the week it is.

Tapescript #8
"Welcome to Our House."
Page 26 and 27, *Daily Routines*

This is the Chung family. Listen as they go through a day in their life. You will need a piece of paper. Look in your Dictionary and write down the times that match what you hear.

1.

Nora: **Wake up,** Dan. Don't even think of going back to sleep. I'm getting up, and if you go back to sleep, you'll be late for work!

Dan: Just ten more minutes. I promise I'll wake up in ten minutes!

[6:00 a.m.]

2.

Dan: Gosh, your mother makes great coffee!

Sara: If it's so great, why can't I have any?

Nora: **Eat** your **breakfast.** You can have coffee in a while—maybe in five years!

Lisa: Here, have some of my cereal.

Nora: No, thanks.

[7:00 a.m.]

3.

Sara: Good-bye, Dad.

Lisa: Good-bye, Daddy.

Dan: Bye. Have a great day in school. Be careful crossing the street.

Lisa: You say that everyday!

Dan: I take you to school everyday!

[7:30 a.m.]

4.

Mr. Drake: Hello, class. Who remembers what we talked about yesterday? That's right. We were talking about the first train across the United States.

Nora: Train… Train… I must have that in my notes. Oh, here it is.

[10:00 a.m.]

5.

Lisa: There's Mom at the window. We're home! We're home!

Sara: She can see that, Lisa!

Dan: Everybody out! I'm hungry!

[6:00 p.m.]

6.

Nora: So how was school?

Sara: Do we have to talk about it now? I'm having dinner. Great dinner, Mom. Really great dinner. I just love this dinner.

Dan: Oh, oh. Bad news!

Lisa: Not bad news. Charlie said hello to Sara today in school! Sara has a boyfriend! Sara has a boyfriend!

[6:30 p.m.]

7.

Sara: Why did you tell them about Charlie?

Lisa: I'm watching TV. My favorite show is on! Don't you have to **do** your **homework?**

Sara: I am doing it! Why did you tell them about Charlie?

Lisa: Let's talk about it later.

Sara: Only if you promise not to mention Charlie again.

Lisa: I promise. I promise.

[7:30 p.m.]

8.

Dan: Gosh, I'm tired. I'm just going to sit here awhile.

Nora: Honey, listen to this. People who **exercise** live longer!

Dan: Are you reading that in the paper?

Nora: Yes. Look. Here's a picture of a man who's 100. He does different exercises every day.

[8:00 p.m.]

9.

Nora: Good night, Sweetie. Are you going to bed now?

Dan: I'm going to bed this minute. The next exercise for me is doing turnovers.

Nora: What is a turnover?

Dan: It's when you **go to bed**, pull up the blanket, turn over on your side and **go to sleep!**

[10:30 p.m.]

Tapescript #9
"Sweet Memories"
Pages 28 and 29, *Life Events*

Martin's widow Rosa is sharing her memories with her grandson. Point to the picture you hear them describe.

Rosa: Come, Ricardo, sit next to me. I have some beautiful pictures to show you.

Ricardo: OK, Grandma. Is this your wedding day, Grandma?

Rosa: Yes, Ricardo. I can still remember Martin saying, "Rosa, it's time to **get married.**" I was 26 years old and we had met only the year before. And…well, we had the most beautiful wedding. Doesn't Martin look handsome in his black tuxedo?

Ricardo: Yeah, Grandma. You look nice too… Hey, is that me in the blanket when I was a baby?

Rosa: No, Ricardo. This is a picture of your grandfather on the day he was born. He was born in Mexico.

Ricardo: Grandma, why did Grandpa Martin leave Mexico?

Rosa: Well Sweetie, he was very young, and his family decided to **immigrate** for a better life. Look, here's a picture with his whole family and the immigration officer. Martin was just a teenager then.

Ricardo: What's immigrate, Grandma?

Rosa: Well, that's when his family moved from Mexico to the United States. Soon after that, the war started.

Ricardo: Hey, cool! Is that Grandpa in the army uniform?

Rosa: Yes, he was a private in the U.S. army. He was very proud to **join the army** in, uh…'44 I think, and…well, the war ended soon after.

Ricardo: Were you sad to see him go, Grandma?

Rosa: I didn't know your grandpa then, sweetie. But the very first day I met him, I just knew we would **fall in love**. Look at this picture. We always loved to walk in the park. Martin would tell me funny stories and we would talk about our hopes and dreams and…

Ricardo: Grandma, look at this picture! What a neat car!

Rosa: Well now, I almost forgot about Martin's first car. He told me he couldn't wait to **learn to drive**. His parents disapproved-said driving was too dangerous. But your grandpa was a very good driver. Well, I helped out with directions now and then.

Ricardo: Grandma, when can I learn to drive?

Rosa: Now dear, you have a few more years to wait! First, you need to finish school. Look, here's your grandpa in his cap and gown. He was so proud to **graduate** high school, and I'll be so proud of you when you graduate, Ricardito.

Ricardo: Grandma, I haven't finished kindergarten yet.

Rosa: Ah, sweet Grandson. Here, look at your grandpa Martin-he was exactly the same age you are now! Where do you think he's going with his notebook under his arm?

Ricardo: He's going to **start school!** Boy, he's sure dressed up for the first day of school. Where's his backpack?

Rosa: I don't think they had backpacks in those days. But look at that beautiful school. Would you like to see your grandpa's village in Mexico someday, Ricardo?

Ricardo: Sure. I can't wait to do a lot of stuff. Like, grow up, and…

Rosa: Ricardo, time goes by very quickly. Soon you'll be a young man. Here, do you see your grandpa? He's a young man in this picture, and soooo serious. See, he's becoming a citizen. First he studied, then took a test, and then he could **become a citizen.**

Ricardo: I can take tests. We had one in school yesterday… Can I become a citizen, Grandma?

Rosa: You <u>are</u> a citizen, dear.

Ricardo: Oh… Hey Grandma, look! It's me! I'm just a baby! And there's Mom, and you! You look really happy, Grandma.

Rosa: I was. And I am, Ricardo. **I have a** <u>wonderful</u> **grandchild.** You know I always wanted a grandson just like you. Now, let's close this album. What about baking some chocolate chip cookies?

Ricardo: Yeah! You're the best, Grandma!

Tapescript #10
"How Do They Feel?"
Pages 30 and 31, *Feelings*

Different people are talking about how they feel. Point to the picture that matches what you hear.

1.
Wife: Darling, I have a surprise for you! We're going to have two! Two babies!! Twins!

Husband: [gasp]

Wife: Sweetheart, are you all right?

Husband: Of course, d-d-d-dearest. I just never imagined two at the same time!

2.
Oh, I can't believe this! It's absolutely disgusting! I can't eat this. I feel sick just looking at it. Ugh. Airline food!

3.
This sun is incredible. I bet I can fry an egg on my shoe! I'm never going to hike out here in the summer again. Whoo-ee!

4.
This is the fourth time this month you've been late, and I won't stand for it. It is unprofessional and unacceptable. I'm docking your salary, Ms. Fields.

5.
Oh, look at this picture she sent. The baby is getting so big. I miss them so much. I want to go home.

6.
104⁰. Oh, this is a very high fever. I wish the doctor would call back. Martita's never been sick like this before. I wonder if I should take her to the hospital. Oh, why doesn't the doctor call?

7.

Can we go on it, Jimmy? Please, I really wanna go on the ferris wheel! Doesn't it look great? Oh, I've been waitin' for this all my life!

8.
Wife: I can't get off this couch. They're just two little kids; they make me feel so…so…what's the word? Honey? Honey? I can't move. Can you make dinner tonight?

Husband: OK…OK, just give me a minute. I don't have the energy to get up.

9.
Ugh—Why did I take this class? I can't pay attention to anything he says. This guy is so boring!

10.
Marsha: Here, I don't want this, and I don't want you!

Jeffrey: But, Marsha, I thought—you—you loved me…

Marsha: You thought, but you were wrong. Good-bye, Jeffrey.

Jeffrey: But you said you loved me. You said… How can you do this?

Unit 3   Housing
Tapescript #11
"Looking to Buy"
Page 34, *Places to Live,* and Page 35, *Finding a Home*

Maureen McLaughlin is a Realtor. She's telling a coworker about her day at the office. Look at the word list in your book. You will need a piece of paper. For page 34, write the number of the place Maureen describes. For page 35, write the letter of the action she describes.

1.
You won't believe the day I had! There must have been 50 people in my office today. And they all wanted me to help them. First, a very nice young woman named Susan came by the office. It was about 8 a.m. She wanted to find a place in **the city.** So many people are moving to the city these days. Anyway, I told her to **look for an apartment** in the classified section of the newspaper. I really don't deal with rentals.

2.
The phone started to ring at 9 a.m. It was the loan officer over at Federal Bank. My clients Mr. and Mrs. Abing were in his office. They were there to **get a loan**. They want the loan for this sweet little **house**-3 bedrooms, 1 bath, great view-that I showed them last week. Of course I told the loan officer what wonderful people the Abings are, so I know they'll get that loan.

3.
I left my office to get a drink of water and bumped into Mr. and Mrs. Nix. They wanted to **make an offer** on that great little place I showed them in Wildwood.

Wildwood is such a great **small town.** I told them that I would write up their offer. They sure were excited.

4.
A little while later the phone rang again. It was Susan—again. This time she wanted to know who to talk to about a place she'd found in **the suburbs,** close to schools and shopping, but away from the traffic and smog. I told her to **talk to the manager** of the building. Managers can give you so much information. I always talk to them.

5.
The next thing I know, Susan comes in here again and asks me to look at her lease. I always tell my friends to read carefully before they **sign a lease.** Once you sign a lease, you have to follow the rules of the **apartment building**. Personally, I like to make my own rules; that's why I don't have an apartment. The lease was OK and I told her she should sign it.

6.
Around 11:00 in the morning, I had to drive my good friends, Rheta and Alan, to their new **townhouse.** It's a beautiful two-story townhouse, near the beach. They're going to **take ownership** today. I love watching people take ownership. It usually makes me cry.

7.
At 11:30 I got a call from those people who just bought the **mobile home.** Remember them? They asked if I had any extra boxes. I told them no. One thing I won't do with my clients is help them **move in.** What a mess! I always tell people to hire movers when they move into a new place.

8.
Anyway, as I was saying, so many people want **to talk to a Realtor.** When I got back from lunch there were 10 phone messages and 2 couples waiting to talk to me. They all wanted to talk about buying a home in the **country.** Now that makes sense to me! The country's a fine place to live. Green fields, blue skies, open spaces, friendly farmers. Hmmmm…I probably should talk to a Realtor about buying in the country! …You know about a place, Bob? [phone rings] Excuse me. Maureen McLaughlin here. Yes, Susan. Uh-huh. Yeah. (I'll talk to you later Bob. This will take a while.) Right, Susan…

Tapescript #12
"The Case of the Missing Wallet"
Pages 36 and 37, *Apartments*

Mr. O'Brien is telling a police officer how he lost his money. Point to the pictures that match what you hear.

Police Officer: So, tell me, Mr. O'Brien, how did you lose your money?

Mr. O'Brien: Well, I was on the **fourth floor**, going into my apartment when I heard a noise—not a loud noise, but a noise. So I went up to the **roof garden**, but I didn't see a thing—except the flowers of course. You should go up there sometime, the flowers are beautiful.

Police Officer: Please, go on.

Mr. O'Brien: Well, the noise got louder. So I go down to the **third floor**, then to the **second**. Nothing. Finally I get down to the **first floor**. Still, nothing. I think I still had my money then.

Police Officer: Why didn't you go back to your apartment?

Mr. O'Brien: I'm the kind of guy who likes to know what's going on. So I think maybe it's something in the basement. I check out the **laundry room**—there's Louie Gonzalez doing his laundry. Nice guy, Louie. Talks too fast, but a nice guy. And his wife. She's folding the laundry. Towels, I think.

Police Officer: Please go on. Did you still have your money?

Mr. O'Brien: Sure—I remember because Louie asks me for some change—which I didn't have, but I look in my wallet. So then I go into the **rec. room.** Two kids are playing Ping-Pong. The **garage**. No one there. Just my car. I love that car! I go out the front and ask the **doorman**. He's a little too friendly for me, the doorman. Talking to this one, talking to that one. He's being real sweet to this new lady. The **manager** is out there too, putting up a sign. They don't know anything. I think maybe something is happening next door.

Police Officer: You went to the apartment next door?

Mr. O'Brien: Yeah. I mean this was a loud noise! I like to know everything. I go check out their **courtyard**. Very pretty, but I don't see anything special. I go back to the **swimming pool**. There's some kids swimming, but it all looks normal.

Police Officer: Did you still have your wallet?

Mr. O'Brien: Yeah. You see, I go back up to the **lobby**. There's Janet Kermit getting her mail out of the **mailbox** and she asks if I have change for a twenty. I give it to her. She goes up in the **elevator**. There's some man in the elevator and I think she wants to get to know him. I take the **stairs**.

Police Officer: Where were you going?

Mr. O'Brien: I just wanted to check out the **hallway** on the second floor.

Police Officer: And what did you find?

Mr. O'Brien: Phil Ford is there putting his trash down the **trash chute**. That's it!

Police Officer: That's what?

Mr. O'Brien: He asks for the ten I owed him. After I give it to him, I help him

hold the trash chute open—my wallet must have fallen down the trash chute! Good-bye, I gotta go!

Police Officer: Where are you going?

Mr. O'Brien: To the **alley**! The alley is right near where they have the **trash bin**. I have to look in the trash bin. That's where my wallet is.

Police Officer: You'd better hurry, Mr. O'Brien.

Mr. O'Brien: Why?

Police Officer: I think that loud noise you heard is the garbage truck coming to collect the trash!

Tapescript #13
"I Love My Home."
Page 38, *A House,* and Page 39, *A Yard*

Chuck Ramirez is describing his new home to his friends. Point to the things Chuck is talking about. For page 38, point to the parts of the house. For page 39, point to the things in the yard.

Chuck: So? You wanna see the pictures?

Annie: You have pictures of your house so soon?

Sam: What do you mean, so soon? He's been in the house for 24 hours. I'm sure he has hundreds of pictures.

Chuck: No, only two. Here they are. You can see the front of the house in this one. And the yard in this one.

Sam: Very nice. OK, Chuck, see you…

Chuck: Wait, you didn't look at the **front door.** Isn't it beautiful? Such a beautiful wooden door!

Annie: Oh! It is a lovely door. Is that your wife?

Chuck: Yes, that's Grace holding open the **storm door**.

Sam: We don't have too many storms here.

Chuck: Well, better safe than sorry. That's me, over by the **garage.** The garage is just the right size for one car. Which is great, because we only have one car.

Sam: And with a new house, you'll have one car for a long time.

Annie: It's a nice garage, Chuck.

Chuck: Well, yes, it is, Annie. Now the tall **hedges** in the yard block the view of the garage from the back. I love those hedges. They're so elegant.

Annie: And you have so many flowers.

Chuck: Yes, we have many kinds of **flowers** in the yard.

Annie: I love flowers!

Chuck: Oh, and I forgot to show you this. Look at this.

Sam and Annie: What is it?

Chuck: You can't tell? It's the **porch light.** It looks great at night. It's right above the porch.

Sam: Usually is…

Chuck: We don't have a porch in the yard, but there's a big **patio** near the

sliding glass doors. I put the **patio furniture** out there right away. I can't wait to sit out on the patio in the evening.

Sam: So, what other features does this house of yours have?

Chuck: Well, there's a **deck** off to the right of the house.

Annie: Oh, a deck!

Chuck: Yep! It's a real nice one. I don't keep my **hammock** there though. I keep my hammock on the other side of the house, on the **lawn**. The yard has a great lawn.

Annie: Your **front yard** looks nice too. I like the shape of your **front walk**.

Chuck: Yes, it's a little different. But look, you have to see this **wheelbarrow** in the yard. It came with the house and Grace and I loved it. It's so shiny.

Sam: Chuck, this house thing is making you crazy.

Annie: I think it's exciting!

Chuck: OK, just look at two more things. Look at the **shutters** on those windows. They're the most beautiful color.

Sam: They're white.

Chuck: Yes, but a beautiful white. Shutters make a big difference on a house.

Sam: All right, Chuck, thanks for…

Chuck: No, no. One last thing to see. Look, I've got a compost pile! My very own **compost pile.** The gardener put her tools against it in this picture, but you can still see all that compost in there.

Sam: Well Chuck, congratulations on your new home! I really can't stay—

Chuck: No problem, Sam. Why don't you and Annie come over this weekend and see the house for yourselves? I'll take you on a personal tour, shutters and all!

Sam: Uhhhhh…

Annie: We'd love to.

Tapescript #14 📼 1: side 2
"A Moving Decision"
Page 42, *A Living Room*

Mrs. Li is moving into a new apartment. She is telling the mover where to put her living room furniture. You will need two pieces of paper. Use one to cover the picture on page 42 and another to write the numbers of the words you hear.

James: Ma, the movers are here! Stop cleaning and tell them where you want the living room furniture to go.

Mrs. Li: OK, James, dear, I'm coming. I can't believe this apartment—so dusty, dust everywhere… wait, I have to wipe this **mantel**. Such a nice place to put my knickknacks and pictures, but it's so dusty.

Mover: Ma'am, where would you like this **bookcase**?

Mrs. Li: Oh, I'mnot sure. Just leave it in the middle for now. I'll have to dust all those shelves first, you know.

James: Gee, Mom, are you going to dust all the furniture? What about your **wall unit**? It's got shelves too, and I see some dust on them…

Mrs. Li: Now, James, stop teasing me. I can't help it. I'm just a little nervous. So many decisions, moving this, moving that…

Movers: Ma'am, what about this large box? It's marked **stereo system**. I don't know how many pieces you got in here. We don't set up electronic components, you know.

Mrs. Li: Oh, don't worry about that. My son James can do that. He's going to hook up my cable **television** so I can watch my favorite show—*Cooking With Klaus*. Have you seen that TV show?

Mover: No, ma'am. OK, look, your **coffee table** is coming off the truck next. Where do you want it?

Mrs. Li: Coffee table? Well, I'm not sure. On the right side. No, maybe on the left. That depends on where I put the **sofa**. This fabric is so pretty, but it gets dirty so quickly. Do you think I should cover it in plastic?

Mover: I don't know, ma'am. Well, where do ya want me to put it?

Mrs. Li: Well, I'm not sure. Maybe over there, by the **window**. Yes, I can sit right here and see the beautiful birds outside. Could you help me open the window? Oh, so dusty.

Mover: Ma'am, I gotta move this piece in here first. Now, you've got a **love seat** on the truck that matches this sofa here… where do you want it?

Mrs. Li: Oh, I can't decide. It only seats two people, so maybe against this **wall**… Or the opposite wall? Oh, just put it in the center of the room, and I'll think about it.

Mover: Whatever you say. Next, you got an **end table**. Don't tell me, just put it in the center, right?

Mrs. Li: Oh no, not there! I have the perfect place for it, right over here. Uh, no, that's not right. Could you move it over there? I can put this beautiful **plant** right on top of it. My sister Viola bought it as a housewarming gift. Isn't it nice?

Mover: Yeah. Real nice, Mrs. Li. Now, ya got some boxes here. One's marked <u>Painting</u>-Fragile. Where do you want yer paintings?

Mrs. Li: Oh, I can't decide about decorating yet. Put that box in the center please. Did you bring in my **drapes**? They're silk, you know, and I wrapped them so they wouldn't get dusty…

Mover: No, ma'am, that box must still be on the truck.

James: Ma!!!! I thought you were telling the mover where to put your furniture! Why is everything piled on the floor in the middle of the room?

Mrs. Li: Now, James, don't get excited. I'm just not sure where I want to put everything. Just give me some time.

Mover: Speakin' of time ma'am, you're payin' me by the hour, and…

Mrs. Li: By the hour? Oh, James, can you help the movers with this box, and…

Tapescript #15
"The Lost Slipper"
Page 44, *A Bedroom*

Graciela is searching for her lost slipper. Point to the items in the bedroom that she's talking about.

Oh dear, what a day it's been. First I lost my glasses. Can't see a thing without my bifocals. Then I misplaced my sewing basket. Now, my slipper is missing! Well, it just has to be in this bedroom somewhere…

I'll start by the **bed**. Well, it's not on the bed. Maybe it dropped behind the **headboard**. No, I don't think so…when I sleep, my feet are on the opposite side, so…well, I could check under the **blanket**. Maybe it got stuck under the blanket while I was lying down, listening to that animal radio program. Hmm, I bet you enjoyed that animal show, didn't you, Whiskers? Well, I have my **clock radio** set to go on exactly when that show starts tomorrow!

Now, if only I could find this slipper. Where else… Well, I should check in the **closet**. I keep all my other shoes in the closet. Well, it's not on the closet shelf with the other shoes.

I know! It could be under my **night table**. Well, now—such a small night table and so many things on top of it! That's your favorite hiding place, under the table, right, Whiskers? No slipper here. Oh, this bending down hurts my knee—maybe it's my arthritis again! Well, while I'm down on the floor, I'll check under the **dust ruffle**. A lot of things can hide in a dust ruffle… no, only dust here.

Where on earth is that slipper? What was I doing in the bedroom before I… oh, yes, I folded some laundry and put it in the **dresser**. Maybe my slipper got stuck between some clothing and I put it in the **drawer** by mistake. Let me see, that second drawer is open…-no. No slipper.

This is just terrible. I feel like Cinderella, hoping for the glass slipper, and…oh, I have an idea. Maybe my slipper is under the **rug**. I vacuumed under the rug this afternoon, but maybe I missed it. No, it's not there, either.

Whiskers?! I know where you usually sleep. Right on top of my **pillow**. Well, you're not sleeping on it now, are you?

Did you see my slipper? Whiskers, did you take my slipper? Whiskers?

Tapescript #16
"And His House Got Very Clean!" (Sung to the tune of "The Green Grass Grew All Around, All Around, and the Green Grass Grew All Around.")

Page 46, *Housework,* and Page 47, *Cleaning Supplies*

This is a song about Mr. Potts cleaning his house. For page 46, pantomime the actions as you hear the different chores mentioned. For page 47, point to the cleaning supplies in your *Dictionary*.

Now Mr. Potts, he **wiped the counter**. He wiped the counter with a big orange **sponge**. He wiped the counter with a big orange sponge and his house got cleaner and cleaner *and* his house got very clean.

Now Mr. Potts, he **cleaned the oven**. He cleaned the oven with **oven cleaner**. He cleaned the oven and wiped the counter and his house got cleaner and cleaner *and* his house got very clean.

Now Mr. Potts, he **vacuumed the carpet**. He vacuumed the carpet with a **vacuum cleaner**. He vacuumed the carpet and cleaned the oven and wiped the counter and his house got cleaner and cleaner *and* his house got very clean.

Now Mr. Potts, he **mopped the floor**. He mopped the floor with a nice **wet mop**. He mopped the floor, he vacuumed the carpet, he cleaned the oven, he wiped the counter and his house got cleaner and cleaner *and* his house got very clean.

Now Mr. Potts, he **washed the dishes**. He washed the dishes with **dishwashing liquid**. He washed the dishes, he mopped the floor, he vacuumed the carpet, he cleaned the oven, he wiped the counter and his house got cleaner and cleaner *and* his house got very clean.

Now Mr. Potts, he **polished the furniture**. He polished the furniture with **furniture polish**. He polished the furniture, he washed the dishes, he mopped the floor, he vacuumed the carpet, he cleaned the oven, he wiped the counter and his house got cleaner and cleaner *and* his house got very clean.

Now Mr. Potts, he **took out the garbage**. He took out the garbage in big **trash bags**. He took out the garbage, he polished the furniture, he washed the dishes, he mopped the floor, he vacuumed the carpet, he cleaned the oven, he wiped the counter and his house got cleaner and cleaner *and* his house got very clean.

Now Mr. Potts, he **dried the dishes**, he dried the dishes with a big **dish towel**. He dried the dishes, he took out the garbage, he polished the furniture, he washed the dishes, he mopped the floor, he vacuumed the carpet, he cleaned the oven, he wiped the counter and his house got cleaner and cleaner *and* his house got very clean.

Tapescript #17
"One House, Many Problems"
Pages 48 and 49, *Household Problems and Repairs*

David Feller is the owner of A-1 House Repairs. His crew is working at a house with many problems. Point to the problems they are talking about.

David Feller: OK, everyone. We only have a few hours. Mary, how is it going?

Mary: I'm OK here. The door is fine but the **lock is broken**. Not too bad—I think the key works, at least.

David: Harry, how about you?

Harry: Shoot, Dave. Look at this fuse box. All the fuses are out. There's **no power** in this house! No electricity, no nothing! I just checked the hot water heater, too. It's broken. There's definitely **no hot water** at this place!

David: Well, fix them, OK? Mike, what do you have?

Mike: No big deal. The **roof is leaking** all right, but I've seen worse. I'm replacing some shingles.

David: Be careful up there! Don't fall down! Hey, Alan, what's happening in the front?

Alan: [mumble, mumble]

David: Take the nails out of your mouth, I can't understand you!

Alan: Sorry. Two **steps are broken**. I'm almost finished with one, and have one more to go.

David: That's great! Jose, how's that window coming?

Jose: Well, this **window is broken** and there are two more, David. It's going to take me at least 15 minutes to fix just this one. Looks like someone who lived here played a lot of baseball!

David: Don't worry, take your time. I'm going inside to check up on Henry. …Hi, Henry—what's going on in there.

Henry: Don't ask! **The toilet is stopped up**. I hate doing toilets. **The sink is overflowing**. There's water everywhere. And **the faucet is dripping** in the kitchen. A little drip like that can add up to a lot of water.

David: That's all?

Henry: No, I forgot to tell you. **The pipes are frozen** too. It was really cold last night.

David: That's OK, I've got the best plumber in town on my team. If you need anything, just yell. I'm going to see how Oleg is doing. …Hey, Oleg. What are you spraying for?

Oleg: [mumble, mumble]

David: Huh? Wait, don't take off your mask. Just nod your head…yes or no. **Termites?** We have termites. **Ants?** Ants aren't so bad. …We have ants, huh? **Cockroaches?** I hate cockroaches. …And cockroaches. How about **fleas**, no fleas right? I know you didn't find any fleas! You need a cat or a dog for fleas. …Hey, where did you come from, little fellow? Hiding under the house, I'll bet. Oleg, spray for fleas, but wait until I get this kitty out of the way! The two of us will be moving in here tomorrow!

Unit 4   Food

Tapescript #18
"Eating the Alphabet—A to Z"
Page 50, *Fruit,* and Page 51, *Vegetables*

Alisha is grocery shopping with her friend Katie. You will need a piece of paper. Close your books. For page 50, write the fruit you hear. For page 51, write the vegetables you hear. Remember you can correct your spelling later.

Alisha: I can't believe we're stuck in the market on Saturday! Thanks for coming with me, Katie.

Katie: It's OK. Hey, what are friends for? Besides, if we can get outta here by noon, we'll still have time to go to the mall.

Alisha: Yeah, now where's that list Mom gave me? Oh yeah, here it is… Let's see…**apples**. Hmm, should I get green or red ones?

Katie: I don't know. Why don't you get both?

Alisha: Yeah. OK, next, uh, three **avocadoes**. I hope Mom makes some guacamole with these.

Katie: Boy, they sure are ugly looking. C'mon, Alisha, what's next on the list?

Alisha: **Broccoli**. Look, the sign says *79 cents a head*. What's a head?

Katie: I dunno. Just get a bunch. Here, I'll hold the bag.

Alisha: Thanks. Now, I gotta find **carrots**. Mom always packs 'em in my lunch. Every single day.

Katie: Yeah, my mom thinks I'm a rabbit, too!

Alisha: OK, let me see… Do you see the **cherries**? Hmm, I bet Mom's baking Dad's favorite pie. Boy, a cherry soda at the mall would be great right now!

Katie: Yeah, and if we hurry up, we can buy one. C'mon Alisha, what's next? You read the list and I'll push the cart.

Alisha: OK, uh, two medium **cucumbers**—look, they're on special, Mom'll like that. And a head of **garlic**. A head? What is that? I'll just get some garlic powder. Same stuff, right?

Katie: Beats me. Hey, look at that guy over there? He's cute.

Alisha: Katie, we're shopping for food, remember? Help me find the **grapes**.

Katie: OK, OK. Here—seedless grapes. Hmm, these look good. Pass me a few, will ya?

Alisha: Katie! We'll eat at the mall, if we ever get there. Push the cart over here. I need two pounds of **lemons**. Can you hold the bag?

Katie: What's your Mom gonna do with those? Make lemonade, maybe?

Alisha: I have no idea. She's been cookin' up all this weird stuff lately.

Katie: Speaking of weird, look at these **mushrooms**! They have, like, tons of dirt or something on them! Yuck. I'll never eat those. Well, maybe on pizza I would.

Alisha: Gosh, Katie, stop talking about food. I'm getting hungry.

Katie: OK, whatever. What's next on the list?

Alisha: A bag of **potatoes**. Wow, this bag must weigh 10 pounds! …Uh-oh, I think the potatoes fell on something. Katie, look in the cart, will ya?

Katie: Don't worry. They're fine. Let's keep going. I can smell the french fries at the mall…

Alisha: All right…oh, yuck! **Prunes**! Where are those?

Katie: Follow me, Alisha. I see them down the aisle. Here's a box. California pitted prunes. Hmm. California. Now that sounds good. Beaches, shopping, cute guys…

Alisha: Katie! Are you helping or dreaming?

Katie: All right, Alisha! Hey, wanna get some **raisins**? I know you like them.

Alisha: Yeah, but they're not on the list. But Mom won't mind. She always puts them in my backpack—says I need more healthy snacks.

Katie: OK, what's next?

Alisha: Oh, yuck, another "healthy food"—**spinach**. Two pounds? I'll get one bunch. Maybe that's enough.

Katie: Yeah, enough for you and Popeye!

Alisha: Very funny. C'mon, help me find the **strawberries**. Yum, I love fresh strawberries! I'll get two baskets. I'm glad they're in season now.

Katie: Alisha, when are we gonna be done? This cart is getting heavy.

Alisha: Just two more things on the list. **Watermelons.** Gosh, these are huge! …Uh-oh.

Katie: Hey, don't worry. You just made a fruit salad!

Alisha: Yeah, right. OK, we just need to find **zucchini**… Oh, here's some zucchini on the top bin.

Alisha and Katie: Uh-oh.

Loudspeaker: Cleanup on aisle 6. Clean up in produce *now*.

Tapescripts

Tapescript #19
"Mary's Restaurant"
Page 52, *Meat and Poultry*

Mary is the owner of the restaurant, Mary's Lamb. Mike is the delivery person who delivers meat from the butcher shop. Point to the meat and poultry items that match what you hear them talking about.

Mary: Hi, Mike! What have you got for me today?

Mike: Well, Mary, let's start with the beef. I brought you **roast beef**—five big roasts. They look really good. And you have here 30 pounds of **steak**, lots of steak. You can grill them, barbecue them, anything you like.

Mary: You mean, anything my customers like!

Mike: Anything you say. Now here's 18 pounds of **ground beef**. You can make hamburger out of it, or that wonderful meatloaf you do.

Mary: How about the pork? Did you bring any pork?

Mike: Oh, sure, here's your **bacon**, 9 pounds, right here. There's not too much fat on it. And I brought you 6 pounds of **sausage**—they come 6 pounds to a box. Here's one box.

Mary: What about the poultry? I still serve a lot of poultry.

Mike: Don't worry, don't worry. You got 20 whole **chickens** and plenty of parts—15 pounds of **breasts**, 10 pounds of **drumsticks.** I know the kids really love these.

Mary: I know, I know. What else?

Mike: 20 pounds of **wings**—you can make those special wings with the hot sauce, too. And I got your **turkeys**, all 60 of them.

Mary: 60? I didn't order 60 turkeys!

Mike: Yes, you said 60 turkeys! I wrote it down.

Mary: 16! I said 16 turkeys! What am I going to do with 60 turkeys!

Mike: Serve them with the **ham.** I brought you lots of ham, just like you asked. You said, "don't forget the ham. I always need lots of ham."

Mary: Ham? I didn't order any ham. *Lamb*, I said *lamb*. Don't forget the lamb! Everyone comes here for lamb! You didn't bring any **lamb chops**?

Mike: Not one chop!

Mary: **Leg of lamb**?

Mike: Not one leg! Well, I gotta go!

Mary: I got to go, too!

Mike: Where are you going? This is your restaurant!

Mary: To find another butcher! One that has some lamb left!

Tapescript #20
"You're Next!"
Page 53, *Deli and Seafood*

Different customers are ordering at a deli and seafood counter. You will need a piece of paper. Write down the items each person orders. Remember youcan check your spelling later.

Katy: OK, number 1. Who has number 1?

Customer #1: Hi, Katy. That pastrami looks great! I'll have a **pastrami** sandwich. If the rye is fresh, I want it on **rye bread**. No mustard. Can I have some **pasta salad** with that?

Katy: You can have any salad you want, love. Number 2!

Customer #2: I'd like something simple—the doctor said no red meat for me. Give me **smoked turkey** on **wheat bread**. No mayonnaise, no onion, no tomato.

Katy: Here you go! Who has Number 3? Your turn!

Customer #3: Well, I can have all the red meat I want. Never go to the doctor! Can I get a **roast beef** sandwich on **white bread** with some **Swiss cheese**? Oh, and a slice of onion. I love onions, and don't forget the tomato. I love tomatoes. Mustard, did I tell you mustard? And extra mayonnaise! Mayonnaise is my favorite.

Katy: Number 4! We're up to 4!

Customer #4: Did you call my number? I just need a few salads for my dinner. I'd like a pint of **potato salad**, and a pint of **coleslaw**. I'll take them right home and put them in the refrigerator.

Katy: Number 5. I'm waitin' on you!

Customer #5: Excuse me, do you take care of the fish counter too?

Katy: For you, honey, I take care of everything!

Customer #5: Great! I'd like a whole **trout**—that big one there. And some **shrimp.** They look nice and fresh. Give me a half a pound of shrimp.

Katy: Number 6. Fish or Deli?

Customer #6: Shellfish, please, if you don't mind. I'd like some **scallops**—they look very fresh. That lobster looks lovely, but it's too expensive. Maybe next time! Just wrap up the scallops.

Katy: Who has Number 7? Oh, Roy! Fish, right?

Customer #7: Right, Katy! That **salmon** looks delicious. Give me a whole one. And maybe some **oysters.** My wife thinks your oysters are the best. About a half a pound? Are the **clams** fresh? Give me a pound, if you don't mind.

Katy: Number 8. Oh, hi. Deli, right?

Customer #8: Not today. The **halibut** isn't frozen, right? I'd like a half a pound of halibut, and the mussels look good… Give me some **mussels**, at least 10 of

them, and a whole **crab**. I'm making fish stew tonight. You know the kids don't like fish, but tonight they're staying with their favorite grandmother!

Katy: They are?!

Customer #8: Didn't I ask you yesterday? I'm bringing them over around 4:00!

Katy: I guess I'd better bring home some deli!

Tapescript #21
"Where Are the Pretzels?"
Pages 54 and 55, *The Market,* and Page 56, *Containers and Packaged Foods*

Customers at Ray's market are talking about different items they want to buy. You will need a piece of paper. Close your books. For pages 54 and 55, write the section of the market each person is in. For page 56, write the container you hear. Remember you can check your spelling later.

1. Young man! Where's the cottage cheese? I'd like to buy a nice **container** of cottage cheese to go with my toast in the morning. I don't see any containers of cottage cheese here. **[dairy]**

2. Dude! I totally need some pretzels. I'm looking at all these bags but I don't see one **bag** of pretzels. This is not cool. **[snacks]**

3. Sir? I'm looking at all of these beverages, but I don't see a **six-pack** of root beer anywhere. Can you assist me in locating a six-pack? **[beverages]**

4. 'Scuse me. Can you reach the wheat bread up there for me? My mom asked me to get a **loaf** of bread, but it's too high for me to reach. Just one loaf is fine. Thanks! **[bakery]**

5. Can I ask you a question? I've been staring at all these cartons in the freezer case for a while now, and I just can't find the vanilla ice cream. I'm thinking, aw geez, I really want vanilla. Do you think you have any cartons in the back? Would you look? I just need one **carton.** **[frozen foods]**

6. Hope you don't mind me asking y'all, but I need a **can** of SeaBrite tuna. You advertised 3 cans for a dollar, but I don't see anything on the shelf. You think you could check for me? **[canned foods]**

7. Oh, now, where is Kitty's food? Hush, Kitty. We don't want the manager to know you're in here. I am looking for your favorite **box** of dry food, precious. Treats for kitty cat, yes, yes, yes. Here's a box. **[pet food]**

8. Let's see. Got that, got that, got that. Oh yeah, paper towels. One **roll** of paper towels. I'm looking, I'm looking. No paper towels. They have to be here. I see napkins. I see paper plates. I see paper towels! Great, one roll it is**.**
[paper goods]

Tapescript #22
"Chef Klaus"
Page 57, *Weights and Measures,* and Page 58, *Food Preparation*

World-famous Chef Klaus explains how to make his special carrot cake. You will need a piece of paper. Close your books. For page 57, write the measurements you hear. For page 58, take notes on the recipe. Remember, when you take notes you can correct your spelling later.

1.
Karl: It's *Cooking with KLAUS!!!* And now, the master of the microwave, the king of cooks, heeeeeere's Klaus.
Klaus: Thank you, Karl. *Willkommen,* Welcome, *Bienvenidos,* my friends. Today we will cook my favorite recipe: the carrot cake. Get your pencils ready. First, use **one quarter teaspoon** of butter to **grease** a cake pan.
Karl: That's one quarter teaspoon of butter, Klaus?
Klaus: Yes, Karl, you don't need a lot of butter to grease the pan, but cover all the edges.
2.
Klaus: Now, **mix** together **two cups** each of flour and sugar and **two teaspoons** of baking soda.
Karl: That was two cups of the flour and the sugar and two teaspoons of baking soda.
Klaus: Be sure to mix all those ingredients well.
3.
Klaus: Next you want to **beat** one extra large egg with **one tablespoon** of water. You don't have to beat it for a long time, but beat it well.
Karl: The egg goes with one tablespoon of water.
4.
Klaus: **Grate three quarters of a cup** of carrots.
Karl: Three quarters of a cup. How many carrots is that?
Klaus: About three carrots will give you three quarters of a cup, but be sure to wash those carrots first and watch your fingers in the grater!
5.
Klaus: **Add half a cup** of oil to the bowl of eggs and add the flour-sugar-baking soda mixture.
Karl: So we're adding one half cup of oil, right?

6.
Klaus: Now **stir** in **half a tablespoon** of vanilla.
Karl: One half tablespoon of vanilla. Can I add some coconut or walnuts?
Klaus: If you like, Karl, but that's not the way I make it.
7.
Klaus: All right, let's **pour** the mixture into the cake pan and sprinkle it with **one half teaspoon** of cinnamon.
Karl: OK, we sprinkle one half teaspoon of cinnamon. Here, I'll open the oven door for you.
8.
Karl: Now we **bake** this fabulous cake at **350° for one hour** and let it cool for ten minutes.
Klaus: This cake is so delicious, my friends. Look at the one I baked last night. Of course, you will need a **quart of milk** to serve with this fantastic taste treat. And so…eat like a king my friends!
Karl: Next week we make Klaus' Krazy Cabbage.

Unit 5   Clothing
Tapescript #23
"The Movie Line"
Pages 64 and 65, *Clothing I*

A businesswoman at the bus stop is talking to her coworker about the people she sees in front of the movie theater. Point to the people you hear her talking about.

Kelly: Just look at all these people lined up to go to the movie. Where do they find the time? Simon, are you sure we couldn't cancel our meeting with Beck and Associates? I really want to change out of this **suit**. I've been wearing the suit all day, and now I have to wear it all night too.
Simon: Can't cancel the meeting, Kelly, you know that.
Kelly: But don't you hate wearing suits to work? Now, don't get me wrong, you look great in a **three piece suit**. But don't you hate wearing it?
Simon: The bus is now 10 minutes late.
Kelly: Well, let's spend our time people-watching.
Simon: Time? What time? We've got to get to the meeting.
Kelly: Well, we could always jog across town like that guy—the one coming at us in **sweatpants** and **sweatshirt**. Wouldn't it be great if we could wear sweatpants and sweatshirts to work?
Simon: Yeah, it would. Now if that bus would just come.
Kelly: Simon, look at those kids. I can't believe he's wearing **jeans** and **sneakers** on a date. In my day, boys dressed up for a date. And the girl is wearing a black **dress!** When I was a teenager we didn't wear black.

Simon: When I was a teenager, buses were on time.
Kelly: Speaking of on time, I wonder how that pregnant woman going into the theater feels. Two kids and one more on the way. You think she likes wearing that **maternity dress**?
Simon: I really wouldn't know.
Kelly: I remember my maternity dresses. They were much uglier than that one. I mostly wore big, old clothes when I was pregnant.
Simon: Where is that bus?
Kelly: You see that woman in a **split skirt**. I bet she wore that to work with the **vest**. She looks great. Maybe I'll try wearing a vest and split skirt to work on Monday. Split skirts feel like you're wearing pants but they're more businesslike.
Simon: Do you think we could get a taxi?
Kelly: Not in rush hour… Maybe I should try wearing what that woman over there is wearing. She looks relaxed. You see her, Simon, the one who's talking? The one in the **tunic** and **leggings**?
Simon: I see her. She's so relaxed that she isn't watching the line. I think that man in the **sports shirt** is going to yell at her soon. I hope this bus comes before they have a fight.
Kelly: Oh, look, Simon. That couple near the teenagers is in love. Look how they're dressed up. She's in that pretty **skirt** and **blouse** and he's in that **turtleneck**. Aren't turtlenecks great, Simon?
Simon: Never liked 'em. Make me feel like I'm choking.
Kelly: Well, you must like his **sports coat**. You never see people in sports coats at the movies! Hey, Simon, where are you going?
Simon: I've had it. I'm not waiting for this bus a minute longer. I'll call Beck's office from inside the theater and tell them we have to reschedule.
Kelly: You're going to the movies, Simon?!! But we…but I…but you… Hey! Wait for me!

Tapescript #24
"Outdoor Fashion"
Page 66, *Clothing II*

People are looking at the clothes in a fashion magazine. You will need a piece of paper. Write the number of the clothing item you hear the people describing.
1.
Teenager: Mom, look at this advertisement in the magazine. This model is wearing my **bathing suit!**
Mother: Well! I can't believe they think it's appropriate to wear a bathing suit at the bus stop. Promise me, you'll never wear your suit in public like that!
Teenager: Oh, mom!

2.

Man: Grayson, look at this ad. The **overcoat** I bought last week is on sale.

Grayson: No, Mr. Findley. Your overcoat is much nicer. This one's beige and yours is gray. And the fellow wearing the coat is much shorter than you are.

Man: Thank you, Grayson.

Grayson: My pleasure, sir.

3.

Dad: Look at this picture in the magazine. This young woman is wearing **rainboots**!

Teenager: Dad, I don't want to wear rainboots on my date.

Dad: This model is wearing them, and she's in a national magazine that you asked me to buy for you! No more arguments. Get your rainboots.

4.

Woman 1: Hey, look! **Leather jackets** are popular again.

Woman 2: Oh, that is one beautiful leather jacket. But, that kind of jacket is so expensive!

Woman 1: I know. We'll just have to wait for a sale.

5.

Tim: Martha, do you think we should each get a **poncho**? One for you, one for me? Bright yellow ponchos like the one in this picture.

Martha: Tim, it's not going to rain on this campout, is it?

Martha: No, no, no. But let's say it did…a poncho is so easy to slip on over your head, one-two-three. And yellow is such a cheerful color.

Martha: You saw something on the weather channel didn't you… Tim? Tim!

Tim: Wellllll…

6.

Fred: So, Jan, you like my **swimming trunks**? They're exactly like the trunks this hunk of a guy in the picture is wearing. Cool, huh?

Jan: Fred, it's the middle of winter. Are you trying to tell me something?

Fred: Pack your bags, Jan—we're going to Hawaii!

Jan: Oh, Fred!

Fred: I knew you'd like the trunks.

7.

Jim: Look! Look at this! They used my picture in this magazine! Now I'm going to be famous for sure!

Tia: This ad? The one with the winter clothes? I don't see you.

Jim: That's me. I'm the one in the **ski mask**.

Tia: Jim! You're wearing a ski mask over your face. No one will know this is you!

Jim: Well, it was snowing and… and my face was cold, and…

Tia: And you put on the ski mask. Oh, Jim!

8.

Jean: Honey, I think you should get one of these.

Josh: I don't want one. I've got enough clothes.

Jean: But look at this picture. This guy in the rain looks great! He looks like he works for the CIA in that **trenchcoat**.

Josh: But I don't work for the CIA, Jean. I'm a teacher.

Jean: Hey, even teachers need trenchcoats!

Unit 6   Health

Tapescript #25 📼 2: side 1
"Morning with the Simms Family"
Pages 76 and 77, *Personal Hygiene*

It's morning and everyone in the Simms Family is trying to get ready for the day. Point to the pictures of the people and the personal hygiene items they name.

Laura: I'm singing in the rain. I'm singing in the rain! What a wonderful… Mom! Mom! Can you hear me? I don't see any **soap**. There's no soap in here.

Ronna: One second, love.

Laura: How can I **take a shower** without soap?

Ronna: Just a minute, Sweetie. Luke is **taking a bath**. Luke, are you ready to get out? The water is probably cold by now.

Luke: I'm almost ready. Do you have my **bath powder**? I like bath powder.

Ronna: Laura! Did you get out already?

Laura: It's OK, Mom. I'll just put on **perfume**! Perfume will make me smell good!

Ronna: That's not the answer. Perfume smells good, but it doesn't get you clean!

Laura: OK, how about some **deodorant**? Where's that green deodorant you use?

Ronna: Deodorant is not the same either. Look, let me just get some…

Pam: Mom! Mom!

Ronna: Is that Pam calling? What is it?

Pam: I'm **washing my hair,** Mom. I'm in the kitchen over the sink. Can you hand me the **conditioner**? I can't see it. My eyes are closed!

Ronna: Which one is the conditioner? Is it this pink bottle?

Pam: Yup.

Mark: Whash all the yelling about?

Ronna: Mark, I can't understand you. Talk to me after you finish **brushing your teeth**.

Mark: I said, what is all the yelling about?

Ronna: We're not…

Pam: Mom, look! I'm **drying my hair** but it's still wet! I don't think this **blow dryer** is working!

Ronna: The blow dryer is fine. Your hair looks OK. Put in a **barrette** and it will look fine!

Mark: [gargling] Ooh—this **mouthwash** tastes awful! Honey, why did you buy this green stuff. I like the other kind.

Ronna: That mouthwash was on sale!

Laura: Mom, do you think red **nail polish** goes with this dress?

Ronna: Nail polish—what are you doing? Are you **polishing your nails** now? This is not the time to polish your nails! It's time to get ready for school!

Laura: I am ready. Look at this magazine picture. Do I look like this model? I think she looks great!

Ronna: For a model, she does. But you're prettier than she is! She has on too much **lipstick**. Look how red her lips are. And she has on too much **eye shadow**, if you ask me. Much too purple!

Laura: Well, she doesn't have to go to school.

Ronna: No, but you do, and so do Mark and Pam. Everyone—time to go!

Tapescript #26
"Ben Knows Best"
Page 78, *Symptoms and Injuries,* and
Pages 80 and 81, *Health Care*

Ben Sheldon is a pharmacist. He is giving his customers advice. For page 78, point to the symptoms and injuries you hear. For pages 80 and 81, point to the health care remedies you hear.

1.

Ben: Ah, Mrs. Switzer. Are you here to renew your **prescription medication**? I just gave you that prescription last week.

Mrs. Switzer: No, no, Mr. Sheldon. I'm not here for that. It's this **rash** on my arm. Look—my arm is red and itchy. Do you think I'm having a reaction to the medicine?

2.

Man: Hello, there. Where do you keep the stuff for a **backache**? My back is so sore, I can't even stand straight. I need some relief now.

Ben: Well, sir, you could take a **pain reliever**. Aspirin works well for relieving symptoms. But backpain could be serious. I could recommend a good **physical therapist**. Physical therapy is very good for the back, and…

Man: Heck, no. I just need to swallow a couple of aspirin. Be fine in the morning.

3.

Woman: Hi, Mr. Sheldon. Little Stevie has an earache—again. Can you believe it? The pediatrician said one **pill** twice a day, but Stevie won't take them. They're too large.

Ben: Well, I'll call your doctor. Maybe he can substitute a **capsule**. Capsules are easier to swallow for some kids.

4.

Ben: Sheldon's Pharmacy, can I help you?

Erwin: Hey, Ben, it's Erwin. Look, I got another **sore throat**. My throat is killing me, I tell ya. Must be this new sales job, talk, talk, talk…

Ben: OK Erwin, slow down. Why don't you come on down here? I've got some **throat lozenges** that will do the trick.

Erwin: Sure thing. Be down there soon.

5.

Ben: Domingo! What are you doing in that **wheelchair**?

Domingo: Well, I was playing soccer, and I **sprained** my **ankle**. Doctor said I gotta stay off my feet for a while, but I'll be needing a **cane** to get around. You got any fancy ones?

Ben: Yes, we have a few canes. But I'm surprised your doctor didn't recommend **crutches** instead. Crutches help keep the weight off your leg.

Domingo: Yeah, well, he did mention it. But I can use the cane to shoot some pool.

6.

Lois: Ben, can you help me? My allergies are acting up again. I feel just lousy. Terrible **nasal congestion**, I can hardly breathe… My nose is so stuffed up…

Ben: Well, Lois, you know the store as well as I do. **Nasal spray**-Aisle 4. You might want to check out aisle 6. I've got an **air purifier** on sale. Doctors recommend those machines for allergies, you know.

7.

Ben: Sheldon's Pharmacy. Ben Sheldon here.

Beverly: Ben, darling, it's Beverly. You know, your favorite sister-in-law. Well, I just got back from Paris, and I have this awful **stomachache**. You know the French, all that cream sauce, and well, what am I to do?

Ben: Well, I've got some **antacids**, Bev, and…

Beverly: Antacids? I don't want **over-the-counter medication**, Ben. My stomach is very sensitive.

Ben: Well, just put a **heating pad** on your stomach, Bev. A sensitive heating pad, that is.

Bev: Ben Sheldon! I think you should have gone to comedy school, not pharmacy school!

Tapescript #27
"County Hospital, 4:00, Channel 14"
Page 82, *Medical Emergencies,* and
Page 83, *First Aid*

Irina and Boris are talking about the television program, *County Hospital.* For page 82, point to the emergency they mention. For page 83, point to the first aid items or procedures as you hear them named.

Irina: Did you see *County Hospital* this week? I never miss a program. It's on Channel 14 at 4 o'clock.

Boris: You can't take it so seriously.

Irina: But did you see what happened to Rita?

Boris: Is she the one who **choked** on some fish at that expensive restaurant? She is with her sister and her sister's boyfriend. She can't talk.

Irina: Yes! And while she is choking, her sister tries to do the **Heimlich maneuver** on her! But she is so nervous, she does it on the wrong woman!

Boris: What happens?

Irina: Her sister's boyfriend, Jason, who is a doctor, does the Heimlich maneuver again. This time it works! So of course, Rita falls in love with Jason.

Boris: The next day while he is on the golf course, Jason thinks he is **having a heart attack**—he is so upset because he loves two sisters!

Irina: I know. The paramedics do **CPR** on him, right? They press really hard on his chest and…

Boris: Well, they go to the wrong place and do CPR on another man. Jason just had a stomachache from that expensive restaurant and he is OK.

Irina: The next day Rita goes to Jason's house.

Boris: What does he say?

Irina: Nothing! All of a sudden there is all this smoke and he **can't breathe**! There is a fire—Jason's mother is cooking chicken soup for him and a towel catches on fire!

Boris: I saw that part. Jason's mother runs out the front door and falls down some stairs!

Irina: She falls really badly and hurts her ankle and can't walk. Jason puts an **elastic bandage** on it, right?

Boris: Right. But even with the elastic bandage, she can't walk very well.

Irina: I know. And then Rita's mother, who is taking care of Rita's son, comes running and screaming looking for Rita. Remember? Rita's son Adolf has jumped into the swimming pool and he can't swim. He is **drowning** and Rita runs back to her house, but Rita can't swim either! She can't swim at all but she jumps in the pool anyway!

Boris: I was so worried!

Irina: But remember this cute pool man named Paul comes just at that time and does **rescue breathing** and saves Rita?

Boris: I know. I cried the whole time. Who saves Adolf?

Irina: The dog! Max, the dog, pulls Adolf out of the pool!

Boris: Then Paul and Rita fall in love.

Irina: From rescue breathing.

Boris: Yes, it is so sweet. And then Paul decides to make a box for Rita for a present. And Rita walks in that very minute to tell Paul thank you for saving her life. Just then Paul cuts himself because he really doesn't know how to use a saw. He's **bleeding** really badly.

Irina: Remember how Rita puts that white **sterile pad** on the cut? And then she puts the white **tape** around it to make sure it stays clean?

Boris: Yes! And then Paul's brother, Ryan, makes some hot tea for Rita and Paul. But while he's making it, he **burns** his hand and his foot really badly.

Irina: He burns his foot too?

Boris: Yes, he isn't wearing shoes! Do you remember how Rita puts the blue **ice pack** on his foot? She loves Ryan too!

Irina: So now Rita loves Jason, the doctor; Rita loves Paul, the pool man; and Rita loves Paul's brother, Ryan.

Boris: Look, I gotta go!

Irina: Why?

Boris: It's almost 4 o'clock. *County Hospital* is on channel 14! See you!

Tapescript #28
"The Patient Doctor"
Page 84, *Clinics,* and Page 85,
Medical and Dental Exams

Listen to Mr. Jack Yee talk about his experience at the Fanfield Clinic. You will need a piece of paper. For page 84, look at the word list and write the numbers of the words you hear. For page 85, point to the pictures you hear described.

1. I had to go to the Fanfield Clinic last week for a check up. It was easy to **make an appointment**. The **receptionist** there is very easy to talk to.

2. Once I got to the clinic, I didn't sit in the **waiting room** long, maybe only 20 or 30 minutes. Then I hear my name, "Jack Yee." So I get up and the next thing I hear is, "I have to **take your temperature**." What was my temperature? Why 98.6, of course. I'm a normal guy.

3. Next they tell me, "Have to **check your blood pressure,** Jack." I like the way they check blood pressure at the clinic. They don't make the cuff too tight. I could see the **blood pressure gauge**, and I could tell that I had 110 over 70. Pretty good for a guy in his 60s.

4. When the **doctor** came in, I was happy to see her. Fanfield has a couple of great doctors: Doctor Brown and Doctor Hidashi. They're not too formal. Doctor Hidashi gave me the examination. She tried to **look in my throat**, but I hate that part. I always start to cough when doctors put that tongue depressor on my tongue.

5. She used her **stethoscope to listen to my heart**. But I just hate how cold the stethoscope feels on my chest. Ugh!

6. She had me read the **eye chart**, and then she wanted to **examine my eyes**…but the light hurt my eyes so she didn't look at my eyes too long.

7. I had to get off the **examination table** to go with the X-ray technician. They make me **get an X ray** once a year. It's not much fun, standing with your shirt off. A person could catch a cold getting an X ray.

8. Well, the last thing Doctor Hidashi did was to order the lab to **draw my blood**. "No thank you," I told her. "I hate **syringes**." And do you know what she said to me? "*Doctor* Yee," she says to me, "you are my most difficult **patient**." Imagine that!

Unit 7   Community

Tapescript #29
"Where Ya' Goin'?"
Pages 88 and 89, *City Streets*

Listen to the people talk about the things they have to do in the city. Point to the places you think they are talking about.

1.
Woman 1: Where are you going for lunch?
Woman 2: I have to deposit some money into my bank account.
Woman 1: Oh, can I go with you? I want to open a checking account.
Woman 2: Sure. Maybe we can grab something for lunch on the way back.
[bank]
2.
Daughter: Where are you off to, Daddy?
Father: I'm going to get a haircut.
Daughter: Don't let the barber cut it too short.
Father: Don't worry, Sweetie.
[barber shop]
3.
Mother: We're going downtown, Fernando. Go get your library books.
Son: Can we check out some more books?
Mother: Of course we can, but don't forget to bring your library card.
[library]
4.
Girl friend: I need to pick up some stamps.
Boy friend: Could you mail these letters for me, while you're at it?
Girl friend: No problem.
[post office]
5.
Son: Mom, could we go see a movie?
Mother: What do you think, Aliseo? Could we catch a 4 o'clock show?
Father: That's a great idea. We haven't seen a movie for a long time.
[movie theater]

6.
Wife: Dick, I'm going to take the car and go get some gas.
Husband: Remember to ask them to check the oil, too.
Wife: Actually, I checked it yesterday. We just need gas.
Husband: Oh, OK.
[gas station]
7.
Friend 1: Are you ready to go work out?
Friend 2: Ugh, I hate exercising.
Friend 1: Come on, you know you like it when you get there.
Friend 2: Yeah, yeah, you're right.
[health club]
8.
Daughter: Mommy, how come you're going to the office today? It's Saturday.
Mother: I know, Grace. I won't stay at the office long. You and Daddy are going to pick me up when I'm done working.
Daughter: You mean I get to ride in the elevator, all the way to the 10th floor? All right!
[office building]

Tapescript #30
"Up and Down the Street"
Pages 90 and 91, *An Intersection*

Different people are doing their daily errands. Point to the places where the conversations are taking place.

1.
Kari: Hi, Mike. I took some pictures at my son's graduation. I can't wait to see them. Can you have them ready in an hour?
Mike: No problem. Come back by 4:00 and they'll be ready for you. Oh, congratulations!
[photo store]
2.
Customer: Excuse me. Do you have any batteries? I need some for a flashlight. I like this store because I can always find things here—but not today!
Clerk: Sure, they're over there—next to the gum and candy.
Customer: Of course—don't know why I didn't see it.
[convenience store]
3.
Customer: I'll take a barbecued chicken sandwich, a couple of cheeseburgers, some fries, and a cola.
Server: Large or small?
Customer: Extra large.
Server: That will be $6.75 at the window. Thank you.
Customer: Could you add a salad to that? Thanks!
[fast food restaurant]
4.
Seller: Let's see—that's two magazines, and the *Daily News*. Anything else?
Customer: Yeah, I'm looking to rent an

apartment—do you have that free newspaper with all the classifieds?
Seller: Sorry, we're all out. Come by this afternoon.
[newsstand]
5.
Wife: Honey, you bring in the detergent. I'll carry in the laundry. Take the bleach, too.
Husband: How much is a wash and dry?
Wife: It's $1.00 for the wash, but the dry is free.
[Laundromat]
6.
Customer: Yolanda, are my pills ready? You called my doctor right?
Clerk: Right, Mrs. King. And they're right here with your aspirin and cold medicine.
Customer: Thanks so much. This drugstore gives the best service. I wouldn't go to one of those big places, Yolanda. No, sir! I mean ma'am.
[drugstore]
7.
Customer: I made 10 copies. How much is that?
Clerk: At 5 cents a copy—it's 50 cents plus tax.
Customer: That's great. I guess color is a lot more.
Clerk: Yep!
[copy center]
8.
Customer: Give me a dozen donuts please.
Clerk: What kind would you like—we got your chocolate, your glazed. Anything you want.
Customer: Plain, please. I'm on a diet!
[donut shop]

Tapescript #31
"Shopping at the Mall"
Pages 92 and 93, *A Mall*

Peggy and Walter are shopping at the new mall. Point to the places you hear them talking about.

Peggy: Oh, Walter! Isn't it just grand! Why, this new shopping mall is beautiful! Oh look, Walter, right on the first floor—there's even a **florist**!
Walter: Florist? Gee, if you want flowers, just pick 'em from our garden.
Peggy: Well, those floral arrangements look so elegant, I… Oh, Walter, there's my favorite **shoe store**. Let's go take a look…
Walter: Shoe store? Peg, you've got enough shoes to open up your own store! …All right, let's go. Maybe I'll have a look at that **food court** upstairs while you're trying on whatever you need to try on…
Peggy: Food court? Why, Walter, dear, you just had breakfast half an hour ago. Remember what the doctor said about your weight.

Walter: OK. Well, then I'll go and check out that **electronics store**. It's right here, on the first floor. Maybe they have clock radios there.

Peggy: Walter, you know how I hate shopping alone. Now you promised not to wander off… I know, let's pick out some presents for the twins. Look up there! I see a **toy store** on the second floor.

Walter: Toy store? I love those boys, Peg, but they really don't need any more toys. Or clothes. Or videos. Or…

Peggy: **Video store!** What a great idea, Walter. We can buy the new science fiction movie they've been talking about. Come on, let's take the **escalator** up and see what else they have.

Walter: Whatever you say, Peg. Hey, while we're up there, let's stop at the **candy store**. Maybe they're giving out free samples of chocolate, or…

Peggy: Walter, honestly! Can't you think of anything besides food? Come on, honey, let's go buy some new shirts at Smith and Co. **Department Store**. I hear their men's department is great.

Walter: Peg, you know I get headaches in those huge department stores. Why don't we check the **directory** on the first floor and see if there are any other clothing stores around, and…

Peggy: Walter, we don't need to look at a directory. Let's take our time and look at all these beautiful stores. Oh, look at those adorable puppies in the **pet store** window! Walter: Yeah, they are kinda cute. Hey, now here's an idea. First, the pet store. Then, let's go to that **bookstore** on the second floor and get a book on animals for the boys. You know, something about dinosaurs or lizards.

Peggy: All right, Walter. I guess I've been so excited about this new mall, I haven't been listening to what you want to do. Oh look, a **jewelry store**. Now, Walter, you did promise me a pearl necklace for our anniversary. Walter, Walter, honey, where are you going?

Walter: I'm going to the **ice cream stand** for a double scoop of French vanilla. I'm hungry, Peg. Then, I'm goin' back upstairs to the **travel agency** and I'm buying a one-way ticket.

Peggy: A ticket at the travel agency? Now just where do you think you're goin', honey?

Walter: Anywhere. As long as it's out of this mall!

Tapescript #32
"Rainbow Day Care"
Pages 94 and 95, *A Childcare Center*

Dorothy Bedlow is an experienced childcare worker. She is describing a typical day at Rainbow Day Care. The first time you listen, point to the actions on page 94. The next time you listen, point to the items on page 95.

1.
So, you want to know about Rainbow Day Care, do you now? Well, I've been here almost 15 years, and I can tell you everything about the little ones, the moms, the dads, and of course our wonderful childcare center. You can **drop off** the little ones as early as 7:30 a.m. For the little ones, we ask that you bring the child's special **formula** and **bottle**.

2.
Oh yes, the older ones need their **baby food**. You're askin' about the feeding schedule? Well, we **feed** the babies every three hours. Look, here's Carlos feeding Carlos Junior. No, he doesn't work here, Luv. That's proud Papa.

3.
Every day I **read** a story to the little ones. Sometimes I read a story from a picture book, and sometimes I just **hold** them and tell them stories. If they get fussy, I give them their **teething rings.**

4.
Some of the little ones need some extra comfort. You can bring in their **pacifiers**, if they're used to havin' one. If that doesn't work, I **rock** them in the rocking chair. While I'm rocking, I sometimes sing a lullaby.

5.
So, what else can I tell you? Oh, you do have to bring in a few more things. We'll be needin' **cloth diapers** if you use 'em, and **training pants** if you have older ones. Yes, we certainly do **change diapers** here—we go through a case every week.

6.
Do you prefer **disposable diapers**? Well, that's fine, Luv, just make sure you bring us a fresh supply every week. There seems to always be little ones on the **changing table**. Oh, that reminds me. You won't be needin' to bring wipes—we have plenty of those too.

7.
You're askin' about the activities? Why, we're busy every single minute! Our staff and children **play** together. Look at those two children with the blocks, and the younger ones have lots of fun in their **play pen**. Our staff pays extra attention to each and every child.

8.
There's always someone close by to help **tie** a shoe. We also teach the children to do as many things on their own as they can. Independence is a good lesson. Why look at that little one—she just learned to shake a **rattle**!

9.
Now, come look at these cabinets. All our supplies, like the **baby powder** and the **disinfectant**, are kept in a locked cabinet. Very safe.

10.
Ssshh! Take a peek at this room—these little ones **take a nap** for about an hour. Aren't they little angels? No, we don't put them in a **carriage**. Later, they'll eat a snack in a **high chair**.

11.
Well, our moms and dads come to **pick up** their little darlins after 4:00 p.m. We charge for late pick ups, you know. And we don't release any children without a **car safety seat**. It's the law, Luv. Make sure you <u>always</u> use that car seat. Oh, I'm sorry, Luv, I forgot to tell you we're all full! We have a wait list, and I'd be happy to…

Tapescript #33
"Officer Lopez Comes to Class"
Page 100, *Crime*, and Page 101, *Public Safety*

Officer Lopez is talking to a class about crime in the area and public safety. For page 100, point to the crimes the police officer talks about. For page 101, point to the various safety tips he talks about.

Thank you for inviting me to speak today. There are many things you can do to take care of yourself and your property. Don't give criminals an easy time.

Now, it's true there is more crime these days. For one, we see more **vandalism**. And vandalism means a lot of things. It can be graffiti painted on walls and fences. It can be someone throwing rocks at your car. But there are things you can do. If someone paints graffiti on your home, paint over it right away. Vandalism brings more vandalism. We also have seen other crimes, but you don't have to be a victim. No, you don't. When you're out on the streets, don't walk alone. **Walk with a friend**. And of course, don't walk on dark streets. **Stay on well-lit streets**.

I know you've heard that there's been a lot of **mugging**—thugs who hit you and grab your purse. **Women, hold your purse close to your body**. Don't let it hang just anywhere. Men, if you don't want someone to pick your pocket while you're waiting for a bus or on the subway, **hide your wallet** inside your clothes—not in your pants pocket. And, of course, don't carry a lot of money with you!

When you're home, protect yourself against burglary. **Lock your doors at all times**—with a bolt lock, if you can. And when someone comes to the door, do not open it. Look through a window to see who it is. If you don't know them, keep it closed. Remember, **do not open your door to strangers**.

Now for the good news. We are doing better against **gang violence**. There are more police in the area and we have a new group called "Families Against Gangs." The neighbors in this group are

Tapescripts

doing their best to keep their children away from gangs. And there is less **drunk driving**. A lot of people are using designated drivers—you know, people who don't drink for the night— when they go to parties or celebrations. No matter what **don't drink and drive**.

There's another way you can help. For all crimes, and especially serious crimes like **assault**, when someone hurts you by hitting you or shoving you, **report it to the police** right away. Do not waste any time. We have a much better chance to catch the person the sooner we know about it. In fact, if you see anything, call us. We are doing what we can, but we need your help. Any questions?

Unit 8   Transportation

Tapescript #34
"LAX to SFO"
Page 110, *An Airport,* and Page 111, *A Plane Trip*

Listen to the passengers and airline employees talking about flights from Los Angeles to San Francisco. For page 110, point to the items you hear the passengers talking about. For page 111, you will need a sheet of paper. Write the letters of the actions you hear described.

1. Oh, I didn't think I'd make it. I can't believe it's only 8:30. I still have time to **check in**. My flight must not be too crowded. There isn't a long line at the **check-in counter** and the **boarding area** looks pretty empty.
2. This is the final boarding call for Skyair flight 444 to San Francisco. Passengers can **board the plane** at **gate** 24. All travelers for flight 444, please board the plane now at gate 24.
3. Final boarding call already? Where did the time go? It's all right. Breathe, breathe… OK, you're on the plane. Now let's just **find your seat** and find some space in the **overhead compartment**.
4. Uh. Uggg-uh. I wish the **flight attendant** would stop playing with the oxygen and help me get my stuff stowed away. It's always hard to **stow your carry-on bag**.
5. (I just know the **passenger** in 14F is going **to request a blanket**. You know he's going to do it.) Yes, of course, sir. You can have a blanket. No problem. (Hah! I knew it.)
6. Miss, don't we have to look for the **emergency exit?** You forgot to say that. I've looked for it, and I see it over there. Now, can you tell me where my **oxygen mask** is? I like to be prepared. I see your mask is on your face, but where is my mask?
7. Ladies and gentleman, the captain has just told us we may **experience** some **turbulence**, so please **fasten your seat**

belts at this time. Put all **tray tables** in their locked and upright position. Thank you.
8. I can't wait until we **land**. I just want to arrive in San Francisco and get to my hotel. What a flight! At least I don't have to go see any customs officers on this trip. **That customs officer** in Los Angeles really made me nervous.
9. Ladies and Gentlemen, on behalf of Skyair, welcome to San Francisco. We hope you have had a pleasant flight. The time is 10:00 a.m. Passengers with checked bags, you **can claim your baggage** on **carousel** 2 downstairs. Your baggage will be on carousel 2. Thank you for choosing Skyair.

Unit 9   Areas of Study

Tapescript #35
"Mr. Porter's Opus"
Page 120, *Music*

Mr. Porter is a high school music teacher. He is describing various musical instruments in the orchestra. You will need a piece of paper. Close your books. Write the names of the musical instruments you hear. Remember you can check your spelling later.

Good evening everyone, and welcome to Central Islip High School's first annual Music Appreciation Concert. Tonight we hope to entertain and educate you as our students play their instruments. Let's hear them individually first…

1.
Notice how this string instrument is held between the shoulder and the chin. Our musicians can use a bow or pluck the strings with their fingers.
[violin]
2.
This woodwind instrument makes a lovely, delicate sound. It's a long thin tube with keys that we call finger holes.
[flute]
3.
Ah, I'm sure everyone knows this instrument. 88 black and white keys. You press a key, a hammer hits a string, and…*voila!* The greatest music ever— classical, rock, jazz, you name it.
[piano]
4.
You can't miss this brass instrument. It's huge, right? Actually, it's a brass <u>wind</u> instrument, since you blow into it. Listen to these really low sounds. Fantastico!
[tuba]
5.
Now, what's an orchestra without these? We've even got congas and bongos for that great Latin beat. You can use drumsticks or your hands. We've got a great percussion section—listen!
[drums]

6.
Here's another brass instrument that you blow into. It's a slim metal tube and it curves to make a "U" shape. At the end there's a larger bell shape. What's unique about this instrument is the slide. See how it moves back and forth?
[trombone]
7.
Have you gone to church or to a baseball game? Well, you may have heard this instrument. The sound you hear comes from pipes that have compressed air. To make the sound, you play one or sometimes several keyboards. Very dramatic, yes?
[organ]
8.
Do you ever dream of playing in a rock and roll band? Well, you'll need one of these—acoustic or electric, take your pick. I mean, you <u>use</u> a pick to pluck the strings, or strum with your fingers. With a little practice, you'll be a star!
[guitar]
9.
Now this is a fabulous string instrument. It's large, so you have to sit down and hold it between your knees. Just like the violin, you use a bow and your fingers. Listen to its sound.
[cello]
10.
Finally, let's listen to this wind-type instrument. You strap it on your chest, so it's portable! It has large bellows that you move in and out with one hand while you play the keys with the other hand. Do you like to dance the polka? This song is for you.
[accordion]
11.
Now, listen when all these marvelous instruments play together. Surely you know what we call this… It's an…
[orchestra]

Unit 10   Plants and Animals

Tapescript #36 2: side 2
"Animals! Animals!"
Page 133, *Domestic Animals and Rodents*

Mark Shepard, famous radio host, and his co-host Debbie are describing the different animals appearing on their radio show. Point to each animal they describe.

Debbie: And now the man who can horse around and get your goat…Mr. Animal himself: Mark Shepard!
Mark: Thanks, Deb. Today on our show we've got animals, animals, and more animals. Who's our first guest?
Debbie: Pink, heavyset, and straight from the farm.
Mark: Wow, she's big. What a porker!

Debbie: That's right, Mark. She's big because she's Penny the…
[pig]
Mark: Our next guest is from the field. She's kind of small, so we'll set her up here on the desk near the mike. That's a pretty long tail she's got.
Debbie: And those cute whiskers!
Mark: Everyone give a big hello to Marsha the…
[mouse]
Mark: Now you don't have to introduce this guest to me. This guy lives in the same house I do. He's a great companion, father of about 20 puppies,
Debbie: Speak boy, speak!
Mark: Everybody, I'd like you to meet Samson, my…
[dog]
Debbie: OK, Mark, here's one of our favorites. She's pregnant and expecting kittens any day now.
Mark: She kinda looks like a miniature tiger, and would you listen to that purr!
Debbie: You better move that mouse, Mark.
Mark: Right, Deb. Ladies and gentlemen, let's have a round of applause for this beautiful…
[cat]
Mark: Let's walk over here, because our next guest is too big to sit down. This tough animal has worked on the ranch and the farm. Please welcome Danny the…
[donkey]
Mark: And who've you got there, Deb?
Debbie: This is Gilda. She's originally from the streams of China and now she lives right here in this bowl. Everybody say hello to Gilda, the…
[goldfish]
Mark: Don't worry, everybody, I've got her and I'll just put her in this bowl over here.
Debbie: Well Mark, are you ready for our last guest today?
Mark: You know I am.
Debbie: Well, here he is, the animal responsible for all those wool sweaters you love so much.
Mark: You mean…?
Debbie: Yes, Mark, it's Sheldon, the…
[sheep]
Mark: Well, it's been great. Join us next week for animals from Australia: the creatures from Down Under.
Debbie: Bye, everyone!

Unit 11   Work

Tapescript #37
"Are They Hiring?"
Pages 136 and 137, *Jobs and Occupations, A-H*

Maureen Serra, a job counselor at A-Z Employment Agency, is telling her clients the jobs that are available. Each client describes the kind of work they want. You will need a piece of paper. Take notes on the different jobs you hear. Circle the best job for each person. Remember, when you take notes, you can correct your spelling later.
1.
Maureen: I have three jobs that just opened up today: **gardener, dockworker,** and **cashier**. The gardening job starts next week. The dockworker position requires a lot of strength, and the cashier opening is in a discount store. What kind of job are you looking for, Mr. Lee?
Mr. Lee: Well, I really like working outside; in fact, I love working near the ocean. And I'm strong, really strong. I can lift heavy things and I have experience operating cranes and forklifts.
Maureen: I think I have just the job for you.
2.
Maureen: Ms. Sarkissian, these four job openings were called in today: **florist, dental assistant, cook,** and **assembler**. Now the assembler position is with a local electronics firm; the hamburger stand on 5th and Central needs a cook. They need a dental assistant at my dentist's office; and, there's an opening at the flower shop around the corner. Let's talk about what kind of work you'd like to do.
Ms. Sarkissian: It's simple really. I just finished school and now I'm ready to work for a dentist. You know, it's always been my dream to work with teeth!
Maureen: Well, that settles it.
3.
Maureen: Yes, Mr. Scarcelli, I did say we had several job openings this week. There's an opening for an **auto mechanic**. That's a job in Clancy's Car Repair. And there's another opening for a **garment worker**. You need to be able to do industrial sewing for that job. Then there's a position open as a **home attendant** for an elderly woman living in the Park Towers. And last, I just got a call from Anna's Pizza; they want a **delivery person**. Are any of these right for you?
Mr. Scarcelli: I'm great with cars. I fixed my dad's car this weekend, and I took some car repair classes at our local community college. I really like that kind of work.
4.
Maureen: Have a seat, Mrs. Armstrong. I see we have three cards from that company that just opened downtown. They're looking for an **administrative assistant**, an **accountant**, and a **graphic artist**. Now, the administrative assistant job requires secretarial and managerial skills. Naturally the accountant needs ability in math and computer skills. And it looks like the graphic artist needs to be able to work with traditional and computer graphics. Which of those positions interests you?
Mrs. Armstrong: Well, I've always been good with numbers. In fact, I kept the books for my husband's office. Did his accounting for years before he hired someone to do it. And now, well, I'd dearly love to get paid for all that time I spent adding and subtracting.
Maureen: OK, let's see what we can do about that.
5.
Maureen: Mr. Fargo, I just got a call from that new restaurant, Casa de Pollo. They're looking for **cooks**, **cashiers**, even **delivery people**. What do you think? I see from your resume that you've been a cashier before, and I'm sure you could do the delivery work as long as you drive. As for the cooking, well, you'd have to be able to do that well to get the job as a cook.
Mr. Fargo: Aw, geez, I'd love to work for that restaurant, but I just don't know anything about preparing food. But, y'know, you're right. I worked in my parents' store while I was in school. I do know how to make change. I like handling money and standing behind a cash register. Let's talk about that job.
6.
Maureen: It must be so hard to think about changing careers, Dr. Murray. Are you sure you want to hear our job listings?
Doctor: Yes, yes. Tell me what you have available.
Maureen: Hmmm…let's see. This week we have openings for a **florist,** a **commercial fisher,** and a **gas station attendant**. Now I just can't picture you working in a gas station. And I really don't see you out on a commercial fishing boat…
Doctor: Actually, I love to fish, but I'm not strong enough to do it commercially.
Maureen: The florist on First Avenue has an opening, but, frankly, I can't see how any of these jobs would be good for you.
Doctor: Well, you're wrong, young woman. I've been working with flowers all my life. I know their common names and their Latin names, and how to take care of them. I would love the opportunity to work in a place filled with flowers. You call that place right now and tell them I'm coming over.
Maureen: Oh—yes, Doctor.

Tapescripts

Tapescript #38
"Castillo's Lamp Factory"
Page 146, A Factory, and Page 147, Job Safety

Arturo Castillo is a factory owner. A county inspector is surprising Arturo with a safety inspection. For page 146, point to the people or things in the factory you hear. For page 147, you will need a piece of paper. Close your books. Write an *H* when you hear a safety hazard. Write an *E* when you hear a piece of safety equipment.

Mr. Tidy: Hello, anyone there? I'm looking for a Mr. Castel, uh, that's Castillo.

Mr. Castillo: Just a minute. Yes, I'm Arturo Castillo. I'm the **factory owner**. How can I help you?

Mr. Tidy: I'm Neil Tidy, the county inspector. I'm here to inspect your factory. Uh, do I need to wear my **hard hat** inside your facility?

Mr. Castillo: Uh, not unless you want to. There's no construction here—we make lamps. Very beautiful lamps. Did you make an appointment with Frank, our **line supervisor**?

Mr. Tidy: No, I didn't. And I didn't call anyone in your **front office**, either. We like to make our visits a surprise. Now, Mr. Castillo, could you show me where you keep **corrosive** materials?

Mr. Castillo: Uh, we don't have anything like that around here. But follow me to the **assembly line**. Everybody wears **safety goggles** and anyone with long hair wears a **hair net**—that's the guys, too. Hey, I had a ponytail once. You know I started here as a **shipping clerk**. Now I…

Mr. Tidy: Uh, that's very interesting, Mr. Castillo. Tell me, how do you handle **flammable** substances around here? Fires can be deadly, you know. And when did you last check your **fire extinguisher**?

Mr. Castillo: Just last month. We've never had a fire. Every single **factory worker** is trained to spot an **electrical hazard**. After all, we make lamps. Wall lamps, floor lamps, gooseneck lamps…

Mr. Tidy: Yes, yes…I see that, Mr. Castillo. Now, I'd like to check the loading dock for **hazardous materials**. And while we're there, I'll check your employees for proper work attire, you know, **toe guards** for their shoes and **back supports** to prevent back injury. Have you had any accidents at the plant recently, Mr. Castillo?

Mr. Castillo, Well, Chuck—he's our best **packer**… See him? He's working really hard now. But last week, well, he couldn't work on the **conveyor belt** for almost a week.

Mr. Tidy: Aha! Was he exposed to some kind of **poison**? I get more poison cases than I can count. Did he wear **latex gloves** to prevent injury to his hands? Did he injure himself on some of those lamp **parts** I see in the factory? You know, your worker may have been exposed to **radioactive** particles. Did he file a medical claim?

Mr. Castillo: Yes! I mean—no, nothing serious like that. Yes, Chuck always protects his hands. He's into safety. He even wears **ear plugs**, 'cause sometimes it's noisy in the **warehouse**. He just, uh, spilled something.

Mr. Tidy: Spilled, you say? Mr. Castillo, we have federal safety regulations concerning **biohazard** spills. I'll need a full report on this accident.

Mr. Castillo: Mr. Tidy, you have the wrong idea. Chuck burned his hand on a cup of coffee! I think he's fillin' in on the **loading dock** today, if you wanna see him. By the way, the catering truck is comin' in five minutes. Can I buy you a cup? Hey, we respect union rules in my factory. When the **time clock** says break, we break. Hey, Clara makes a pretty strong cup of java. Maybe you need to wear your **safety vest**? Just kiddin', you know.

Mr. Tidy: OK, Mr. Castillo, maybe a cup of coffee is just what I need. I'll just fax in this report, and…

Mr. Castillo: Call me Arturo. Hey, would you like to see our new reading lamp? It's our latest model, a real beauty…

Unit 12   Recreation

Tapescript #39
"Where Do You Wanna Go?"
Page 152, Places to Go

Tim and Ellen are discussing their weekend plans. Point to the places you hear them discussing.

Tim: Ellen, let's go to the **movies** this weekend.

Ellen: I'd love to, Tim, but we just can't take Sam to the movie theater. How about the **zoo**?

Tim: I'm tired of the zoo. We go there all the time. What about going to a **baseball game**? It'd be fun to sit at the top of the stadium, with all the people.

Ellen: I don't think so. All those people… Sam doesn't like crowds…

Tim: Yes, of course, you're right, but what…

Ellen: …about a sitter? Great idea. We can get someone to watch Sam and then you and I can go downtown to **the art museum**. There's a new sculpture exhibit.

Tim: That would be a great idea, if the exhibit were open. It doesn't open until next month. What do you think of a **swap meet**?

Ellen: Too crowded again, and I don't want to shop for anything. What about the **botanical gardens**?

Tim: Wrong time of year, my allergies are killing me, and with all those fl-fl-flowers… [ha-choo!] Makes me sneeze just to think about those flowers, plants, and trees. We could try the…

Ellen: Oh, Tim, I just remembered. The **county fair** starts today. We could go there!

Tim: That's a great idea. Animals, exhibits, rides: it sounds like a perfect day to me.

Ellen: To me, too. I'll go get Sam ready and then we'll go.

Tim: I'll help. Come on, Sam. Come on, Sammy. Come on, good boy! That's a good boy. We're going to the fair!

Tapescript #40
"Take Me Out to the Beach, Please."
(Sung to the tune of "Take Me Out to the Ball Game.")
Page 155, The Beach

Listen to the song and point to the things at the beach that you hear.

Take me out to the beach, please
Take me out to the **sand**
Summer's the time for a walk on the **pier**
There's lots of fun where the **ocean** is near

So it's time to pack up a **beach chair**
Relax in the **shade** or the sun
Don't forget your **sunblock**—it's hot
And we'll have some fun!

Take me out to the beach, please
Take me out to the **sand**
Where there's a **lifeguard** you'll never sink
Open that **cooler** and get me a drink

So let's bring a shovel and **bucket**
And find a **seashell** to save
Get your **surfboard** ready—let's go
Ride the next big **wave!**

Take me out to the beach, please
Take me out to the **sand**
Look at that guy with his **diving mask**
Using a **scuba tank's** no easy task!

But it's fun to dive in the **ocean**
You never know what you'll see
Put your **wet suit** on and stay warm
Come and swim with me!

Take me out to the beach, please
Take me out to the **sand**
Climb on a **rock** and enjoy the view
Colorful kites and a **sailboat** or two

So let's plan a little vacation
We need a day to unwind
Grab your **beach towel**—ready, let's go
And we'll have great times!

Tapescript #41
"The Oakwood News"
Page 156 and 157, *Sports Verbs*

Karl and Gina are the sports editors for their high school newspaper, *The Oakwood News*. They are deciding what sports pictures to put into the newspaper. Point to the pictures you hear them talking about.

Gina: Gee, Karl, we had a great week this week! Which picture do you like the best? I like the one from the women's basketball. Look at Nancy Booker **shoot** the ball. She looks great!

Karl: I like the one of Maxine better from the same game. She **dribbles** really well. I got a good picture of her dribbling down court.

Gina: I don't know. Here, look at this one of Mario Mendez pitching. He's **pitching** his fastball. He struck out 7 batters! That's a great record.

Karl: Maybe. But I think it's time for the football team. Here, look at Neil Peters **kick** that football. With that extra point, we won that game, too!

Gina: Time for the football team? We always do football. What about something different? Here is Carla Rapilli running for track and field tryouts. She **runs** like a racehorse! And, look—she has a sister, Candy, who plays tennis. Look at this picture of her sister on the tennis court. She **serves** the ball so well nobody wants to play against her. We can do a story on the Rapilli sisters.

Karl: It's almost spring. I think we have to do something from the swim team. See this one of Mark Spencer? He **swims** five hours a day. That's a lot of swimming.

Gina: Yeah—well, look at Natalie Nava. She **dives** seven days a week! That's a lot of diving!

Karl: Forget diving. You know, golf is becoming a big thing. How about this one of Tiger Forest? He **swings** a golf club just like the pros!

Gina: Maybe because his father is a professional golfer. You know some kids went on a ski trip last week. Here's a picture of Brian. He **skis** really well. Look at him coming down the mountain. And here's one of Katya. She doesn't **skate** that well. But she was having fun on the ice!

Karl: You said you wanted something different! What about one of the teachers?

Gina: Teachers?! One of the teachers?! What are you talking about?

Karl: Look at this. Sally found this picture of Mr. Slavak in a race when he was in high school. Here he is, **starting** the race. See—he's number 12! Here he is **racing**. He's going pretty fast, I think. And here he is **finishing** the race.

Gina: I really don't think he would like to have this picture in the paper. I really don't!

Karl: Why not?

Gina: He finished last!

Tapescript #42
"Coach Wilder, Lakewood High"
Page 158, *Team Sports,* and Page 161, *Sports Equipment*

Coach Wilder is talking to all the 12th graders who have physical education at Lakewood High. For page 158, point to the sports you hear him talking about. For page 161, point to the sports equipment you hear him say.

OK, everyone, listen up! I don't want to repeat myself. If you signed up for **football**, you go to the weight room. I want you to start lifting some **weights**. But don't start too heavy. For tomorrow, Adam, you're in charge of the football equipment. Take enough **helmets** for everyone—we want to protect those heads of yours! And I think we have plenty of **footballs** for practice. Adam, make sure you get all the footballs. Your first meeting is at 3:00 today. You're not on the field today, that's tomorrow. Got it? Football in the weight room! Go!

OK, let me see. **Volleyball**. If you signed up for volleyball, your practice begins right now. Here's the volleyball and the net. Go set up outside, on the volleyball court. Start out with some stretching—especially your legs!

Soccer. Raise your hand if you signed up for soccer. You guys—that means the girls too—you guys meet right on the soccer field. Take the **soccer ball** and start practicing your passes. Wait a minute! Anyone not wearing **shin guards**? No shin guards, no play! We got to protect your legs so you don't get hurt.

Anyone here who signed up for **water polo**? Water polo? No one? Oh, yeah, they must be at the pool already. OK, let's go on.

Baseball players. Who's playing baseball? Go on out to the field. Take a look at these new **bats**. I know you'll hit great with them. Take the **gloves**, too. Here, Yoshi, you have a big hand. This glove is for you. Who's catcher? Take the **catcher's mask** and the chest protector. The **balls** are in the bucket. Divide into teams and get started. Lynn, what are you doing with that **flying disc**? We're not playing flying disc. If you throw that one time, you're on the bench!

Softball. Where's my softball team? You're on the other field. Pitchers, I want you to practice throwing underhanded.

OK, I think that does it. Oh yeah! **Basketball**. Basketball people, you're with me. We're going into the gym right now. Sophie, take the **basketball**. Today is coed. Did you see the picture in the

paper from yesterday's game? Here, look. See me standing up? I never understand why a **coach** would sit during the game. Look at that **score** at half time: 60-45. We did great! John, love the way you got the tip off! You out-jumped the other guy, big time!

Tapescript #43
"Who's Doing What?"
Pages 162 and 163, *Hobbies and Games*

People in two different families are talking about their hobbies and crafts. Point to the person you hear speaking.

Grandmother: Well, I sure hope you like this doll, honey. I didn't know when I bought this doll kit that it would take me so long to make it.

Young girl 1: I love it, Grandma! And look what I made for you! This paper chain's got all your favorite colors. I love to do crafts with you, Grandma.

Son: Yeah, well, I love to play games. Kablammm! Got him. This video game system is the best, Dad. And this Math Monsters cartridge is the best! Wanna play, Dad?

Oldest girl: Hey, Ben, stop bugging Dad. You play your game and let him concentrate on this game. He has to concentrate if he wants to beat me at Monopoly!

Mother 1: Excuse me, but who moved my figurine? I put her over here this morning, and now she's in a different spot. Please, everyone, don't touch my collection. These figurines are very important to me.

Father 1: It's my fault, Sandy. I was looking for the dice. I thought I put the dice on the shelf near your collection. Sorry.

Mother 1: Oh, that's OK. It's just a collection. You are my family, after all. Just don't do it again.

Young girl 2: And SuperJaclyn leaps into the air, she's flying, she's going to save the world. You know what, Grandpa? I'm going to be an action figure someday…

Grandfather: That's nice, dear. All right. I think you have the ace of hearts, but I don't know what else. So I'm going to get rid of the ace of diamonds. What do you think of that?

Father 2: Lester, you always do that, and that's why I beat you every time we play cards.

Mother 2: Now if I put the red here in the corner, and I paint a little green down here…hmmm, this is looking very nice. What do you think of my painting, Keisha?

Older girl: It's great, Ma. What do you think of my scarf? I like the color of the yarn, but I don't know if I have to knit this differently. I'll go inside and ask Grandma's opinion.

Father 2: Keisha, you knit that scarf anyway you want. That's what's great about a hobby: you can do things your way. And, speaking of my way, I win, Lester! Aces and nines.

Tapescript #44
"Channel Changers"
Pages 166 and 167, *Entertainment*

The Petrenko family is trying to find a television show to watch together. Point to the pictures you hear them talking about.

1.

Mom: Well, this is nice! Saturday night and we're all together at home. Let's watch something together on TV, OK?

Michael: Yeah, there's a snowstorm and we're stuck inside. OK, pass me the remote. Here, let's watch *Frontier Cowboys*. I like the sheriff. He really shows those bad guys. Even his horse is cool.

[western]

2.

Dad: Now, Michael, you know your mother hates guns. Let's have a look at this TV page. Aha! 8:00 p.m. on channel 28, *Animal Discovery*. This week's program is endangered gorillas. Interesting... our animal friends, huh?

[nature program]

3.

Michael: Not really, Dad. Mom's not too crazy about those animal programs. Hey, Mom, remember last week's show, "Splendid Spiders"?

Mom: How could I forget! Now, I'm sure we can find something entertaining... Aaaah! It's Carmen Sotos, singing the aria from "La Viking Romantica." What a divine singing voice!

Michael and Dad: Noooooooo!!!!!

[opera]

4.

Mom: All right, all right. So you're not a fan of classical music. How about Channel 13, *Guess That Tune?* You know, there are two contestants and they try to win prizes by guessing songs. I like the host of that show, and well, I think last week the grand prize was a vacation in Hawaii.

Michael: Gee, Ma, that show is boring. Anyway, it's already over, see?

[game show/quiz show]

5.

Dad: Hey, speaking of Hawaii, did you hear about that volcano on the Big Island? How about we watch *World Tonight*. That reporter, Ron Dather, may have some late-breaking

information about the volcano. And then, we can hear the local weather report for tomorrow.

Michael: Weather report? Dad, just look out the window. That's all the information I need to know. C'mon, pass over the remote.

[news]

6.

Michael: Great! *They Came from Outer Space*. This is really neat. Watch how the aliens land on Earth. They take different people in their spaceships, and they want to learn about Earth's food and plants, so they...

Mom: Oh, dear! Space monsters and spaceships... You don't really believe this story, do you, Mikey?

[science fiction]

7.

Michael: Ma, you promised to call me Michael, remember? OK, forget that show. Hey, here's something "real": that Jenny Rivera lady. The TV page says, "Jenny's topic tonight: Teenagers in Trouble. 'Why are teenagers bored on Saturday night?'"

Mom and Dad: Michael!

[talk show]

8.

Michael: OK, OK, just joking. But Dad, we'll never agree on a program.

Mom: I have an idea. Look! Here's *On Stage Tonight*. We all like music, right? Well, this is a concert with a rock group, a jazz trio, and a classical pianist.

[concert]

Dad: Well, I love jazz. Turn it up, would you?

Michael: All right, but I have a better idea. Let's buy another TV!

Tapescript #45
"Where's the Party?"
Page 168, *Holidays*, and Page 169, *A Party*

Listen to different people leaving party invitations on answering machines. For page 168, point to the pictures of the holidays you hear. For page 169, you will need a piece of paper. Close your books. Write the dates and times of each party.

1.

Pat: I can't come to the phone right now. So please leave a message.

Amy: Pat, this is Amy. I'm calling to find out if you are free on the 14th. I'm having a Valentine's Party that day and I'd like you to come. I'm planning to decorate the house with hearts and serve lots of chocolate. Call me back and tell me if you can come this Saturday, February 14th, from 11:00 to 2:00.

2.

Tracy: Hey, Tracy can't get to the phone. Leave your name at the tone.

Roy: Tracy, this is Roy. I thought it would be nice to have a New Year's Day party at my house, say around 2:00 p.m. I'll make snacks and we'll watch the parade. You can invite a guest if you'd like. Right, then, that's January 1st at 2:00 for New Year's Day. Hope you can come.

3.

Answering Machine: This phone is being answered by a t-com answering system. Leave your name and message when you hear the beep.

Laura: Chrissy, hi. It's Laura. Listen, I'm calling to invite you to my party this Friday. It's on the 31st at 8:00—y'know, October 31st, Halloween? Oh, and everyone's wearing a costume. Call me when you get this message, OK?

4.

Dr. Keeshen: This is Dr. James Keeshen. I'm either away from my desk or on another line. Leave me a message and I'll call you back as soon as possible. If this is an emergency, you can page me at 555-1575.

Alonso: Dr. Keeshen, this is Alonso. I'm calling to let you know that this year Mercy Hospital will be having a party for all the children in the hospital on Christmas Day. Everyone working on December 25th is asked to attend. The party is at 3:00 p.m. Please wrap a small gift and bring it to the party. Call Hospital Services at 525-1225 to RSVP.

5.

Susan: Leave your message after the beep. Thanks.

Lynn: Susan, this is Lynn. I'm making a 4th of July surprise party for Margaret. Her birthday is on the 4th and I thought a group of us could have dinner at 6:00, then go see the fireworks at 9:00. Call me back if you can't make it. Bye!